*the*
# HIGHLAND RAILWAY

# *the* HIGHLAND RAILWAY

DAVID ROSS

TEMPUS

Also by David Ross

*Scotland: History of a Nation*
*Ancient Scotland*
*Scottish Place-Names*
*The Willing Servant: A History of the Steam Locomotive*
*An Illustrated History of British Steam Railways*

First published 2005

Tempus Publishing Limited
The Mill, Brimscombe Port,
Stroud, Gloucestershire, GL5 2QG
www.tempus-publishing.com

British Library Cataloguing in Publication Data.
A catalogue record for this book is available from the British Library.

ISBN 0 7524 3479 9

Typesetting and origination by Tempus Publishing Limited
Printed in Great Britain

# CONTENTS

| | |
|---|---|
| Introduction | 9 |
| Note on Currency and Measurements | 11 |
| Acknowledgements | 12 |

PART I

*Chapter One*

| | |
|---|---|
| The Great Scheme and its Failure | 13 |
| The Inverness & Nairn Railway | 19 |
| The Inverness & Aberdeen Junction Railway | 24 |
| 'Further North': The Inverness & Ross-shire Railway | 33 |
| The Great North Withdraws | 36 |

*Chapter Two*

| | |
|---|---|
| The Inverness & Perth Junction Railway | 38 |
| Formation of the Highland Railway Co. | 44 |

*Chapter Three*

| | |
|---|---|
| The Sutherland Railway | 47 |
| The Caithness Railway Co. | 50 |
| The Highland Railway, 1866–70 | 54 |
| Dingwall & Skye: the First Phase | 56 |
| The Duke of Sutherland's Railway | 62 |
| The Sutherland & Caithness Railway | 64 |

*Chapter Four*

| | |
|---|---|
| The Highland Railway in the 1870s | 70 |
| Dingwall & Skye: the Second Phase | 76 |
| The Steamship Venture | 78 |

*Chapter Five*

| | |
|---|---|
| The Highland in the 1880s – Territorial Defences | 81 |
| The Portessie and Strathpeffer Branches | 86 |
| New Western Schemes, and Frontier Skirmishes | 88 |
| The Kyle Extension | 93 |
| New Branches: Hopeman Extension, Black Isle, Fochabers and Fort George | 95 |

*Chapter Six*

| | |
|---|---|
| The Resignation of Andrew Dougall | 96 |
| Double Track over Druimuachdar, and the 'Direct Line' | 103 |
| Light Railways in the North: Dornoch, Wick & Lybster | 106 |
| New Men and New Attitudes: The Highland Railway from 1896 to 1914 | 110 |

*Chapter Seven*
The First World War 118
The Last Years 126

PART II
*Chapter Eight*
Mitchell's Road 130
Operations 137

*Chapter Nine*
Motive Power – The Early Years 143
Motive Power – The Classic Era 148
Motive Power – The 'Modern' Era 156
Lochgorm Works 160

PART III
*Chapter Ten*
The Community of the Railway: The Staff 162
The Community of the Railway: Directors and Shareholders 173

*Chapter Eleven*
Passenger Trains 178
Passengers 187
Through Carriages, the Sleeper War and the 'Caravans' 190
Goods Traffic 192

*Chapter Twelve*
The Postal Subsidy and the Mail Wars 198
Mixed Trains and Continuous Brakes 205

*Chapter Thirteen*
The Railway in the Community 210

*Appendix A:* Some Notable Accidents 221
*Appendix B:* Hotels and Refreshment Rooms 224
*Appendix C:* The Strange Story of the SS *Ferret* 226
*Appendix D:* Proposed, but Unbuilt or Uncompleted Railways in the
              Highlands 228

Notes and References 233

Sources and Bibliography
Bibliography 1: Books and Articles on the Highland Railway 247
Bibliography 2: Other Works consulted or referred to 248

Index 250

*For Fynn*


'Many shall go to and fro, and knowledge spread over the face of the Earth.'
*Daniel*, xii, 4; quoted at the celebrations of the arrival of the Inverness & Ross-shire
Railway at Dingwall, 13 June 1862

'The day will come when long strings of carriages without horses shall run between
Dingwall and Inverness, and more wonderful still, between Dingwall and the Isle of
Skye.'
Coinneach Odhar ('The Brahan Seer', fl. sixteenth – seventeenth century)


God made the Highland Railway,
But not for mortal men
Who up and down from town to town
Hasten, and back again –
Nay, rather for the shining ones
Whose worth transcends all rhyme,
Who travel in eternity,
For ever out of Time.
Anon.

# INTRODUCTION

Two things need to be said in opening. First, although this is a history of a railway, it is written for people who are interested in the Highlands as well as for those who are interested in railways. The advent of railways had a far-reaching effect on the life of the Highlands: greater, indeed, than would have been the case in a more populous and 'developed' area. The second follows on – in intention, this history of a railway is also a small contribution to Scottish history. In the second half of the nineteenth century, the Highlands and Islands were in a bad way socially and economically. Emigration – both permanent and seasonal, low and uncertain incomes, inbred ideas and occasional outbreaks of violence and intolerance marked the late throes of a process, centuries-long, of decline, in which an ancient social framework had been brought, through internal decay and a combination of interference and neglect from outside, to a state of complete decrepitude. Even after governmental prejudice and neglect had ceased, official attention and subsidies did not attack the root of the problem, which was landownership. One consequence was the parallel and paradoxical existence of population 'congestion' in some areas and a human vacuum following population clearance in others. The intentions of 'Improvers', for bringing industry to the people by such schemes as the extracting of oil from peat or fish, were swept aside not merely by an inhospitable climate and a remoteness from markets, but because such localised attempts to introduce an alien system simply could not be patched into the fabric of a society in collapse. In such circumstances, it was a remarkable achievement to construct and operate railway lines through the extensive and mostly rugged mainland terrain. The part played in the region's economic and social life, during the years from 1854 to 1923, by the successive railway companies with their headquarters in Inverness, has hardly been explored. W.H. Marwick's *Economic Development in Victorian Scotland* does not mention the Highland Railway, and indeed hardly mentions the Highlands. From Mackenzie's and Mitchell's histories of the Highlands, published around the end of the nineteenth century, one would suppose Highland history had petered out 100 years earlier. T.M. Devine's 1994 study,

'Clanship to Crofters'War', ignores the economic and social impact of the railway, as does James Hunter's otherwise very detailed *The Making of the Crofting Community*, though the crofting/fishing communities were by no means unaffected by it. These omissions are not wholly explicable by the 'mainstream' historian's view of transport history as a subject of marginal significance. The railway company was by far the single biggest commercial concern in the Highlands from the 1860s into the 1920s. It is of course very easy to take the presence of railways for granted, but one must at least venture the thought that the fact of the creation and successful running of a railway service, through local initiatives, and paid for very largely by the 'lairdly' class (for whatever motives), cuts against the conventional grain of the historiography of the region. Whatever epithets might be applied to the Highland Railway, it can scarcely be regarded as part of a campaign to make the Highlands more 'exclusive', or as a planned instrument of official or social repression.

The Highland was one of Britain's smaller, if more idiosyncratic, railway companies, and few general histories give it much attention. In locomotive histories it normally fares better, though E.J. and G.J. Larkin's *The Railway Workshops of Britain, 1823-1986*, makes no mention of Lochgorm Works, Britain's most northerly site of locomotive building. Its history and impact are sketched in Vol. XV of *A Regional History of the Railways of Great Britain*. But the Highland Railway has always been of interest to railway enthusiasts, and has its own society, which publishes a regular journal. A number of books have been written about Highland locomotives, and Neil T. Sinclair has written a history of the Inverness – Perth line. Histories of the Dingwall & Skye line, by John Thomas and David McConnell, have been published, and Mr McConnell has also written an account of the lines to Wick and Thurso. Two general histories of the Highland Railway, by H.A. Vallance and O.S. Nock, have also been published and reissued; my reason for offering a third is partly that, like many other readers, I would have wished them to be longer. Also, since their day, railway history has acquired more of a social element, which is reflected in the present book. Details of these books, and of many others which make reference to the Highland Railway, will be found in the Bibliography.

A railway company is a complex organisation, with several main facets of importance and interest. There is no ideal way in which to structure its history, if one wishes to do justice to all these aspects. This history of the Highland company is divided into three parts. First, and longest, is the company's history as an institution – its founding and extensions; its place among other railways; the ups and downs of its existence as a business and its survival as an independent joint stock company. Part One is also intended to provide a general background to the events, machines and individuals described or appearing in the parts which follow. Part Two is an account of the railway's physical existence – its tracks and structures; also its locomotives (famously good). Its carriages (for long legendarily bad) are covered in Part Three, which also examines the Highland Railway's operations – the role it played in the counties where it operated a monopoly service and its relations with its own employees and the people of the region. Within these divisions there are overlaps and asides of various kinds. These are intentional, to keep a sense of underlying narrative, as well as inevitable, because it is impossible to completely separate all the different facets of corporate life into compartments. Finally, the Notes and Appendices cover a variety of interesting aspects that are best treated separately.

The briefest personal explanation may be of some relevance. The author of this book first became aware of railways by growing up within sight and sound of the 'Further North' line. By then it had been for a few years part of the nationally-owned British Railways, and only three or four former Highland engines remained in service. Venturing into the engine shed at Wick in the summer of 1952, one could see an old engine, slumbering in the dimness as if forgotten, carrying the name *Ben Alder* lettered in flaking yellow paint. This and other personal recollections of a time well within living memory, in which, although already long after the formal winding-up of the Highland Railway Co., much of its ethos and practice was still preserved – and when the railway still played an important part in the local economy – underlie the research, observation, selection and presentation of information in the pages which follow.

# Note on Currency and Measurements

The Highland Railway accounted for its moneys in pounds, shillings and pence. There were 20 shillings in a pound, and 12 pennies in a shilling. These were old ' pennies', and 2.4 of them made up the face value of the present-day penny. The conventional abbreviations were 's' for shillings and 'd' for pence; thus today's £1.50 would be set out as £1 10s. The purchasing power of money in the period between 1855 and 1923, though it gradually became less – especially after 1914 – was always very much greater than it is today. Throughout most of its existence, most of the Highland Railway's staff were paid around £55 a year.

Distances on the railway were measured in miles, furlongs, chains and links. The mile, then as now, was 1,760 yards, or 1.609 kilometres. A furlong was 220 yards (201.12m); a chain was 22 yards (20.12 metres), and a link one hundredth of a chain. Heights and widths were measured in feet (.3048 metres) and inches (25.4 millimetres). Land area was expressed in acres (4,840 square yards, or .405 hectare) and roods, which were quarter-acres.

Weights were measured in tons (equivalent to 1.016 metric tonnes) and hundredweights, of which there were twenty to the ton, approximately .05 of a metric tonne. Boiler pressure in locomotives was measured in pounds per square inch (psi).

# ACKNOWLEDGEMENTS

Grateful thanks are owed to those who have allowed me to draw on their work or who have helped in other ways: particularly David Stirling, who has been generous with his prodigious knowledge of the HR, also Philip Atkins, David Rose, Neil T. Sinclair and Iain Sutherland. Any mistakes, along with the opinions expressed, remain the author's sole responsobility. I am also very grateful to Keith Fenwick, Hon. Librarian of the Highland Railway Society and Editor of its *Journal,* and Reg Carter, Hon. Librarian of the Stephenson Locomotive Society; also to John Holm, and George and Isabel Ross for sight of John Ross's Diaries; Gail Inglis at the North Highland Archive, Wick, and the staff of Wick Public Library; the staff of the National Archives of Scotland at Register House and West Register House, Edinburgh; and of the Post Office Archives at Mount Pleasant, London; Bob Steward, Archivist of the Highland Regional Council, and the staff of Inverness Reference Library; the staff of the Special Collections at Aberdeen University Library where the O'Dell Transport Collection is housed; and Lynne Thurston at the National Railway Museum Library. Lillian King kindly gave permission to quote from 'Dalnaspidal Recollections'. Lesley Junor trawled the Highland Photographic Archive for possible pictures, most of which I have gratefully used; and Paul Adair did the same at Perth and Kinross Museums. Howard Geddes also gave valuable help with illustrations from the Highland Railway Society's collection. The epigraphic verse is from a poem published in *The Scotsman* on 9 October 1933 (full text in *HRJ*, No.13). I am also grateful to Iain Sutherland for the 1864 map of Caithness railways; and to Mrs C.G.W. Roads, Lyon Clerk and Keeper of Records at the Court of the Lord Lyon, Edinburgh, for information on Scottish railway heraldry; to Kay Lucas for hospitality in Edinburgh, and to John Yellowlees of Scotrail for help with travelling the modern Highland Lines.

# PART I

# ONE

Inverness, in the year 1845, was a town of some 11,000 people – the remotest urban centre of any size in Great Britain. Once a royal site of the Pictish kingdom, it had been a royal burgh since at least the reign of King William the Lion in the thirteenth century, and was long-established as the principal commercial, legal and social centre of a vast region, encompassing the four northern counties of Ross, Cromarty, Sutherland and Caithness, as well as its own shire, the largest in Scotland, with the Isle of Skye, the Small Isles, and the Outer Hebrides, and the small county of Nairnshire. This enormous hinterland, most of it in a state of severe economic and social depression, formed the greater part of Scotland's *Gaidhealtachd*, the Gaelic-speaking Highlands.

Though Gaelic was daily heard on its streets in the nineteenth century, the town had, for centuries, been an enclave of non-Gaelic speech and customs: the Gaels were not town-builders. It was always a king's centre, with none of the local magnates being quite dominant enough to control it, and its castle was the seat of the often-precarious authority of a royal sheriff. A small mercantile community had developed there in order to both serve the needs, and exploit the resources, of the Highlands. Several times in its history the town was plundered and burned by the Lord of the Isles. Its ill-treatment in 1746 by the Duke of Cumberland and his army in the vicious aftermath of Culloden was by no means forgotten by the townspeople a century later. Being so far from any larger town – the nearest, Aberdeen, was 110 miles away; and Edinburgh was two days' journey by stagecoach – had always fostered a spirit of self-reliance. Its importance as a social centre was signified by the Northern Meeting, an assembly of the Highland gentry and their associates, which took place over several days each autumn. Of all the provincial centres in Great Britain, many of them much bigger, Inverness was probably the most accustomed to fending for itself.

Its great natural advantage was its situation, where the long-level gash of the Great Glen, slicing south-west to north-east across the country, met the coastal strip between the mountains and the sea. The narrows at the mouth of the Beauly Firth made it convenient to operate a ferry to the Black Isle – in fact a peninsula – on the other side, while the level terrain at the seashore made east – west travel relatively easy. Land routes from north, south, east and west converged on Inverness, and its harbour provided for coastal and foreign trade.

This small metropolis harboured both civic pride and entrepreneurial spirit. Its sense of isolation had been somewhat lessened by the work of the Commissioners for Highland Roads and Bridges during the earlier decades of the nineteenth century. They had built the Caledonian Canal, linking the three lochs of the Great Glen with the sea at each end. Old Highland footpaths, and the narrow military roads built by General Wade after 1715, had been replaced by wider roads and more substantial bridges. Around 875 miles of road were constructed, and over 1,300 bridges, mostly small but including many which spanned the larger rivers. As a result of this activity, the people of Inverness and its environs were well used to the presence of engineers, and a new career was opened to young men who previously might have passed their lives as labourers, or joined the army, or emigrated. One such was John Mitchell, born in Forres, and trained as a stonemason, whose diligence attracted the favourable notice of Thomas Telford, supremo of all the works. Mitchell was appointed as chief superintendent of all the Highland Roads in 1806. His eldest son, Joseph, was also born in Forres, in 1803. He attended Inverness Academy, which had been founded in 1791 and was a flourishing school. Showing some aptitude for technical drawing, he was sent to Aberdeen for a year's tuition in drawing and architecture. It became clear that engineering would be his profession and, at the age of seventeen, he was employed as a trainee mason at the canal works then under way at Fort Augustus, on the south end of Loch Ness. As the son of John Mitchell, he was already on a fast career track, and from here he was taken to London by Telford, who liked the idea of a couple of 'raw Scotchmen' to act as his clerks and learn engineering at his house-cum-office. Joseph's years with Telford in London taught him a lot about dealing with officialdom, the rich and the nobility, as well as about engineering. In 1824, John Mitchell died, and Telford thought sufficiently well of Joseph to secure his appointment, aged only twenty-one, as his father's replacement. Over the next twenty years, Joseph Mitchell acquired an unparalleled knowledge of the Highlands and Islands, as an engineer planning, contracting, supervising and consulting on virtually every work of significance from new paving in the streets of Inverness, and the setting-up of the town's gasworks, to laying out roads and building piers in the Orkneys. By 1844 he was a prominent and highly respected member of the Inverness community, a director and co-founder of the Caledonian Bank, and involved in many aspects of life in the town and the countryside beyond.

Mitchell was something of a glutton for work and rarely refused any offer of supplementary employment. James Hope, W.S., the Edinburgh-based Law Agent to the Commissioners for Highland Roads, first got him to apply his professional talents to railway construction in 1837. Well beyond the Highlands, he surveyed an alternative route for the Edinburgh & Glasgow Railway through the Earl of Hopetoun's grounds. From then on, Mitchell maintained an interest in railways, and noted in 1841 that the government had instructed Sir John McNeil to survey and lay out the main lines of railway in Ireland. He felt that the same thing could be done in Scotland through the already-existing agency of the Commissioners for Roads and Bridges. At Mitchell's urging, the provost and Town Council of Inverness made a proposal on these lines to the Treasury, and encouraged other town councils to do the same, but nothing came of it. Official guilt about the Highlands had not yet set in. The *Railway Times* commented:'These hill-people have been too long accustomed to draw on the public Treasury for the expenses of all their local improvements.'[1]

Steamboats had been operating on the Caledonian Canal from as early as 1820, and between Inverness and Glasgow from 1822. Mitchell saw that steam railways would come to his part of the country sooner or later, and was determined to be the man who would make it happen. In 1841 he made a proposal to a dynamic solicitor of Elgin, James Grant (later provost of the town), to build a railway linking it with the harbour of Lossiemouth, six miles away. Mitchell would undertake the engineering, and Grant would organise the company. Mitchell carried out a survey, and had a contractor ready, but he recorded that, 'although Mr Grant held meetings, and made considerable efforts at the time, the public did not seem then to appreciate the advantages of the proposed scheme.'[2] Mitchell's next railway venture was to propose the building of the Scottish Central Railway, to link Perth to the Edinburgh and Glasgow Railway, at Larbert. This would seem to be outside his Highland stamping ground, but it is likely that he was already thinking of securing the southern basis of a route into the Highlands. He noted of the project that, 'It would bring Perth and the whole north in direct railway communication with Edinburgh and Glasgow'.[3] Its prospectus was issued on 30 March 1844. On 14 August of the same year, a public meeting was held in Inverness, noted as the first meeting 'for the promotion of railway enterprise in the northern counties'.[4] Mitchell surveyed the Scottish Central line for its promoters at his own cost, on condition of being appointed engineer, but here he ran into the sharp and heavy end of railway politics. The promoters of the Caledonian Railway acquired an interest in the Scottish Central as a northward extension of their own line, and insisted on their engineers, Locke and Errington, being installed on the SCR project. Locke was a big name, considered second only to George Stephenson as a railway engineer. Mitchell, an obscure provincial engineer with scant railway experience, was at a severe disadvantage. Refusing to act in a subordinate capacity to the interlopers, he withdrew, receiving £1,500 for his work. Although disappointed and annoyed at the time, he was philosophical about it later. It was late 1844, and the 'railway mania' was on the point of breaking out; many people were about to lose a lot of money (though the Scottish Central, absorbed into the Caledonian in 1865, was always a profitable line).

He did not lick his wounds for long. The excitement of the 'mania' was causing all kinds of railway schemes to be brought forward, with 9,000 miles of line being authorised and over £550,000,000 of largely non-existent capital being pledged. To buy and quickly sell at a higher price was the aim of many; others held on to their expensively-bought shares believing that they were on to a sure winner. As the atmosphere became more feverish, expectations were pushed higher and higher, and numerous hopeless or fraudulent schemes were launched, simply to make money for their promoters. While the mania was still mounting, in March 1845, two railway schemes were advanced from Aberdeen, Scotland's third city. It was already anticipating rail connection from the south via the Aberdeen Railway, joining up with the Scottish Midland Junction. Meanwhile, it became known that plans were being drawn up, and a prospectus prepared, for rail access to the city from the north. This was for a line to link Aberdeen to Inverness, passing through the intermediate towns of Huntly, Keith, Elgin, Forres and Nairn. Its name, The Great North of Scotland Railway, suggested ambitions even beyond Inverness.

Mitchell now acted swiftly. His road-surveying work in the central Highlands had left him convinced that a railway line through the region was perfectly feasible. Such a line would be sixty-five miles shorter from Inverness to Perth than the Aberdeen route. There was an obvious advantage in costs and time. But there was also a proper Invernessian urge to do things in that town's own way, and manage its own affairs. The northern counties were considered to be the hinterland of Inverness, not of any other town. It did not fit their view of themselves to be at the end of a long branch line from Aberdeen. Mitchell found support from a local solicitor, Peter Anderson, and they formed a committee for the promotion of a railway company which would build a direct line from Inverness to the south. Mitchell's plan was to begin with what he called a 'base line' from Inverness to Elgin, along the relatively level Moray Firth coast. This would serve the dual purpose of creating a feeder line, and of keeping the Aberdeen party at bay. Anderson and Mitchell were authorised by the committee to go to Edinburgh and issue a prospectus for the Inverness–Elgin line, which was done on 24 March 1845 – a week before the Great North's document. The response from the Highlands was overwhelming, with applications for £2,000,000 of stock against a proposed capital of £300,000 for the line. The gratified committee thereupon empowered Anderson and Mitchell to go to London and issue a prospectus for the main undertaking, the line from Inverness to Perth, diverging from the coastal line at Nairn. Prospectuses for the Perth & Inverness, and Inverness & Elgin were issued on 9 April 1845, just as the railway mania was rising. The number of shares was set at 48,000, priced at £10, with a deposit price of £2 10s each. The brokers, Foster & Braithwaite, riding in arrogance on the wave, demanded: 'power to dispose of half the shares of the Company to such parties as they might approve of; the other half might be reserved for subscribers in the northern counties.'[5] Among railway schemes, this was a bold one, but far more dubious projects were selling at high prices, and the brokers demanded another quarter of the shares. Anderson demurred, but Mitchell insisted the aim was to sell the shares, and so in less than a week the whole stock was placed, and there was £120,000 of deposit cash in the bank. Lord Cockburn, the judge, noted in his *Circuit Journeys* of 1845 that, 'From Edinburgh to Inverness the people are mad about railways. The country is an asylum of railway lunatics. The Inverness patients, not content with a railway to their hospital from Aberdeen, insist on having one by the Highland road from Perth.'

The two promoters returned with some satisfaction, and the committee now set about the serious business of arranging for surveys, providing for wayleave and land purchase, and working out the details of traffic and materials. Enthusiasm for railways, they found, was not strong among certain Highland landowners whose territory would have to be traversed. Some, like Capt. Grant, the Earl of Seafield's factor, believed that trains would scare away the grouse; and the dowager Countess of Seafield simply detested railways – 'posting, in her opinion, with four horses was the perfect style of travelling,'[6] Mitchell was informed by the lady herself – and others merely held out in anticipation of a large cash offer. There was much need for persuasion and diplomacy, especially with the Duke of Atholl, whose agent at first refused to permit a survey. Nevertheless, by October the survey was completed, and Joseph Locke, with whom Mitchell appears to have buried the hatchet, came to inspect and approve. Locke, as Mitchell would have known, was a man who believed in cutting straight through, unlike his old master, George Stephenson, who preferred to go round major obstacles and who, if applied to, would have certainly preferred the Great North route to the direct line. By 30 November, the plans, checked and completed, were deposited with Parliament as required by standing orders. The legislation governing railway construction was based on that developed for canals; by obtaining an Act of Parliament authorising the construction, along a defined and mapped path, the company could exercise compulsory powers of purchase against a recalcitrant landowner, though the exact route, and the price of the ground, remained negotiable. At the same time, the Aberdeen party had been preparing its own scheme, and once this was published many hours were spent in Inverness checking its details and accuracy.

At the beginning of February 1846 some thirty of the Inverness party, promoters, solicitors, valuators, engineers and others who might be called on to give testimony in support, gathered in the Colonnade Hotel, in London's Haymarket, to await the summons of the Parliamentary Committee. Their number included the town clerk of Perth, Mr Reid, an important ally. The support of the considerable town of Perth, as southern terminus of the line, was valuable. For Perth, which already had the Scottish Central, a direct line from Inverness was a bonus. Never sure when the call would come, they cooled their heels until 29 April, such was the pressure of railway business. 'We were an idle and a jolly party,' noted Mitchell.[7] But he was displeased when other members, led by Reid, agreed with the Great North promoters, also in London for the same reason, that neither party would oppose the other on standing orders: that is, on alleged defects or deficiencies in their plans. Having closely perused the Aberdeen proposals, he had noted enough discrepancies and errors to give powerful ammunition to the Inverness counsel, but the agreement ruled this out. When the committee sat, it took the evidence for the Great North scheme first, and then considered the Inverness plan. William Austin, the barrister appearing for the Great North of Scotland, and a specialist in railway bills, was described by Mitchell as, 'very eloquent and very unscrupulous'. He rose to heights of sarcasm about the proposal, picking on the untried Mitchell rather than the expert railway witnesses, who included John Hawkshaw, engineer of the trans-Pennine Manchester & Leeds Railway, as well as Locke:

Ascending such a summit as 1580 feet,' he said, 'was very unprecedented. Mr Mitchell, the engineer, was the greatest mountain climber he ever heard of; he beat Napoleon outright, and quite eclipsed Hannibal. He read a book the other day, of several hundred pages, describing how Hannibal crossed the Alps; but after this line will have passed, he had no doubt that quartos would be written about Mr Mitchell. Besides the decision of the committee in its favour, there was only one other thing that would surprise him – that was the making of the line.[8]

Two weeks later the decision was given. The Great North's Aberdeen–Inverness scheme was passed, but 'the preamble[9] of the Perth, Inverness and Elgin Bill was not proved.' Austin's attack had struck home. It was the altitude and what the committee described as the engineering character of the line, that had brought the parliamentarians' negative decision. A separate though related proposal, the Strathtay and Breadalbane Railway, intended to make a branch to Aberfeldy from the main line at Ballinluig, was passed unopposed. The jolly party returned north in a state of depression, which Mitchell wickedly purported to see shared by those landowners who had driven hard bargains for their loss of amenity.

In 1847 came the crash. The collapse in railway share prices sent shockwaves of dismay and distress through the country. Stock purchasers, approached for the balance of payment on their deposits (at the original price) lost huge sums or were bankrupted. Every railway company struggled to survive. The Great North of Scotland, whose notional capital was £1,500,000 in 30,000 shares at £50 apiece, had allocated large proportions of shares to its promoters and directors, and now found itself in severe difficulties, exacerbated by its unhappy merger with the Aberdeen Railway in 1847, which was nullified in 1850. It was late 1853 before it amassed sufficient funds to contract for a line from Aberdeen as far as Huntly, about forty miles, and it was November 1852 before construction began. Inverness, kept waiting for its rail connection, soon became impatient. The *Inverness Advertiser* of 21 August 1849 published a lengthy 'Open Letter to Sir Robert Peel' (the Prime Minister, then on holiday at Eilean Aigas on the Beauly River), setting out the case for a railway from Perth to Inverness and further north, asking: 'Is a third part of the lineal extent of Great Britain to be permanently cut off from a participation in these facilities of transit, which, within the last twenty years, have grown into a very necessity of modern civilisation?' The anonymous author did not believe the Highlands could do this with their own resources, and 'substantial assistance from the Imperial Government' was requested. Frustration increased when in August 1852 a railway line opened between Elgin and Lossiemouth, promoted by James Grant, now Provost of Elgin, but achieved without the participation of Joseph Mitchell. Elgin, with a population of 7,500, was regarded in Inverness as a somewhat rundown place, but here it was, with the North's first railway. Mitchell, who had returned to his post with the Commissioners of Roads and Bridges, formed a new committee in 1851 with Peter Anderson, and joined by a local landowner, Eneas Mackintosh of Raigmore (known, in Highland style, by his estate's name as 'Raigmore'), with the initial aim of getting railway companies in the south to back the direct line. Forty-five members eventually joined, including Dr Grigor, the dynamic leading citizen of Nairn, and its chief promoter as a resort town, as well as merchants, solicitors, landowners, tacksmen (tenants entitled to sublet), and the manager of the Caledonian Bank. Alexander Matheson of Ardross, who had returned from Hong Kong with a fortune (he was nephew of Sir James Matheson, co-founder of Jardine, Matheson) and was now MP (Liberal) for Inverness Burghs, was also persuaded to join.

The new committee was more cautious and circumspect than that of 1845. Around £400 was subscribed to enable the three leaders to make new overtures to the landed proprietors and to the railway companies to which the line might be both a feeder and extension. Chief among these was the London & North Western Railway, then managed by Capt. Mark Huish. A bad enemy to competing companies, Huish had no reason to be other than cordial to his Highland visitors. Approaches to Joseph Locke and the great railway builder, Thomas Brassey, also resulted in support and advice. Brassey, if given the building contract, would take a third of the stock as part payment. Locke reckoned that the southern companies and the directors could feel confident about purchasing another third, and that the rest should be sold to the public. The landowners were also mostly supportive. Mitchell dusted off his plans and estimates of seven years before, for Brassey's inspection and approval. In April 1853, a public meeting was convened in Inverness to report on the committee's activities.

The economic background was still sombre; the country was in recession and money was not readily available. Mitchell urged the need for financial prudence but proclaimed his confidence that the line could be built – as he had worked out in 1845 – at £8,817 per mile. This was far less than the £30,000 per mile of the Caledonian, or even the £20,000 of the Dundee & Perth, but Mitchell insisted that the line should be constructed as in America,[10] a single track, at a cost suited to the requirements and the limited traffic of the country. As he himself later recorded, the actual cost was £8,850 per mile. It was unanimously agreed that a new prospectus should be drawn up.

## The Inverness & Nairn Railway

Meanwhile, the Great North of Scotland was still building its line to Huntly, but it had almost totally reorganised itself as a company, and had renewed its original Parliamentary powers in 1852. Mitchell's advice to the Inverness Committee was to proceed gently. In a report to it on 15 September 1853 he advised that the crucial ground, now as in 1845, was that between Elgin and Inverness:

> By possessing this latter portion of the line, the Great North of Scotland Company cal-
> culated to divert the entire northern traffic to the Aberdeen route.
>
> They have now abandoned this project, solely because they do not possess the means
> of constructing their line so far north, and for which they had obtained renewed
> Parliamentary powers.
>
> It appears to me therefore that the present time is favourable for those interested in
> promoting the direct Highland Railway taking possession of this ground, which in fact

forms the key to the North, and the possession of which will secure to the proprietors of the northern counties the means of constructing the through short line whenever the opportunity arises... I am decidedly of opinion, therefore, that as the first step in the great scheme, we should proceed to Parliament for power to construct the portion of the main line, between Inverness and Nairn, the Parliamentary plans and documents being almost all prepared.[1]

Mitchell's reason for claiming that the GNSR had abandoned Inverness–Elgin is unclear; it certainly had not been formally renounced.[2] This most important document also seems to be the first to refer to a Highland Railway, though the title was not to be formally adopted for eleven years. At this time, he was also active in preparing plans for the direct Perth line, negotiating with the landowner at Killiecrankie, Mr Butler, who was objecting to the projected route through the pass. The committee accepted Mitchell's proposal for the Nairn line. In his memoirs, Mitchell makes it seem as if the scheme breezed along effortlessly, but in fact considerable pains were taken to placate the Aberdonians, who, if not in a position to advance their own line, were unhappy to see Inverness taking advantage of their weakness. Objections were to be expected. Mitchell was also watching matters at the southern extremity, where the Scottish Midland Railway was proposing a branch line up the Tay valley to Dunkeld. This line had been approved by Parliament in 1846, but no construction had been undertaken. A line to Dunkeld was considered acceptable, but if the Scottish Midland proposed to go as far north as Pitlochry, it was to be resisted.

Committee minutes survive from 16 July 1853. At this time, they were meeting every few days to deal with immediate issues and keep matters rolling. A prospectus for the Inverness & Nairn Railway was issued in November. The capital of the new line was to be £85,000 in £10 shares, with a deposit of £1 10s per share payable on subscription. Brassey, through his Perth associate James Falshaw, was prepared to build the line for £65,000, taking £20,000 of it in stock. The other £20,000 was for land purchase, rolling stock and other items. It was very much an Inverness enterprise: even its bank was the Inverness-based Caledonian Bank. Further public meetings in Inverness and Nairn endorsed the project. On 6 December a public meeting in Inverness Castle carried two resolutions by acclaim:

1. Railway Communication has become indispensable to the interests of this Community.
2. That formation of a Line from Inverness to Nairn is the best possible commencement of the Railway System in the North.

In the Nairn court house two days later, someone asked if the Aberdeen company meant to oppose. Mitchell replied that he and Raigmore had met Mr Anderson, solicitor to the Great North, in Edinburgh, who had said that the Great North would be glad to witness the success of the Inverness & Nairn. Soon, however, it was being minuted by the committee that GNSR men were combing through the plans and making field observations; it was emphasised that the Inverness & Nairn was prepared to give 'every facility' to the GNSR, 'consistent with the interests of their own [I&N] shareholders'.³ The same meeting noted that Mr H.A. Welsh, an Inverness landowner, was objecting to the line taken through his grounds at Millburn.

By the end of January 1854, the new company had 210 shareholders, mostly from Inverness and around; the number reveals how small the pool of relatively well-off individuals really was. Brassey and Falshaw each had 1,000 shares; Joseph Mitchell had taken 250. Some of the big landowners, like Macpherson of Cluny, subscribed only the 25 minimum needed to be on the committee, but Raigmore took 800, and Capt. Fraser-Tytler of Aldourie, 500. The majority of shareholders held less than 10 shares; many had the minimum of 2.⁴ On 7 February, the *Inverness Advertiser* noted with regret that the GNSR had 'seen fit to show a bad animus' by lodging a memorial against the I&N line on standing orders. In anticipation of this, the I&N's Parliamentary agent, Theodore Martin, had been supplied with information to lodge a tit-for-tat memorial against works the GNSR was proposing in Aberdeen. An armistice was made by the 10 February, and both sets of objections were withdrawn. Still concerned about Aberdonian opposition, the committee sent Charles Stewart, an Inverness solicitor, with Raigmore to London, to meet with representatives of the GNSR, 'with power to agree to such terms for the purpose of preventing opposition, in Parliament, to the further progress of the Bills of this Company... and for making such arrangements in regard to the future relations between the two Companies as they may think best for the interests of this Company...'⁵ With such a very open brief, Mitchell for one must have waited with anxiety for the result. A draft heads of agreement was drawn up, giving the GNSR running powers over the I&N line, from such time as the companies' lines met, and allowing for it to have facilities for a booking clerk in the station at Inverness, and on this basis, the Great North withdrew its opposition. The document, drawn up on 25 February 1854, was approved by the I&N directors. But it was to be the cause of controversy later.

The Inverness & Nairn Bill duly received its second reading, and the committee felt it was safe to proceed. Mr Welsh was still causing difficulties, and negotiations were also going on with the Inverness and Nairn county Turnpike Trusts, both of which claimed recompense for anticipated loss of revenue. A deputation of Inverness-shire territorial grandees, including Cameron of Lochiel, met the railway directors, and a payment of £2,000 was speedily agreed.⁶ With Nairnshire, a small county less furnished with notables, but also with a roadways debt of £2,000 to pay off, apart from future loss of earnings, there was a long wrangle, but ultimately the railway company paid another £2,000. Mr Welsh – whose attitude was making him deeply unpopular in Inverness, which was longing for its railway – refused to withdraw his objections. Having at first, to Mitchell's surprise, agreed to have the line pass in front of his house, he now adamantly opposed this and wanted it built so far behind the house that it would have to be carried offshore, on an embankment, to a terminal point far from the town centre. Mitchell had offered to sink the railway in a low cutting and to provide access by means of a bridge and level crossing. With obstinate determination,

Welsh took his objections to the House of Commons and, when they were rejected, to the House of Lords, with a petition that the railway was not necessary at all. This last eccentricity was ruled out of order, but the company had to spend much time and money defending its plan. The bridge and crossing were duly built, Welsh taking his time about accepting a suitable bridge design.[7] In due course, expansion of the railway yards swallowed up the bridge, crossing, and most of the Millburn grounds. A signboard, 'Welsh's Bridge', in the Inverness station yard, still commemorates the railway's opponent.

The railway got its Act of Parliament on 24 July 1854, and on 21 September, the new board of directors, with most of the population, came down to the site of the inaugural ceremony, just east of Millburn House. The press of people and their enthusiasm was such that the barriers built to separate the nobs from the plebs were quickly knocked down, and official guests had some trouble in claiming their reserved seats. But the crowd was good-natured, and once some order had been restored, the Rev. Dr Macdonald offered up a prayer and Cluny, as chairman of the board, made a speech. The Countess of Seafield (not her anti-railway mother-in-law) duly cut the first sod with an ornamental spade, and Cluny, in full chieftain's fig, wheeled it away in an ornamental barrow. The countess too made a speech, expressing the hope that the line would extend over the Highlands for the benefit of all the people; and other orators expressed similar feelings. The magistrates and persons of distinction paraded through the town, and further speeches, with the multiplicity of toasts normal on such occasions, followed at a dinner in the town hall. The railway had no need for a full-time mechanical engineer, and on Mitchell's recommendation, Alexander Allan, Locomotive Superintendent of the Scottish Central, was retained at a fee of £150 to supervise the provision of locomotives and rolling stock.[8] Allan is an engineer whose stock has gone down somewhat in recent decades, but he appears to have done a sound job for the Inverness & Nairn. On 24 January 1855, a tender from Hawthorns of Leith for two engines, at £2,375 apiece, was accepted. At the board meeting on 7 February, Mitchell reported that rolling stock to the value of £4,436 was also on order: three first-class, four third-class, carriages, and a van from Brown & Marshall; two carriage trucks and two cattle and sheep trucks from Faulds of Glasgow; and two horse-boxes, six timber trucks, and twenty open wagons from Watsons of Errol.

So relatively short and level a line was no problem for Messrs Brassey and Falshaw, and work went ahead, with completion anticipated within twelve months. It was single track all the way, though accommodation was made for eventual double tracking. The directors were disappointed to have to record delays, however. They had hoped that their meeting of 18 August would record the completion of the works, but they had to wait until November. The problem was not with construction of the line but with manufactured items which had to be supplied from the south. Whatever the reason – perhaps only pressure of orders – signalling equipment and turntables were not delivered when due. But the Aberdeen Steam Packet Co., engaged to take these items from Aberdeen, was in no apparent hurry. The owners of coastal steamship lines had no cause to love the railways, which had already killed off their lucrative

Edinburgh and Glasgow to London passenger services. In the end, a local vessel, the *Isabella Napier*, had to be chartered in order to bring the equipment from Leith Docks to the quay at Inverness.

The *Inverness Advertiser*, on 4 September, reported that a first locomotive had been landed at Inverness and this began making runs with ballast wagons from 18 September. By this time a general manager had been found. With Mitchell playing the main part in a selection process involving thirty candidates, Andrew Dougall, of the Dundee & Arbroath Railway, was appointed on 6 September 1855, at a salary of £200 a year. He was also secretary and cashier, and would have a long career in Inverness. The line was inspected on 3 October by Lt Col Wynne for the Board of Trade. He reported that, though well-laid and in good order, it was '... deficient in signal posts and turntables, and as yet the Company are unprovided with passenger carriages, and have but one engine',[9] and required opening to be deferred for a month. By 13 October, a set of Rules and Regulations for the guidance of company servants had been compiled and printed. In hiring men with some experience, Dougall had perforce to look south. Inverness' first stationmaster, Thomas Mackay, came from the Edinburgh & Glasgow Railway; Nairn's, James Hall, from the Dundee & Arbroath. The Locomotive Superintendent, William Barclay, aged thirty-one, had been proposed by Alexander Allan, who was his uncle. With only two engines to look after, the skills of 'a good practical mechanic' were all he needed to display. It was 27 October before the turntables were installed, and the Board of Trade finally passed the railway as ready for public use on 31 October. The terminus at Inverness, with a single platform some 20 yards long, though at the edge of the town, was quite centrally placed, with the line curving in through open ground to a building set slightly back from Academy Street, and located between the Academy grounds and the Falcon Ironworks. The governing body of the Inverness Academy had wanted £5,000 for this site, described as 'waste garden', but by an agreement of March 1855 the railway company took it on a feu tenancy, at 4s per foot of frontage per annum.[10] At opening the company had paid-up capital of £43,476 and loans of £14,300; expenditure was £56,540.[11]

On 5 November the railway opened for business, amid scenes of celebration. A huge crowd came to see the first public train leave Inverness for Nairn, drawn by the railway's two engines, which were decorated with evergreens, flowers and flags, while their crews were 'turned out in spotless white'. Two small guns went off and a row of flags across the line was 'hitched some yards higher'.[12] There were pauses at the three intermediate stations,[13] Culloden, Dalcross and Fort George. Most of the 800 or so passengers were in open wagons but the November chills did not dampen their ardour. Reporting the events, the *Inverness Courier* noted that: 'Almost all the way back they sang songs in loud chorus and testified by the general exhilaration of spirits that they were not unacquainted with the barley-bree of Nairnshire. There was however no excess'.[14] Next day, an excursion was run from Nairn to Inverness, the train reputedly reaching a speed approaching fifty miles an hour. In the first five days, passenger numbers totalled 2,733 – over 130 per train. The initial service was four trains each way daily, but from 1 December it was reduced to three, the journey lasting forty-five minutes.

The half-mile harbour branch linking Inverness Station with the quay on the Ness Estuary opened some time after the Nairn line.[15] A goods service on the latter began from 1 December 1855, by which time a number of wagons had been delivered. But while the response of passengers had been satisfactory, the daily goods train was little used. Though trade was always low in the winter months, Mitchell's estimate of freight traffic was over-sanguine. He had conducted thorough surveys of road traffic between Elgin and Inverness, and knew that some 30,000 passenger journeys had been made each year by coach and cart. All of this and more was now using the train for the Nairn–Inverness section. His estimate of annual revenue was £9,600, of which he expected passengers to provide £4,325 and other items carried by passenger train: mails, parcels, carriages and horses, to account for £1,335, with general merchandise, manure, fish and livestock bringing in around £4,000. In fact, passenger traffic earned three fifths of the I&N's revenue, a pattern which would be maintained as the Highland lines were extended.

### The Inverness & Aberdeen Junction Railway

Even as the Nairn line was building, plans for extension were already in hand. During 1854, a committee had been got together to promote a line from Nairn to Elgin, to be known as the Inverness & Elgin Junction Railway.[1] This proposal was at first resisted by the Great North of Scotland Railway, whose line to Huntly opened in September 1854. The GNSR deposited a new Bill to build its own line between Huntly and Nairn, but negotiations took place through 1854, resulting in an agreement to jointly complete a line between Nairn and Huntly. The plan was for each company to build its own section, meeting at an end-on junction in the middle of a viaduct over the Spey. Isambard Kingdom Brunel was to be consulted on the bridge works. Elgin was to be the exchange point for trains or locomotives.[2] It was decided that if agreement over the site of the bridge could not be reached in time for the two companies' Bills to be passed in the current session, both would be withdrawn for the time being, except that part of the GNSR Bill which gave it powers to build between Huntly and Keith. The agreement was announced at a meeting in Inverness on 5 December, and the new line was to be known as the Inverness & Aberdeen Junction Railway.[3] Discussions on the Spey Bridge and the precise routing of the line between Keith and Elgin became protracted, and the two Bills were consequently withdrawn as agreed. But the initiative rested with the Inverness party. In the spring of 1855, they instructed Mitchell to survey a line from Nairn to Elgin,[4] and secured the services of Locke as consultant engineer.[5] Two large proprietors, the Earls of Seafield and the trustees of the Earl of Fife, each agreed to subscribe £30,000 towards the undertaking. The obtaining of this aristocratic and financial support was a coup for Inverness as the two earls might have been expected to look to Aberdeen for the provision of their railway. Perhaps to the surprise of the Inverness promoters, the board of the Great North of Scotland Railway now seemed to take the view that the Invernessians were not going far enough. They pointed out that the Inverness proposal would serve the richest part of Morayshire, while they would be left to build an expensive line from Keith through the rough, hilly district to the west, involving a stiff climb in both directions and a crossing of the wide river Spey. In fact, the GNSR, chronically short of money and in no state to raise additional capital, could not possibly have undertaken this task, and the Inverness Committee realised that Aberdeen was looking for ways to delay the project. In Inverness there was strong determination to see things through, and a little group of promoters met regularly through the early summer of 1855 in Martin's offices at New Palace Yard, Westminster. On 14 June, the Hon. Thomas Bruce, commissioner for the Earl of Seafield, wrote on behalf of the committee to Sir James Elphinstone, chairman of the GNSR, to state their position:

> Since last year some very important interests in the North have taken up the scheme, and we now form a body incomparably more powerful than last year, and, as I am assured, fully capable of carrying out our plans.'

He went on to say that:

> … in order to avoid any discussion between the Companies as to the Spey crossing, which might indefinitely postpone the completion of the line, we propose, instead of meeting at the Spey, to construct the whole line from Nairn to Keith, and shall trust that you will take stock in our line to the extent to which you proposed last year[6]

Among these important new interests was the marquess of Stafford, heir to the Duke of Sutherland, whose family owned almost the whole large county of Sutherland, and who was interested in a steamboat link between a railhead on the Moray coast and a harbour on his estates. The Inverness Committee consisted of Seafield as chairman, Stafford as deputy chairman, Lord Berriedale (later Earl of Caithness), James Duff MP and W.J. Tayler (both as trustees for Lord Fife), Thomas Bruce, Capt. Fraser-Tytler, and Eneas Mackintosh of Raigmore. Elphinstone returned a cautious but negative reply[7] to Bruce's letter, expressing a wish to stick with the agreement of December 1854. The committee reiterated its will to proceed, one way or the other, but stating that if necessary, they would go to Parliament to get powers for a Nairn–Keith line (extending the same running powers to the Great North as already agreed). Stafford wrote to Elphinstone on 18 June 1855, hoping for 'the most cordial understanding' between the companies and reiterating Bruce's invitation for a GNSR deputation to talk things over in London. The GNSR were in no hurry to do this, and they meantime continued to dispute the Keith–Elgin route, preferring a line via Rothes rather than follow the Mitchell plan to cross the Spey at Boat o' Brig, which gave a more direct but more steeply graded line. This was a tricky point, as the Seafield and Fife interests also would have preferred the Rothes line, which would have served their own properties better; but they agreed to go along with the Boat o' Brig route which was favoured by the rest of the committee. The Fife estate's costs in having a Rothes line surveyed were accepted by the committee.[8] On 18 July, Bruce reported to the committee that a private letter from Sir James Elphinstone had expressed great satisfaction with the proposed plans, and it was agreed to lose no time in bringing the undertaking before 'the public and the Proprietors'.

A new I&AJR prospectus was issued in Inverness and the first meeting was held on 21 August 1855. The capital was to be £300,000 in £10 shares, with a deposit of £1 10s per share, and the GNSR was invited to invest £50,000 and have two seats on the board of the new company.[9] Shares could be applied for at the offices of banks or writers (solicitors) in Inverness, Aberdeen, Dingwall, Cromarty, Tain, Golspie, Wick, Grantown, Kingussie, Perth, Edinburgh, Glasgow, Newcastle, Liverpool, Manchester and London. Elgin was added to the list a few days after the first issue of the prospectus. Bruce 'also undertook in a letter that they would abide by all the agreements come to in 1854', which, to the Great North, included running powers all the way to Inverness.[10]

Local committees were formed in the northern counties to help the subscription drive, but there was displeasure in Elgin: the new prospectus specifically mentioned 'a Line to Burghead' as part of the company's plan. In reply to a letter from some leading citizens of Elgin, the committee explained that the capacity of Burghead harbour, 'affords the Committee an assurance of the propriety of the courses which they have adopted.'[11] In other words, this was to be their steamer port for Littleferry, at the mouth of Loch Fleet on the Sutherland estates. Provost Grant of Elgin, now promoting a southwards extension of his Morayshire Railway from Elgin to Rothes, saw no reason why another harbour should be preferred to that of Lossiemouth for the Sutherland steamer, despite its greater distance. Nairn joined the debate, proposing that its harbour should be developed for the same purpose. Grant was a powerful agitator and he too could command some big guns. Although Burghead had been the connecting port for the Sutherland estates since 1809, George Loch, the duke's factor, eventually proposed to a Committee meeting on 6 November 1855 that the Burghead branch should be dropped, and this was agreed, with a protest only from Robert Milne, of the GNSR, which at that time had no involvement with the Morayshire Railway.

This meeting was at Inverness, where all the committee's gatherings had been held since 21 August 1855. The GNSR, after much foot-shuffling debate over gradients and curves, had finally given up argument and come in with a pledge of £40,000 in return for two seats on the board, on 20 October. A revised prospectus, confirming that the I&AJR and GNSR lines would meet at Keith, was issued on 15 November. On 14 December, it was agreed that the company should purchase locomotives from Hawthorns of Leith (on a basis of shares rather than cash), and carriages and wagons from Brown, Marshall of Birmingham, hopefully on the same basis. At this point, no Act for the new railway had been obtained, though there was little doubt in anyone's mind that it would be secured. Tough negotiations lay ahead with certain landowners. Brodie of Brodie, between Nairn and Forres, demanded large sums in compensation for the loss of his amenity. Another grandee reared his head, the Duke of Richmond and Lennox, who controlled the tolls of a bridge over Spey, and also wanted the railway to come nearer to Fochabers than Mitchell's plan allowed. A deviation was agreed,[12] The Morayshire Railway set aside its plan for an Elgin–Rothes line and instead requested running powers between Elgin and Orton, from where it proposed to build a branch to Rothes (this was opened on 23 August 1858); powers were granted on a basis of a mileage payment plus a proportion of total earnings between Rothes and Elgin. The Morayshire Road Trustees, the Trustees of the Findhorn Suspension Bridge, the Morayshire Turnpike Road Trustees, the Spey Bridge and Fochabers Road Trust and the Boat o' Brig Trust all lined up to demand compensation. By this time, there was considerable evidence that railway development had little adverse effect on road traffic, and the committee held out against these demands. Other factors helped to add to costs: the Board of Trade required five bridges where level crossings had been planned. By the time the Bill for the I&AJR got its second reading, only two objectors were recorded: the Duke of Richmond and Mr Stewart of Auchlunkart. On 12 July 1856 a committee of the House of Lords proved the Preamble of the Bill, but awarded £2,500 to their ducal colleague in respect of his bridge. Brodie finally agreed to an arrangement of forty-five years' purchase at an average of £1 9s an acre, plus a station (Brodie) to be built close to his West Lodge. He went on being a nuisance, later demanding a bridge for a farm track, unless he was given £160, in which case he would accept a level crossing. On 21 July the Bill received the royal assent and became an Act. The authorised capital was £325,000,[13] with loans of up to £108,300. A board of directors was elected, with Alexander Matheson as chairman, Lord Seafield as deputy, George Loch, Eneas Mackintosh of Raigmore, W.J. Tayler of Rothiemay, Sir Alexander Gordon Cumming, the Hon. T.C. Bruce, Alexander Inglis Robertson of Aultnaskiach, the Earl of Caithness, Capt. Fraser-Tytler, Lord Stafford, the Hon. George Skene Duff of Miltonduff, Sir James Elphinstone, and John Blaikie; the last two being the GNSR nominees. As befitted a grander enterprise, the company furnished itself with armorial bearings: those of Macduff, the Duke of Fife, and Skene, with Seafield's wild men as supporters. Lyon King of Arms was not asked for his permission; and they also took Fife's motto, *Virtute et Opera*, 'By Virtue and Works'. By early August, building from Keith and Nairn was under way, with Mitchell, Dean & Co. in the eastern section (no relation to Joseph Mitchell), and Brassey & Falshaw between Nairn and Elgin. The works were again made to accommodate a double line, but only one line of rails was laid. The GNSR was also building its line from Huntly to Keith, which was opened on 11 October that year. Mitchell, determined to keep to his cost estimates, kept a close eye on progress. Later he wrote that Falshaw, 'never forgave me for compelling him to execute the works in terms of his contracts.'[14] It had always been the intention, in Inverness at least, that the new line should work hand-in-glove with the Inverness & Nairn, and on 20 August Andrew Dougall was formally appointed secretary of the I&AJR, in addition to his duties with the Inverness & Nairn.

Meanwhile, far to the south, the Perth & Dunkeld Railway had opened its line from Stanley Junction to a terminus at Birnam. The plan for a railway to Dunkeld had come to fruition, not through the Scottish Midland Junction but through a local initiative, whose backers were a similar social group to the Inverness/Nairn party, county landowners and Perth city merchants, with the Earl of Mansfield as chairman.

It obtained Parliamentary powers on 10 July 1854 and had a somewhat tense and strained association with the SMJR, which was to work the line. The eight-mile line left the SMJ just beyond the weaving village of Stanley, and ran, keeping to the south-west of the Tay, to a terminus at Birnam. The little town of Dunkeld was across the river here, but the bridge had a toll, belonging to the Duke of Atholl, and the duke had no intention of losing any income by permitting the railway to actually reach Dunkeld. The P&D line entered difficult country at the Pass of Birnam where the Tay is confined between steep hills, and a short tunnel was cut through the rock at Byres of Murthly, half-a-mile west of Kingswood. The line's engineer was John Stewart of Edinburgh and the contractors were Davidson, Leslie & Oughterson, their tender being £50,000. Unlike the Inverness lines, whose buildings were designed by the engineers, an architect was employed for the stations at Murthly and Birnam, Andrew Heiton of Perth. The cottage-style building at Murthly was the only brick station on the line. A private halt was constructed at Rohallion in 1859 for the benefit of the landowner, Sir William Drummond Stewart. Construction began in July 1854, and the line was officially opened on Saturday 5 April 1856. From 7 April, a daily service of three trains each way ran between Birnam and Perth, operated by the Scottish Midland Junction, which merged with the Aberdeen Railway in June of that year to become the Scottish North-Eastern Railway.

Even a modest railway needed works facilities, and expansion of the terminal and other railway buildings at Inverness began from a very early stage. A substantial amount of extra carriage and wagon stock was ordered – twenty-nine passenger carriages, three carriage trucks, three horse-boxes, and sixty-two trucks and vans – at a cost of £12,900, all approved at the Junction Co.'s board meeting of 9 February 1857. At the behest of the GNSR, the goods wagons were ordered to be fitted with spring buffers, as otherwise they would not be allowed to run south of the interchange station at Keith. To cope with the increase in rolling stock, a carriage repair works was set up at Needlefield, just to the north of Inverness Station, and a further part of the academy's grounds were acquired under feu. An attempt to have the railway pay for the complete relocation of the academy was successfully rebuffed.[15] Despite its pleasure at being on the railway map at last, Inverness Town Council was keen to ensure the line paid its due fees. As a royal burgh, the town was entitled to charge 'petty customs' on goods brought in, and the railway company had to account for, and duly pay, the tolls on all items. This provided cause for much petty wrangling over the next decades.

Terms of accommodation between the Nairn Co. and the I&AJR had to be sorted out. Though it was intended that the new company should take over all train working, the line from Nairn to Inverness and Inverness Station would remain the property of the Inverness & Nairn, and it was responsible for extensions and alterations at Inverness. For four years, the two companies cohabited, sharing some directors and senior personnel. Despite the close relationship, the Working Agreement took some time to thrash out: the I&N shareholders wanted to make sure their position was safeguarded in the new set-up and the eventual amalgamation terms. Their movable items and equipment were to be rented by the Junction Co., which would also buy all new plant. On 21 February 1857 the I&AJR board approved the building of a new locomotive shed, a repair shop and a smithy on the site known as Lochgorm, adjacent to Inverness Station, on the left-hand side of the track. This whole area was a marshy one and no doubt there had been a pond there at one time, as the name suggests. The new workshops and sheds were to be rented from the Nairn Co., but the latter refused to place orders until the agreement was signed and sealed. The I&AJR proposed on 16 March 1857 to:

> take over the whole undertaking of the Inverness and Nairn Co. with its assets and liabilities and to put the Ordinary stock already subscribed for in that Company on the footing of a Preference Stock and guarantee a dividend of 4 per cent per annum on that stock for the first two years and 5 per cent thereafter.

If the ordinary dividend of the I&AJR should exceed that, the larger amount would be paid. This was approved by the I&N board on the following day, 'as the basis of an arrangement between the companies'. Amalgamation had in fact to wait another four years. Argument on a Working Agreement continued, until the I&N board meeting of 14 July was able to minute that agreement had been reached. The I&AJR was to work the Nairn line on a basis of working expenses not to exceed 45 per cent of gross receipts, and to be given the use of Inverness and Nairn stations for the purpose. Workshops and running sheds would be erected at Inverness by the Nairn Co. and rented to the Junction Co. Engines, carriages, trucks, wagons, and all workshop and warehouse plant belonging to the I&N would be bought by the I&AJR and paid for over three years. The agreement would last for ten years, and would come into effect as soon as the Junction Company commenced its service.

In anticipation of a Working Agreement, the I&NR obtained a new Act, on 26 June 1857, re-incorporating the company, and with an arrangement to pay the town council of Inverness an agreed sum for tolls, rather than on an item-by-item basis. The Act also provided for the creation of 2,500 additional £10 shares, as preference shares at 5 per cent in perpetuity. These were to be offered first to existing shareholders at a proportion of five to two existing shares; and the issue was, unsurprisingly, highly successful. These resources were useful, as in the course of 1857 the I&AJR was running short of capital and it was proposed that a loan should be raised, with security guaranteed by the directors. The idea was opposed by George Loch, and dropped. At an extraordinary Shareholders' Meeting in Inverness on 18 August it was, however, agreed that the company should raise its permitted total of £108,300 by mortgage or bond. At the end of September a debenture loan of £45,000 was raised in Edinburgh, over two years at 5 per cent per annum. The directors agreed this time to give personal guarantees against the payment of interest, though a minute of the board meeting of 16 October specified that if required to pay up, they would have, 'complete releif [sic] and recourse against the said Railway'.

From early 1856 Inverness had had a Station Hotel, owned by the I&NR, whose board meeting of 1 December 1855 authorised the manager to seek a tenant for 'the two dwelling houses at the Inverness Station'. These were 77 and 78 Academy Street, and in January, Mr Mackie of the Union Hotel took on the lease at an initial £50 per annum, 'rising to £90 in the last four years of the lease', inclusive of running the refreshment rooms. Mitchell organised the necessary alterations to the buildings at a cost of £184. The hotel was soon in need of extension, and by 1859 had hot running water and a hand-operated lift to take luggage and other items to the upper floors. Although the hotel was profitable, Mackie on occasion had to be chased by the HR lawyers to pay his termly rentals.

The I&AJR's half-yearly meeting on 31 October 1857 was turned into a special meeting in order to consider the terms of the Working Agreement with the I&N. The necessary three-fifths majority was obtained, with £128,510 of capital in favour and £65,650 against. The prime objectors were the GNSR, who thought the agreement, with its charge for working the I&N's traffic not to exceed 45 per cent of receipts, and the proposed amalgamation terms, too kind to the Inverness & Nairn Co. The latter's shareholders had agreed the terms at a meeting on the previous day.

By the end of November at least four locomotives had been delivered from Hawthorns, to supplement the I&N's pair. By December it was clear that insufficient rolling stock would be delivered to work the traffic, but the resourceful Alexander Allan was able to arrange to get an additional twenty-five wagons built in central Scotland and delivered by the end of January 1858, at a modest £8 to £9 each. Dougall was busy hiring staff: the stationmaster for Dalvey (to transfer to Forres) came from Eskbank on the North British, at a salary of £60 plus an allowance of £7 10s for a house; the stationmaster at Brodie got £45 plus £5. Both were also allowed to sell coals from the end of March 1858, so long as this did not interfere with their prime duties, and 'during the pleasure of the Company'. The night-watchman at Dalvey got 15s a week, inclusive of Sunday work; the platform porter received 13s. Inevitably, as before, experienced men had to be recruited from the south, bringing a modest influx of new faces to small communities.

On 22 December 1857 the line was opened from Nairn to a temporary station at Dalvey, on the west bank of the Findhorn River, about a mile from Forres. Construction of the bridge here was delayed by legal action brought by the owners of salmon fisheries on the river. Fares between Nairn and Dalvey were 4s (first class), 2s 7d (second) and 1s 11d (third); the first-class return fare was 6s and in third, 3s 11d. On 9 December the engineer was instructed to build wooden stations at Kinloss, Carsewell (opened as Alves), Lhanbryde, Orton and Mulben at £80 to £100 each; the larger station at Forres was budgeted at £200. In the first five days, 592 passengers travelled between Inverness and Dalvey, and takings for the week ending on 2 January were £207 3s 8 ½d. Following the completion of the Findhorn Bridge, the new line was fully open between Inverness and Elgin from 28 March 1858, and Dalvey Station was closed, its staff transferring to Forres.

On the new line, substantial bridges had to be built over the Nairn, Lossie, Findhorn and Spey rivers. The former two were masonry, the latter pair of iron-girder construction. The Spey crossing, a 230ft wrought-iron-girder structure, with six-side arches to accommodate flood-water, was the longest and by far the most expensive, costing £34,482. 'A formidable and difficult work' in Mitchell's words, it caused problems with the Board of Trade inspecting officer. On 16 August, Capt. Tyler of the BoT approved the line, specifically excluding the Spey Viaduct, which the company had indicated it would not use for the time being.[16] It was in fact not yet completed, and through 1858 and 1859 a technical argument on box-girder bridge construction went on between Tyler, who had been shown the specifications and drawings, and William Fairbairn, the ironworks contractor and builder.[17] Thomas Bruce, who had replaced Seafield as deputy chairman, was keen to get the trains and revenues rolling, and a temporary structure had been built with the aim of carrying the line and providing scaffolding for construction of the viaduct proper. Mitchell wrote that:

> The Board of Trade would not sanction the opening of the line for carrying the traffic over the scaffolding erected for the construction of the Spey Bridge. The directors, however, determined to take their own way notwithstanding, and they opened the line and carried on the traffic on the timber scaffolding.[18]

He formally disclaimed responsibility for any consequences. On 18 August 1858, the Elgin–Keith section opened for business, and the Inverness–Aberdeen railway was at last a reality. But the I&AJR was using the Spey Bridge without official sanction. When the temporary wooden bridge began to sag, the trains were stopped at each side. The passengers were made to get out, and walked or were 'bussed' over the nearby road bridge. Work continued, urged on by the directors, who wanted to speed up the mail train from 1 February 1859, and instructed the engineer to make every effort to have, 'the Spey Bridge completed… absolutely necessary for fast train'.[19] From that date, though the BoT was not informed, the bridge was in regular use. The 'Fast Mail' ran from Inverness to Aberdeen in five hours fifteen minutes, compared to five hours fifty-five minutes for the merely 'Fast' train. Late in April, Tyler inspected and tested the bridge, with a 204-ton train on each of the tracks, and an extra 56 tons of rails laid on the deck. He reported: 'I consider that it is weaker than it ought to be, by at least two-fifths of its present strength, even to carry a single line'.[20] Fairbairn, an accepted authority, continued to dispute the captain's formulae. On 31 May, the board suavely reminded the I&AJR that it was liable to a fine of £20 a day for using the viaduct without official approval; Dougall responded on 14 June to say that, '… the Directors have given instructions to Mr Fairbairn and their engineer to take immediate steps for strengthening the bridge, so as to bring it up to the requirements of their Lordships'; and that the viaduct would not be used at present for a double line.[21] The board waived the fine. Although correspondence between Tyler and Joseph Mitchell continued for some time, there was no further inspection. The company laid only a single track over the viaduct, and Tyler wrote to his board on 11 July:

> I do not know how far their Lordships consider it judicious to interfere further at present with regard to this bridge. It was opened in the first instance without sanction, and they

have no power now to interfere with the Company in any arrangements that they may think proper to make for its improvement so long as it is employed for a single line only.[22]

Through trains were not operated between Inverness and Aberdeen; I&AJR services terminated at Keith and passengers transferred to the Great North. Four trains ran daily each way between Inverness and Keith, three giving an Aberdeen connection. The increase in traffic made additional demands on infrastructure, which the Nairn company watched carefully. An I&N Board minute of 19 October 1858 agreed to a request relayed via Mitchell that a crossing loop be installed at Dalcross, 'but only on the distinct understanding that no additional works of any description, involving an outlay of expenditure to this Company, shall be undertaken on the line between Inverness and Nairn, without the knowledge and consent of this Board thereto'.

The line's first serious accident happened as a result of a derailment at the Spey Bridge, and Joseph Mitchell blamed the premature opening. On 4 September 1858, as the 4.45 train from Inverness stopped at the platform on the east side, the pointsman put a block behind one wheel of the brake van. When the train started, the locomotive set back momentarily, and the brake van was jerked off the track. The driver took his train on to Keith without it, saying nothing at Mulben about the incident. He then returned, on his own authority, with five additional men, to re-rail and collect the brake van, running his engine in reverse. From Mulben Station down into the Spey valley there is a 2.5-mile incline at 1 in 60, and to prevent runaways, a set of catch points led into a siding. Except when set for the passage of trains, these points were kept open to the siding, and the driver, unaware or forgetful, ran his engine straight into the siding and it crashed against a bank of earth and gravel. Three men, pinned between the boiler backhead and the tender, were killed by a horrible, slow broiling. The driver was jailed for six months and the Keith pointsman, who admitted the engine to the line, was also held responsible.[23] Mitchell growled in his *Reminiscences* that the real guilty parties were those who authorised the traffic to be carried on, 'in defiance of the Board of Trade and their own engineer'.[24]

On 16 April 1860, a short line of three miles was opened, linking the coastal village of Findhorn to the I&AJR. Joseph Mitchell was employed as engineer, and Charles Brand of Montrose was the contractor. The wood-built station at Kinloss was moved some 300 yards to the location of the junction. The Findhorn Railway, which got its Act of Parliament on 19 April 1859, was a local venture and worked its own line with its modest locomotive, until the I&AJR made an agreement for working it, on 4 March 1862, commencing 30 March. The income did not cover the I&AJR costs, reckoned at £800 a year, and the agreement was renegotiated by the Highland Railway in March 1866, and again in 1867, when the Findhorn directors reluctantly agreed to be responsible for making up any deficiency between the HR's costs and revenue. They withdrew this guarantee in January 1869 and from the end of the month, regular services were withdrawn. Kinloss Station was moved back to its original location. The Findhorn Railway closed completely in 1881. Silting of the small harbour, killing off its timber export trade, was the main cause of its demise. The tiny engine outlived it.

The I&N Board continued to meet regularly, though now chiefly concerned with property and finance. It had always anticipated amalgamation, and the lapse of time before this occurred was due to the I&AJR's problems. Consummation came in 1861, when at a special meeting on 13 April, the shareholders of the Inverness & Nairn Railway unanimously agreed to amalgamation with the I&AJR, on the terms set out in 1857. In 1861 its directors were Eneas Mackintosh of Raigmore, chairman; Major Fraser-Tytler, deputy; Ewen Macpherson of Cluny; Col Findlay of Millbank; Robert Fraser of Brackla; Charles Stewart, solicitor, Inverness; Charles Waterston of the Caledonian Bank, Inverness; Neil Maclean, Inverness; Alexander Forbes, Inverness; Provost Colin Lyon Mackenzie of Inverness; Col Hugh Inglis of Kingsmills, and Thomas Ogilvy of Corrimony. Raigmore, Fraser-Tytler and Inglis were also on the I&AJR Board, but the original company had a much stronger representation of Inverness citizens than its successors ever did. In their final half-yearly report, to 28 February 1861, the directors declared a revenue of £5,509 11s 5d, an operating profit of £1481 0s 5d, and a dividend of 5 per cent. As a final gesture, before the company ceased to exist, the meeting agreed that it should subscribe for and hold £10,000 worth of shares in the Ross-shire Railway.

## 'Further North': The Inverness & Ross-shire Railway

The Keith line was hardly open when another was under survey by Mitchell and his assistant Murdoch Paterson. This time they were working north of Inverness, on behalf of a provisional committee formed, in Inverness, in January 1859, to promote a railway as far as Invergordon, in Ross-shire. Though the line passed through fairly easy country, it required the bridging of the river Ness, the Caledonian Canal, and the Beauly, Conon, Sgitheach, Allt Graad, and Alness Rivers. A northern line had been under discussion for two decades, with strong support from the two Ross-shire royal burghs of Dingwall and Tain. A Bill for the railway was prepared, using Theodore Martin as before, and was passed unopposed on 3 July 1860. The estimated cost was £215,000, to be met by the sale of 21,500 shares at £10. Powers also included the ability to raise a mortgage of £75,600 once half the capital was secured. The I&N and the I&AJR were allowed to subscribe 1,000 and 1,500 shares respectively, and, on doing so, to appoint two directors each, and it was anticipated that an agreement would be made with the I&AJR to work the line. The directors of the new railway were recorded on a slab in the old Ness Viaduct: Alexander Matheson, chairman; the Master of Lovat, deputy; Sir Kenneth Smith Mackenzie of Gairloch; Sir James Matheson; Eneas Mackintosh of Raigmore; R.B. McLeod of Cadboll; Sir Alexander Gordon Cumming; Major Fraser-Tytler; T.C. Bruce; and Provost Colin Lyon Mackenzie of Inverness. The I&N nominees were Bruce and Gordon Cumming, and the I&AJR's were Fraser-Tytler and Lyon Mackenzie. The start of work was marked by a public gathering in the Academy Park in Inverness, and a procession through the town. The navvies were prominent in the march, and were later entertained to beef, bread and ale in 'a specially erected booth [1]'. The quality went to the Station Hotel for a lunch that lasted from 1 p.m. to shortly after 10 p.m. Mrs Alexander Matheson gave the contractor, George Meakin of Birkenhead, a purse of £20 to distribute among his men. Meakin had been chosen as contractor at the behest of Joseph Mitchell, although his tender was not the lowest. Mitchell pointed out that he named sureties 'of undoubted means'. These probably included Brassey, an early patron of Meakin. There were many horror stories of contractors going bankrupt and causing long delays and extra costs. The engineer was also anxious to ensure high-quality masonry in the big bridges he had designed for the line, especially those crossing the Ness and the Conon. To save money, the Beauly bridge was of timber. In *The Railway Navvy*, David Brooke notes that north of Perth, most of the workmen were Scots. Many west-coasters, from Applecross, Ullapool and Gairloch, worked on the Ross-shire line. Their inexperience and Mitchell's keen contract price combined to make their pay low, and there was some trouble. Work stopped for a day on the Ness viaduct on 20 November 1860, when they went on strike to get a rise from 3*d* to 4*d* a day; and the *Inverness Advertiser* of 21 June 1861 reported 'a day of turmoil' at Alness, when some of the workmen were charged with intimidating their fellows. A novelty in railway engineering in the north was the swing bridge over the Caledonian Canal, just north of the Muirtown basin at Inverness. Built after close consultation with the Canal Co. and the Admiralty, it allowed a free span of 40ft when open. Although the Act provided for the company, if required, also to build swing spans over the Ness channel and the Dingwall Canal, these were not pursued. In return for a payment of £500 and the building of a wharf on the seaward side, Dingwall Town Council gave up the swing bridge, and felt it had got a bargain.[2] The line reached Dingwall in June 1862, was inspected and passed by Col. Yolland for the Board of Trade on the 10th, and opened on the 11th. Two new 2-2-2 engines, No.12 *Belladrum* and No.13 *Lovat*, were built for this line, and *Belladrum* was there in time for the opening; No.13 appeared in July. Like Inverness, Dingwall as a royal burgh exercised the right to levy 'petty customs' on goods coming into the town, and the railway company also had to compound for an annual payment in respect of these. On 13 June the town council held a lunch in the National Hotel, and Provost Falconer described the arrival of the railway as '... beyond all comparison the most momentous event that has ever occurred in its annals since the title of 'royal' was conferred upon it by Alexander I in 1226'.[3] Inverness to Dingwall by coach (inside rate) had been 7*s* 6*d*; now by train the first-class return was 4*s* 6*d*, and a third-class return only 1*s* 6½ *d*.

Invergordon, only thirteen miles further along the Cromarty Firth, was reached almost a year later on 23 May 1863. The delay was partly caused by protracted argument with a Dingwall landowner, and I&RR shareholder, Colin Mackenzie of Findon, who demanded a bridge rather than a level crossing where the Ferry Road crossed the railway. In the end a lightweight lattice metal bridge was put up. This line, passing through agricultural countryside and tapping the cattle-market site at Muir of Ord, was at first seen more as a feeder to the still-projected direct line southwards, rather than as a 'further north' main line. One of its effects was to kill off the ferry service between Invergordon and Fort George: except in calm summer weather, passengers preferred the circuitous route by train.

The Inverness & Ross-shire Railway's independent existence was short. Just after completion to Dingwall, it amalgamated with the Inverness and Aberdeen Junction by an Act of Parliament of 30 June 1862. A Memorandum of terms for the amalgamation had been produced in October 1861. The Ross-shire had capital of £245,000, of which £83,000 had actually been called up at that point. The I&AJR had capital of £675,000, of which £560,000 was paid up. The paid up Ross-shire shares were to be converted into shares in the combined company at a dividend of 3 per cent in the first year after opening and thereafter, '½ per cent additional per annum until the dividend reaches a sum equal to that paid by the Junction Company on their Ordinary stock, and then *pari passu*'.[4]

Further extension had long been assumed; in February 1862 Tain Town Council bought 150 shares in the Ross-shire Railway to help with the northwards progression. On 11 May 1863, an Extension Act was passed, allowing continuation of the line from Invergordon via Tain to Bonar Bridge, on the south bank of the Kyle of Sutherland, and granting the I&AJR facilities to raise a further £160,000 of capital and loans to the value of £53,000. The prime mover in this was the Duke of Sutherland, Bonar being the gateway to his domains, and he contributed £30,000 to the costs of this section. The inner reaches of the Dornoch Firth have steep banks, and the extension required a causeway below the tideline under Struie Hill, between Easter and Wester Fearn. The terminal station was at Ardgay on the Ross-shire side, but was named for the nearby road bridge at Bonar, tapping the routes leading west and north-west into the interior of Sutherland. There was some industrial trouble on this line also: it was reported that the navvies had gone on strike for an extra 2s a week, and had marched into Tain. Granger, the contractor, compromised with 1s, and they returned to work.[5]

The eastward-tending layout of Inverness Station was not suitable for the new north line. To get trains facing the westward run along the shore of the Beauly Firth, two new platforms were built, curving sharply to the west and resulting in the V-shaped layout which the station, though extended on various occasions, still retains, with Lochgorm Works between the arms. A linking line, later known as the Rose Street curve, was built, but despite many suggestions a set of through platforms was never built on it. Instead, trains from the north used to follow this link line into the main station yard, and then reverse back into an eastern platform, enabling passengers to make an easy transfer if that was their intention, and giving engines a speedy release to the running shed.

The Duke of Sutherland's requirements and his financial contribution effectively ensured the main characteristic of the 'Further North' line. It was not an express line designed to bring Wick and Thurso into the speediest possible contact with Inverness and the south, as envisaged by the first proponents, who had thought in terms of a line which would bridge the Dornoch Firth – not a major engineering challenge, as the Admiralty did not require a high-level bridge, and the waters were shallow – and make for Wick by as direct a route as the rugged hills of the Ord of Caithness would allow;[6] instead, it was an access line designed to bring railway communication to as large an area of the county of Sutherland as possible, by winding through its tundra-like landscape and offering the maximum number of access points.

## The Great North Withdraws

While these 'Further North' developments were being projected, the affairs of the Inverness & Aberdeen Junction Railway were not proceeding harmoniously, and the northern venture was partly the cause. There were difficulties in Aberdeen also. In 1859 there was still no physical link in that city between the Great North of Scotland Railway and the Scottish North-Eastern's line to the south.[1] Passengers and goods destined for places south of Aberdeen had to be transported between the termini. Some were diverted to go by sea from Aberdeen harbour. Delays were inevitable, and the hotelkeepers and hauliers of the Granite City duly benefited, while consignees and passengers from the north fretted. Meanwhile, the two GNSR directors on the I&AJR Board rarely seemed to concur with their colleagues.[2] The plans for expansion north of Inverness were under intensive discussion at this time, but the Aberdeen members had little interest in this, at least in the form proposed. They resisted one proposal to increase the company's capital by £200,000, as it would devalue their £40,000-worth of stock. The investment of £15,000 in the Inverness & Ross-shire Railway was also opposed, with a counter-suggestion that the GNSR should have a much greater degree of involvement, buying the plant, lending the money (from what resources is unclear) and even working the new line. It was clear that the joint line was not an axis of peace between Inverness and Aberdeen, and that the Great North had by no means forgotten its early ambitions. According to Mitchell's memoirs, acrimony came to a head at the board meeting held on 5 January 1860. Matheson, in the chair, was so infuriated by the Aberdeen members that he offered there and then to write out a cheque for £40,000 to buy back the Great North's shares. To the surprise of the Invernessians, Mitchell remarked, the offer was accepted.[4] Though this episode became part of Highland Railway lore, and was even repeated by a later general manager, Thomas Addy Wilson, in a press interview in 1905, it is pure folklore. If anything of the kind happened, it was in private, though high words are not unlikely. Matheson, as a Ross-shire proprietor, had an obvious interest in the Ross-shire Railway, and the GNSR directors on his board might well object to what they saw as him hustling the Junction Co. into support for it. However, at the next board meeting, on 25 January, Matheson, with some suavity, presented a very different picture. From the chair, he stated that after the last general meeting:

> ... a statement had been thrown out on the part of the Great North of Scotland com-
> pany that they would not be indisposed to part with their interest in this Company.
> Conferences had subsequently taken place between the Hon. Mr Bruce and
> Mr Stewart[6] and Mr Anderson of Aberdeen, in which the views of the Great North were
> more definitely ascertained. On the chairman's arrival in town [London], Mr Bruce had
> explained these views to him, and after careful consideration of all the circumstances,

and in particular the importance to this Company of being relieved [sic] from all further obstruction and interference to what they had already experienced, and also of being able to carry through their money bill without opposition, and also taking into account the fact of the steady increase of the traffic of the Company, they had worked to submit a proposal to the Great North for the purchase of their shares.

The proposal, made on 3 January 1860, offered the sum of £40,000 to be paid in two bills of £20,000 each, one payable on 1 January 1861 and the other exactly a year later. During the currency of the bills, the Junction Co. would pay interest, 'at a rate corresponding to the dividends receivable upon an equivalent value in the said shares taken at par.' Provision was also made for earlier payment if such should occur. The GNSR would immediately deliver up its share certificates and vacate its board seats. Its directors, for once, did not haggle: a letter from their solicitors of 18 January stated that the GNSR 'begged to close with these terms'. As it happens, the value of the shares at that time was somewhat under par – around £9 to £9 10s – so that, as Barclay-Harvey observed, it cost the Highlanders some £4,000 to get rid of their troublesome colleagues.[7] Nevertheless, Matheson's official version of events was received with acclaim. The uneasy alliance was over, and one imagines that the Highland oligarchs attended their Burns suppers that evening in particularly cheerful mood.

The Act of 3 April 1860, which was obtained to ratify the separation, still provided for Working Agreements between the two companies, but apart from this, both were free to square up to each other, a stance which seems to have been congenial to many of the directors and officials on each side. The Great North could continue to scheme for its own ways to push past Inverness. Working arrangements between the Junction Co. and the Morayshire Railway had been anything but harmonious and the Morayshire, in concert with the Great North of Scotland, obtained a Bill for a direct Elgin–Rothes line in July 1860. This was completed by the end of 1861, and by 1 July 1863 the GNSR had its own alternative route, via Dufftown, between Aberdeen and Elgin. Meanwhile, the proponents of a direct line from Inverness to the south – Joseph Mitchell among them – could use the deficiencies of the Aberdeen link, and the depravities of the GNSR (which had always refused to quote a through fare via Aberdeen for fear of getting an insufficient share) to push for the Grampian route.

# TWO

*The Inverness & Perth Junction Railway*

A new sense of urgency was rising about the Perth line. Mitchell reported that two schemes were in hand for surveying new lines, one along the Spey linking the Elgin–Rothes line to Grantown and one up the Tay-Tummel valley between Dunkeld and Pitlochry.[1] Both Aberdeen-sponsored, these would tap the only sizeable communities on the planned direct line to Perth, with negative effects on the railway's economic prospects. A committee was formed, of Mitchell, Fraser-Tytler, Raigmore, Sir Alexander Gordon Cumming and the law agents, Stewart, to spearhead developments and enlist the support of landowners. Pre-eminent among the latter was the Duke of Atholl, whose wide domains would be bisected by twenty-four miles of the new railway. On 9 June 1860 the committee met the Duke at Dunkeld. Atholl was polite but frosty. He did not want railways in the Highlands any more now than he had in 1846. He regarded an Inverness–Perth trunk line as less of an evil than the proposed Pitlochry branch, but reserved all judgement until he had seen the plans.[2]

The duke's obstinacy was notorious, but almost certainly here he was merely adopting a negotiating position. Mitchell felt he had to be won over, and thirty-six years of dealing with temperamental landowners had made the engineer an expert. With the duchess already on his side, a set of trim white route-marking flags, a few soothing words, and a sketch of a handsome lodge for the north end of the castle park, helped him to gain acceptance of the plan. The duke may also be thanked for one of the railway's most striking features, the high-level viaduct leaping both road bridge and river at Struan. This was designed by Mitchell to satisfy Atholl's request that his trees and riverside pathways should not be affected at this beauty spot.[3] Though Mitchell claims Atholl did not drive a hard bargain, employing a professional and respected arbitrator, Mr Elliott, to establish the value of the ground traversed by the line; the board decided on 25 August 1863 to protest against an award of £3,000 as compensation for loss of the duke's amenities.

Mitchell records[4] that two Badenoch proprietors, The Mackintosh and the laird of Glentruim (Col Macpherson), offered land to the railway at no charge, an offer which the company did not take up. Speedy completion of the plans was no problem and they were lodged within the deadline for the current Parliamentary session, 30 November 1860. The only important change from the original plan of 1846 was that the direct line now began at Forres instead of Nairn. The consideration here was that Forres was a more central point, to which traffic from Moray could be attracted, as well as the Northern traffic. Though it added fifteen miles to the journey from Inverness, it also served to fight off the threat of a Speyside line coming southwards from Elgin. The new route rejoined Mitchell's original proposed line south of a 1,052ft summit on Dava Moor.

The Bill for the Inverness & Perth Junction Railway was passed, despite opposition from the Great North of Scotland Railway, on 22 July 1861. It provided powers for a takeover of the Perth & Dunkeld Railway. The Scottish North-Eastern had begun defensive manoeuvres in Strathtay, proposing purchase of the P&DR and extending it to Aberfeldy, but the Inverness & Perth managed to achieve a friendly agreement, with the SNER being reimbursed 75 per cent of the costs of its defensive plans.[5] The P&DR was fully amalgamated with the Inverness & Perth on 28 February 1864, its shareholders being recompensed with I&PJR Preference Stock at 6 per cent; and the latter was also authorised to build the branch line from Ballinluig to Aberfeldy. Running powers between Stanley Junction and Perth, over the Scottish North-Eastern Railway, and the right to use the station at Perth, were encompassed in the Act. The running powers were initially subject to a toll on each passenger conveyed. Even for a single-track line with only essential fixtures, the new main line was going to cost a lot of money: £600,000 was Mitchell's estimate. The I&AJR invested £50,000 in the Perth company, and it was agreed that the I&AJR would work the line, for 50 per cent of the gross receipts, for a period of ten years, 'failing an amalgamation'. Such a failure was hardly to be anticipated, and the arrangement saved the new company from investment in locomotives, rolling stock and staff. Finance was a major concern. At one time it had seemed possible that the Scottish Central and Edinburgh & Glasgow Railway companies would take £200,000 worth of stock, but this never materialised.[6] Two I&PJR loans were negotiated, £110,000 from the National Bank of Scotland in January 1861, and £60,500 from the Commercial Bank in August. At the start of 1861, subscribed share capital was £135,000. With a very large shortfall looming, the first contracts were let at the end of August 1861.

While the I&PJR was busy building the main line to the south, further I&AJR activity was going on east of Inverness, often involving the same people. After being deprived of it in 1856, Burghead finally got its rail connection on 22 December 1862, with a line from Alves Station. There was an intermediate halt at Wards, renamed Coltfield Platform from 1 January 1865. Ignoring the charms, or perhaps avoiding the harbour dues, of Lossiemouth, the Sutherland Steam Packet Co. had been running the *Heather Bell* between Littleferry and Burghead since 1860. On 8 June 1863, an Act was obtained for a six-mile line from Fochabers to Garmouth, on the west side of the Spey close to its estuary. Though backed by, and to be worked by the I&AJR, this was nominally an independent line, and had been included in the GNSR's plans back in

1846. Nothing was done about building the line, whose purpose was merely as a spoiler to prevent the GNSR from making it. On 7 November 1865 the Highland Board decided to apply for a time extension of their powers, but the Bill was withdrawn in March 1866, on account of 'the strongest objection from Lord Redesdale' (chairman of the Lords Select Committee). The project was finally abandoned in 1868, when the Directors' Report of 31 August frankly admitted that it had been 'the only line ever promoted by the Directors for defence purposes'. Fochabers in the meantime had to make do with its inconveniently placed station on the main line.

With the passing of the Inverness & Perth's Bill, a meeting was immediately convened to appoint directors to the company. Mitchell records that while it was the general expectation that Alexander Matheson, chairman of the I&AJR, would also chair the I&PJR, this did not happen. In something of a Moray-men's coup, the Hon. Thomas Bruce, son of Lord Elgin, was proposed and elected, and this was not to the liking of the officials, who considered Bruce an interferer in their own domain. Mitchell adds that the initial arrangement did not last long and that in a few weeks Matheson assumed the chairmanship.[7] This was not the case: Bruce remained chairman of the I&PJR until its amalgamation with the Inverness & Aberdeen in 1865. On 23 April 1862 he promised in the Shareholders' Report that: 'Your Directors are resolved to push forward the Works with the utmost rigour'. Mitchell blamed Bruce's pressurising for a paralytic seizure which afflicted him on 4 May 1862, in the middle of the works, and which kept him away from the railway until the end of the year. From October 1863 Bruce also took on an executive role, described as that of managing director, at £500 a year while building was in progress, dropping to £250 a year once the line was built. In a dry line, Mitchell commented that 'Mr Bruce is an able man and devotes about ten days per annum of his time to the company.'[8] But that was much later: during the building, Bruce was, from the engineer's point of view, uncomfortably active.

Lady Seafield again cut the first sod, in a ceremony at Forres on 17 October 1861, though work was already in hand on the viaduct across the Divie and the 350 yard-tunnel at Inver, near Dunkeld. Work proceeded from each end. No railway of such length, through such terrain, had been built in Britain before, though similar work on a much greater scale was proceeding at the same time in North America. The 104 miles of line were subdivided into nine contracts, and eventually work was going on simultaneously in every section. Material could be supplied from both ends, from the railhead and harbour at Perth and from Inverness. On 6 June 1862, the *Inverness Advertiser* noted, perhaps with some exaggeration: 'In a few weeks there will be not less than ten thousand men employed on the line'. They were quartered in temporary hutted blocks, Spartan places, with six beds for twelve men. Driven on by Bruce, who was 'urgent for progress'[9] construction was remarkably quick. The entire task was completed in just under two years, at a cost of £919,204, or £8,860 per mile, including the cost of land and Parliamentary proceedings. Mitchell's 1852 estimate of £8,117 a mile held up pretty well. It was a good price, and the structures of bridges and embankments still remain to testify that Mitchell made his contractors build solidly and well. But it was a single-track line, with relatively few stations, and surprisingly few major viaducts: only three, the seven-arched Divie Viaduct near Dunphail, the ten-arched curving viaduct at Killiecrankie, and the single-span girder bridge over the Tay near Dalguise. There were many smaller bridges and culverts, but far fewer road bridges than on most railways in Britain. The two short tunnels at Inver and Killiecrankie were both amenity works, cut through solid rock. Alongside the rails, telegraph poles and wires were set up, since traffic over the whole line would be controlled by the electric block instrument system, as with the I&AJR. With construction going on apace, the Working Agreement between the I&AJR and I&PJR was finalised by the companies on 28 October and 6 November 1862, respectively. The I&AJR Board had spent considerable time discussing and making dispositions for working the new line, down to such minutiae as who should be entitled to issue free travel passes.

A debenture issue was made in November 1862 by the I&PJR, raising £118,007 from 160 investors. The list[10] reveals that they came from all over Scotland, around half from the more thinly populated area north of Perth. Aberdeen and the north-east are significantly under-represented, and only one or two holders from south of the border are noted. A perhaps surprisingly large number of clergymen appear on the list, though in some cases it may be as representing Kirk Sessions rather than themselves, as Kirk Sessions also appear on other lists of debenture holders, along with Masonic Lodges.

Further works were required at Inverness in order to service the new line. On 4 October 1862, the company's engineer was instructed to prepare plans for a new running shed, capable of holding twenty locomotives. Up to now, locomotives had been stabled in or at the workshops. Mitchell designed the new locomotive shed in the American style, a C-shape with tracks radiating from a central turntable into the locomotive stalls. Extensions on either side could readily be added. It was built by John Hendrie of Inverness, at a cost of £4,952, plus £1,144 14s 5d for the iron roof. Mitchell reported the shed as completed by 18 March 1864, with room for twenty-four locomotives (at this time the company was about to own fifty-five engines in total). The access track passed under a 45,000-gallon water tank mounted in a handsome masonry arch – a unique feature in the workaday architecture of locomotive depots, and expressive of the pride felt in the Inverness railway's sudden doubling of its length, and in the achievement, at last, of the direct line to the South. Expansion was also needed at Forres, where the station had to be rebuilt; in May 1863 a tender of £2313 was accepted from Squair & Mackintosh for erection of a new station house, engine shed for four engines, water tank and turntable. In January, a deal had been made with the Scottish North-Eastern for temporary locomotive and carriage accommodation at Perth. Locomotive sheds were also built at Blair Atholl and Aviemore.

The Dunkeld-Pitlochry section was opened on 1 June 1863, Forres–Aviemore on 3 August, and the entire line was ready for working on 9 September. Refreshment rooms were set up at Forres (let at £70 p.a.) and Kingussie. At the October half-yearly Shareholders' Meeting back in 1861, the manager of the Caledonian Bank,

Charles Waterston, had successfully moved that £1,300 be voted to the directors on the eventual opening of the new line: this was £100 each to Bruce, Matheson, Atholl, Seafield, Gordon Cumming, Loch, Fraser-Tytler, Sir Kenneth Mackenzie of Gairloch, Sutherland, Cumming-Bruce of Dunphail, Raigmore, Cluny and the Master of Lovat, a useful morsel of pocket money in addition to their share of the directors' modest annual remuneration of £500, divided 'as they saw fit'. Eight of them, incidentally, were also on the Inverness & Aberdeen board, with Matheson and Bruce as chairman and deputy chairman.

On 9 September 1863, the complete line was approved by Capt. Tyler for the Board of Trade. That same day, according to Mitchell, the directors ordered that traffic should begin. The engineer commented that, 'It was much against my will... no preliminary trains had been run through to test the line and the working of the engines; and the drivers were new men, unacquainted with the line and the gradients'.[11] A train left Inverness at 10.18 a.m. with placards proclaiming such destinations as York, Euston Square and Kings Cross. In Mitchell's rather sour account:

> Another train was to start from Perth for the North in the middle of the night. The clerks at the different stations could not work, or worked very imperfectly, the telegraph, and at Dunphail, where I stopped, we had no trains and no communication the first day.
>
> The engineman from Perth arrived at Struan, where for some cause or other the engine refused to ascend the incline, and there he was, he and his passengers, in a mountainous country, unknown, in the dark, within hearing of the adjoining Falls of the Garry.[12]

Recalling events forty years afterwards, a correspondent in the *Inverness Courier* of August 1903, said the stalled train was a goods. It was eventually got into a siding, but then the telegraph system broke down, which meant that no trains could run between Struan and Kingussie. The writer joined the first passenger train from Perth at Forres, which got into Inverness at half-past midnight on the morning of 10 August.

It was the opening of the Keith line over again, the same haste – not without good reason – to get cash flowing in. Despite these initial difficulties, for Inverness it was 'the great consummation',[13] and Matheson and Bruce were both made freemen of the burgh. A celebratory banquet was held in the Northern Meeting Rooms on 10 September, with about 350 persons present. An elderly, eminent Liberal statesman, the Right Hon. Edward Ellice MP, proprietor of the Glenquoich estate, presided, and Raigmore paid tribute to Mitchell, Paterson and their men. Mitchell responded suitably, affirming his pleasure that the long-cherished scheme had been achieved:

> The work was now accomplished, he hoped, effectually, and it remained only for him to express his acknowledgement for the support and consideration he had received under the many difficulties they had to encounter, and also his thanks to his staff of engineers for their earnest and energetic labours to complete the work, without which it could not have been accomplished in the time.[14]

If his eye rested on Bruce at the mention of 'many difficulties', it is unlikely to have been noticed by their fellow-diners. His semi-detached existence as engineer continued, but he was no longer closely involved in other company business. He was not an employee but was retained by the company to provide the functions of an engineer: from 1862 this had been organised through a company, Joseph Mitchell & Co., in which Murdoch Paterson and his brother William were junior partners.

On 25 June 1862, Andrew Dougall and Alexander Allan had met at Perth to consider the motive power needs of the new line. It was agreed to obtain tenders for eight passenger engines, 'to carry 172 tons up a gradient of 1 in 70'; and ten goods engines, capable of pulling 200 tons on the same gradient. This was an unprecedented order and intensive shopping around was done. Two passenger engines came from Hawthorns as part of an earlier agreement; the rest from Neilsons of Glasgow; the goods engines were from Sharp, Stewart of Glasgow. The total bill was £56,670, and this took the locomotive stock from seventeen to thirty-five. Payment was to be made half on delivery, a quarter after running 1,000 miles, and a quarter after three months. Allan was to receive 1.5 per cent on cost 'for supervision of new plant'. He, however, had to advise the Locomotive Committee at the beginning of June 1863 that delivery was going to be late, 'due to shortage of skilled operatives at the engine-builders' works.' On the opening of the new line, only one of the goods engines and none of the passenger engines were delivered, and the I&AJR had only twenty engines to work all its main line trains. Engines had to be borrowed from the Scottish Central and the Caledonian (which, with remarkable generosity, made no charge for its three) to work the southern part of the Perth line.[15] Locomotive deliveries were not completed until November, but it had already become clear that the orders placed in 1862 were not sufficient, and the board meeting of 24 September 1863 authorised the purchase of twenty additional locomotives, ten goods and ten passenger, for delivery by April of the following year.

Through unforeseen circumstances, Queen Victoria was one of the first people from England to travel on the Inverness & Perth line. On 15 September she travelled from Perth to Blair Atholl and back again, breaking her journey to Balmoral from Windsor, to visit the Duke of Atholl, who was fatally ill with cancer of the throat.

In the last half-year before the Direct South line opened, the I&AJR reported a revenue of £35,935 19s 7d, of which £20,149 13s 2d was accountable to passenger traffic. The operating profit was £18,052 16s 5d, and after the Preference shares received their dividends, 5½ per cent was paid on Ordinary stock. For those who had invested in the Ross-shire Railway, a pleasant consequence of amalgamation was the dividend of 3 per cent on their shares even before the line was completed. In April 1865, the Inverness & Perth also gave a good account of its half-year from August 1864 to January 1865. Revenue was £52,030 13s 8d, of which passengers contributed £25,611 11s 8d and mails a further £2,824 17s 3d. Its operating costs were £38,807 4s 9d, including the 50 per cent of receipts due to the I&AJR. It paid 4 per cent on its Ordinary stock. Already, the Perth line was out-earning the Aberdeen line. But sterner times were round the corner.

Work was still in progress in the counties to the north. On 1 June 1864, the terminal point was advanced to Meikle Ferry, two and a half miles north-west of Tain, and about a mile from the ferry point across the narrows near the mouth of the Dornoch Firth. Four months later, the line was complete to Bonar Bridge. The importance of the ferry began to dwindle, and once the railway had reached Golspie in 1868, it and the station experienced very little traffic and the station closed in 1869. Local passenger trains were instituted on the Inverness Harbour branch in June 1864, in connection with steamship traffic, but were terminated in June 1867.

The 8.73 mile-branch line from Ballinluig to Aberfeldy, provided for in the Inverness & Perth Junction Railway Act was finally opened on 3 July 1865, after much local indignation over the delays in starting work. Following the south bank of the Tay, it required a bridge over that river and another, almost immediately, over the Tummel. These two girder bridges, with thirty-nine other bridges or culverts, and numerous cuttings and embankments brought the final cost of the branch up to £12,000 a mile. There was an intermediate station at Grandtully, almost exactly halfway. In September 1866, after protracted haggling, the HR agreed to pay an additional £9,600 to the contractors, McDonald and Grieve, for work required beyond the terms of the contract. This problem, with an even longer dispute over the cost of the Dunkeld–Pitlochry section, especially the tunnel at Inver, cooled relations between Mitchell and the Highland board. Arbitration was resorted to and an interim ruling in December 1866 awarded £4,000 to the Dunkeld section contractors, Gowans & Mackay. Perhaps it was not surprising that when Mitchell submitted a request for £500 on account against his own outstanding bill, the board agreed to pay it 'as soon as the state of the Company's finances warrants'.[16]

## Formation of the Highland Railway Co.

The Highland Railway Bill, for the amalgamation of the Inverness & Aberdeen and Inverness & Perth Junction Railways, was introduced in the new Parliamentary session of 1864. Vigorous opposition was mounted by the Great North of Scotland Railway. During the deliberations of the Parliamentary Committee, the question came up of GNSR running powers into Inverness, which had been agreed in 1854 and reiterated, if not in so many words, in 1857, but never granted. The Inverness company resisted the claim for running powers, and Bruce asserted he knew nothing about such an agreement. The GNSR was able to produce a copy of the 1854 document, which subsequently was lost.[1] In any case, never having been sealed by either company, it was not a binding legal document, but the disowning of the old Inverness 'promise' long remained a source of bitterness to the Aberdonians. The GNSR succeeded in ensuring that the Act did provide for it to maintain a ticket office in the station at Inverness, and also for traffic to and from the Great North to have equal rights, powers and privileges to Highland traffic, and for the Highland to concur with the Great North in fixing through rates, if called upon to do so. The Highland Railway Act was passed on 29 June 1865. A new emblem was devised for the company seal and to mark company property: 'An Eagle displayed, bearing two shields, charged with the arms of the City of Perth (Gules, the Holy Lamb passant regardant, argent, carrying a banner of St Andrew, proper, within a double tressure flory-counter-flory, argent) and the Burgh of Inverness (Gules, Our Lord upon the Cross, proper)'.[2] The share capital of the combined organisation was £3,305,000 and it had loans of £1,107,780. Its board met formally for the first time on 2 August; consisting of Alexander Matheson, the Hon. T.C. Bruce (elected chairman and vice-chairman respectively), William Fraser-Tytler, by now a Colonel, Col. Inglis of Kingsmills, Lord Seafield, the Duke of Sutherland, Alex Robertson of Aultnaskiach, Sir A. Gordon-Cumming, Mr Duff MP, George Loch, the Master of Lovat, William Tayler of Glenbarry, R.B. McLeod of Cadboll, Major Cumming-Bruce of Dunphail, James Merry MP, and Cluny Macpherson. Merry, an ironmaster from the central belt who had bought the estate of Belladrum, near Beauly, was something of a wasp among the bluebottles.[3] It was resolved that 'the arrangement which had existed between the Board and Mr Bruce prior to the amalgamation be continued'. This was Bruce's part-time role as managing director. The immediate concern was money, and it was resolved to raise £400,000, as provided in the company's Act, through the issue of 40,000 £10 Preference Shares, to be known as Class B, at 5 per cent. The next meeting accepted the tender of John Hendrie, Inverness, for the building of extensions to the workshops, for the sum of £4,456. Tools and equipment came to another £2,000.

The toll charge of the Scottish North-Eastern Railway for use of the line from Stanley into Perth Station had been the subject of discussion with that company. It came up with a revised suggestion of a fixed annual charge of £5,000, which, though less than half the likely tollage, did not find favour at Inverness. At the I&PJR Shareholders' Meeting on 28 March 1865, Fraser-Tytler also complained of long delays, with some trains arriving in Stanley on time, but reaching Perth half an hour late. The board decided to start the necessary procedures for the HR to build its own line into Perth.[4] Negotiations were also going on to acquire land from Lord Kinnoull's estate, north of Dovecotland Road in Perth, where the HR could lay out sidings and a yard. It was acquired in feu in August 1866, at £25 per acre.

On 17 October 1865, the amalgamated company issued its first half-yearly report, and the board had to express regret that it was much less favourable than that of the separate companies. They blamed the cost of completing the works, which had 'very substantially exceeded the amount contemplated', but added that the works 'have been completed in a manner so substantial as to render it improbable that any large amount will be required in repairs for many years'. The combined revenue was £103,950 7s, of which passengers accounted for £51,182 16s 9d, and mails £6,076 7s 7d. Tollage to the Scottish North-Eastern amounted to £5,343 0s 7d. Expenditure amounted to £24,448 10s 10d, and after the Preference shares had their dividends paid, only 2 per cent could be paid on the Ordinary shares. Despite this, at their meeting of 7 November, the directors requested the secretary to look into the cost of fitting out a luncheon room adjacent to the boardroom. Ten days later, the secretary put himself on the agenda, and reported that the Caledonian Railway, with which the Scottish North-Eastern and Scottish Central were now amalgamated, had offered him a 'high appointment' at £2,000 per annum, 'with the prospect of a large increase'. The directors were loath to lose Dougall, and knew, too, that a replacement of the necessary calibre would cost them dear. By 29 November, all was done. They expressed appreciation at his 'pecuniary sacrifice' in staying with the Highland, at an enlarged salary of £1,000 for seven years, but with the intention to raise it 'when the Company should be doing better'. This kind of promise in a poke was popular among directors, especially when made to a man who, like Dougall, was in a position to exercise close control on costs. Dougall himself perhaps appreciated being a big fish in a small pond: to the outside world, he was the Highland Railway.

At the end of August 1865, the newly combined company owned twenty-four passenger and twenty-nine goods locomotives, and two small tank engines. It had 124 passenger carriages and 1,150 assorted goods vehicles, four Post Office vans, and a travelling crane. Geographically, it was now an extensive system with just over 238 route miles. Its new southern main line was a very demanding one, and the small 2-2-2 passenger locomotives supplied by Alexander Allan were struggling to fulfil requirements. Breakdowns were frequent. The directors, themselves among the most regular users of the line, complained, and pressure was put on William Barclay to do something about it. But Barclay was out of his depth and, perhaps because he had a good subordinate in David Jones, who had been his assistant since 1858, was also wont to take days off to go fishing. In May 1865, after one outing too many, he was dismissed with three months' pay,[5] and Jones ran things while a replacement was being sought. On 19 June, William Stroudley, an Englishman of thirty-two, who had been with the Edinburgh & Glasgow Railway, was appointed, at £500 a year. The board recorded its satisfaction with the interim supervision of the Locomotive Department by awarding Jones a special payment of £25.

Apart from a steady stream of such relatively minor business as approving the discharge of the Nigg stationmaster for issuing an 'old ticket' to a first-class passenger to Inverness; the installation of a timber siding at Bogbain, just beyond Fearn, and another of 150 yards to Mr Munro's manure works at Invergordon; and granting £25 to pay for an annual staff festival or social meeting, the board at this time, in late 1865 and early 1866, was much involved in the financial diplomacies of railway building in the far North. With Mitchell and Paterson both engaged on work north of Inverness, the company employed an additional civil engineer, J.W. Buttle, formerly of the Scottish North-Eastern Railway, employed as superintendent of ways and works in October 1865, his charge being the lines already opened.

# THREE

*The Sutherland Railway*

Though Bonar Bridge was not seen as anything other than a temporary terminus, it was provided with an engine shed and a turntable. Beyond Bonar, the railway could have followed the turnpike road round the north shore of the Dornoch Firth, passing close to the little town of Dornoch. Instead, it took a more difficult and circuitous route following the Oykell and Shin river valleys to Lairg, from where roads and tracks diverged north and north-west, and then climbing to a summit of 400ft before dropping again to near sea-level at The Mound. It was intended to cover the whole distance from Bonar Bridge to Brora, 32.75 miles, and obtained its Act on 29 June 1865; among the various provisions was one allowing the Highland Railway Co. to subscribe funds. The *John o' Groat Journal* reported on 25 May an admiring comment picked up at an I&AJR meeting in Inverness, on the safety of investing in the Sutherland Railway, because 'there was scarcely a fashionable lady or nobleman in London who had not taken shares'. Building work began straight away. Andrew Dougall had placed advertisements in the local newspapers in early May, inviting tenders for three contract sections, Ardgay–Lairg; Lairg–Pittentrail; Pittentrail–Kirkton, near Golspie (in fact two miles short of Golspie; a fourth section was not advertised). Drawings and specifications were to be had from J. Mitchell & Co. Joseph Mitchell, largely recovered from his stroke, had been put in charge of the works. On this line, far more than any other, he had a single patron who was both a director of the railway company, the principal shareholder, and the owner of virtually all the territory it traversed. George Granville William Sutherland Leveson-Gower, whom we met earlier as Marquess of Stafford, was now third Duke of Sutherland. Aged thirty-six, he owned 1,300,000 acres of that county, 99 per cent of its total area, as well as 32,000 acres of coal-rich land in Staffordshire, the main source of his enormous wealth. Mitchell estimated his annual revenues at £200,000. True to the Whiggish traditions of the family, he was a Liberal in politics and an enthusiastic improver of his northern estate, with particular concern for the harbour township of Brora, whose shutdown coal pit and brickworks he intended to reinstate.[1] His immediate forebears, through their local agents

(George Loch's father, James, had been a leading figure in this), had systematically emptied Sutherland's interior of most of its indigenous population in some of the most infamous episodes of the Highland Clearances. The third duke had had no part in that, but he had to live with the social and political consequences. Fascinated by mechanical things, above all by fire engines – his steam fire engine can still be seen at Dunrobin Castle – he was a keen railway enthusiast, and his investment was made all the more readily because this was going to be in every way 'his' railway. Mitchell by this time had a habit, possibly tiresome, of reminding all Highland grandees of how well he had known their fathers and even grandfathers, but he and the duke got on well enough. The duke was more interested in engines than in civil engineering, and, though he wanted his railway, he did not want to pay a penny more than he had to. John Fowler, an eminent English civil engineer who had acquired an estate at Braemore in Wester Ross in 1865, was retained to inspect and comment on the works. Despite the economy with which the Perth line had been built, Fowler said that Mitchell was 'addicted to extravagance' and his bridges were unnecessarily ornate. The Sutherland railway, he said, should not cost more than £7,000 a mile. Nettled, Mitchell pointed out that the contracts had been let, inclusive of two substantial viaducts, for 24¾ miles at £5,773 per mile, making a total of £142,393. But he neglects to add, in his *Memoirs*, that he had underestimated the costs and the funds ran out by the time the line reached Golspie, in 1868, six and a quarter miles short of Brora. Thereafter, nothing could shake the duke's view, which he reiterated to members of the Highland Railway Board, that Mitchell's lines cost more than they should. [2] Mitchell's reputation as a creator of well-surveyed, excellently engineered, and soundly-built lines through difficult country is safe enough for it to be noted that he had no special formula on cost beyond keeping his estimates low, driving a hard bargain with contractors, and maintaining a close watch on their activity. In addition, the lines were single track, the extent of sidings very small, and buildings normally of wood. Some stations were not built until after the line was opened. Most of the smaller bridges were originally of timber. But Mitchell still took the American railroad as his model – get the track down and the line in business, and refinements can follow; if he had not adopted this policy, the lines might never have been completed.

Mitchell was destined to have further troubles with Fowler, but in the meantime, having spent the winter of 1866-67 in Italy for his health, he withdrew from the Sutherland project in May 1867, leaving Murdoch Paterson to complete it. A dispute then ensued between Mitchell and the duke, who refused Mitchell's bill of £5,500 for his professional services and offered £4,000, which, after a long wrangle, was reluctantly accepted.

In the winter of 1865-66, with the Sutherland Railway's cash difficulties becoming plain, the duke, through his commissioner (and fellow-HR Director) George Loch, was putting heavy pressure on the Highland Railway to subscribe £30,000. The board resisted this, not without some squirming, deploring the circumstances in which 'even a casual difference of opinion should arise between the Directors and His Grace', in a long, delicately phrased letter recorded at its meeting of 2 January

1866. To subscribe £30,000, an Extraordinary Shareholders' Meeting would have been needed, and approval was far from certain. A directors' meeting in London, of Matheson, Bruce, the Master of Lovat and Merry,[3] expressed regret to learn that the Board of the Sutherland Railway had resolved to put a stop to further works, but made no commitment about a Highland Railway contribution. The county of Sutherland was well known to be a thinly populated wilderness and the feeling, never uttered in so many words, was that the colossally rich eponymous landowner should fork out for 'his' railway himself. In fact, this was what the duke then proposed to do: a letter from Loch to Matheson, of 9 June 1866, stated that the duke would buy £30,000-worth of stock in the HR, on condition that it would be applied in payment of their subscription to the Sutherland company. The board regretfully declined, pointing out that the increase in its capital could not be expected to generate the necessary increase in revenues, and suggesting action should be delayed until they were in 'a little better position', when a Shareholders' Meeting would be much more likely to agree.[4] At this time they were seriously worried about the HR's own financial state. With some candour, they added that:

> The Company… can hardly meet the present charges on their Capital Account – and these are only provided for by the personal security on part of the Directors being interposed to a large amount to meet the debts of the Company. The whole of the unissued Capital of the Company is held by the Directors who have subscribed their Bills as a security for the advances guaranteed by their signatures.

These directors, of course, included Sutherland himself. At the meeting of 9 October that year, Loch reported that the duke would take up £30,000 worth of the company's unissued 4½ per cent preferred stock, 'to put the Company in funds to invest £30,000 in the Sutherland Railway as allowed for in that Railway's Act'. After almost a year's hammering from its biggest shareholder, the board caved in, and agreed to submit the offer to the forthcoming General Meeting, so long as the Sutherland company continued its line to Golspie at once, and completed it to Brora within the time prescribed by the Act. James Merry, who himself had an outstanding loan of £50,000[5] to the HR, formally dissociated himself from the decision. At the half-yearly Shareholders' Meeting on 30 October, the transaction was formally approved.

As the businessman Merry realised, the duke and his agent had battered their way into a very favourable deal. The Sutherland Railway got its cash injection (though it never completed the line to Brora) and the duke had an attractive extra parcel of shares in the Highland Railway, which would also work the trains over the SR. Quite soon, however, the board's policy of keeping in with the ducal house was seen to make sense. At the same time as the discussion with the duke was going on, the HR was trying to raise a loan in the Edinburgh and Glasgow money markets, and not finding it easy. In August 1866, the board meeting was told that the Caledonian Railway's own financial difficulties prevented it from acquiring £50,000 of Highland Railway Ordinary stock, 'as suggested by them last year'.[6] In November 1866, a temporary overdraft of £20,000 had to be arranged with the Caledonian Bank to enable interest payments to be made. But later that month, the Trustees of Lords Ronald and Alfred Leveson-Gower, sons of the duke, agreed to lend the HR £100,000 at 5 per cent over five years, on security of the Directors' signatures guaranteeing the interest payments.[7]

The Sutherland Railway opened for business on 13 April 1868, the line being worked as an extension of the southern lines, with through trains between Inverness and the terminus at Golspie, the service provided by the Highland Railway. The turntable and engine shed at Bonar Bridge were sold to the Sutherland Railway, for use at Golspie.[8] Mr Macdonald, stationmaster at Dunphail, was transferred to Golspie at a salary of £80 plus a house. On opening day, the first train to Golspie was at 12.00 from Bonar Bridge. It returned to Bonar Bridge at 6 p.m., but at 4.30 p.m. a special arrived from Inverness, having left at 1.00 p.m. The duke got on at Rogart and took command on the footplate. At Golspie the banners, pipes and drums were waiting, and a procession went along the street, heading for the banquet that had been prepared. From then on there were two trains daily each way between Golspie and Inverness, shown on the original poster[9] as: Up Mail at 6 a.m. and Mixed at 3.15 p.m., arriving 9.50 a.m. and 7.20 p.m.; Down Passenger at 9.15 a.m. and Mail at 2.45 p.m., arriving at 1.20 p.m. and 7.20 p.m. Probably all were mixed; by the 1871 timetable they are all shown as such, with slightly altered times.

## The Caithness Railway Co.

After Inverness, Wick, the county town of Caithness, was the largest town in the north of Scotland, with 7,475 inhabitants in 1864. Thurso had 3,426, making it of comparable size with Nairn and Forres. Caithness as a whole then had a population of 41,100. Though much of the ground was undrained bogland, there were also arable and pastoral farms, and flagstone quarries. Scrabster harbour had been built for the flagstone trade in the early 1840s and since 1856 it had also been a steamer port for Orkney. Wick was on the Leith–Aberdeen–Orkney–Shetland steamer route, and an important herring and white fish industry was also centred there, with a number of secondary harbours round the coastline. The population, a long-established blend stemming from indigenous Picts and colonising Norse, also included many east-coast Scots, with a substantial recent influx of Gaels from the Mackay country to the west. Since late medieval times the Sinclairs had been the dominant family, still represented by the Earl of Caithness and sundry related gentry families. It was farming as well as crofting country, and its farmers were mostly tenant smallholders, who had done much to improve their land in the course of the nineteenth century. Land values and rentals had gone up sharply as a result. It was very different territory to Sutherland and Ross. Such a district might have been expected to show interest in railway construction, and a scheme to link Wick and Thurso had been mooted locally in 1845 but vanished in the mania years. Serious interest resumed in the 1860s, with the building of the line into Ross-shire. In September 1864 the earl took the lead in forming a committee to promote a railway to join with the line coming north from Inverness. (The earl was another steam enthusiast: as a scientist and inventor, he had been elected a Fellow of the Royal Society). The Duke of Sutherland of course took an interest, and Joseph Mitchell was 'requested by the Duke of Sutherland and the heritors of Caithness' to make a preliminary survey of a line from Helmsdale to Wick and Thurso.[1] With the speedy publication of Mitchell's survey in October, controversy began. There were two sources of contention: the route, and the funding.

Immediately north of Helmsdale, the mountain chain separating Sutherland and Caithness reaches the sea, in the Ord of Caithness, a rugged mass of hills and incised valleys, reaching a height of over 1,000ft. Though certainly not impassable by railway, such a line would need massive and costly engineering works, including tunnels, deep cuttings, and viaducts. The alternative was a great detour, following the inland straths and passing to the north of the hills, with a summit of around 700ft. The direct line from Helmsdale to Wick was thirty-seven miles; the inland route, as first surveyed, was seventy-seven miles. Mitchell's 'flying survey' opted for the inland line. While his book refers only to engineering difficulties at the Ord,[2] Mitchell's own ideas (like the duke's) might have been in favour of a line that opened up a huge tract of inland country to potential development. But his verdict met furious opposition in Wick. Most of the committee wanted the shortest line from Wick to the south, which meant a coastal route via the Ord. This was the way taken by the turnpike road, and it passed through well-populated agricultural countryside between Wick and Dunbeath, as well as serving fishing stations at Lybster and Dunbeath. Though Mitchell's plan also indicated the possibility of an alternative (or additional) line from a point between Forsinard and Altnabreac down to the coast at Latheron and thence via Lybster to Wick, this did not answer the Wick objections. Their route made their town the nerve-centre of the far-north railways, as terminus of lines from Thurso and from Inverness. A local engineer, Alexander Doull, was commissioned to make an alternative survey, but his report was in general agreement with Mitchell's. In January 1865, however, the committee secretary, Mr Miller, reported the receipt of a plan from Mr Donald Ross, of Thurso, to carry the line over the top of the Ord, 1,074ft, by means of a gradient of 1 in 40 for a distance of seven miles. Ross also proposed a stationary engine to cope with the formidable 1 in 10 slope at Berriedale: the part Mitchell considered to be the real problem. The *John o' Groat Journal*, considering the options, commented on 12 January that:

> Mr Ross thinks that even if the line should cost £10,000 a mile between Helmsdale and Dunbeath that route would be preferable to the inland one, but he does not offer to construct it for £10,000 a mile. At any rate, Mr Mitchell's proposal would unite Wick and Thurso with Helmsdale for nearly the same sum, or perhaps less, than would be required between Helmsdale and Dunbeath.

No more was heard of Ross's plan, and a *Groat* editorial of 5 June on 'The Railway Question' was categorical: 'Mr Mitchell was right and the carpers were wrong. There is no way into Caithness or out of it but the one left by Nature for the purpose'.

But even for the less expensive, though lengthier, route, it was far from clear where the money would come from. The Duke of Sutherland saw no reason why Caithness should not pay its share for its railway, and expected it to raise £100,000. But Wick, with its seaborne export trade of salted herring to Danzig, Königsberg and other Baltic ports, had no enthusiasm for being at the end of a railway that wound its way through the empty wastes of Sutherland. None of its merchants showed any interest. The *Groat* had helpfully drawn landowners' attention to the Improvement of Land Act of 1864, which enabled them to get a government grant to invest in railway construction; this would be useful because '... many of the landowners in Caithness are in such a position that, however anxious they might be to see a Railway in the county, they are absolutely unable to give it that amount of pecuniary support which a Caithness Railway scheme must meet with ...'[3]

At this point, a new figure was drawn into the scene, and for a short time the Caithness Railway promoters hoped they might get their line for nothing, or at least for much less than they had supposed. The kite was flown by George Loch, in a letter of 21 August to Nethan Giles, agent for the railway contractor Thomas Brassey. By this time it was quite common for new railways to be built as 'contractors' lines', in which the contractor bore the building costs and leased the line to an operating company, or sold it in exchange, or part-exchange, for a large shareholding. Several lines traversing rural Wales were built in this way. Loch's letter does not make such a proposal directly, but its tenor is clear:

> Dear Sir, I have been considering very anxiously, as you may believe, the best means for promoting the extension of our Sutherland Railway to Wick and Thurso – for, until this be accomplished, we cannot look for a sufficient return on the capital that will be expended in Sutherland, nor can we expect for the country the full advantages to be derived from a system of railways, until it be completed by establishing communication with the principal places of business in this distant part of the world.
>
> The Duke of Sutherland shares in these views, as is proved by his offer to subscribe £50,000 towards an extension of the line to Caithness, over and above the similar sum which he contributes to the scheme as far as Brora, already in course of construction. 'An unexpected difficulty has, however, occurred in the inability of the Caithness public to bear their fair proportion of the cost of such an undertaking; and though the railway companies to the south would probably afford pecuniary assistance, I fear the project will fall to the ground unless aid be obtained elsewhere. 'I have no right to suppose that Mr Brassey would turn his views in this direction; but being well acquainted with his enterprise, and with the power he possesses of giving it effect, I would ask you to bring the subject under his consideration...

Brassey's response was prompt and positive, and so was that of Lord Caithness when he was informed. Mitchell's plans were made available to Brassey, who had the line re-surveyed. A meeting was then held at the Highland Railway headquarters, including the duke, Loch, the earl, Brassey, and Giles. While Mitchell's general plan was followed, some deviations within Caithness were agreed, mainly to provide a Wick–Thurso line running to the north of Loch Scarmclate, with a short branch to Castletown. Brassey offered to construct the line, taking part of his payment as £100,000-worth of shares. The duke would provide his £50,000, on condition of the Highland Railway doing likewise; but Caithness was still expected to subscribe £100,000. The earl reported all this to a meeting of the Caithness County Road Trustees on 30 September, and quoted an estimate of costs as around £6-7,000 a mile.[4] Over the total projected distance of eighty-two miles, this produced a grey area of £82,000. A new Caithness Railway Committee was formed, but until the funding position was more definite, it decided initially to seek Parliamentary powers only for the Wick–Thurso and Castletown line. Criticism was not long in coming. The *Groat* published a letter on 5 October, datelined London, from 'A well-wisher to the Caithness Railway', observing that: "It may be very grand to be associated with eminent financiers and contractors, but depend on it, those who travel in such company pay dearly for their whistle'. The storm broke on 9 November, with a letter of furious opposition from Sir Tollemache Sinclair (who made no secret of his friendship with and support for Joseph Mitchell), denouncing the "local" line ('I myself will not subscribe a farthing to the proposed local line'), and, though declaring himself for Mitchell's inland route, condemning the proposal to give £100,000 of shares to Brassey, pointing out that Brassey's estimate was £127,000 more than Mitchell's. A similar letter from Mitchell himself followed on 16 November.[5] Nevertheless, the proposal went ahead. Following receipt of a letter from the earl, the HR Board agreed on 29 November 1865 to subscribe £10,000 to the project, though this was not put to a Shareholders' Meeting until 27 June 1866, when it was approved, on assurance that it would only be given to support a line built to join the Highland system. The committee made their application for a Bill on 28 December 1865, with Thomas Brassey Jr among the promoters. The railway duly received its Act on 30 July 1866, but against a nominal share capital of £130,000, the value of shares subscribed was only £27,000. The Duke of Sutherland had ceased to concern himself once it was clear that Caithness was not stumping up. Consequently, the Caithness Railway was unable to undertake any construction, though as a company it continued to hold regular meetings until 1870, making itself available rather like an increasingly elderly and impecunious bachelor hoping a rich widow will somehow turn up.

As a footnote to the general *débacle*, Mitchell had been asked to follow up his 'flying survey' with the working survey for the full line, but Lord Caithness reported to the committee that he had 'asked too much'.[6] In fact Mitchell had been invited by Loch to undertake the task at his own risk and cost, to be repaid if the Caithness people raised their £100,000 and if the railway's Bill were passed; in which case he would be paid two-thirds in cash and one-third in shares.[7] Mitchell's assessment of the Caithnessians' response was canny enough for him to turn down this offer. Instead, two other engineers, McLean and Stileman, were employed, and paid on a more conventional basis: they received £4,000 in cash for their work, rather more than twice what Mitchell would have charged. Mitchell believed that Brassey and the earl had had to find this out of their own pockets.

## The Highland Railway, 1866-70

The Caledonian's proposed investment suggests that informal talks about a merger may have been taking place in 1865.[1] Certainly in the early part of 1866 the HR senior officials were sufficiently alarmed about their own futures to submit a Memorandum to the Board, asking that their interests be protected in any amalgamation with a 'Southern company'. The board disclaimed all contemplation of such a step, but agreed, 'in the event of such a contingency, to do their best'.[2] Terms for a three-year loan of £40- or £50,000 from the Scottish Provident Institution had just been agreed. No more was heard about amalgamations. At that time, with the American Civil War just ended and transatlantic trade still disrupted, with economic depression at home driving claims for more industrial and political reform, and with war going on in Europe, all prudent company managers were pruning their costs, trimming their ambitions, and waiting for better times to resume. For the Highland directors, exposed as they were by their guarantees on interest payments, the need for the business to be conservatively run was paramount.

Among the few new works to be put in hand were a crossing loop at Brodie, 'to help with the altered timing of the Up English Express Goods' which had had to be made to fit in with changed timings of its southern connections. A link was also authorised at Forres, to enable through carriages to run direct from the south on to the Elgin line: the station's triangular layout dated from this. The link was horse-operated at first.[3] In March 1866 tenders were accepted for refreshment rooms at Invergordon and Nairn, at rentals of £25 and £30 a year respectively. A softening in relations with the Great North of Scotland at this time resulted at last in an agreement on through rates for southbound traffic off each company's lines, via Dunkeld or Aberdeen as the case might be. The GNSR also agreed to run a 7 a.m. train from Aberdeen to connect with the Highland's 9.40 a.m. from Keith to Inverness. Money was still tight and a 1 per cent dividend on the Ordinary stock was declared for the half-year ending 28 February 1866. In the Directors' Report, to the cry of high interest rates was added the new problem of Cattle Plague, which had spread throughout much of the Highlands. The market at Muir of Ord had been suspended, cattle traffic receipts were down disastrously and an increase in sheep traffic merely made up for much of the loss rather than providing a useful extra. Thirty per cent of the company's capital, £669,128, was held in Loan Capital and Debenture stock. Against such a background, the thought of proceeding with the Highland's own line into Perth received no encouragement. Mitchell's estimate for its cost had been £124,000, and the compromise arrangement of an annual toll of £5,000, irrespective of traffic load, over the Scottish North-Eastern line was agreed by the board on 8 May. Compromise had been the advice of the companies' chosen arbitrator, James Grierson of the Great Western Railway. A Westminster directors' meeting on 7 June sealed the agreement and also agreed to withdraw the tactical opposition the company had adopted to the amalgamation of the SNER with the Caledonian. The plans for an independent line into Perth were withdrawn.

Setting their faces against all perks for the staff, the board had refused the request of William Stroudley, the locomotive superintendent, for a free pass for his wife; but they unbent a little in the case of the platelayers employed on the line. Their request for a pay rise was turned down, but those working between Struan and Newtonmore, and Dunphail and Grantown, were granted free passes for weekly visits to the nearest village station.[4] Dougall reported that the Morayshire Railway had closed its branch between Rothes and Orton on 31 July, and the Board, reminded that since 1858 it had paid out £4990 for facilities to handle transfer traffic at Orton, delegated authority to Martin & Leslie, the company's Parliamentary agents, to pursue the matter. Another 1 per cent dividend on the Ordinary shares was declared for the half-year to 31 August. While the Orton claim was being pursued, a new junction, with the Strathspey Railway, a GNSR protectorate, was opened on 1 August, as provided by the Strathspey's Act. The two lines converged south of Broomhill, about four miles north of Boat of Garten. The HR refused to contribute towards the cost of operating a signal box here, and after two years of argument the junction was lifted in June 1868, the Highland laid an extra track alongside its own, and the two parallel roads were worked as separate single track railways to a junction at Boat of Garten.[5] In theory, the Strathspey line enabled the GNSR to tap Highland territory, but no one from Grantown, which now had two stations, was likely to go south via Craigellachie, Elgin and Aberdeen rather than via Aviemore.

In September 1866, the northern section of the HR had its first royal passengers when the Prince and Princess of Wales, in a train provided by the GNSR, travelled from Keith to Bonar Bridge, en route for the Duke of Sutherland's castle of Dunrobin. A Highland engine was attached at Keith, and the senior officials, in the standard railway protocol for such occasions, travelled on the train. This underlining of the duke's status and connections may have played a modest part in the ongoing discussions on funding the Sutherland Railway. The HR's £30,000 was confirmed at a special meeting on 30 October.

In December 1866 Mr Critchley, stationmaster at Inverness, requested and received a pay rise of £10. An Englishman, he was a popular and highly regarded figure, always conspicuous on the platform when the Perth trains came in. Yuletide generosity on the board's part was a little less evident when the tenant of the Nairn refreshment rooms wrote to say she was now engaged to be married to the stationmaster, and hoped that her tenancy might nevertheless be continued. It was agreed to maintain it on a trial basis until Whitsunday. In February 1867 – the year in which the GNSR would finally make a physical link with the Caledonian in Aberdeen Joint Station – a committee was formed to consider acquisition of the Morayshire Railway, which was still independent though very much a GNSR satellite. Nothing came of this gambit.[6] A curious and unexplained item was recorded in the company's expenditure on 5 April 1867, of £9 4s 1d 'to pay stipend due Minister of Dingwall'.[7] Later in that year,[8] another unusual gesture was made, when the board awarded a Free Pass for life to John Fowler, in recognition of his 'very efficient assistance', especially when the direct line into Perth had been under consideration. (Joseph Mitchell had an annually renewable free pass). At the half-yearly Shareholders' Meeting on 27 April, a dividend of 1 per cent on the Ordinary shares was announced. Expenditure was still under tight control, but Buttle reported the building of two houses at Dava for the accommodation of workmen during snowstorms, and Stroudley reported that the company's two fire engines had been tested and painted and were now in excellent working order. At the end of September 1867 Buttle reported two breaches in the line north of Struan Station, of 24ft and 18ft respectively, caused by flooding after heavy rain. A single large culvert was built to replace two smaller ones.

The Directors' Report for the half-year to 31 August 1867 recommended a dividend of 2 per cent. At that time the HR's authorised and created capital was £2,209,180, with debentures and loans of £708,880 6s. The toll arrangements from Stanley with the Caledonian were modified, with an agreement made in December 1867 and backdated to 1 August, for a 'mutual interchange of traffic'. In effect the toll was waived as long as the HR delivered at least two thirds of its southbound goods traffic to the Caledonian.[9] At the board meeting of 7 January 1868, T.C. Bruce's salary (which seems to have remained at £500) was reduced, at his own suggestion, to £250. He was about to become a director of the London & North Western Railway, and was also planning to go abroad in the spring; but he continued to be managing director. During July, the board received an anonymous letter informing them that John Buttle was using the company's men and materials in building a new house, Carleton Villa, at Millburn. Enquiry showed this to be true, and it also emerged that Buttle had not accounted for Grass Money, paid in 1865, to the extent of £16 15s. A special meeting of directors on 11 June felt that 'their confidence in the future usefulness of Mr Buttle was destroyed', and he resigned a week later, though at the Board's request he stayed in his post until a replacement was found. Sixty-seven people applied for the position of resident engineer: a measure of how the railway industry had grown. Mr Peter Wilson of Glasgow, was appointed on 5 August, at a salary of £300.

In the course of the later 1860s, the dividend payable on Ordinary shares began a modest upward trend, with 3 per cent paid for the half-year to August 1868 and 2.5 per cent for the following winter half-year, when takings and profits were traditionally less. The lists of debenture holders provided also show how investment in the HR was spreading beyond the Highlands and Scotland: the company's performance and reputation were steady enough for it to be recommended to investors looking for a reliable return. Capital and loans remained stable, but interest payments running at over £60,000 a year made a heavy drain on revenue. Nevertheless, the HR was seen to be a well-run concern, by contrast with, for example, the much bigger North British Railway, on which a shareholders' inquiry in 1866 had revealed a 'careful and most ingenious fabrication of accounts'.[10]

### Dingwall & Skye: the First Phase

What were railways in the Highlands *for*? The simplistic answers, that a railway is a means of conveyance of people and goods from place to place, and a railway company is a business intended to make money for its investors by providing such a transport service, were only rarely the full story in other places and certainly were not such in the Highlands. The moving spirit of the Dingwall & Skye line was Alexander

Matheson, Ross-shire's largest landowner, who in addition to his Ardross estate had another at Duncraig between Loch Carron and Loch Duich. His experience with the Inverness & Aberdeen Junction Railway had shown him that a railway line in the north of Scotland could pay its way very well. Family connections with the Isle of Lewis, where his uncle, Sir James, was the territorial magnate,[1] made him familiar with the north-west coast and the northern Hebrides. Lewis, Harris, and even Skye were still relatively densely populated in the mid-1860s, with substantial, if impoverished, crofting communities. The Ross-shire interior had been largely cleared of its human population apart from a few small fishing villages and crofting townships on the sea-indented west coast, the largest being Ullapool, with 908 inhabitants in 1865. The nearest thing to an industry was at Letterewe, on the northern shore of Loch Maree, where Black's *Guide to Scotland* (1864) records that a tramway had been constructed to bring limestone down. It was burned at a place still known as Furnace, then brought across by boat to the public road. The proposed railway was to serve neither of these places, but to strike south-west towards Loch Alsh, the narrow sea-lane, or kyle, between the mainland and Skye, where there was a ferry and an inn, but nothing else. Here a port would be set up to concentrate the traffic both of Skye and of Lewis at the railhead. At that time, there was some hope of industrial development in the Hebrides apart from the cottage industry of tweed weaving: Sir James Matheson had set up the experimental Lewis Chemical Works outside Stornoway, to extract hydrocarbon oil from peat; and the proprietor of the Talisker Distillery on Skye was one of the D&SR promoters. Thus the Dingwall & Skye Railway had quite a different intention to the Sutherland Railway: in a real sense it was, like Inverness–Perth, or Chester–Holyhead, conceived as a trunk line. The configuration of the Wester Ross valleys meant that two stations, Garve (for Ullapool), and Achnasheen (for Gairloch), on the railway acted as convenient railheads for these other coastal settlements. Any further 'opening-up' of the countryside would be quite incidental, and, in fact, something to be ferociously resisted by the majority of landed proprietors in Ross and Cromarty (still two separate counties in 1864). Most of the land here was already turned over to 'deer forest', with isolated shooting lodges. The proprietors' interest was to keep people away, not to encourage an influx. They accepted the convenience of the railway for themselves, and lobbied for private stations on it, but even the keenest had none of Matheson's or Sutherland's enthusiasm for 'improvement' (Matheson, though he too had his deer forests, was an ardent land developer).

The first meeting of the promoters was held in London, on 26 April 1864, with a handful of proprietors, and Matheson brought Joseph Mitchell and Andrew Dougall to help put the case for a railway. Mitchell had already carried out a physical survey. Dougall produced a traffic estimate, though, as there was no existing traffic on the route to speak of, it was inevitably a rather aspirational picture that he drew. At this time the Oban & Callander and West Highland lines did not exist, and there was no rail-connected port on the west coast north of the Clyde. (For the promoters, a warning note might have been sounded by the failure of a scheme to build a railway from Fort William, on the sea at Loch Linnhe, to meet the I&PJR at Newtonmore.

Though backed by the area's prime landowner, Cameron of Lochiel, lack of subscription support meant that it could not even get a Bill in Parliament and the project sank from view in the autumn of 1863). Fish, sheep and tourists formed the traffic staples in Dougall's presentation. He also drew attention to the potential of Strathpeffer, with its chalybeate springs, as a spa resort. Though it was only four miles away from Dingwall, its visitors might very well go on to explore the region beyond. He expressed a confidence possibly greater than that which he actually felt, that the line could yield a dividend similar to that of the I&AJR, around 4.5 per cent. Two days later a Provisional Committee was formed, thirty-seven strong, with Matheson as its chairman; and the prospectus was launched at a well-attended public meeting in Inverness on 15 July, with MacLeod of MacLeod in the chair, a token of the Skye and Hebridean connection. But after that, progress was extremely slow. No deposit was called for in the purchase of £10 shares, of which 10,116 were subscribed for by 6 October, the date of the promoters' first business meeting. A notional £101,160 was far from enough to build a sixty-three-mile railway. Even at Mitchellian rates per mile, much more was needed (the eventual cost of opening the line was £286,534 for fifty-three miles, plus £7,480 for the pier works at Strome). Despite these difficulties, the committee persevered. With the help of a loan from the Commercial Bank of Scotland to cover the costs, a Bill was entered to Parliament for the 1864–65 session. The opponents were Lord Hill (who offered to withdraw his objection if a new house were built for him), Lord Salisbury, as trustee for Mr Balfour of Strathcarron, Sir William Mackenzie of Coul, and Duncan Davidson of Tulloch (both of the latter had been members of the Provisional Committee). Counsel for the promoters, Serjeant Merewether, made a clever speech, anticipating and demolishing the opposition's arguments,[2] and the Bill was passed on 5 July 1865. The company was duly formed, empowered to have a share capital of £450,000 and to raise loans to the value of £150,000; its powers also including the right to acquire or lease the ferry at the Kyle, and to build a hotel there. Arrangements had been made with the Highland Railway which was to contribute £50,000 to the project, and with the Caledonian, which was also to subscribe £50,000.[3] The first directors of the new company were Alexander Matheson as chairman, MacLeod of MacLeod as his deputy, the Master of Lovat, A.G. Dallas, of the Hudson's Bay Co., London (he was also owner of Dunain House, near Inverness); Eneas Mackintosh of Raigmore, and Capt. William Fraser of Kilmuir, Skye. Andrew Dougall was interim secretary. A minimum investment of £1000 was required to be a director. When the first £2 *tranche* of share capital was called up, many subscribers defaulted and the company had to resort to law to force them to pay. One of the non-payers was the deputy chairman, who had mistakenly relied on getting the money through the Land Improvement Act of 1864 (he disappeared temporarily from the board but was allowed to settle for 200 rather than 700 shares at £10). Troubles were only beginning, however. At the eastern end of the proposed railway, continued refusal to accept the surveyed line through Dingwall, by Davidson of Tulloch; and through Strathpeffer, by Mackenzie of Coul, effectively prevented work from starting at all. Dougall and Mitchell, giving their time and energy for nothing, until such time as the company could pay them, found the Dingwall & Skye project a headache when both had plenty to cope with in other ways.

Incoming landowners, mostly of the new-rich sort, with a colonial or industrial fortune, might be expected to object to the intrusion of a railway across their deer forests, but most were happy to claim a hefty amenity payment and their own private halts. Mackenzie, with Brodie of Brodie, was one of the very small number of intransigently obstructive landowners of Highland descent. While Brodie's motive was pure greed, Mackenzie's professed concern was for his amenity. If a railway were to pass through his territory, he wanted it to be invisible. The railway's Act had gone to great lengths to placate him, including the provision of a tunnel or covered cutting 510 yards long. There is a local tradition that Mackenzie's father, Sir George, had had a personal animus against John Mitchell, from some old grievance related to road-building.[4] Sir William's own crusty conservatism was a local joke. His and Davidson's refusal to agree to any proposals from the company meant that no work could begin, since no link could be made with the Ross-shire Railway. In January 1866, Mitchell was instructed to survey an alternative route, avoiding Dingwall and Strathpeffer altogether; following the river Conon to Marybank and Contin, and meeting the original line at a point west of the Falls of Rogie.[5] This was a jump from the frying pan of Coul into the fire of a grander Mackenzie, the Brahan estates of the Earl of Seaforth, and though the survey was done, no more was heard of it. The financial stringency of 1865-66 was a further blow. On 30 October 1866, Matheson had to report on behalf of the directors to the annual Shareholders' Meeting that: '… in consequence of the state of the money market during the last twelve months the works have not been commenced and they regret to say that the difficulty in arranging with certain landowners on the line alluded to in their last report still exists'. In February 1867 The MacLeod resigned and two new directors, Sir John Stuart of Lochcarron, and Lord Middleton, of Applecross, were elected. There was no action until September 1867, at which point the company's receipts were £10,293 and its expenditure £3,833.[6] A meeting of major shareholders from the west, including Lord Middleton, Sir John Stuart, and Matheson, at Jeantown (now Lochcarron) on 5 September, resolved to urge the board to find a way round the disputed areas and to terminate the line where it first met deep water, at Attadale, near the head of Loch Carron, rather than go on through extremely difficult terrain to the Kyle of Lochalsh. Spurred into action, at the General Meeting of October 1867 the board announced that the line had been examined and partially re-surveyed, with a view to reducing the expense. 'By effecting alterations and deviations at several parts of the line there will be a great saving in the cost but the route will be unobjectionable to these landowners who felt themselves compelled to oppose the original scheme.' The building cost was now estimated at £220,000 and a new subscription drive raised £26,160 in shares on top of the £91,000 of original subscription which Dougall still considered collectable. Some of the more amenable proprietors exchanged land for shares: thirty miles at £200 a mile, making another £6,000. Apart from the still-anticipated Highland and Caledonian contributions, it was hoped that other, unnamed, railway companies would subscribe to the tune of £30,000 and on this somewhat uncertain basis a new Act was obtained on 29 May 1868, which reduced the capital to £400,000, and gave powers to mortgage up to £143,000. Construction was at last put in hand, with a modest ceremony at Dingwall on 2 September 1868. Now, instead of passing to the south side of the spa village of Strathpeffer, the line avoided it completely, swinging across the floor of the strath in two sharp curves and climbing steeply up the Heights of Dochcarty on the north side, passing into a great defile below the crag of Raven Rock, at a summit of 458ft, and following the upper course of the Rogie Burn down towards Loch Garve. The station named 'Strathpeffer' (Achterneed from 1884) was two miles away and up a steep hill; the agricultural district of Contin was also now completely bypassed. The line was divided into two construction sections: Dingwall to Achanalt, and Achanalt to Attadale. The eastern section was awarded to J. & A. Granger of Perth, for a tender of £63,583 16s 3d; the western side to A. & K. Macdonald of Glasgow, for £62,798. Both were obliged to take some payment in shares, of a value of £2,000 to Macdonalds and £1,500 to Grangers.

With this resumption of activity, Joseph Mitchell bowed out, and the company hired Murdoch Paterson as its engineer, at £500 a year. Paterson was still at work on the Sutherland Railway, but like his mentor he was a man of abundant energy and had also acquired great knowledge of the topography of the Highlands and the psychology of the local gentry. Mitchell's exit may have been made with some relief, since John Fowler of Braemore, who was a shareholder in the Skye line, was proferring advice which was almost always contrary to Mitchell's. Fowler (who was elected a director of the D&S in August 1868) had been strongly in favour of a narrow-gauge, 3ft 6in line, which would have been cheaper to construct, but Mitchell felt that a break of gauge at Dingwall would cause inconvenience and extra working expenses far into the future.[7] As on the Sutherland Railway, his departure was marred by a dispute over his professional fees; instead of the £5,000 he claimed, he had to be content with £3,500, payable in a year's time, and fifty shares in the company.

John Fowler, a first-rate engineer, despite his concern for economy did not feel that Attadale was the right place for a terminus and pier. Even as the contractors were getting down to work, having first criticised the plans for a station and hotel there, without persuading his co-directors, he went on to assert that it was completely unsuitable. His standing as an engineer of docks as well as railways compelled the board to listen, though he annoyed them by departing to the Mediterranean for the winter of 1868-69 and it was not until the meeting of 23 March 1869, following his return, that the matter could be resolved. At that time it was decided to extend the line a further 4.5 miles along the south shore of Loch Carron to Strome, where there had long been a passenger ferry across the loch. The Macdonald contract was extended by this length and by the modest sum of £5,232 4s 10d to effect it. But savings at Attadale were expected to contribute. For businesslike characters like Matheson and Dougall, the confused management of the Dingwall & Skye project seems odd, but Matheson had other concerns and Dougall was finding ever-increasing calls on his time. But no director, it seems, had a watching brief, unlike Thomas Bruce on the Perth line, or the Sutherland & Caithness Railway, where Kenneth Murray received an honorarium of £250 for his participation in the construction committee. Fowler's role appears to have been a self-appointed one. In Spring 1869 it was evident that the company's funds were insufficient to complete the line. Debenture issues brought in some cash, but it was an expensive way to raise funds.[8] The pier works, entrusted to Donald McGregor of Dingwall, were reduced to the barest simplicity. A shortfall in working capital of £29,632 was met by a loan from the Commercial Bank of Scotland, against shares to the value of £105,000. Even this only sufficed to get the line to Attadale and Macdonalds were demanding an additional £2,000 for the works to Strome. The lack of an adequate port on the west coast made the delivery of supplies difficult, and Macdonalds were falling behind. The rail suppliers, Gilkes, Wilson, Pease & Co., of Middlesbrough, having quoted a freight-inclusive rate, now demanded an extra 8s a ton for delivery, and their contract was cancelled. Instead, Head, Wrightson of Stockton supplied rails (of iron: steel-topped rails were allowed only for points and crossings).

While it had always been anticipated that the Highland Railway would work the Dingwall & Skye line, a Working Agreement had to be established. Fowler took an interest in this, and there were lengthy discussions in the autumn of 1868 before a ten-year agreement was concluded on 4 January 1869 (in his absence). The HR would operate two trains each way daily, at a cost of 2s per mile, and any additional trains at 1s 10d per mile, in fact the same arrangement as with the Sutherland Railway. Trains would be mixed passenger and goods. In addition, the D&SR agreed to pay £200 a year for use of the station at Dingwall, where the Highland Railway was constructing an engine shed and turntable for the benefit of the D&SR. The HR Board explained as the basis of the Agreement that: '… the Directors do not believe it is the wish of the Shareholders to secure a large profit by working the Skye line' (James Merry, not for the first time in a minority of one, dissented), but also pointed out (in the half-yearly report of 30 October 1868), that 'These rates are higher than those at which the Highland line is worked'. The Agreement was approved by a large majority of the HR shareholders present at the meeting.

Despite its chronic shortage of cash, the D&SR went ahead in 1869 with an imaginative business idea. This was to build the line with sufficient clearance to transport fishing boats from east to west, and vice versa. Fishing vessels, sailing craft of the 'Zulu' type, were not of great bulk or weight, and masts could be stepped. The Moray Firth fleets regularly went to the Hebridean fishing grounds, and a route which avoided Cape Wrath, and offered a shorter transit time and lower rate than the Caledonian Canal, looked like a potential winner. Special 15-ton cranes were to be installed on the Dingwall Canal and on Strome pier, to hoist boats on and off specially designed wagons. The design work was done by William Stroudley at Lochgorm. To allow boat trains to pass each other, the loop at Garve was built with a 10ft-gap between the tracks, rather than the usual 6ft. Two boat cranes were ordered on 4 March 1870 from Cowans Sheldon at Carlisle, at £243 each. But the delayed opening of the line meant that the date for the fishers' migration was missed, and the order was postponed to 1871. By that time, the D&SR had neither the capital nor the confidence to proceed with the idea, which fell into limbo.[9]

The opening of the line was scheduled for 1 July 1870, but Paterson reported that this would be impossible. A new date, 10 August, was agreed, but Capt. Tyler, inspecting the line for the Board of Trade on 9 August, refused to grant a certificate because the line was not fully fenced as required by Act of Parliament. The banquet arranged at Strome for 10 August had to be hastily cancelled. After completion of the fencing, the line was finally opened on 19 August, and station staff installed in rudimentary accommodation at Strathpeffer, Garve, Achanalt, Achnasheen, and Strathcarron. Mr Baxter, stationmaster at Murthly, was transferred to the other end of the system to take charge at Strome Ferry at £100 a year plus a house. The delayed opening feast was held on 7 September, when a special train left Inverness for Strome Ferry at 8 a.m. Tickets for train, banquet and a short steamer trip cost 17s 6d (first class) and 12s 6d (third class). The Peacock Hotel of Inverness undertook the catering, with 470 places laid in the draughty barn-like terminus at Strome. As the first of several speakers, Matheson, who had been born at Attadale, recalled how, as a boy, his first journey to school at Dingwall, in 1819, had taken him two days.

Strome Ferry was now the only western railhead north of the Clyde. Sanguinely, the directors of the D&SR had assumed that the established steamer operator, David Hutcheson, would be ready to make their pier a port of call for the Skye and Lewis traffic. This was not the case. To Hutcheson, the proposed connection meant a loss of business from Glasgow, as well as a twelve-mile detour each way from the existing route through Loch Alsh, and, though the water was deep, there were numerous rocks and islets in Loch Carron forming a hazard to navigation. Late in the day, the D&SR found it would have to provide a connecting steamer service by itself. Two small vessels were purchased from William Sloan & Co., of Glasgow, *Jura* and *Oscar*, and with these a service was begun on 20 August. Down trains left Dingwall at 10.15 a.m., reaching Strome at 1.15 p.m., with an arrival at Stornoway at 10.45 a.m. next day; and 4.15 p.m., reaching Strome at 7.15 p.m., with an arrival at Portree at 11.15 p.m. Up trains left Strome at 8.15 a.m., with passengers who had left Portree at 4.15 a.m., arriving at Dingwall at 11.15 a.m.; and at 3.15 p.m., with passengers who had left Stornoway at 5.45 that morning, and arriving in Dingwall at 6.15 p.m. Three hours for fifty-three miles, averaging 17.6mph, was hardly commendable for 1870, but the line was new, the signalling rudimentary, the locomotives small, and the need for economical working paramount. Shunting might be required when goods wagons were taken on at intermediate stations. It was epoch-making in any case to get from Stornoway or Portree to Inverness within a single day.

## The Duke of Sutherland's Railway

Through his marriage with the Mackenzie heiress to the Cromartie estates, the duke was proprietor of large tracts of the counties of Cromarty and Ross (confusingly, much of Cromarty consisted of scattered enclaves of territory within Ross) and in that capacity, he subscribed £15,000 to the Skye Railway. But his prime interest continued to be the line through Sutherland, whose terminus was at the south end of Golspie from April 1868. The duke was frustrated by the situation. Nothing was happening with the Caithness Railway project, though its powers were still valid. The Sutherland Railway Co. had no money to continue beyond Golspie, just north of which, separated by a ridge of rugged ground, lay the ducal demesne of Dunrobin, and then a relatively easy shoreline route to Brora and Helmsdale. The fishing industry, especially herring, was reaching a peak. The sandstone measures around Brora held unexploited coal reserves. Determined to exploit the resources of his land, the duke resolved to go it alone. On his own account he promoted a Bill for a railway between Golspie and Helmsdale. Mitchell had already surveyed the line. No one was likely to oppose The Duke of Sutherland's Railway, through the duke's own domains, and it received its Act on 20 June 1870. The duke had not waited for this formality, which was mainly concerned with establishing the line's links to the Sutherland Railway Co., taking over its responsibility for the Golspie–Brora section. Under a local contractor, William Baxter, construction had begun on 16 February 1869, with the first sod being cut at Clynemilton, Brora, by an octogenarian local lady, Mrs Houstoun of Kintradwell. Local men were employed and the early start was noted as 'a measure of relief' since unemployment was high, but one can also perhaps detect a certain eagerness on the promoter's part to get his own railway into being. By October 1870 the line was completed between Dunrobin and a temporary station at Gartymore, named West Helmsdale,[1] with intermediate halts at Brora and Loth, the latter serving the Lothmore and Lothbeg crofting townships. In September 1870 the duke asked if the HR would give a third-class carriage and four wagons to provide trains. They were duly 'given' at standard Railways Clearing House hiring rates, and hauled two miles from Golspie to Dunrobin, by a traction engine. Later, the Highland Board agreed to withdraw the hire charge.[2] A 2-4-0 well-tank locomotive was purchased from Kitsons of Leeds and delivered by sea to Helmsdale; again a traction engine appears to have dragged it to the northern railhead. It was given the name *Dunrobin*. A saloon coach was ordered and delivered in the same way. Capt. Tyler, for the Board of Trade, inspected the line on 31 October and declared it 'in excellent order'. Tyler also noted the part played by Kenneth Murray of Geanies[3] in supervising the works, along with the duke. The cost of the seventeen-mile line was £5,077 a mile: a very modest rate, though of course no land purchase was required. But there were nineteen bridges, described by the inspector as all being of 'a substantial character' and including the 60ft masonry span of the bridge at Brora. On 1 November 1870 the railway was inaugurated by Princess Christian, in a ceremony at the temporary West Helmsdale Station, down at the seashore. *Dunrobin* operated a twice-daily service each way, taking forty-five minutes, until the completion of the end-on junction at Golspie in June 1871. From 19 June 1871, the Highland Railway took over services under the same terms of working as with the Sutherland Railway, and through trains between Helmsdale (the 'West' was dropped in July 1871) and Inverness were instituted. Dunrobin then became a private station for the castle, and the duke retained the engine and saloon carriage for his own use, together with the right to run his own train over the entire line to Inverness.[4]

*The Sutherland & Caithness Railway*

Having taken a scunner to the inland rail route in 1865, Wick's merchants and burgesses did not repent or recant. In justice to them, it was partly that, though a stagecoach had run between there and Inverness with the mails since 1816, 'Herringopolis' was accustomed to doing its trade by sea, and its merchants put their money into shipping. In 1879, five years after the railway came, there were over seventy trading vessels registered in Wick, some of several hundred tons.[1] A direct railway down the coast to Helmsdale was no more on offer in 1871 than it had been in 1865. The chief promoter of the proposed Sutherland & Caithness Railway was the Duke of Sutherland, and his route was the one first surveyed by Joseph Mitchell, swinging sharply away from the sea, climbing up Strath Ullie into the deep interior, then bending eastwards to run through the centre of Caithness to Wick, with a branch to Thurso. The duke was still intent on opening up the country. He had no vested interest in Lybster or any of the coastal communities between the Ord and Wick. His great meander would still beat the stagecoach and gain the mail contract, and he also expected the Thurso branch to tap the short sea-route to Orkney, drawing some of the traffic that mostly went by steamer to Aberdeen or Leith. Only these final extensions to Wick and the Pentland Firth would turn his railway into something other than a remote branch ending at the edge of a fishing village.

The Caithness Railway Co., perhaps spurred by the opening of the Dingwall & Skye line and the impending arrival of a railway at Helmsdale, held a Shareholders' Meeting in Wick on 30 September 1870, at which it was unanimously resolved that a railway should be built 'from the point at which the Sutherland Railway terminates northward to the authorised line in the neighbourhood of the Loch of Watten'. All necessary arrangements with the Highland Railway and the Duke of Sutherland were to be made. This was all very well, but purely aspirational while the matter of finance remained unresolved. Nor had the concept of the Wick–Castletown–Thurso line been dropped: this was 'the authorised line'. The Duke of Sutherland's patience had been stretched over five years, and now it snapped. His line to Helmsdale was almost complete, and Loch, ever-vocal as the ducal mouthpiece, embarked on public criticism of the Caithness Railway, terming it a 'sham', without shareholders; and of the earl's apparent continuing hope that Brassey would somehow rescue the venture. Relations between the two northern magnates became somewhat tense for a time. 'Dear Sutherland', wrote the earl to the duke, 'I have sought his [Brassey's] aid only because of our difficulties in raising the necessary capital. If it can be obtained by subscribers, then, as I stated to the meeting, we don't want what is termed a contractor's line'.[2] He also pointed out that it had been Loch who first of all had brought Brassey into the business. But Loch and his employer had moved on from that. Now the earl proposed that the Sutherland Railway should be extended to the County March, using 'a fair proportion' of the £50,000 to be contributed by the HR, and the Caithness Railway would build on from there to meet the Wick–Thurso line, using the rest of the Highland's £50,000 and otherwise 'at our own expense'. Sutherland had had enough pie in the sky, however. On 27 October, Loch wrote to inform the earl that the duke had given him the authority to instruct Murdoch Paterson to make another Helmsdale–Wick–Thurso survey,

> … with a view to the preparation of plans for a railway, that may be deposited in time for an application to Parliament, to be made in the next Session, a complete scheme from Helmsdale on the one hand, to Wick and Thurso on the other …the Duke has been induced to take this step by seeing the hopelessness of the efforts hitherto made having this important objective in view. He is prepared to contribute a large sum, probably £50- or £60,000…

Even for the outspoken Loch, this was straight from the shoulder. The Caithness company was being brushed aside like a cobweb – but then, it was hardly more than that. Sir Tollemache Sinclair added his voice, hoping that: 'the so-called Caithness Railway Company will now abandon their illusory and ruinous scheme'.[3] This was not to be, however. In November 1870 the Sutherland & Caithness Railway applied for a Bill, while the Caithness Railway applied for resuscitation of the powers granted to it in 1866, which were due to lapse in 1871. Earl and duke had locked horns. Two hundred years before, armed clansmen might have been sent across the Ord of Caithness, but times had long since changed: both these noblemen had had English public-school educations, and their battleground was a committee room of the House of Commons. In public opinion, though, the S&CR became Thurso's line, and the CR became Wick's. A public meeting in Thurso on 31 January 1871 called on the earl to withdraw his Bill; one held in Wick on 3 March supported the Caithness Railway Bill. Both Bills were considered by the Select Committee on 3 and 4 May. Even during the evidence and speeches, there was little doubt about the outcome. The Committee unanimously favoured the Sutherland & Caithness's Bill, which went on to receive the Royal Assent on 13 July 1871. The Caithness Railway Co. was left to unwind its affairs and pass from the scene. It was abandoned by the Board of Trade order on 23 January 1873.

The Bill was for a standard-gauge railway, though during the survey the duke and Paterson had seriously considered the idea of a 2ft 6in line, narrower than that proposed by John Fowler for the Skye Railway. The potential saving in construction and operating costs was tempting, but, again, the problem of trans-shipping goods and passengers, with all its cost and inconvenience, prevailed.[4] The duke might be forgiven for taking a rather teasing attitude to Wick in his speech at the opening of his own railway at Helmsdale. Referring to plans for further extension, he commented on a notable lack of share applications from the county town of Caithness: '… The second subscription to be remembered is a little donation from Wick, and till these subscriptions are made up we cannot expect much railway accommodation. Perhaps indeed we may manage to begin our works and go to Thurso, leaving Wick where it is at present'.[5]

Extending from the end of the duke's line at Helmsdale (with a new station higher up on the valley side) the S&CR was sixty miles long to its terminus at Wick. It

seemed odd to many people at the time, and since, that the main line stopped at
the town boundary of Wick, and the Thurso branch likewise at the edge of town,
without giving access to Wick harbour or Scrabster pier. Joseph Mitchell, in his
letter to the *Inverness Courier* of 28 November 1866, had castigated as 'a fatal and
unaccountable error' the fact that the McLean and Stileman plan had omitted these
harbour connections. In the case of Wick,[6] there might have been a difficulty in
passing through the town to reach the quays; the reason for not going to Scrabster
is less obvious, but it is likely that in both cases it was felt sensible to wait and see
what traffic developed, before extending the line. The S&CR shareholders, led by
the economical duke, would not have wanted to inject any further capital until a
return was safely predictable. Once again the deep Sutherland coffers had had to be
tapped. The duke put £60,000 into the new line. The Highland Railway guaranteed
£50,000. The board held its first meeting on 19 September 1871, the directors being
the duke, Sir Tollemache Sinclair, George Loch, Kenneth Murray of Geanies, and
Donald Mackay, a farmer, of Thurso. After Sutherland's 6,000 shares at £10, the next
largest shareholder was Sir Tollemache, with 600. Fifteen investors, mostly landowners
and farmers, had between 120 and 20 shares each, and a further thirty-two had from
10 to a single share. These were almost entirely tradespeople and householders of
Thurso, like George Macdonald Carnaby, watchmaker, with his one share, and James
Gerry, pavement merchant, with five. Not one shareholder came from Wick.[7] At this
point, 7,603 shares had been issued, at a value of £76,030.

Construction of the line[8] was split, with the Caithness section under Murdoch
Paterson, who had relinquished his connection with the now-finished Dingwall &
Skye Railway to Peter Wilson, the Highland Railway's civil engineer. His headquarters
were at Halkirk, later at Georgemas. The Sutherland section (to the County March)
was under William Baxter, the Brora engineer who had built the Duke of Sutherland's
Railway. He worked from a hut, moving along as the line extended. Paterson as senior
engineer was paid £500 a year, and Baxter, £350. On both sections the contracts
were divided into a multiplicity of small portions, often entrusted to local or northern
companies and tradesmen, like John Scott of Coupar Angus, Hector Mackenzie of
Turriff, John Ross of Fearn, John Matheson of Dunnet. In fact it was the complete
opposite of how Brassey or Falshaw would have gone about things. Between 400 and
560 men were employed in each main section, many being local or from elsewhere in
Sutherland. They departed so far from the conventional image of the railway navvy as
to combine among themselves to pay for a preacher to come on Sunday: no minister,
whether Established or Free, apparently troubled himself about the spiritual welfare
of these men. In order to provide accommodation for them, the planned houses for
isolated surfacemen were built early, and those on the Caithness section were listed by
Paterson in a letter to the board on 23 October 1871: four permanent blocks of three
houses each, near the ruined shielings 1¾ miles north of County March; at Altnabreac;
at Culmaddy burn, seven miles from County march; and at Dorrery, eleven miles
from County March. Additional wooden huts, double-walled with moss insulation,
were built on both sections where necessary. Policemen were engaged to patrol the

line and to check on the 'order and cleanliness' of the cottages. Construction was frequently held up by bad weather, especially rain, but both engineers kept the board well informed. A letter from Paterson of 23 October 1871 notes that:

> We have immense tracts of peat moss to contend with from the County March to Dorrery – a distance of 12 miles, and I have sounded the depth of it at every fifty feet. There are many parts where the moss is very soft, and is termed "flow" moss and we have done all in our power to escape it with the line, as, from its softness, it can not be properly drained…

Two miles west of Dorrery the flow was unavoidable, '… but the softest portion of it is only seven feet deep and the deepest part at any point 11 ft 9ins. The length of this 'flow' traversed by the line is ¾ of a mile.' Baxter suggested that the contractors as well as the men be paid fortnightly, and that provisions and clothing be supplied for ready money by merchants to be approved of: 'the Railway Company building the Provision Shops and the several Contractors would be taken bound to fall in with the means which would thus be provided'. The duke had a hand in this – he detested the 'truck' system by which contractors paid their men in tokens which could only be exchanged for goods at the contractors' own store. The modest degree of amenity for men working on the line shows how things had moved on from a decade before. Paterson's quite commodious station building at Georgemas[9] included an enginemen's and guards' room, in contrast to the non-existent facilities for crews at Bonar Bridge.

As with the Sutherland railways, strict economy was maintained in the construction but the work was done well. Baxter made use of £460-worth of surplus permanent way material from the Duke of Sutherland's Railway; and also acquired the Sutherland Railway's now-redundant engine shed at Golspie for £55, using it in different locations as a temporary workshop. One of the most unusual of railway board meetings was held in a workmen's bothy at the County March summit on 10 June 1873, with the duke, Loch, Kenneth Murray, Andrew Dougall and the two engineers in attendance. They decided on the purchase of rails from the Stockton Rail Mill Co., to be of iron with crystallised steel tops, to be delivered at Helmsdale, Scrabster and Wick. It was also resolved to purchase an additional locomotive to be used in construction of the Caithness section, and to, 'arrange with Mr Sacré [Charles Sacré, Chief Engineer of the Manchester Sheffield & Lincoln Railway] to get one he knows of in Liverpool, which is stated to be in excellent condition, and little used'; the price was £750 exclusive of shipping, and it was to be delivered to Wick. Part of the deal was that the engine could be returned at valuation after completion of the works. The first standard-gauge locomotive to run in Caithness had been landed at Scrabster in early March 1873 and was in service hauling ballast trucks from the 24th of that month.

In June 1874, the duke entertained a large party of visiting mining and mechanical engineers at Dunrobin. They travelled on the new line as far as Georgemas, and saw some of the duke's other enterprises, including a machine for converting peat into charcoal, and steam ploughs for land reclamation at Lairg and Loch Shin. They descended the now reopened coal pit at Brora where a 4ft-seam was being energetically worked (around 40 tons a day was the current output), and finally saw a display of dynamite blasting. Among the guests were Francis Webb, chief mechanical engineer of the London & North Western Railway (of which the duke was a director) and David Jones, once a pupil of that line's Crewe Works, now locomotive superintendent of the Highland.

The S&CR's Working Agreement with the Highland Railway was modelled on those already made by the Sutherland and Dingwall & Skye Railways, providing for a rate of 2s per train mile, for two daily trains in each direction, 'whether such trains run or not', and 1s 10d per train mile for each additional train. But the first train to traverse the new railway from end to end was the duke's. He drove his locomotive *Dunrobin* into the new station at Wick on 9 July 1874, two days after the last rails had been laid. He was expected at around 3 p.m. but arrived ninety minutes early. On the news of his arrival, the Provost and a few local worthies turned out to greet him, but it was a somewhat constrained reception for, as the *Groat* caustically observed, 'they do not in their corporate or personal capacity hold a single £10 share of the railway among them'.[10] In the carriage were some select friends, including Mr Carter of *The Times*; William Baxter came on at Helmsdale and Murdoch Paterson at the County March. The duke regarded the visit to Wick as a piece of business, to inspect the works. His train then went to Thurso, where a crowd estimated at three thousand was waiting, with two bands. A banquet had been prepared, at which the duke was a somewhat reluctant guest of honour. Sir Tollemache Sinclair had organised a collection to make him a presentation to mark his contribution, but the duke deprecated the notion, saying he had enough silver plate already, and asked that Sir Tollemache's collection be distributed among 'those poor fellows who have borne the burden and the heat of the day in pushing on the works as they have done. I refer to the workmen on the line'. On the way back to Dunrobin, at 'the embankment of Mer-na-caber… we found Mr Scott, the enterprising contractor, in charge of two hundred stalwart navvies, mounted on a string of wagons, whose hearty cheers as the Duke passed made the welkin ring'.[11]

The Caithness newspapers advertised a special train from Wick to Inverness, for the Royal Highland Show, on 31 July, 'If the Sutherland & Caithness Line is opened'. The line was inspected on 20 July for the Board of Trade by Col. Rich, who declared himself fully satisfied, and opening was set for Tuesday 28 July. The first train for the south left Wick at 5.10 a.m. on that day, 'without even a cheer'.[12] The number of passengers was estimated at between 70 and 80. On the opening day, the Wick burgh council went so far as to arrange for the town bell to be rung at intervals, and suggested that the merchants might give a half-day holiday to their shopmen, but there was no civic ceremony for the arrival of the first train from Inverness at the northern terminus.

By 31 August 1874, a month after the opening of the line, the authorised capital was £480,000, comprising £360,000 in Ordinary shares and £119,960 in loans. Of the Ordinary shares, £284,254 had been issued, including £72,000 'for Stock issued in Security'. The directors now were the duke, as chairman, Sir Tollemache Sinclair, as his deputy, James Henderson of Bilbster, Col. Charles Guthrie of Scotscalder (who had given the railway free access to his ground), George Loch, Kenneth Murray of Geanies, Alexander Matheson of Ardross, MP, and the Hon. T.C. Bruce, MP. The HR Board was thus well represented. Andrew Dougall had taken over from the Golspie Writer, Donald Gray, as secretary in 1873, wielding the company's seal which blended the arms of Sutherland, Wick and Thurso. In 1876 the Earl of Caithness, a conspicuous absentee from the first shareholders' list, purchased shares and was elected to the S&CR Board. The Sutherland Railway, the Duke's Railway and the S&CR all retained their separate independence for ten years, during which time they were worked, and staffed, by the Highland Railway under the Working Agreements.

# FOUR

*The Highland Railway in the 1870s*

All things considered, the 1870s, and to a lesser extent the 1880s, were the Highland Railway's most successful period. For a railway serving an agricultural region, this is perhaps surprising, but in the early years of the 1870s the farmers of the central and eastern Highlands seem to have fared better than those further south. Specialisms like growing seed potatoes, and barley for the distilleries, and breeding pedigree livestock were already developing. If unlikely to bring about a new era of general prosperity, they were providing local pockets of economic success and were not over-prone to market fluctuations. Fish, coal and timber remained the staple traffics, after passengers. In the west, the self-sufficiency of crofting was not likely to be affected by cheap grain, meat and wool from North America and Australia.

The Locomotive Superintendent, William Stroudley, resigned at the very beginning of 1870. He had been offered a similar post with the London Brighton & South Coast Railway, at £800 a year. While he intimated that he would stay at Inverness if the HR would match this, the board was unwilling to make a commitment, which would be likely to involve salary rises for other senior officers. Stroudley had had scant chance to show his mettle as a locomotive designer, but he had made himself useful in many ways, including the contriving of a 'wagon ramp' for putting derailed wagons back on the track, which the Board Meeting of 7 January 1868 authorised to be provided to all guards, 'at a cost of £3 or thereby'. He left with many praises, and went on to pursue a distinguished career, but his successor at Inverness was also to prove himself a locomotive engineer of first-rate ability. Forty-three engineers applied for the post, and after reducing this number to six, the board appointed David Jones, currently Stroudley's foreman, at £500 a year, inclusive of any extra responsibilities for the D&SR. Now aged thirty-six, he knew the line and its needs, the works and their capacity, the company and its limitations, better than anyone.

A useful chunk of capital came in 1870 when the company was awarded £40,000 compensation for the loss of its telegraph business, following the Telegraph Act of 1868 which put the public telegraphs into the charge of the Post Office. The poles and lines were to be maintained by the railway company at a rate agreed for five years, varying according to the number of wires. For three wires, it was £1 per mile per annum.[1] More than half the lump sum went in settlement of the long-disputed claim by Gowans & Mackay over the building of the Inver Tunnel, in which arbitration was awarded against the HR, at a cost of £22,603. In the following year, the original seven-year mail contract was up for renewal, and was eventually renegotiated at £21,000 a year for ten years.[2] Little in the way of capital expenditure was needed, as the locomotive works had recently been refitted, and the locomotive and rolling stock was enough to fulfil the needs of the service. Cost-reduction was still a preoccupation, and in April 1869 the small turntable at Newtonmore was exchanged for the large one at Dalwhinnie, to reduce the number of pilot engine movements. Interest levels fell from the high points of the 1860s. War between France and Germany in 1870-71 discouraged continental traffic and helped push up tourist numbers in the Highlands – it seems only reasonable that the HR Board agreed to ship seed corn to distressed districts in France at no charge.[3] In October 1870 officials' salaries were duly reviewed. Dougall's rose from £1,000 to £1,600; his assistant, William Gowenlock, went from £160 to £195. The two goods managers, Thomas Macray at Inverness, and Thomas Lowson at Elgin, went from £325 and £250 respectively, to £400 and £300. Waged staff received no increase at all, but the company's donation to the employees' annual festival was raised from £25 to £40. For the half-year to 31 August 1870, the dividend on Ordinary shares was 4 per cent, with £3514 14s 8d held over to even up the balance on the normally shorter dividend of the winter half.

On 31 January 1872 *The Times* noted that the Highland Railway, 'an undertaking which, though of considerable standing, has not hitherto had its stock quoted on the London Stock Exchange', had made a formal request for a quotation. What with one thing and another, by March 1872 the company was in the happy situation of having paid off all its loans and having a modest surplus in the bank, to the relief of the directors who had pledged their personal credit against the interest payments. For the half-year ending on 31 August 1872, an unprecedented 6 per cent was paid on the Ordinary shares: the payout on these, of £33,213 12s 7d, was just over twice the interest payments of £15,500 16s 10d. Not everyone got what they felt they deserved, or had earned. Joseph Mitchell was still pursuing payment of his professional account, from which the company was busy deducting every extra payment it had had to make against claims made by contractors with whom he had made agreements. For the rest of the decade the dividend never went below 4.25 per cent, except in the winter half-year of 1874-75, when it fell to 2 per cent. At that time, Matheson was obliged to explain to the shareholders that for two successive half-years, traffic receipts had been over-estimated. The need for estimates was because of the delay in precise figures being obtained from the Railways Clearing House. Commenting on the company's results, *The Times* of 5 May 1875 remarked: 'It appears that the figures given from week to week are those of a month or two back'. It added, ominously: 'This kind of publication can only tempt speculation by those in the secret... No system could be worse than that of the Highland Railway.' Twenty years later, it would be seen that nothing had been done to reform this practice.

Of course, the availability of ready money was accompanied by demands for capital and other expenditure. A good deal needed to be done to keep pace with the expansion of services. In the first half-decade of the 1870s many staff cottages were built, mainly for surfacemen, station porters and pointsmen. The relative prosperity of the company could scarcely be kept from its workforce, especially when approval was given for a new head office building at Inverness, on 1 April 1873. The Locomotive Superintendent passed to the same board meeting a letter signed by 136 of the "principal artisans" of the workshops, intimating their intention to cease work on the 5th of the month unless their working hours were limited to 51 hours per week "as has been conceded in other Railway Workshops throughout Scotland". Jones said that he could not guarantee replacing these key workers, and the men's request was acceded to, with effect from 1 May. This was the first known occasion of the Highland Railway's employees combining, and the immediacy of the strike threat suggests that Jones had been withstanding the request for some time, presumably on the advice of Andrew Dougall. On 25 April, the Secretary reported to the Board that a Memorial had been received from the guards, porters, pointsmen and surfacemen, requesting a pay rise of 3s per week. Again the company moved quickly, and the Finance Committee resolved to revise the classification of workmen in the Traffic Department, by reducing the period between minimum and maximum pay levels from two years to one year, and also allowing an extra 1s a week extra to men of two years' or more service. It was calculated that this would add £550 a year to the Traffic Department's costs. Pay scales for surfacemen were also revised. Men working between Stanley and Struan got 1s a week extra, those between Newtonmore and Forres got 6d, except for foremen, who got a shilling. The Inverness squad of six men got a shilling, and all surfacemen on other sections got 6d. The total cost of these increases was reckoned at £480 a year. That month the tenders for the new offices were agreed, at £9,512 1s.[4]

On 6 January 1874, anticipating the opening of the line through to Wick and Thurso, and the arrival of ten new locomotives of the 'F' class, extensions to the roundhouse at Inverness were authorised, at a cost of £2,300. Five additional tracks were added at each end of its arc, making a total of thirty-one. At the end of the year Peter Wilson died, and Murdoch Paterson, already acting as locum, was appointed engineer at £600, on condition he gave the post his whole time and attention. The new offices were built in 1875, adjoining the station and on the opposite side of the square from the Station Hotel. The Inverness architects Matthews & Laurie, who had already designed the extended hotel in 1859, were retained for this, and they provided a handsome Classical design of ashlar stonework, rising to three storeys and fronting on to the square. On Academy Street, the façade was recessed, with arches between the Corinthian columns and carved decorations by the stone-carver Thomas Goodwillie of Elgin, including three decorative wheel-spoke designs above the windows. Inside, the boardroom was impressive, with a coffered ceiling and downwards-pointing bosses, and lofty windows looking southwards. In October 1875 the board voted £500 for a portrait of Alexander Matheson to hang in the boardroom; in February

1878 it voted to spend £50 on decorating its ceiling with gold leaf. The building still stands, and though its interior has been remodelled, it is still possible to admire the handsome staircase, lit by tall windows with coloured glass side-panes. Between October 1876 and 1878 the station itself was improved. The public concourse and the pitched iron and glass roofs, with the long-familiar gabled façade, date mainly from this time, and cost £3,000. The overall roof was relatively short and the company never provided awnings along the platforms.

Lochgorm Works were also enlarged in 1876, and again in 1879. From 1876 until the 1890s, apart from the general programme of maintenance and light and heavy repairs, the company's own shops built at least one or two locomotives in most years. Throughout the 1870s and 1880s, steady progress was made in renewing rails and sleepers, with from ten to twelve miles of new 75lb iron track laid in most years, with steel track at the most heavily used locations. At stations like Pitlochry or Struan, where the gradient steepened virtually from the end of the northbound platform, slipping driving wheels could cause rapid damage to the rails. The board meeting of 30 August 1876 approved the ordering of 80,000 sleepers, enough for around sixty miles of track. The standard 9ft-sleeper cost 2s 6d if cut from larch, 1s 10d if from natural Scots pine, and 1s 8d if from planted Scots pine. Half a mile of track was added to the system with the construction of a branch from the Ross-shire line to the east side of the Muirtown Basin, close to the north end of the Caledonian Canal. The goods-only branch opened on 9 April 1877, though it was not legitimised by Parliament until the HR Further Powers Act of 4 July 1890. At this time there were regular canal steamer services, daily to Fort Augustus, and weekly to Glasgow, carrying freight and passengers. In the Working Timetable of 1884, the branch was serviced by a daily train leaving the Inverness yard at 4.15 p.m., shunting for thirty-five minutes and returning at 5.20; while the Harbour branch had three trains daily. No regular service on the branch is shown in the 1922 Working Timetable.

In August 1876 the HR Board consented to Andrew Dougall becoming a director of the Caledonian Bank, and in September Charles Waterston, the managing director of the bank, was elected a director of the Highland Railway, taking the seat of Kenneth Murray of Geanies, who had died in August. Waterston was immediately co-opted on to the Finance Committee. Later, in October, the Duke of Atholl also became a director, though his appearances at board meetings were at first rare. Normally it was only death that removed a director from the Highland Board, once elected. James Merry died in April 1877, and Sir George Macpherson-Grant of Ballindalloch was elected in his stead.

In the first half-year of 1876, the company for the first time carried more than half a million third-class passengers.[5] There were 500,255, bringing in a revenue of £44,573 1s 6d. Second-class passengers numbered 27,776 and brought in £7,208 8s 5d, while first class numbered 84,436 and brought in £21,409 19s 4d. A 5 per cent dividend was paid on the Ordinary shares. More passengers also created more demands, and there was a steady flow of minor improvements to station facilities. On

3 April 1877 the board agreed to a petition from the inhabitants of Dunkeld, that a gentlemen's waiting room be erected on the west platform, and urinals were installed at a number of larger stations over the next few years. The same meeting accepted a petition from the Night Pointsmen that their uniforms be made of strong cloth, not corduroy, for warmth. The extra cost was duly noted, at £1 4s 7d per suit, or £24 11s 8d a year. A more expensive but vital step was taken that day when, following the report of an accident at Kincraig Station to the 9 p.m. Down Goods on 17 March, the engineer was asked to report on the expediency of interlocking points and signals. This was a matter that the Board of Trade had been pressing for some time, together with that of fitting passenger trains with automatic brakes. On 4 September 1877 the board resolved that: '… the Directors will be prepared to adopt the Brake found most suitable by the large Companies in the South.'[6]

An important decision was taken at the board meeting of 2 October 1876, when it was agreed that the company would give up leasing the Station Hotel at Inverness and take it into direct management. The hotel had been considerably extended and improved and the company had spent a lot of money on it, without ever feeling that the rental justified the expense or was adequate to the potential. The current tenant, Mr Macdonald, late of the Sutherland Arms at Golspie, was given notice, and a manager, Charles Spinks, formerly of the Caledonian Hotel in Inverness, was appointed at £400 a year, this salary to include his wife's services. Due to Mrs Spinks's poor health, he resigned in March 1878, and from sixty-six applicants, Edward Cesari of the Devonshire Hotel, London, was appointed, on the same basis. Cesari, a hotelier to his fingertips, took the establishment in hand and it made a steady profit for the company. Other large hotels were built in the town, but the Station retained its pre-eminence.

'A student of transport needs no *leftish* bias to appreciate the almost feudal powers exercised over their wages staff by mid- and even late-Victorian railway companies', wrote Hamilton Ellis in *British Railway History*.[7] The early years of the 1870s had seen the formation of the first railmen's union, the Amalgamated Society of Railway Servants, coinciding with a period when the laws of supply and demand in the labour market seemed to move a little way to favour the workforce. By the end of the decade the position was different. In June 1878 the Highland Railway Board resolved to follow the practice of the North British and Caledonian Railways, by extending working hours at their workshops from fifty-one to fifty-four hours a week, as from 1 July. Surfacemen's pay was to be reduced from between 6d to 1s a week, at the engineer's discretion, and their hours extended to fifty-four. The Traffic Department was unaffected. Other than copy-cat behaviour, there seems no reason for this action. The company was not in trouble and no other economies were called for. The Lochgorm Works were the nearest thing in the Highlands to a concentration of industrial workers, and the directors perhaps felt conscious of this large group as a potential source of turbulence, and had no compunction about pre-emptive action. The surfacemen were isolated groups. Exact arrangements for implementing the cuts were remitted to the Finance Committee. From 1 August 1878, the workshop and surfacemen were offered the choice between either a 5 per cent reduction in wages between 17s and 24s a week, and of 7.5 per cent on wages of 25s a week or more; or the extension in working hours. On 6 August, Jones reported to the board that his men had opted for the pay cut. The pressure continued. In the winter of 1878-79 the question of wage cuts or longer hours arose at each board meeting and was deferred to the next. But on 4 March 1879 the board again proposed to increase artisans' and surfacemen's hours to fifty-four, or to implement 5 per cent reduction to all wages over 16s per week. Again the Traffic Department seemed immune, and there was no suggestion at all of any decrease in officials' salaries. On 1 April it was reported to the board that the men had accepted the increase in working hours but requested a pay rise in consequence. This latter was deferred, and did not come up at subsequent meetings.

In the Directors' Report of 25 April 1879, the wage bills for the half-year to 28 February were recorded as:

| | |
|---|---|
| Permanent way staff: | £10,492 15s 11d |
| Locomotive department: | £5,516 0s 3d |
| Locomotive repairs: | £3,101 9s 7d |
| Carriage and wagon repairs: | £3,132 2s 10d |

The total, £22,242 8s 7d, was 25 per cent of the company's gross expenses, excluding steamers and other charges not directly concerned with operations. Gross revenue for the period, excluding steamers, rents and so on, was £147,586 19s 6d. The dividend on Ordinary shares was the lowest in the decade, at 3.5 per cent, but this was ascribed in the report to prolonged snowfalls, which, even though the lines had been kept clear, had blocked access roads to stations and so disrupted traffic. The task of keeping the tracks clear was of course shared by the surfacemen and locomotive men.[8]

Towards the end of the 1870s a number of changes were made to the board, for the usual reason. George Loch had died in 1877 and, as he was the Duke of Sutherland's nominee, the duke replaced him with Samuel Bateson of Cambusmore, who died after a few months and was replaced by Sir Arnold Kemball, commissioner of the ducal estates. Col. William Fraser-Tytler, another of the original directors, died in 1878 and was replaced by Lord Thurlow who had extensive estates around Dunphail (Fraser-Tytler's son would later join the board). In March 1879, J. Grant Peterkin of Grangehall was elected in place of Robertson of Aultnaskiach.

The Working Agreement with the Dingwall & Skye Railway was due to terminate in 1880 and the future of that line was under intensive discussion in the latter half of 1879. The likelihood of amalgamating the problematic D&SR with the Highland Railway clearly caused some concern to the Duke of Sutherland, and on 20 October 1879 the HR Board pledged itself to make an amalgamation with the Sutherland Railway, the Duke of Sutherland's Railway, and the Sutherland & Caithness Railway, on or before 1 June 1884.

## Dingwall & Skye: the Second Phase

Fifty hundred thousand pounds was a very large sum in the nineteenth century, equivalent to some £2,500,000 in 2005. For the Caledonian Railway to contemplate an investment of this scale in the Dingwall & Skye Railway suggests some wider motive. But in the event, the D&S's expectation, repeated in Bradshaw's *Shareholders' Guide* over several years, of attracting investment from the Caledonian was never realised.[1] That company's interest switched to the Oban line, which had a starting point from the Caledonian's own station at Callander. For its part, the Highland Railway invested £35,000 in D&S stock in 1872, acquiring two seats on the board.

A few months' operation was enough to show that the D&S was unlikely to be as profitable a railway as the I&AJR. From 1 November 1870 the winter service was reduced to a single mixed train each way between Dingwall and Strome, which often earned barely enough to meet the HR mileage rate. The steamer service was a loss-maker from the start. It was quickly reduced to three sailings a week between Strome, Broadford and Portree; and one between Strome and Stornoway. *Oscar* ran aground at Applecross on 9 November 1870, and though no lives were lost, the vessel was declared a total loss (it was ultimately refloated but the company was paid the insurance value). Further requests to Hutcheson to take over the steamboat service from Strome were politely declined: '... we could not run a steamer or steamers specially in connection with the Dingwall & Skye Railway without a serious loss of money', he wrote to Dougall on 21 November 1870; Dougall was already sadly aware that the same was true of the railway company itself. Between direct runs to Stornoway, *Jura* operated a twice-monthly service up the coast to Gairloch, Aultbea and Poolewe and then across the Minch. Two of its Portree calls each week connected with the Hutcheson steamer *Clansman*, and an agreement on through fares to the Outer Hebrides was made with Hutcheson. The little North British Railway paddle steamer, *Carham*, of 159 tons, built for the shallow Solway Firth, was acquired in 1871 for £3,000 to work the Portree route, and on its arrival *Jura* was sold, for £3,500. Stornoway sailings were dropped. *Carham* operated alone until 1873, having to be replaced or supplemented by charter vessels when it broke down or required refitting or could not cope with the peaks of sheep traffic. A mail contract worth £1,250 a year from September 1871 helped to stem the losses, and the company also received £4,250 from the GPO for its telegraph business in 1872. But by the end of 1873 *Carham* needed a complete overhaul, including a new boiler. At the beginning of 1874 a larger and more up-to-date vessel of 347 tons, with the unprepossessing name of *Ferret*, was put in service, having been acquired from the shipowners G&J Burns of Glasgow for £15,000. The new ship was able to do a daily run (except Sundays) to Portree, a weekly one to Stornoway; and also to fit in trips to Gairloch (fortnightly) and the Loch Ewe villages (monthly). *Carham*, refitted at a cost of £4,000, was available as a reserve and for special charters, though only because the company failed to find a buyer who would offer a reasonable price. Quite apart from the capital expenditure involved, the D&S shipping accounts record a trading loss for every year from 1871 to 1877.

These losses merely compounded an already critical situation. The line had been built to minimal acceptable standards, and further works were constantly needed. Bridges over streams and rivers, mostly timber structures, needed maintenance and renewal. Platforms were unpaved and unlit. No houses had been built for station staff or surfacemen. The wooden pier at Strome soon needed reinforcement. From November 1870 Peter Wilson put some urgent work in hand. In the winter of 1872 double sets of surfacemen's cottages were built, at seven locations between Achanalt and the terminus. The principal stopping point was Achnasheen, where Alexander Matheson had acquired land for refreshment rooms (later a hotel) opening on to the platform. Engine water columns were also installed here. Over a period of several years, houses were built for stationmasters at Strathpeffer (later Achterneed), Garve, Strathcarron and Attadale. Private stations were opened at Lochluichart, Glencarron (in return for an investment of £2,000 in the D&S Co.) and Achnashellach, all of which in time were also opened for use by the general public.

With two trains a day each way in summer, and one for the rest of the year, plus occasional extra services when fish or sheep traffic required them, the Dingwall & Skye made a precarious living through the 1870s. Its best year was 1877, when its receipts totalled £17,423 (passengers £8,443, parcels £1,296, mails £1,250, goods £4,288, cattle and sheep £2,026, miscellaneous £120). Operating expenses were £6,430 to the Highland Railway, and £5,133 for steamers, leaving a surplus of £510.[2] This might have seemed a Micawberish sufficiency, were it not for the fact that the company had to pay interest on its loans: at the end of 1876 these totalled £128,058. At that time, shares in stock amounted to £229,058 against a notional share capital of £400,000, with Ordinary shares at £114,000. The company was perilously under-capitalised.

As a trunk line, its survival was more remarkable than its performance. Inevitably the disappointment of some investors caused complaints and recriminations. In 1871 Fowler and Stuart resigned from the board, and in 1872 they joined two discontented shareholders, Mr Banks and Capt. R.J. Tennant, in a self-styled Committee of Investigation into the joint management of the line by the Highland and the D&SR. Two highly critical documents were published by the committee in the spring of 1872, alleging mismanagement and misappropriation of funds. The D&S Board responded by convening a public meeting in Inverness on 13 July, to which the committee were invited. Matheson, in the chair, said that: 'The whole of the allegations... had arisen from the disappointment alone of two former directors, who appeared to think their opinion was law'. Only Stuart appeared, to find himself in a minority of one. Having unanimously passed a resolution that the committee's actions had been 'irregular and wholly unwarranted', and expressed its confidence in the D&S Board, the meeting disbanded.[3] At the end of 1872 Fowler apologised to the Highland Railway Board. He was a mercurial figure, whose biographer records that: '... in his less guarded moments he was apt to be impulsive, passionate and even arbitrary'.[4] Tennant, who still owed the D&SR for two special trains he had had run to his station at Achnashellach in 1871, was still being pursued for payment in 1873.

In 1877 the D&S was relieved of a burden when the Highland Railway acquired its shipping interests.[5] The total of £13,450 it received for *Ferret* and *Carham* – plus £130 for smaller boats – was used to pay off some of the company's debt, but even so, it was plain that only further borrowing could keep the business from insolvency; and no one was likely to make a loan in these circumstances. With the Highland a large investor, two HR directors on the D&S Board, HR officials in charge of operations, and HR trains operating the service, there were only two possibilities – amalgamation with the Highland, or closure. A few lingering glances may have been directed at Aberdeen, where the GNSR was getting its house into good order, but the Highland would unquestionably have wrecked any such move. The Highland and D&SR Boards opted for amalgamation and applied for a Dingwall & Skye and Highland Railways (Amalgamation) Bill in the 1879-80 session of Parliament. Andrew Dougall provided his board with 'Notes on the Proposed Amalgamation' in October 1879: the Skye company's debenture and temporary loans by now amounted to £200,000, at 4.5 per cent interest. Dougall reckoned they could be replaced by HR debenture stock at 4 per cent, with a consequent saving in interest payments. Furthermore, he estimated that the HR would make £4,000 on the debenture issue. His paper anticipated that over ten years, an amalgamated D&SR would bring in a surplus of £26,000 to the Highland Railway.[6] Unanimous approval of the HR shareholders was not forthcoming, but a substantial majority supported the decision. Forty-eight shareholders, representing £109,335 worth of stock, opposed. An Act was obtained on 2 August 1880 and the Dingwall & Skye Co. was formally amalgamated into the HR on 1 September. The Highland Co. was authorised to raise £74,000 of debenture stock to pay off the immediate D&S debts, and it acquired the residual borrowing powers of the D&S. Fifty pounds worth of HR Ordinary shares were issued for every £100 of Dingwall & Skye, which was not a bad deal for shareholders in a company that was technically bankrupt. No D&S directors joined the HR Board, apart from those who were already members, but no doubt Alexander Matheson, Esq., of Ardross and Lochalsh, MP for Ross & Cromarty (in the Liberal interest), felt quite able to look after the interests of the West Coast.

*The Steamship Venture*

Andrew Dougall had achieved a handsome pay rise in 1870, but there is no doubt that the Highland Railway made him work for it. Each new extension, Working Agreement and amalgamation laid more onus on the slenderly staffed office of the general manager and secretary. Quite apart from railways, from 1870, the agreement with the Dingwall & Skye had required him to become instantly knowledgeable on the business of purchasing, supplying and operating ships. In 1876 he had to pursue the board's will in a further nautical undertaking, under the Highland Railway (Steam Vessels) Bill, which became an Act on 24 April 1877 and gave the company authority to provide and use steamships from the harbours of Strome Ferry, Gairloch, Poolewe, Aultbea, Ullapool and Glenelg to Skye and the Hebrides; and from Wick, Scrabster and Thurso to the Orkney and Shetland Islands. The board's view was only moderately sanguine; its report to the Shareholders' Meeting on 24 October 1876 announced that: '... the Revenue to be derived from the Traffic... combined with subsidies from the Post Office for the conveyance of Mails, will protect the Company against loss...' For the western isles, the board had resolved to acquire the vessels owned by the Dingwall & Skye Railway. For the North, it was going to build its own ship.[1] A marine engineer, James Grier, of Glasgow, was retained as adviser, and in December 1876 he was authorised to prepare plans for a screw steamer of 384 gross tons, 175ft length, and capable of 11 knots. It was built at Gourlay Brothers yard in Dundee, at a cost of £12,750, and was launched in April 1877 as *John o' Groat*. Trials were carried out satisfactorily on 22 June and the ship was duly delivered to Inverness, its port of registration, though the intention was for it to work between Scrabster, Stromness and Kirkwall. The service began on 27 July, with a wagonette conveying passengers between Thurso station and the pier. Goods transport was provided by Wordies. The steamer's funnel was painted yellow,[2] and this style was applied to the other two members of the fleet, *Ferret* and *Carham*, bought at Grier's valuation.

Mail contracts were seen as an essential underpinning of the steamer services. Dougall made a proposal to the Post Office for a service from Strome Ferry to Harris and Lochmaddy on North Uist, but this was turned down.[3] However, £2,000 a year was agreed by the GPO for the carriage of mails between Scrabster and Stromness.[4] The Orkney steamer service was seen as a natural extension of the Thurso line, but Hutchesons were a serious rival on the west coast.

Unfortunately, the HR's experience as a steamship operator was no happier than the D&SR's. Strome remained an inconvenient and difficult harbour on the west; and *John o' Groat*, despite being a modern ship, failed to draw an adequate share of the Orkney traffic, which, for much of the year, was very small in any case. At a board meeting on 1 April 1879 it was resolved to sell *John o' Groat*, and replace it with a smaller ship; also to sell *Carham*. Finding buyers for ships was not easy, however, and both vessels remained in service with the HR. By this time the Highland had become keen to dispose of its shipping services altogether. David Hutcheson & Co. had become David Macbrayne Ltd in June 1879 when the partner of that name acquired the business. Macbrayne was more willing to listen than his predecessor had been, and the Highland more willing to do a deal than in 1870. In January 1880 a Working Agreement was made for Aultbea and Gairloch services from Strome to be operated by Macbrayne, and this was followed by all other western services from 17 April. A Heads of Agreement was signed by Macbrayne and Dougall in Glasgow on 18 March, the terms of the document showing clearly which side held the cards. Macbrayne was to run a steamer service between Strome and Portree, calling at Plockton, Broadford and Raasay, to connect with the HR trains, at a frequency of three sailings a week each way, increased to a daily service between July and September, and would pay £50 a year for the use of Strome Pier. Clause 7 engaged the railway company to haul steamer coal to Strome for the Macbrayne ships at the same rate it would have charged itself. Once the agreement had been concluded, the Highland still had *Ferret* and *Carham*, which, it seems only now to have transpired, Macbrayne did not intend to buy, though he did acquire the Strome ferryboat and other small lighterage vessels at Plockton, Broadford, Aultbea, Gairloch and Poolewe. *Carham* had grounded at Raasay on 30 March 1880 and had to be taken to the Clyde for repair. *Ferret* followed it there. Carham was not finally sold until 1882 when it became *Queen of Thanet*. The fate of *Ferret* was far more peculiar and is narrated in Appendix C. The Highland Railway continued to operate the Scrabster–Orkney service until 27 July 1882, when it was taken over by the North of Scotland, Orkney & Shetland Steam Navigation Company. They did not require the *John o' Groat*, which was sent first to the Clyde, then to Liverpool for sale; and was eventually bought for £10,200 by a Spanish firm, and renamed *Fé*. All in all, the shipping venture had been an expensive failure, and though occasionally the receipts exceeded the operating costs, more typical was the half-year to 28 February 1879, when the steamers earned £3,742 11s 11d, and their running cost was £4055 19s 7d. The Highland Railway was in no hurry to enter the water again. Even when it acquired the Kyle–Kyleakin ferry in 1897, it leased the operating rights.

# FIVE

*The Highland Railway in the 1880s – Territorial Defences*

Early in 1880, the HR received solicitations from Perthshire and Dundee urging it to construct two new lines, a branch from Ballinluig eastwards over the hills to Bridge of Cally, and a trunk line from Stanley to Dundee. Both were largely expressions of discontent with the Caledonian Railway's hegemony of Strathmore, and the Highland politely turned the opportunities down.[1] On 30 June the railway to Oban, worked by the Caledonian, was completed, and the Highland Board resolved at its meeting of 3 August to spend £2,600 on extensions and improvements at Strome Pier to counter competition from the new railhead. Although trading conditions were not particularly propitious – the half-yearly report to 29 February 1880 had referred to a 'General depression of trade and agriculture' – the Finance Committee also approved an outlay of £5,450 on extensions to the Station Hotel, and also plans for a new parcels office, third-class ladies' waiting room, stationmaster's office, and closets, at Inverness Station. Consideration of automatic train-braking systems was still going on. For the half-year ending in August 1880, the Highland reverted to the 5 per cent standard, paying out £39,061 on Ordinary shares, the largest amount yet. It had carried a total of 667,009 passengers for a revenue of £74,166 0s 3d; mails at £10,000; parcels, horses and carriages at £11,560 18s 3d; merchandise at £46,217 0s 6d; livestock at £9148 18s 7d, and minerals at £14,506 4s 4d.

Snow struck hard at the railway in the winter of 1880-81. On 17 December a mixed train going south from Forres was immobilised in drifts north of Dava. The passengers were able to struggle on to the station, where they found others from an oncoming Down train which was snowbound south of Dava. Efforts to free the cattle from five wagons on the mixed train were a failure, and as drifting continued, and the train became buried completely, all the animals were suffocated. Several days elapsed before the line was cleared. Blizzards returned in January, February, and March, blocking the line to Wick for a week between 17–24 January, and that to Perth between the 17–23 January. At that time, and at the beginning of March, service was further disrupted by the collapse of telegraph wires. The effect of the delays was to push down even the winter levels of revenue, and the dividend on Ordinary shares paid at the end of February 1881 was down to 3.5 per cent. Though it was under no legal obligation, the HR paid half the value of the dead cattle, but wrangles with the farmers of Easter Ross, who wanted full restitution, went on for a year.[2]

In March 1881 the locomotive men sent in a request for a pay increase of 7.5 per cent; after checks with other Scottish railways, this was deferred by the board on 5 April. That month, one David Ross, a fitter, wrote directly on behalf of the Lochgorm workmen to the board, to ask for a general pay increase. Ignoring him, the directors replied to Jones, instructing him to say that, 'the time has not arrived for the moment'. On 27 July, however, an increase was made to the pay of iron-workers only, totalling £267 a year.

On one or two occasions, the company had received representations from the Free Church Presbytery of Lochcarron, protesting about the unloading of fish at Strome Pier on Sundays. The reply had been that Sunday work was only undertaken when essential. A different request was received from the Church of Scotland, asking if the train shed at Strome could be used for church services on Sundays during the summer months of 1881. The community there was a new one, dependent on the railway, and there was no church within easy access. The board, however, turned it down on 5 April. Although in May 1867 it had followed the example of other Scottish railways in allowing the National Bible Society to install collecting boxes at larger stations, the HR normally kept a secular detachment from all denominations and moral causes. Regular appeals from temperance societies for the company to serve only soft drinks, or at least, no ardent spirits, in its refreshment rooms were allowed to 'lie on the table', and it had declined a request from Bishop Eden that the peal of bells for Inverness's new Episcopalian cathedral, St Andrew's, should be carried free of charge from Perth.[3]

The first attempt since 1862 to promote a direct railway from the south to Inverness began in 1882, with the formation of a prospective Glasgow & North Western Railway Co. It proposed to make a railway from Glasgow, via Loch Lomond and Glen Coe, to Ballachulish, Fort William and on through the Great Glen via Foyers to Inverness. It would cross the Callander & Oban line at Crianlarich. The plan aroused great enthusiasm in Lochaber, well off the railway map following the collapse of the Newtonmore–Fort William proposal in 1863. With the backing of the North British Railway, a Bill was put before Parliament in the 1882-83 session, and strongly opposed by the Highland Railway. The NBR involvement caused some embarrassment to Sir James Falshaw, a director of the NB as well as of the Highland; he resigned, then withdrew his resignation, from the Highland Board. The main shortcoming of the G&NW was the fact that it was a speculative contractors' line, proposed by a London firm, Wilkinson & Jarvie, with no experience of Scottish railway construction and with very little support from the landowners. They would build and then lease or sell the line to an operating company. The C&O also opposed the plan, and it joined the HR in pointing out, from experience, the defects in planning and the over-optimism in cost-forecasting of the proposal. Among the supporters of the project was Inverness Town Council, despite the fact that the Highland Railway was its largest single source of income. Part of its case was that competition would reduce fares and freight costs. After much intense and ill-tempered argument, the Parliamentary Committee rejected the Bill, but the Highland had a price to pay. One of the better arguments for the G&NW was that its line from Glasgow (a city by now much grown from the 1860s and still expanding vastly) would be forty-five miles shorter than the Caledonian–Highland route via Perth. This was a strong point, and T.C. Bruce informed the Select Committee that the Highland Railway was considering a diversion line between Kingussie and Inverness, to shorten its route from Perth.

The thought of another railway reaching Inverness warmed up the ancient ambitions of the Great North of Scotland Railway, which was engaged in building its coastal line via Portessie to Elgin (partially opened in April 1884 and completed in 1886). The GNSR was already irked by the Highland's refusal to concede it running powers between Elgin and Forres (see Portessie line, below) and also by the Highland's insistence on retaining Keith as the transfer station between the companies, rather than Elgin. On 9 May 1883, the Highland, trying to avoid war on two fronts, signed a Memorandum on Traffic Exchange with the GNSR. This provided that traffic to and from all Great North stations, except Aberdeen and stations west of Keith, should be exchanged at Elgin, unless specifically consigned via Mulben on the HR. Traffic from south of Aberdeen would be exchanged at Keith or Elgin, depending on whether it had come by the Caledonian or North British respectively. William Moffat of the Great North reckoned his company would profit by £600-£750 a year.[4] By these and some other minor concessions, the Highland prevailed on the GNSR not to support the Glasgow plan. But peace did not last long: in the Parliamentary session of 1884 the Great North was back with a New Lines Bill, for a line between Nethy Bridge and Inverness to be jointly owned with the HR. There were still men of the Highland Railway who remembered the last joint line; but even without that, the HR had no intention of letting any other company into its sanctum. At the same time, the Highland presented its own Bill for an Aviemore–Inverness line, for which a survey had been carried out in August 1883. The sensitivities of Inverness were further inflamed by yet another Bill, presented by a group of Aberdeen and Angus landowners, led by the Marquis of Huntly, for a lofty railway to be built right through the Grampian massif, to link the Deeside Railway at Cambus o'May with the GNSR at Nethy Bridge. This, however improbable in reality, in combination with the GNSR's proposed new line would provide a complete alternative Aberdeen–Inverness railway. Dubious as he was about this 'Landowners' Line', Moffat hoped that a Dundee–Perth–Ballater–Boat of Garten–Inverness railway would be built, and worked by the Great North.[5] Such a line would draw off traffic to and from the north which would otherwise go via Perth. It may be a mere historical aside that more blood had been spilt in Highland warfare over land rights than anything else, but the HR Board was thoroughly roused and alarmed. In front of the Parliamentary Committee, accusations of blackmail were levelled at the Great North, which replied by saying that if the Highland should get powers to build the direct line from Aviemore, it would be in no hurry to use them. T.C. Bruce, as the Highland's spokesman, put forward a powerful case, emphasising that the local landowners supported the HR's direct line. In the end, the Highland's was the only one of the three Bills to be accepted, becoming an Act on 28 July 1884, and Murdoch Paterson was duly instructed to make a full survey. The Act also formally established that traffic on the Great North for west of Elgin, if forwarded via Elgin, could be transferred there and not at Keith; and the GNSR was also allowed to have its own agent at Inverness Station.

The Highland had seen off the invaders, and the GNSR prophecy proved correct: the direct line from Aviemore promptly went into abeyance. Barclay-Harvey comments:

> It is not easy after a lapse of fifty years to understand why the Highlands of Scotland held out such attractions to would-be railway builders towards the end of last century, yet not only private individuals but also Scottish Railways fell victims to this allurement. The Highland, which was there, knew all about its limitations, but the Great North of Scotland on one side and the North British on the other seemed to have altogether exaggerated ideas of the value of Highland traffic.[6]

However, there is some evidence that the GNSR had no real intention of building an Inverness line of its own: its Parliamentary agents, Dysons, advised the chairman, William Ferguson of Kinmundy, that it would not work simply demanding running powers on Highland tracks; the Great North 'must be in the field with a new through line'.[7] This does not imply an intention to build; the hope was that by proclaiming its readiness to build a line of its own, the GNSR would be given running powers on the new Highland direct line, or that Parliament would insist on a joint line. On 26 July 1883, Moffat wrote to Ferguson, *à propos* of the Highland's Aviemore direct line, that:

> ... it seems pretty clear we shall have no locus standi unless we have a scheme similar. And that means shutting us out, perhaps from all time, from Inverness; and I fear will prevent the plan of a through line between Perth, Dundee and Inverness under our control from ever being carried into effect.

He does add, referring to such a line: '... the question is whether it is practicable.'[8] The Great North's long-unrequited passion for physical union with Inverness had not wholly blinded it to economic realities. The Highland's half-yearly statements, available to all shareholders, showed the extent of its traffic perfectly plainly. Only by getting the mail contract and creaming off the tourist traffic could a rival line hope to survive, and that would be the death of the Highland Railway. This was understood very clearly at Inverness.

During the campaign to protect the Highland's territory, Joseph Mitchell died in London, at the age of eighty, on 26 November 1883. For years he had had no direct involvement in the company, although he continued to be a shareholder. His relations with it, in the latter years of professional work, had not been particularly happy. But he would certainly have been on its side in the battle to preserve its livelihood. In the last year of his life, he published two volumes of *Reminiscences*, for private circulation, in the second of which he recalls some of his railway work, especially in the early days. Not all his recollections are accurate, and much is written in a spirit of understandable self-justification, but the *Reminiscences* remain a valuable account by the man who, more than any other, was the creator of the Highland Railway.

The boundary disputes at Keith and Elgin did not go away, and the Highland refused to time trains to connect with the GNSR coastal route between Elgin and Aberdeen. The Aberdeen company took the matter to the Board of Trade, in July 1885, but the board, though it instructed the Highland to operate proper connecting services, also fixed Keith as the exchange station. Eventually, in 1886, William Moffat and Andrew Dougall concluded one of the longer lasting truces between the companies, which endured for seven years. Joint meetings were held at Elgin on a monthly basis, but the minutes of these reveal a sad state of relations. Discussions on building a joint station to replace the GNSR's ramshackle one at Elgin proved fruitless and the Great North built its own station, with a connecting link to the HR station, in 1902. There were endless minor disputes over traffic handling, largely to do with the Highland diverting traffic consigned via the GNSR. The HR rarely conceded any complaint from the Great North, unless it was about something too blatant to resist, and the phrase, '… whereupon the Great North Company intimated an appeal', was invoked 199 times. James Grierson of the Great Western Railway was the arbiter until his death in 1888, when Henry Tennant of the North Eastern took on the job, which was no sinecure. Henry Cripps, the Great North's Westminster agent, summed up the Highland's attitude: 'I believe however they will go on fighting to the last over everything rather than concede anything however slight and however reasonable'.[9] Meanwhile, the GNSR took what advantage it could. Its large advertisement in the Highland Railway's *Handbook* for 1892 shows it taking bookings at Inverness Station for: 'Passengers, Parcels, Horses, Carriages &c.' and offered travellers the chance of going one way by the Highland and the other by the GNSR, via Aberdeen, at the same fare as via Dunkeld both ways.

In 1884, Thomas Bruce, for long the deputy chairman and managing director, was elected chairman of the board, on the retirement of Matheson, who had become Sir Alexander in 1882. On 27 July 1886 Matheson died, at the age of eighty-one. Bruce, who had been a young man in a hurry in 1862, was now an elder statesman. Indeed, the continuing presence of Bruce, Raigmore, Dougall and Sutherland shows how relatively young the leading figures had been in 1855. Then, the railway had been a young men's affair. But they had grown old with the company. The summer half-year figures for 1884 did not suggest that their stewardship was failing, however. The dividend on the Ordinary shares was 5.25 per cent, amounting to £44,987; the company's total revenue was £191,303 11s 10d and its expenditure £94,323 4s 6d, less £11,744 as working cost of the northern lines. Future growth was envisaged, and twenty-two acres of ground beyond the Rose Street connecting line, known locally as 'Cyprus', were bought for present and future expansion. A new director, Lord Colville of Culross, chairman of the Great Northern Railway of England, was elected to the board in 1885 – a sign of the HR's widening horizons.

At the same time as it obtained its New Lines Act in 1884, providing for the direct line to Inverness and the Strathpeffer branch, the HR also obtained an Act for the amalgamation of the northern lines. By this, the Sutherland Railway Co., the Duke of Sutherland's Railway, and the Caithness & Sutherland Railway Co. all became part of the Highland Railway on 1 September 1884. The mortgages on the SR and S&CR were converted into HR debt and the HR was empowered to issue £200,000 of debenture stock to cover the liabilities of these lines. The Ordinary stock of the Sutherland Railway, its capital value £211,852, was converted into HR stock at 60 per cent, and that of the S&CR, £433,266, at 50 per cent (though no dividend on the latter was to be payable before August 1886). None of the northern lines had been profitable for their investors: the Sutherland Railway had paid no dividend for its first seven years, and in the year to 31 August 1882, its revenue was £10,780, its operating expenses £6,063; and it paid a 1 per cent dividend after interest payments. The Sutherland & Caithness never paid a dividend at all. Although in 1882 it made a respectable operating profit of £5,940 on a revenue of £19,363, its accumulated debit balance at that time was £63,643. The duke received additional HR stock to the value of 87 per cent of the £72,182 he had expended on his own railway, and he and his heirs were entitled to be directors of the Highland Railway as long as they held at least £100,000 worth of stock in it. This was enshrined in the Act, which makes no mention of his right to run his own trains, though this was continued by formal or informal agreement with the HR. The change made no difference to the working of these lines or to the involvement of HR staff, though it provided a welcome simplification of life in the secretary's department.

The Highland's lethargic attitude to the Aviemore direct line infuriated the Aberdonians. In 1888 they reopened a campaign to get running powers on the new line, on the basis that services via Boat of Garten would be reduced. Dougall wrote to Moffat on 30 October 1888 that the Forres line would remain a main line, adding:

> As the object of my Board is simply to give a shorter route for the existing traffic between Inverness and the North and Perth, and it is necessary for this object to have the absolute control of its working, they cannot consent to any proposal for its joint ownership or joint use though they will take care to do full justice to the marketing of your traffic.

## The Portessie and Strathpeffer Branches

During 1881, the Highland Railway was receiving, and sympathetically considering, representations from the Provost and Town Council of Buckie about a rail link. The alternatives were a 'coast line' like the abandoned Fochabers project, involving a bridge over the lower Spey, or a direct line from Keith. At a special meeting of directors on 14 September 1881, both were considered, and it was decided to promote a Bill for the Keith line. On 12 July 1882 an Act was obtained by the HR authorising a railway of thirteen miles three furlongs, from Keith to Buckie and Portessie, empowering the company to raise additional capital and loans of £100,000 and £33,600 respectively. Simultaneously, the GNSR obtained the Act for its coastal line from Portsoy to Elgin, passing through both Portessie and Buckie. This Act provided for a junction with the Highland at Portessie, and for the HR to have working powers from there to the new Cluny Harbour at Buckie. The HR 'Buckie Line' was intended to tap the fish trade of the Banffshire ports, but it is hard to see why it was thought necessary to build it. Some notion of making the most of the company's position at Keith presumably played a part, as well as a reluctance to see the Great North monopolise a rich fish trade. The Great North's Act also provided the Highland with running powers between Portsoy and Elgin, and the GNSR with running powers between Elgin and Forres. These powers could come into effect only if both companies agreed to exercise them: something the Highland took care never to do. Perhaps because of this, its Portessie line always seemed something of a neglected child. From Strathisla at Keith it had to heave itself up among bare hills to a summit at 670ft before descending almost to sea level. The planning seemed to anticipate considerable traffic. Intermediate stations were to be at Forgie, Enzie, Rathven, and Buckie. Two crossing loops were provided, at Forgie and Enzie, but after an altercation with the Board of Trade, which demanded that the line should be worked by the staff system as well as by block telegraph, the Highland announced it would be worked by a single engine. A further station was built at Drybridge in 1885. The HR reached Portessie in July 1884 and the line opened on 1 August, almost two years before the GNSR's. Four mixed trains each way daily were the normal service. Forgie Station was renamed Aultmore in 1899, probably as a result of the establishment of the distillery of that name, which began production in mid-1897. The line was closed under wartime regulations on 9 August 1915, with staff shortages given as the reason, and as a temporary measure.[1] In 1917 the GNSR's Working Timetable provided for it to run goods wagons from Portessie as far as Rathven on occasions, but by the end of 1917, the rails on the entire branch had been lifted, for use on the admiralty lines by the Cromarty Firth. Portessie–Buckie was relaid in 1919, when the GNSR again operated a goods service to the Highland station at Buckie. The branch is not mentioned in the HR Working Timetable operative from 2 October 1922. After the Grouping, the LMS relaid the entire branch, and renamed Drybridge as Letterfourie, plainly with the intention of re-establishing a passenger service. But the reopening never happened. The branch had a desultory freight traffic for a few years, but the rails between Aultmore and Buckie were removed in 1937. From 1 April 1944 the Portessie–Buckie section was also declared closed. The goods line from Keith to Aultmore remained in operation until 3 October 1966.[2]

One of the ironies that beset the Dingwall & Skye Railway was that its great enemy, Sir William Mackenzie of Coul, died before it was completed to Strome. His heir did not share his prejudices, and was keen to maintain the growth of the village as a spa resort. The Act for a branch line to Strathpeffer was obtained by the Highland Railway without opposition on 28 July 1884. Only two miles four furlongs in length, its track continued straight on from the sharp bend at Fodderty, making the Kyle line look like the branch, and terminated at the lower end of the village. J.&A. Granger of Perth, one of the original D&S contractors, were engaged to build the line, for £5,019 5s. Opening day was 3 June 1885, and the new baronet of Coul was said to have been on the engine of the first train from Dingwall, where a bay platform was built. The former Strathpeffer Station was renamed Achterneed. The first engine to work the branch was a veteran dating back to 1862, the 2-2-2 *Belladrum*, converted to a tank engine in 1871, since when it had been called *Breadalbane* and worked the Aberfeldy branch. In 1885 it was given a replacement – but not new – boiler and became the first *Strathpeffer*. The village already had three large hotels, and the train brought about an increase in the number both of hotels and boarding houses, and, on a modest scale, it became a flourishing summer resort. The station itself was built handsomely, as a long, one-storey wooden structure with an eleven-gabled platform awning. Six trains were run each way daily, except Sunday. Soon the hoteliers were complaining about the Spartan four-wheel carriages the Highland was using on the branch trains from Dingwall. Their grumbles had little effect until the arrival of the publicity-conscious Thomas Addy Wilson as general manager in 1898. In the early twentieth century the HR worked hard to promote the charms of Strathpeffer, and in 1908–09 there was a London–Strathpeffer through sleeping carriage. In 1911 the HR opened its Highland Hotel in a commanding position in the village centre. By this time, Strathpeffer had upwards of 500 hotel rooms available, more than any other place on the Highland Railway except Inverness and Pitlochry, and the seasonal influx of visitors (listed weekly in the *Ross-shire Journal*) and catering staff more than doubled its population. The 'Strathpeffer Spa Express', a Tuesdays-only fast train from Aviemore, northbound only, was introduced as a summer service in 1911 and continued until the summer of 1915. This was the only scheduled passenger service, outside wartime, to bypass Inverness Station, using the Rose Street curve. Connecting with the 11.50 a.m. fast train from Perth to Inverness via Forres, it left Aviemore at 2.30 p.m. and ran non-stop to Dingwall, arriving at 4 p.m., and reached Strathpeffer at 4.15 p.m. The First World War closed off the village as a tourist centre from 1916, and though its hotels reopened in 1919, the spa's best times were already in the past. The 1922 timetable showed six trains each way on weekdays, two of them mixed; but apart from special excursions, the through carriages were no more. It was closed to passengers on 2 March 1946, and completely on 26 March 1951.

*New Western Schemes, and Frontier Skirmishes*

By 1889, significant changes to the Scottish railway map were in the offing. The Forth Bridge was well on the way to completion, and its opening would mean a substantial speeding-up of the east coast London–Edinburgh–Aberdeen route, and so also of London–Inverness by the same route. A new company, the West Highland Railway, was applying for powers to build a line from Craigendoran, outside Glasgow, to Fort William, entering the southern end of the Great Glen at Spean Bridge. The Highland at first opposed the proposal but withdrew its objection, partly because a proposed western extension from Fort William, which would have competed with the Strome line, was abandoned; and partly after diplomatic talks with the West

Highland promoters and their North British Railway backers. The Highland's fear was that once the Fort William line was built, a proposal for a line up the Great Glen to Inverness would naturally follow. A pact was made that neither side would promote a line through the Great Glen for ten years from 1899.[1] At the time, William Acworth wrote in *The Railways of Scotland*:

> The apple of the Highland Railway's eye is Inverness, and a railway at Fort William, or, what was worse, on the banks of the Caledonian Canal a dozen miles nearer than Fort William, is perilously close to Inverness itself… By some means or other not easily intelligible to the outside observer, the opposition of the Highland Company was disarmed, the West Highland Act is now safely passed… the position in which the Highland Company finds itself is no enviable one. If on one side it is liable to be pressed hard by the West Highland, on the other, the Great North, a line which has enormously improved within the last few years, is… doing its utmost to get access to Inverness and Dingwall. No amount of genius can extract much sustenance for railways any more than for man or beast from the barren hills of Perthshire or Inverness. The Highland must always depend for a dividend on its through traffic.[2]

Acworth had identified the nub of the matter, but he overlooked the possibility of government grants and other forms of financial support, including dividend guarantees, which stimulated railway schemes in districts not yet served by a railway line. In 1884 the plight, anger and desperation of the crofting communities, ever-more marginalised by the extension of deer forests, resulted in the formation of a Royal Commission under Lord Napier, and its report, issued in 1886, acknowledged that the western Highlands and the Islands were in dire need of economic and social resuscitation. This led to the formation of the Crofters' Commission and the strengthening of crofters' and smallholders' rights. It also led to government money being available for the improvement of communications – one of the Napier findings had been that poor communication links exacerbated the poverty of the crofting districts, and new railway building was among its recommendations.[3] In August 1889, following a tour of the north west and the Hebrides, Lord Lothian, the Secretary of State for Scotland, recommended to the Treasury that £150,000 should be spent on the development of fisheries and in the construction of roads, railways and piers. By 1892, when the Conservative government left office, £237,291 of government money had been assigned to development schemes in crofting areas.[4] With such resources to be tapped, the flurry of new railway schemes is less surprising. James Hunter comments that government policy at this time, 'produced a lasting improvement in the region's communications system… with undoubted beneficial effects on crofting life.'[5]

Of these, the one that seemed most likely to succeed was the Garve & Ullapool. Its story is worth recording since it clearly shows the Highland Railway's attitude and tactics. Although the first intimations of this project came as a memorial from the inhabitants of Lochbroom, Elphin and Assynt parishes, in January 1889, requesting the HR to build a railway from Garve to Ullapool, it seems to have had local proprietors in the background. The Highland, well aware of the limited traffic on the Strome line (but currently dusting off the original plan to reach Kyle of Lochalsh) made no initial offer of support other than to work the line, if built, 'on reasonable terms'. The proposal brought back into the HR's ambit Sir (as he by now was) John Fowler, engineer-in-chief of the Forth Bridge, whose Braemore estate would be traversed by the Ullapool line. At Fowler's instigation, the HR instructed Paterson to make a 'flying survey' of the line, and also lent assistance with a Bill, which was passed on 14 August 1890, allowing for the building of a line of thirty-three miles, five furlongs, four chains and fifty links, terminating on a steamer pier at Ullapool, and to be worked by the HR. As Ullapool was a potential port for a short sea-crossing to Stornoway, there was a strong Lewis landowning interest, and the promoters of the new company were Lady Matheson of Achary and the Lews (the first appearance of a woman in such a role: she was the widow of Sir James), Donald Matheson, Maj. Duncan Matheson, John A. Fowler (son of Sir John) and Maj. James Houstoun. Sir John's by now lustrous name was added as consulting engineer. Share capital was set at £240,000 and loans at £80,000. It was understood that the scheme was dependent on Government support, and, pending some announcement of this, nothing happened.

If the threat from the West Highland had been at least temporarily seen off, there was still trouble from the east. The Great North of Scotland Railway, with dogged determination, and encouraged by the imminent opening of the Forth Bridge, returned to the attack in the autumn of 1889, when it prepared to submit a Bill to Parliament for three new lines, all in 'Highland' territory. One was for a separate line from Elgin to Inverness; one was for an isolated branch on the Black Isle, from the Highland line at Muir of Ord to Fortrose; the third was for a line from Elgin to Hopeman and Burghead. A ferry service from Fortrose to a rail-connected pier at Ardersier (then known as Campbelltown) was also included. There had been extensive discussion between William Ferguson and James Fraser, an Inverness civil engineer, about the Black Isle branch. The Highland Railway was preparing to set up strong opposition, when a letter was received from the Great North to suggest that 'a new solution' might be found to the difficulties between the companies if the GNSR were allowed to exercise running powers between Elgin and Inverness for a number of through services from Aberdeen. This was strongly redolent of blackmail. The Highland replied with some guile, raising the stakes by proposing that the two companies should consider an amalgamation, and that pending such a discussion, all hostile schemes should be withdrawn (i.e. the Great North's triple Bill). In reply, the GNSR accepted the idea of merger discussions, but they insisted on having an Amalgamation Bill drafted before they would withdraw their Bill. With equal degrees of elaborate insincerity and mutual mistrust, the amalgamation idea, or ruse, fell by the wayside. The two companies remained at odds. The GNSR presented its Bill, which was strongly opposed by the Highland, whose basic argument was that the agreement reached in 1886 made an additional Elgin–Inverness line unnecessary. The Highland had also discovered a solicitude of its own for the inhabitants of the Black Isle, Hopeman and Ardersier, and introduced its own Bill for a branch to Rosemarkie, just beyond Fortrose, an extension of the Burghead branch to Hopeman, and a short branch to Fort George. The Parliamentary Committee accepted this, and it became an Act on 4 July 1890. The GNSR withdrew its Bill.

Then in 1891 the Great North was presented with an exciting new opportunity. The directors of the Garve & Ullapool, still waiting for news of their government funding, had become increasingly disenchanted with the Highland Railway. In 1890 a Royal Commission had been appointed to review transport in the Western Highlands. It had held twenty-eight local meetings and also private talks with interested parties, including the Highland company. If government cash was going to be available for railway projects, the HR was certainly interested. The board authorised Andrew Dougall to meet the commissioners, and to offer to extend the Skye line to Kyle of Lochalsh; and he duly reported that he had, 'offered on behalf of the Highland Company to extend the line from Strome Ferry to Kyle, and erect a suitable pier there, for £120,000 '. [6] The commissioners, however, made no formal recommendation, merely noting that the most advantageous developments for the district would be:

> ... to construct two lines of railway: one running to Loch Laxford or some point near the angle of the coastline at Cape Wrath, so as to serve the North as well as the West coast; the other running to Loch Ewe or some point on Loch Broom nearer than Ullapool.

If only one line were to be considered, it suggested a compromise route from Culrain to Lochinver.[7] Ullapool was thus dismissed, but it remained strongly supported by Lord Lothian, who urged its case with W.H. Smith, First Lord of the Treasury. But Smith had persuaded in favour of the Achnasheen & Aultbea scheme, and would not hear of Ullapool.[8] This deadlock between Cabinet Ministers led in 1891 to a further commission, of transport experts,[9] with a narrower brief: of six projects nominated for review, only one would be selected for official backing. One of the six was the Highland Railway's proposal for a ten-mile extension from Strome Ferry to Kyle of Lochalsh, the Garve & Ullapool was another.[10] W.L. Jackson MP, Financial Secretary to the Treasury, was instructed to obtain guarantees from the G&U that its proposed line would be completed and maintained. The Highland Railway, after meetings in London on 13 and 14 April 1891, refused to confirm construction without personal guarantees from the G&U directors.[11] The directors refused, and unhappy with such an attitude, and conflict of interest, on the part of the company with which they already had a Working Agreement, they opened secret negotiations with the Great North. Moffat, Ferguson of Kinmundy and the GNSR Board jumped at the chance. By 23 April there was a draft Agreement; by the summer, they were discussing a complete GNSR takeover, and a draft Bill for this, including the provision of running powers between Elgin and Garve for the GNSR, was presented to Parliament. Long before this time the Highland knew what was going on, having been briefed on 24 April, at W.H. Smith's request, by W.L. Jackson, whose support Moffat had vainly hoped to enlist.[12] On 1 May, Andrew Dougall confirmed to Jackson that the HR was, after all, willing to build and work the G&U line on the same basis as the GNSR[13]

News of this was received with pardonable bitterness by the other camp; as Henry Cripps wrote to Jackson: '... it would be even more to their interest to prevent the line from being made at all than to be in a position to control it after construction'.[14]

The report of the commissioners, early in 1892, was a dispirited and depressing document. Confronted by empty acres of heathery moors, peat bog, innumerable lochs and lochans, bare mountains, steep wet valleys, a rocky coast punctuated by isolated small villages and strung-out crofting townships, and an indigenous population rich only in a sense of long grievance, the members concluded that: 'None of the proposed railways can be regarded as possessing a commercial basis or the elements of success as ordinary undertakings'. Their only recommendation was the provision of £45,000 towards the Kyle extension.[15] General disappointment and anger greeted the report, especially in Lochbroom and Assynt. The Highland Railway and Andrew Dougall as its spokesman were regarded as wreckers. Although the Ullapool promoters and the GNSR persisted with their plan, there was no hope of subscribing the capital without a Government guarantee on earnings; and eventually an Act of Abandonment was passed on 4 August 1893, only a few weeks after the Act authorising the HR's Kyle extension was passed, on 19 June.

The board had been weakened by the death of Thomas Bruce on 26 November 1890, at the age of sixty-five. The senior director, Eneas Mackintosh of Raigmore, was elected chairman. Raigmore, aged seventy-one, had immense experience of the company, having been a director from the very beginning, but he was not a businessman of the calibre of Matheson or Bruce. The Highland directors between 1890 and 1898 have been subject to some criticism, especially with regard to the laxity in financial controls revealed in 1895. But during this time, the board had to take some very important and difficult decisions, not necessarily palatable to shareholders. The pressure of other companies' manoeuvrings at the time was such that extreme vigilance and stout defensive measures were needed. The Highland does not come out of the G&U affair with any grace, but it got the result it wanted. The GNSR continued to latch hopefully on to other proposed railway schemes in the north west, including the Achnasheen–Aultbea line which had also been on the Special Committee's short list, but none came as near fulfilment as the Ullapool line. The inadequacy of the HR management became more apparent in the summer of 1893 when the company indicated its intention not to renew the seven-year agreement on traffic made with the Great North in 1886. Two years of non-co-operation, altercation, and inconvenience to customers and passengers ensued.

Access to Inverness was still the crucial issue, but the needle of contention swung again to the south with the potential new threat of a line from Fort William to Inverness. Confronted with the need to make an increasingly unavoidable decision, the Highland Board resolved to actually build the cut-off between Aviemore and Inverness. However, it span the process out for as long as it could. Through the 1890s, there was sparring over the Great Glen. On 7 August 1894 the West Highland Railway opened between Fort William and Glasgow, and in the same year applied for powers to build a forty-five-mile extension to Mallaig on the western seaboard, facing the south-eastern tip of Skye. This line had active Government support, with the Treasury giving the company a guarantee of a minimum return of 3 per cent on a capital of £260,000 over thirty years, though Opposition (Liberal) objections to the generosity of this provision held up the passage of the Bill until 1896. By 1894, the Great Glen pact was under too much pressure to survive and the Parliamentary session of 1894-95 saw Bills from both the West Highland and the Highland for a railway to link Fort William and Inverness. Each was an attempt to pre-empt the other. The Inverness papers carried articles about 'The Great Railway War'. For the Highland in particular, with the Aviemore cut-off still uncompleted, there seemed no good reason to embark on a Great Glen line. In the event both Bills were withdrawn, due to the diplomatic activity of the Marquis of Tweeddale, chairman both of the NB and the West Highland, who convened a meeting between the companies in Edinburgh in February 1895, which procured peace for a short time.

In 1895, after almost two years of indefensible obstructiveness and provocation by the Highland, the Great North again entered a Bill to allow it running powers between Elgin and Inverness. Its case was that with its two lines to Elgin, the number of passengers exchanged at Keith and Elgin had risen by 78 per cent in the ten years to 1894, while goods traffic had gone up by 63 per cent. This was despite the Highland's refusal to provide a proper connecting service. All that apparently mattered to the Highland was that its own trains from Keith and Elgin should connect effectively with the Perth trains at Forres. But, as the GNSR pointed out, the Highland trains were grossly unpunctual. Lengthy and often heated arguments were expounded on both sides before the Parliamentary Select Committee. But in the end the committee, though it roundly and unanimously condemned the Highland's behaviour − it had placed 'undue obstructions in the way of the development of traffic', and its alterations of train times and general dealings with the Great North of Scotland were considered 'vexatious' − refused to accept the Bill and merely expressed the hope that the two companies could sort out their differences in the spirit of the 1886 agreement. A meeting between the two followed in August 1895, but failed to reach any new agreement. At the Highland's suggestion, the matter was referred to the Board of Trade, which appointed the Railway and Canal Commissioners to arbitrate.

## The Kyle Extension

Forty-five thousand pounds was, as it turned out, not a very large contribution from central government, in terms of the cost of building ten miles of railway round the edge of the Lochalsh peninsula.[1] The estimated cost was well above the first estimate quoted by Dougall, £233,873 plus £37,099 for the harbour works at Kyle, and the HR obtained an Act on 29 June 1893, to issue new share capital of £200,000 and extend its borrowing powers by £66,600. The engineer in charge was Murdoch Paterson, for the railway company, and the contractor was John Best, of Edinburgh, whose tenders were accepted both for the railway and the harbour works. The new line cut through around 150 crofts that skirted the loch shore, and both the crofters and the landowner, Sir Kenneth Matheson, claimed substantial compensation for the survey work and the actual construction. Work began in September 1893 and was completed by 28 October 1897, after long delays caused by severe weather and the migratory habits of many of the workforce, local men who left the railway works to take in the harvest on their crofts. Others were professional Irish navvies, and there were numerous fights between the two groups, ending up at Dingwall Sheriff Court. As was also the case with the direct line from Aviemore, the number of workers was reduced by the employment of steam-powered machinery, and, given that much of the line was cut through hard, ancient quartzite and gneiss, the use of explosives. Between 600 and 800 men were employed, of whom four were killed in working with machinery or gelignite, and many more injured. The station and yard at the terminus were entirely cut out of rock or built out on the new pier. The result was a far more extensive layout than Strome Ferry, where the wooden pier was demolished, though the roofed-over station was retained. In fact, with its neat buildings right on the pier, the loch beyond, and Ben na Caillich looming up on the Skye side, it was one of the most attractively sited stations in Britain. A cost of £23,000 a mile, including land, should have made Joseph Mitchell rise from the grave, but the Highland Railway had really no alternative. Whichever way the directors reasoned it, the answer was uncomfortable. The establishment of a second western railhead at Oban, far down the coast, in 1880, had already had a negative effect on traffic on the Skye line – the arrival of the West Highland at Mallaig would be far more damaging to business at the inconveniently sited Strome pier To keep the terminus at Strome would not merely be to give up that struggle, but would also certainly bring the Great North pushing in with some scheme of its own to reach the west coast. Kyle it had to be, and the Highland bit the bullet with some style. The new pier, 125 yards long and 75 yards wide, with a low-water depth of 25ft, was well equipped to handle livestock, fish, coal and general goods, with three travelling cranes; while passengers had a short walk to the ship or to the Kyleakin ferry. On the Skye side, £3,000 had been spent on a new jetty. The company had bought Kyle House, overlooking the ferry jetty, from Sir Kenneth Matheson for £1,500 in August 1895, and commissioned Ross & Macbeth, of Inverness, to design it into a hotel, which opened on 18 December 1897. Intermediate stations were provided at Duncraig (at first a private platform for the Matheson estate), Plockton and Duirinish. At the opening ceremony, Sir George Macpherson-Grant, the Highland chairman, remarked that: 'This line has been opened with no niggard hand'. It was true, and a striking contrast with the Strome Ferry line. With a more than two-year head start on Mallaig, there was time to develop traffic, but inevitably the West Highland Railway, with its shorter and cheaper route to Glasgow, drew off a substantial share. With three companies, the HR, the Caledonian and the North British, all vying for the highly seasonal west coast fish, livestock and tourist traffic, it was a perfect paradigm for competition. But on the Kyle line, services languished, though never quite to the 1870s level. Two mixed trains between Dingwall and Kyle each way on weekdays formed the service for most of the year. The line's mail contract, now at £1,750 a year, helped to sustain the finances.

*New Branches – Hopeman Extension, the Black Isle, Fochabers and Fort George*

The HR had shown no interest in the fishing village of Hopeman until the GNSR did. But it went ahead quite quickly with the two-mile extension from Burghead, which opened on 10 October 1892; the station at Burghead being remodelled as a through one, and the harbour line reduced to the status of a siding. Despite the short distance an intermediate station was built at Cummingstown (Cummingston to the HR). This was closed on 1 April 1904, not before having been burned down and rebuilt in 1898. (The old Burghead Station had also been destroyed by fire, on 10 February 1871). A siding was opened to the adjacent Cummingstown sandstone quarry. Neither Burghead nor the new terminus had a turntable and the line was worked by tank engines, as the original branch had been since 1862.[1] On 19 November 1890, work began on the thirteen-mile, forty-five-chain Black Isle branch at Muir of Ord. Though the Act specified Rosemarkie as the terminus, rails were not laid beyond Fortrose, a mile short, where a turntable was installed. Intermediate stations were at Redcastle, Allangrange, Munlochy and Avoch: all agricultural hamlets except the last, a small but active fishing port, whose catch was usually landed at Inverness, just across the firth. Construction of the line is recorded in the preserved diaries of John Ross, the contractor, who was on the site virtually every working day. To look after his workmen, he engaged the services of Dr Finlayson of Fortrose, for £30. The pace of construction was slow, and the line was not opened until 1 February 1894. None of the stations had crossing loops, and the line was worked on the basis of 'one engine in steam'. Seven trains each way, on weekdays only, of which four were mixed, provided the first service, which was reduced by 1897 to five, with two mixed. Unlike the Aberfeldy branch, which had a daily through service to Perth, all passengers had to change at Muir of Ord. Most trains took from forty-five to fifty minutes for the journey. The shortest of the branches authorised in 1890 was that to Ardersier, only a mile and a half long. The station was named Fort George, though it was almost two miles from the actual fort, and the former Fort George Station was renamed Gollanfield, the junction facing the Nairn direction. The Highland was in no hurry to build this branch, and the powers had to be renewed in an Act of 7 August 1896; it was not completed until 1 July 1899, three days before expiry of the renewed powers. On 27 June 1892, at the same time as an Act was obtained for a deviation in the direct line, at Culloden, powers were granted for a three-mile branch to give a better service to Fochabers. The line opened on 23 October 1893, with an intermediate station at Balnacoul, and the former Fochabers Station was renamed Orbliston Junction. From 1 July 1894 the new terminus was called Fochabers Town, a piece of mendacity, as it was situated in Mosstodloch, with Fochabers still a mile away, on the other side of the Spey. The HR never called an engine 'Fochabers', but from 1895 the line was worked by the 2-4-0T *Gordon Castle* (the original *Dunrobin*), and from 1905 by the new Lochgorm-built 0-4-4T *Gordon Lennox*. None of these branches required the raising of extra capital. The Black Isle line was the most expensive; Ross's diaries[3] show that he was paid a total of £57,560, around £4,260 a mile. The Hopeman extension was closed on 31 December 1957, the Fort George line on 11 August 1958, and the Black Isle branch on 13 June 1960.

# SIX

*The Resignation of Andrew Dougall*
In February 1894 the Earl of March was elected to the Highland Board, to replace
J.W. Kynoch of the Keith woollen mills, and the next vacancy was promised to
James Douglas Fletcher, who had inherited and enlarged a family fortune based
on rubber and tea, and was owner of an opulent mansion at Rosehaugh, between
Avoch and Fortrose (it duly acquired its own Halt in 1905). His turn came only two
months later, when Lord Thurlow resigned. Fletcher was thirty-seven, a man used to
boardrooms and the ins and outs of commerce, and, like James Merry of the previous
generation, had no diffidence about asking awkward questions or taking a line of his
own. Between February and August 1894, the Highland Railway for the first time
carried over a million passengers in six months: 984,119 third class, and 52,740 first.
A dividend of 2 per cent on the Ordinary shares was declared. The Directors' Report
noted a loss of £7,272 on account of the 'Scotch coal strike',[1] and the company also
believed it was receiving £12,000 a year less than it should from the distribution, via
the Railways Clearing House, of the railway companies' earnings from carrying Post
Office parcels. Other railways were resisting the Highland's demand for arbitration. At
this time, the company had capital in stocks and shares of £4,173,113, and in loans of
£1,723,013. It was a substantial business by any standards.

Symptomatic of the fact that the HR was no longer seen as a bravely struggling
little railway was the news imparted by the Railways Clearing House, and reported
to the board on 6 March 1895, that the Great Northern, London & North Western,
North Eastern, and Midland Railways were ceasing to pay bonuses on southbound
passenger traffic off the Highland line, as from 1 January of that year. These bonuses,
partial rebates on the element of through fares payable along these companies' routes,
had usefully bumped up the HR's passenger income since the 1860s.

In July 1895 the HR Board obtained an Act of Parliament to raise further capital
of £300,000 and raise loans up to £100,000. This sum was partly needed to prepare
for the junction of the new direct line at Inverness, when Welsh's bridge would be
demolished. But other works were in progress or under consideration at this time,

including the Aviemore direct line, and plans for the complete rebuilding of Inverness Station with through lines, and of the locomotive works and running sheds. It was a busy time, and the Board Meeting of 4 September dealt with numerous issues, including the granting of three months' sick leave to the locomotive superintendent and the purchase for £300 of the Duke of Sutherland's old tank engine *Dunrobin*. The minutes, taken by Andrew Dougall, are supplemented by a letter from Raigmore to William Gowenlock, the deputy secretary:

> Before the close of our last Board Meeting a Protest was moved by Rosehaugh, and seconded by Aldourie. It was also supported by Dochfour. This should have been placed upon the Minutes. The fault was mine, for omitting to look at the Minute Book before going away. Would you be so good as to place this Note in the Book, until the matter can be put right.

Fletcher's protest related to the share issue of June 1893, when £200,000 of new stock had been created in connection with the Kyle extension. The omitted Minute, as inserted, stated:

> It was resolved that in the opinion of the Board the action of the General Manager in connection with the issue of the Company's stock was most irregular, and much to be regretted, and that steps be taken to prevent the recurrence of such irregularity.

A special board meeting held on 22 October listened to a statement from Dougall (who was not present), read by Raigmore, but resolved to adhere to the censuring Minute of 4 September.

If the chairman hoped that the matter would end there, he was to be disappointed.[2] The following day was that of the half-yearly Shareholders' Meeting, normally a good-natured and uncontroversial occasion. Raigmore opened the meeting in a self-deprecatory manner, saying he thought it his duty, 'to carry on the business of the Company on the lines laid down by far abler men who sat in that chair before him'. For the company, he was bullish, looking forward to towns at Kyle of Lochalsh, and Lochinver, and a good harbour at Gills Bay.[3] A 5 per cent dividend on the Ordinary shares was announced. But Fletcher was far from satisfied. He stood up and formally announced his resignation from the board before proceeding to accuse Dougall, in detail, of irregular share-dealing and doctoring the accounts. He referred to the manager's dealing in £150,000-worth of company stock in 1893, and went on to produce figures showing that, '... during the past twelve months the Company had debited no less than £34,000 to its reserve, instead of revenue, account. But if the above sum had been debited to revenue, as it should have been, the Company would only have paid 2 per cent instead of 3½ per cent'. He ended:

> ... That is the way in which the Board are treated by the General Manager, and it is entirely a question for you whether you are satisfied with the condition of things. I am

not, and I cannot remain any longer on the Board if such a state of things will continue, and if you allow dividends to be paid out of capital, as has been done for years past, you are only encouraging the Board to go on in a way that can only end in inevitable and irretrievable disaster.

Dougall, who was present, made no statement. Two shareholders, Francis Darwin of Muirtown, Inverness, and William Keith, of Castletown, moved that a Joint Committee of shareholders and directors be appointed to examine Fletcher's accusations. This was agreed, and Fletcher consented, in the meantime, to withdraw his resignation. A special Shareholders' Meeting was convened for 5 December to consider the report. The Joint Committee consisted of Darwin, William Keith, and John Macpherson-Grant, younger, of Ballindalloch (son of a director) for the shareholders; J.D. Fletcher himself, J.E.B. Baillie of Dochfour, and Thomas Yool, for the directors.

Fletcher's bombshell generated alarm and intense interest. Highland Railway shares fell heavily on the Stock Exchange, in anticipation of terrible revelations. An angry letter from 'An Ordinary Shareholder' in the *Inverness Courier* of 29 November pointed out that Fletcher appeared to be both accuser and judge. The company's affairs proceeded uneasily for six weeks, with Dougall continuing to carry out his normal duties. On 31 October he issued a lengthy letter, addressed to Francis Darwin, chairman of the investigating committee, but circulated to all shareholders and to the local press, setting out his defence. But at the board meeting of 4 December, having read, or been informed of, the committee's report, he tendered his resignation. He had been general manager, secretary and cashier for forty years. The board accepted it, and deferred a decision on whether he should be asked to continue while a replacement was sought.

Next day came the special meeting, with 133 people squeezed into the boardroom. Raigmore took the chair; a phalanx of thirteen other directors was present, and all six members of the Joint Committee. The Marquis of Breadalbane moved adoption of the committee's report, and Lord Colville of Culross seconded. Colville announced that he had the support of the Duke of Sutherland; the fourth duke being still the largest shareholder in the company. He also startled the meeting with the news that Francis Darwin had been elected a director of the company on that very morning.

The report set out three charges against Dougall. First, that he had taken advantage of his position to allot £150,000 of the 1893 4 per cent preference stock to himself, without informing the board. He had then on 12 September 1893 written a letter in the board's name, but without the board's knowledge, agreeing that a dividend on this stock should be payable at once, instead of in two and a half years, as had been intended. In this way he had realised a profit of £21,300. Dougall had claimed that this was a personal transaction of his own, paid for with a loan from the British Linen Co.'s bank, with the shares as security; but, the committee found, all the banks and brokers involved believed that they were dealing with him as the representative of the Highland Railway. Dougall pointed out that he had had the £21,300 paid into the company's bank account, not his own. However, the committee noted that on several occasions he had expressed a view that this money was rightly his. The first of these was when he told Raigmore of the transaction, in February 1894. The chairman consulted the company's legal advisers, who replied that Dougall had no right to the £21,300. Dougall, however, reiterated his claim in the statement he had sent to the board on 22 October, in which he hoped that 'it would not be forgotten'. In his published letter of October 31, a week later, he waived all claim to the sum.

The second charge was that Dougall had overstated the traffic receipts of February 1895 by the amount of £7,238. Because of the delays in accounts coming through the Railways Clearing House, it was normal for the half-yearly receipts to be partly based on an estimate, taking previous performance and any unusual circumstances into account. When the overestimate became known, the manager ordered Mr Lamond, the audit officer, in the name of the board (but without the board's knowledge) to debit the amount to the reserve account, rather than to the revenue account. Lamond did this under protest, and his reservations about this practice were expressed in the half-yearly statement of April 1895.[4] The effect was to inflate the revenue account, so that, the Joint Committee said, '… the Directors were induced to recommend a larger dividend than the profits for the half-year would have justified'. The declared dividend was 3½ per cent, and would otherwise have been 1½ per cent.

The third charge harked back to 1890. When the board gave an order for the issue of £265,000 convertible 4 per cent preference stock, being part of £515,000 of such stock authorised for issue on 29 October 1890, a further sum of £100,000 was issued by the manager without direction from the board. The Joint Committee's view was that Dougall had been irregular in doing this, although he had the chairman's authority to do it, and the action was reported and approved at the Board Meeting of 31 May 1892.

The committee found Dougall at fault on all three charges, the first being regarded as 'most serious', the second as 'also grave', the third as 'of less importance since the Manager acted in accordance with then practice – however irregular'. But it pointed out that no sufficient reason for the unauthorised issue of stock had been shown. The committee finally stated that:

> In making this report – a very painful one – the Committee feel that the necessity for this enquiry would not have arisen had a more vigilant control been exercised over the management, and they trust that this report will induce the Board to examine carefully into the various departments of the Company with a view to amendments, in the detail of management, where they may be found desirable.

Dougall made a dignified reply. On the first charge, he regretted that the committee appeared to have wholly set aside his own letter to them of 31 October (This letter had pointed out, among other things, that the company had lost nothing by his purchase of the shares, at the price set by the directors; and that there was no rule against company officials buying shares in the company).[5] He pointed that he had had the £21,300 paid to the company's account and had not had a penny out of it;

and also produced a letter to the bankers, of 1 September 1893, which refers to the transaction as his own, without mentioning the Highland Railway. On the second charge, he took full responsibility for the over-estimate, but said:

> I certainly did not anticipate that the amount would be so large, but at the time there was reason to hope that a claim for our proper share of Parcel Post receipts would be so settled as to entitle us to take credit in the following half-year for an even larger sum than was over-stated in February.

On the third charge, he took up the point about the reason for issuing the extra stock:

> It was of importance to the Company to get the stock taken up whenever an opportunity offered as the money would be needed in the following year for the works then in hand. Although not immediately required, I must point out that the stock was not to bear dividend, and be a burden on the Company, for twelve months; while, on the other hand, as its price was deposited at a good rate of interest, it brought to the Company in that time a profit of £4882.

He represented himself as a faithful steward of the company's interests:

> In sometimes acting on my own responsibility in name of the Board, I may have erred, and I regret now that I did so, but I never abused the privilege for my own ends or to injure the Company. It is, I believe, by no means unusual for others in a similar position to act occasionally in name of the Board when carrying on their companies' business. I have served you to the best of my ability for forty years, and I have every confidence that you will at this time take no strained view of the actions complained of, which at the worst may be called errors of judgement, but were not intentional wrongs.

From the floor, Mr James Anderson then moved an amendment:

> That this meeting thanks the Committee for their report and labours, and having unabated confidence in the Directors, remit the report to them to take such action thereon, if any, as they consider necessary.

There was applause when he objected to Fletcher's presence on the Joint Committee. Anderson, a lawyer, asked what proof and documents the committee had, and proceeded to make the case for Dougall, on the basis that he had done no wrong and made no profit. His amendment was seconded by Sir Henry Macandrew, of the Rose Street Foundry company, who felt the board was the only proper body to deal with the matter. Dougall was also supported by Anderson's partner, Duncan Shaw, who accused the committee of being wholly one-sided in their view. Darwin spoke trenchantly for his committee, at one point brandishing a file of papers and saying, 'The evidence is here', adding that he thought it would be a 'very unwise act' to print and circulate the evidence, as it would lead to other questions. He then addressed himself to Dougall's defence, making first the most obvious point: 'he could not conceive that it was right for any servant or paid official of the Company, with a knowledge that the outside world did not possess of the affairs of the Company, to use that knowledge for his own benefit'. He pointed out the inconsistencies and ambiguities of Dougall's letters to the banks and brokers, which could be read as from himself or from the Highland company. The various assertions by Dougall of his right to the £21,300 profit were witheringly exposed; on 31 October he had waived all claim; on 4 November he wrote that the company were appropriating money 'earned at my risk and expense'. On the second charge he damningly quoted Dougall's own evidence to the committee: 'That sum was chosen... merely to provide such a sum as I could recommend the Directors 2 per cent dividend on, as the drop from 3¾ dividend to below 2 was so serious that it would have alarmed the shareholders.' Darwin told the meeting that: '... it was merciful and right of the Committee not to say all they could have said'. His final flourish was to produce a letter from a most eminent shareholder, William Ewart Gladstone, approving of the inquiry and expressing his support for the committee. In the north of Scotland, the voice of Gladstone was second only to that of God. Fletcher followed Darwin, even more belligerently and, like his colleague, made veiled hints about other matters: 'The Committee treated Mr Dougall as leniently as they possibly could, and if they had gone into other matters they might have made out a report which would be far more serious for Mr Dougall'.

Not the least embarrassed person in the room was the chairman, Eneas Mackintosh of Raigmore. Though almost every speaker took time to make a courteous and complimentary reference to him, his easy-going chairmanship of the board was revealed as incompetent if not negligent. Clinging to the shade of T.C. Bruce was no defence. Darwin's accusation that Dougall had 'shielded himself behind the Chairman'[6] was in itself a reflection on Raigmore's judgement. The special meeting came to an end with Dougall seemingly forgotten, in some sharp little spats between Lord Tweeddale, who felt the company's auditors should have been more vociferous in resisting dubious practices, and Darwin, who defended them; and between Raigmore himself, who while honourably accepting his share of responsibility for the transfer of the £7,238 to the reserve fund, made an unfortunate reference to what he clearly saw as excessively '*doctrinaire* financing', and Tweeddale, who jumped on his comment, saying, 'he would not sit and listen to the doctrine of the Chairman with regard to the Reserve Fund. The chairman would recognise that he had addressed him on the subject on more than one occasion. It really was very bad financing.'

At the end a vote was taken, and on a show of hands, the motion for adoption of the committee's report was carried, statedly by a large majority. The committee had made no recommendations about Dougall and the board – perhaps encouraged by Lord Tweeddale's view, expressed at the extraordinary meeting, that he had no corrupt motive – kept him on pending a replacement. Until February 1896, he continued to attend board meetings as general manager, and the familiar 'AND. DOUGALL' appeared at the bottom of all company notices and advertisements. At board meetings held consecutively on 5 and 6 February 1896, the directors refused to pay the £21 5s 9d it had cost Dougall to circulate his letter to shareholders. No one would second a motion to pay him a third of his salary as a retirement pension. Peterkin and Colville moved that he be given a year's salary. Fletcher and Baillie moved that he receive nothing. In the end a majority of seven to two gave him a year's pay, and he was also allowed to keep his Gold Pass. At the meeting of 5 February Raigmore resigned as chairman and his deputy, Sir George Macpherson-Grant of Ballindalloch, took over. On 18 February, Charles Steel joined as manager, from the North Eastern Railway, at £1,500 a year; Gowenlock had already been appointed secretary in January, at £800.

The company could move on, and its erstwhile general manager could feel himself battered but not broken. Any assessment of his case has to bear in mind that the Joint Committee was neither independent nor impartial: it represented the views of a significant number of mostly recent arrivals on the board, and they wanted the general manager out. Fletcher's and Darwin's dark hints of further iniquities have no corroboration – but Dougall, a proud and not a poor man, did not take the course of suing them for defamation. This could be set down to his undoubted loyalty to the company and unwillingness to prolong its difficulties, as much as to any inference of guilt. There were two quite separate issues. His venture into share speculation – probably in conjunction with Waterston, who was silent throughout the drama and whose resignation from the board immediately afterwards was unaccompanied by the usual tributes[7] – had a half-hearted aspect, typified by his inability either to grab or let go of the £21,300 profit. He seems to have convinced himself that the speculative aspect – the price *might* have fallen – justified his action, and ignored how shoddy such reasoning was when he had known very well the price would rise. Here he fell far below the personal standards to be presumed of a man who had disciplined or dismissed peccant stationmasters and clerks over four decades. His manipulations of the dividend rate, using the reserve fund, though as a shareholder he might himself benefit, had a different motivation. From early years the company had been concerned about the imbalance between the summer and winter revenues and dividends. Despite the criticisms of *The Times* in 1875, the system had gone on working; Bruce and Matheson had known and approved, and it was not done to excess. If T.C. Bruce had also approved of charging interest on the investment in new works to revenue, why should an upstart director like Fletcher parade his objections? But the company had grown too big for such tinkering, and expectations and conditions of good management and governance had changed. It was a tribute to Dougall's abilities that one man could still be general manager, secretary, and cashier, but it had gone on too long for his own good, as well as the company's.[8]

Raigmore refused the board's wish to have his portrait done for the boardroom.[8] In many respects, however, the record of his board in the 1890s was not unimpressive. Perhaps another, more adept, chairman might have exposed the element of bluff in the GNSR campaign, and thus removed the need to build the direct line, but the Great North was not wholly bluffing, and the threat of a rival Great Glen line was very real. And after all, it was Thomas Bruce himself who had pulled the rabbit of the direct line from his hat. As it was, the board under Raigmore and then Macpherson-Grant built it, and undertook the double-tracking from Blair Atholl, and introduced the most powerful locomotives in Britain; they added several useful branch lines to the system, installed the electric tablet method of train control, and made many other improvements of detail. Having found an element of disorder in the company's management, they did not lose their nerve, but created a new order, with some able new men at the top. In the following decade, with a new and strong chairman, and an innovative general manager, the HR was far less expansive.

## Double Track over Druimuachdar, and the 'Direct Line'

On 6 August 1897 the Highland Railway (Additional Powers) Act was passed. This gave the company authority to double the track on its line from Stanley Junction to Aviemore (from where the new cut-off was under construction). The issuing of new capital of £750,000, and additional borrowing powers of £250,000, were included, though much of this was probably to be set against the direct line. The doubling was always intended to be done by stages, and the July board meeting authorised the letting of contracts to John Best for Blair Atholl to Dalnaspidal. This was of course the most difficult section for train working, with the fifteen miles at one in seventy of Struan Bank, and further complicated by the movements of pilot and banking engines, requiring to be detached at Dalnaspidal or the County March, and returning down the single line to Blair Atholl. At the board meeting of 1 December 1897, the estimated cost of the work was put at £97,000. While doubling the track, and thus increasing the line's traffic capacity, can be seen as part of the HR's defensive strategy, there were other reasons too. In the 1890s, though the introduction of new carriages made trains both longer and heavier, there was also something of a general speeding-up in main line services. The Highland, as northward extension of the old Caledonian trunk route from the south via Stirling; and of the new North British route via the Forth Bridge and Glenfarg, was under pressure from public opinion and the southern companies to improve its very poor record of punctuality. Although delays often began south of Perth, the single-track Highland line invariably compounded them. In addition, passenger numbers were increasing greatly. Additional capacity on the line was badly needed, and further crossing loops were also installed on the single track: the *Inverness Courier* of 21 May 1897 noted that Chisholm's of Dingwall were building new loops at Inchmagranachan and Moulinearn, north of Dunkeld and Ballinluig respectively; and at Inchlea between Dalwhinnie and Newtonmore. These had no station facilities, and were used in the summer season only.[1]

By 2 July 1900 doubling had been completed from Blair Atholl to the crossing loop at Dalnacardoch in Glen Garry, and was through to Dalnaspidal by 13 May 1901. In the meantime, it had been decided to carry the double track as far as the County March crossing loop, and this was reached on 10 June of the same year. After several years, a further stage was authorised, from County March to Dalwhinnie. This section, first of all to the crossing loop at Balsporran, and from there to Dalwhinnie, was made by the HR's own permanent-way staff under William Roberts, and the last stretch was ready by 17 May 1910. 'County March' disappeared as a name, and was replaced by the variously spelled Drumochter or Druimuachdar Summit (Gaelic – 'ridge of the high ground'). Twenty-three and a quarter miles of double track in the central section of the Inverness–Perth line made a welcome easing to train control; though overall speeds do not seem to have altered to any significant extent,[2] delays were now reduced. Although full doubling between Stanley and Aviemore remained an official ambition of the company, and its Parliamentary powers to undertake the work were extended in 1905 and again in 1915, no more was done, though the direct line was built with double track between Inverness and Daviot.

For the HR, the most important development of an eventful decade was the construction of this thirty-four and a half-mile cut-off between Aviemore and Inverness. For six years from obtaining the necessary Act on 28 July 1884, the company managed to stave off any real action, although by 1886 agreements about land acquisition were made with proprietors, who were largely co-operative, though a minor deviation at Moy was agreed, and the route past Culloden was altered twice before the landowner, Duncan Forbes, was satisfied. Altogether four extensions of time to complete the line were granted – two before and two during construction. In almost a self-parody of the supposed '*mañana*' attitude ascribed to Highlanders, the secretary wrote to a shareholder on 2 March 1886 to say that the board, 'will proceed with it when the proper time arises, but there is no intention of pressing it forward unduly.' 'Small blame, however, to the Highland Company that it hesitated', wrote William Acworth in 1889; '... the construction of the new road will mean to them: in the first place, a capital expenditure of some hundreds of thousands of pounds; secondly, the cost of working some thirty additional miles; thirdly, no additional traffic whatsoever; and lastly, the reduction of the passenger fares by as many pence as the new road will be shorter in miles than the old.'[3] But, in its efforts to maintain its monopoly on Inverness, the board had painted itself into a corner. As long as it failed to build the direct line, it was leaving Inverness open to some other company, and it was vulnerable both to the Great North and the West Highland. There was undoubtedly also a bullish element within the board that felt the new line would stimulate additional traffic. At the very end of 1889 it finally advertised for tenders for the first stage, Aviemore to Carrbridge, let to John Ross of Fearn.

Murdoch Paterson, who had surveyed the line, was engineer; and in his positively final appearance with the Highland Railway, and in a positive role, Sir John Fowler acted as consulting engineer. John Ross's diaries give a daily account of his own doings from January 1890 to the end of 1898, and show how close and regular the liaison with Paterson was. From his yard at Boat of Garten, Ross ranged widely, not only managing his workmen but looking in the hills for stone, and going to sales for second-hand equipment.[4] On 8 July 1892 the line to Carrbridge, of six and three quarters miles was opened, and operated by a tank engine as a branch line, with very little traffic. Work began on the more difficult section from Carrbridge to Tomatin, under John Munro, on 11 April 1890.[5] In September 1892 Ross was negotiating with Paterson on the contract for the Moy section, Tomatin–Dalmagarry–Culdoich; his price was £87,000.[6] Once again there was an 'advancing army of labour' and Inverness Christians raised £100 to pay a missionary.[7] Workers on the new stretch seem to have been fairly decorous. In *The Railway Navvy*, David Brooke notes the fact that many of them were quite elderly compared with their predecessors: in 1891 around 40 per cent of the men working on the direct line were aged over forty or more; fifty years before, more than two thirds of railway navvies were under thirty. Skill and experience were now of more value than brawn. From 16 July 1897,[8] Daviot became the temporary end of a remarkable branch which included the spectacular threading of the narrow defile of Slochd Mhuic, 'the Pigs' Den' with a combination of lofty embankments, deep cuttings, a high viaduct, and the HR's second-highest summit at 1,315ft. A few miles on was the curving lattice girder bridge over the Findhorn, a separate contract in itself, its masonry columns by William Alexander & Co. of Inverness; the girders by Andrew Handyside & Co, of Derby; and a short distance further was the 143-yard nine-arched Tomatin Viaduct. The Culdoich to Inverness section had been let on 5 October 1892 to Mackay & Mackay. Even for a railway in no great hurry, there was a deeply unwelcome delay when they went bankrupt in July 1894, in the middle of their job. The contract was acquired by Charles Brand & Sons on 10 August and work resumed. In October 1897 it was decided to extend the double track from Inverness as far as Daviot,[9] which involved widening the track and some bridges between Culdoich and Daviot Station. The great 600-yard viaduct across Strathnairn was steadily rising, but before it was quite finished, Murdoch Paterson died, aged seventy-two, in the station house at Culloden Moor, on 9 August 1898[10] The Highland lines still stand as a memorial to Paterson and his mentor, partner and friend Joseph Mitchell. The two were not very alike: Mitchell somewhat reserved and remote, a grey eagle hovering above the everyday world, thinking his own thoughts which went far beyond engineering, while Paterson was a cheerful figure, more of this world, and a good leader. He is remembered not only in stone and steel, but in anecdote, especially as the man in charge when washouts or snow-blocks occurred, who knew when to pass round a reviving nip of whisky to keep the team's spirits up. He was succeeded by his assistant William Roberts, whose Oliver Hardyesque bowler-hatted figure appears in many contemporary photographs of the line.

On 29 October 1898 the HR directors were shown the completed direct line,[11] and lunched with the contractors at Carrbridge. It opened for traffic on 1 November 1898. Though its gradient, with a maximum of 1 in 60, was steep, Paterson's third and final plan (authorised on 7 June 1892) for the great swing across Strathnairn and down to sea level made a fitting end to the passenger's long northward journey past moor and mountain. There was a sudden vista of the sea, far below, and of a great expanse of mountains and hills stretching away to north and north west, before the train plunged downhill through cuttings, sweeping over the Keith line, to emerge among sidings and sheds, with the arch and the roundhouse on the left. There still remained the final surprise for the uninitiated: the apparent by-passing of the station, followed by reversal to the long arrival platform, and the modest yet not unworthy terminal buildings in the centre of Inverness.

*Light Railways in the North: Dornoch, Wick & Lybster*

The Light Railways Act, which became law in 1896, created a rush of interest in new railway schemes, not least in the Highlands. The Act allowed promoters to obtain a Light Railway Order for construction, a much simpler business than obtaining an Act of Parliament. The concept of a 'light railway', operated at slow speed in rural country, was not new but an LRO also carried with it compulsory land purchase powers, as with the traditional Act. Even more enticing was the availability of grants of public money to assist with the building of light lines in impoverished districts. Although Hamilton Ellis pointed out that 1896 also saw the abolition of the requirement for motors to be preceded by a man with a red flag,[1] the railway was still universally seen as the prime means of land transport. At this time, numerous local initiatives for light railway projects emerged in the further north region. Of these, only two became realities, the Dornoch and the Wick & Lybster Light Railways.

Dornoch, with a population of around 2,000, and sharing county administrative offices with Golspie, had dreamed of a rail connection since the 1840s, when the advocates of a bridge over its Firth would have put it on the main line to Wick. When the Sutherland Railway was built, the town council agitated successfully for a connecting station at The Mound, and a gig service for passengers and mail was run from there to the town.[2] The third Duke of Sutherland had died in 1892, but his heir inherited something of his father's mechanical interests, and his seat on the Highland Railway Board; and saw the possibilities of developing Dornoch, with its splendid beach and golf links, and its historic cathedral, as a tourist resort. In early 1897 a Dornoch Light Railway Co. was formed, with the duke as its chairman. The Sutherland County Council offered to contribute £1,000 – in 1889 these elected bodies had replaced the old oligarchic commissioners of supply, but Sutherland remained in many ways a ducal dominion – and Dornoch burgh council found £500. The duke was to contribute £5,000, and also gave most of the ground free; in recognition of this he was entitled to appoint another director additional to himself. The Treasury was asked for £9,000. A prospectus was issued in November 1898, announcing an authorised capital of £30,000. Shares were £1, and 9,501 were taken up (by 1912 paid-up share capital had reached £13,071). Everything looked promising. It had been supposed that the Highland Railway would work the line, which the HR was indeed disposed to do, but strictly on its own terms. It offered to put in a junction at The Mound, at a charge of £1,000. The DLR had thought the Highland would do this at its own expense, and after protest, it did. The Treasury grant was conditional upon the Highland, as the working company, guaranteeing to work the line for ninety-nine years. The HR refused to do this unless the Dornoch directors gave personal guarantees against any operating losses; they declined. Application to the Treasury brought the period down to fifty years, but still the Highland was obdurate. A telegram from Wilson, read to the Dornoch Board on 29 August 1899, stated that the HR could not legally incur any risk in working a line which did not belong to itself, without a specific resolution of shareholders, 'and, in the present state of the Highland Company's finances', he thought it most improbable that such a resolution would be carried. The duke guaranteed the first fifteen years, and the HR, rather surprisingly, agreed to risk the second fifteen. Twenty years were unaccounted for, until finally the duke set up a guaranteed trustee fund of £3,000, to last for thirty-five years. The Treasury was also prevailed upon to raise its grant to £14,945. On 4 October 1899 a Working Agreement was signed. The HR was to be paid the actual cost of working and maintaining the line, out of receipts, which it of course gathered. After five years it was entitled to demand 50 per cent of net receipts, 'or in their option the actual cost of working and maintaining the line'. Section 13 allowed the duke to run his own engine on the line. Chisholm & Co. of Dingwall contracted to make the line, apart from rails and buildings, for £11,573. Then in November 1900 the promoters' nightmare occurred: Chisholms went bankrupt. Work on the line came to a standstill for eighteen months until matters were settled, and a new contractor, Roderick Fraser, took over in July 1901. On 17 October that year, the Highland Railway confirmed its plan to build a large hotel in Dornoch. This was the Highland's first purely resort hotel, for a seasonal trade. With sixty-five rooms, it duly opened at the end of June 1904. Guests' laundry went by train to the Station Hotel in Inverness for washing, at no extra charge. The Highland also subsidised the Golf Club with £50 a year, though there was a dispute in 1913 when the board withheld its subvention, 'until the recent resolution of the Town Council has been rescinded'.[3]

The HR staffed the new line, with Douglas Mackenzie, stationmaster at Georgemas, moving to Dornoch. The first directors of the DLR were the duke, and Donald Maclean, his factor; John James Barrow of Northfield, W.S. Fraser, merchant, Dornoch, Rev. Donald Grant, Minister of Dornoch, George R. Kennedy, Links House, Dornoch, and John Mackintosh JP, bank agent, Dornoch. The number of local men is interesting, as is the lack of any involvement of HR directors. This railway was also unique in having a minister of the Kirk on its board. Sunday services were not to be a feature of the DLR. The secretary, Hector Mackay, writer of Dornoch, found himself involved in almost perpetual wrangling with the HR, which collected all revenues, on the deductions for operating costs and shared services, until a Supplementary Agreement in 1906 established a fixed sum of £153 2s 6d per annum plus 10s per week for any extra carriages required.

The branch, seven and three quarter miles long, was passed fit on 29 May 1902, and opened on 2 June 1902. There were intermediate halts at Cambusavie, Skelbo and Embo. Dornoch was provided with a wooden locomotive shed and a carriage siding. In classic light railway fashion the line was run on the 'one engine in steam' principle, which removed the need for crossing loops and signals. Three services each way ran on weekdays between Dornoch and The Mound. A through carriage from Inverness was conveyed on the 12.50 a.m. train in 1905, and a through Pullman sleeper was run from Glasgow to Dornoch every Friday night in June.[4] However, with the opening of the hotel in 1906, the HR laid on a dedicated train, the 'Further North Express', which ran from Inverness to Dornoch on Fridays only, during the months of July–September. It was technically non-stop between Inverness and The Mound, but would have taken on water at Tain or Bonar Bridge. There was no corresponding return service, so the train must have returned empty to Inverness. From October 1906 and in subsequent years to 1912 the 'Further North Express' became a Wick train, with a southbound train operating on Thursdays, returning north on Friday. Dornoch passengers had to change at The Mound, unless an entire carriage had been reserved from Inverness. The DLR made a modest annual operating profit until 1921, when earnings of £4868 11s 9d were overtaken by costs of £5612 16s 3d. It was necessary to draw on the company's reserves of £800, but by then the end was in sight. The LMS paid £75 for every £100 of Dornoch 4 per cent Debenture stock (total £1,652), and £15 per £100 of the Ordinary stock (£13,072).[5] The branch was worked by HR tank engines until 1957, and was closed in 1964.

A line from Wick to Lybster and on to Dunbeath had been proposed at least since 1864. With the proposal for a Wick and Lybster Light Railway,[6] yet another duke rose above the Highland Railway's horizon. This was the Duke of Portland, whose Cavendish–Bentinck family had owned the Langwell estate, on the edge of the Ord of Caithness, since 1859 and had gradually extended their possessions northwards. In 1883 the duke had had the harbour at Lybster rebuilt, in an effort to maintain the local fishing industry. But despite this, Portland was by no means an operator on the Sutherland scale, and he was not the sponsor of the railway. The final scheme began with Caithness County Council, which proposed the line to the Secretary of State for Scotland, under the Light Railways Act, on 5 March 1896. The council was prepared to find a fifth of the necessary £75,000 share capital.[7] Although the government had approved grants for the Dornoch line, and for the Forsinard, Melvich & Portskerra Light Railway (see Appendix D) in 1897, it was 27 November 1899 before a Board of Trade order was received, with details of a ten-year interest free loan from HM Treasury of £20,000. Problems in negotiation between the Highland Railway and the Duke of Portland were at the bottom of the delay: it was felt that the HR, which refused to contribute to the costs of a survey, and which was demanding a working rate of 2s 1d per train mile, was being obstructive. The biggest shareholders in the Wick & Lybster company were the County Council and Portland, each with £15,000-worth. Wick Town Council invested £1,500, as did Pulteneytown Burgh Council (not yet amalgamated with Wick). By January 1901 there were sixty-five shareholders, of whom fourteen held £10 or the minimum amount of £5, in £1 shares. The county MP, R.L. Harmsworth, had 1,000 shares; the member for the Northern Burghs, Sir Arthur Bignold, had 500. The great majority of personal shareholders were from Lybster and the communities between there and Wick, including Georgina Forbes, dressmaker, Lybster, who took twenty shares, and William Henderson, crofter, Osclay, who took five. The original seven directors were John Miller, chairman of the County Council, John M. Sinclair, Lybster (also a council nominee), J. Harling-Turner, 'General Estate Agent on His Grace the Duke of Portland's Scotch Estates', George King, Berriedale (also a ducal nominee), provosts Nicolson and Wilson of Wick and Pulteneytown, and John Mowat, banker, Lybster. William Roberts was temporarily seconded from the Highland Railway as engineer. Eight thousand shares were still unsubscribed on 28 March 1900.

An agreement on the same terms as the DLR's was made with the HR on 27 November 1899, by which the HR, 'shall construct and form the said Railway', but like the Dornoch company, the Caithnessians found the Highland tough and not over-scrupulous in negotiation. Having taken responsibility for construction, its main concern with the Lybster company was to make sure enough funds were secure for this, and on 24 January 1901 the HR vice-chairman, William Whitelaw, came to Wick to demand irrevocable guarantees for £70,000 of construction money, failing which the HR would withdraw from any agreements already made. The directors, who had prised another £5,000 out of the Board of Trade in 1900, reluctantly gave guarantees,[8] and were further upset when the Highland, having first offered Roberts's services for free, now required payment. A new Working Agreement was signed on 27 February 1901. On 21 May of that year, the Directors' Report noted that they had:

> … hoped that the construction of the line would have commenced nearly a year ago, but the work was delayed on account of controversies which arose between your Directors and the Highland Railway Company regarding the providing of the money to meet the cost of the line.

There was a benefit however: in that period the cost of rails fell sharply and a saving of almost £6,000 was made by the delayed purchase. Work at last was under way. The main contractor was William Kennedy, who supplied his own Glasgow/Irish labour force. Rails were shipped to Wick, while sleepers and other equipment came by train. All station buildings were of wood, with Lybster the most expensive at £200 14s 2d, plus £117 1s 5d for the engine shed and £55 12s 5d for the water tank. Thrumster Station, still standing in 2005, cost £93 8s 9d to build. The line, thirteen miles, three furlongs and nine chains 'or thereabouts' long, was opened by Mrs Miller on 1 July 1903.

Troubles with the Highland did not go away. The HR's interpretation of the Working Agreement, including depreciation charges on a locomotive proudly named *Lybster* but already ten years old (and carrying a boiler built in 1862) and some venerable rolling stock, was a constant source of friction until an annual lump sum payment was agreed on 4 December 1907. In 1909 the Treasury loan period was extended by five years. The line was no more than moderately successful, its dividend never exceeding 1.5 per cent, though it experienced a modest boom in passenger traffic when Wick voted to go 'dry' in May 1921, and the pubs of Lybster benefited accordingly. The W&LLR was never absorbed into the Highland Railway, and in the post-war grouping, it, with the Dornoch Light Railway, was treated as a 'worked line' and its compensation claim for wartime wear and tear was handled through the Highland, which kept the modest £190 awarded, 'to offset debts and alleged sums due for running costs'. The LMS paid £12 10s for each £100 of the company's Ordinary stock (£42,515).[9]

*New Men and New Attitudes: The Highland Railway from 1896 to 1914*

The half-yearly results to 29 February 1896 gave the shareholders a cold whiff of what 'doctrinaire financing' meant: the Ordinary dividend was half of 1 per cent. The Directors' Report spelled out the reason: the company was no longer crediting interest on the cost of new lines to the revenue account: 'The Accounts now submitted show the actual net cost of working the line for the past half-year'. The following summer half-year paid 3 per cent; the winter to February 1897 paid nothing at all on the Ordinary shares. All departments had been subject to close investigation, and a Liverpool accounting firm, Harmood Banner, had scrutinised the company's books but gave its finances a clean bill of health. Fletcher, Darwin and Baillie kept up the pressure and formed a sub-committee to check the accounts and monitor expenditure.[1] Board committees, focusing on traffic, ways and works; estates, and law, as well as the old finance, stores, locomotive and hotels committees, were strengthened. They all met regularly and sent in their Minutes. The new puritanism seemed all-pervasive; on 3 April 1896 the general manager informed the Traffic Committee that he was taking steps to obviate the excessive rate of speed down the inclines between Dava and Forres and from Dalnaspidal to Blair Atholl. Only one thing seemed unchanged in the post-Dougall era: a profound suspicion of the Great North of Scotland Railway and its ambitions. Joint meetings were still going on, and in January 1896 it had been agreed to plan for a new joint station in Elgin, but in August the HR was seeking an interdict to prevent the GNSR from employing a representative at Inverness, 'to assist passengers travelling by way of Aberdeen'[2] The cause of the trouble was local passengers on the Highland section choosing to use the superior GNSR through coaches meant for passengers for the Aberdeen line, and it was resolved by agreement.[3]

On the western approaches, the precarious peace established in 1895 was violently rocked by an independent proposal for a line from the West Highland at Spean Bridge to Fort Augustus, at the south end of Loch Ness. To be known as the Invergarry & Fort Augustus Railway, its main sponsors were Lord Burton, a local sporting tenant on a large scale, and Charles Forman, the engineer of the West Highland line. A supporting voice came from the British Aluminum Company at Foyers, whose manager, Mr Ristori, said that: 'It was of immense importance to the Co. that there should be a railway connecting the works with the southern centres and markets'.[4] But the BAC made no investment. Despite opposition from the Highland and West Highland, the I&FAR obtained their Act on 14 August 1896. Bruce Lenman notes with minimal exaggeration that the line served: '… a Highland terrain which for a radius of 50 miles around Fort Augustus was 99 per cent deer forest and 1 per cent arable'. It cost £344,000. The arrival of this cuckoo in the nest immediately prompted three schemes to complete the thirty-mile gap along the steep shore of Loch Ness: from the I&FAR itself, the WHR, and the Highland, the two latter involving running powers over the Invergarry line between Spean Bridge and Fort Augustus. All were presented to Parliament in the 1897 session. A special correspondent in the *Inverness Courier* pointed out the old HR objections to a Great Glen railway, and asked what was different now? For him, 'The enormous advantages of competition to Inverness are so clear as to quite outweigh the private interests of the Highland Company'. He also believed that if the HR won the battle, it would not build the line.[5] Inverness Town Council backed the I&FAR proposal; most other northern towns, like Dingwall, supported the HR, though Wick did not. Its provost said that its people had 'many complaints' about the Highland Railway.[6] Everyone, on whichever side, was confident that a line would be authorised. In February, the Commons Select Committee accepted the Highland Bill and rejected the others. By the time the Lords Committee was considering the Bill, in July, the Highland had come to an agreement with the North British, but the I&FAR vigorously opposed, claiming a conspiracy by the bigger companies.[7] The chairman of the committee, Lord Brougham and Vaux, was clearly hostile to the HR. The Lords Committee rejected the Bill, and it is unlikely that there was much grief in the boardroom at Inverness.

Throughout 1896 the HR was receiving representations, deputations and petitions from all over the north of Scotland, Skye and Lewis, relating to light-railway schemes for places as yet unattached to the network. To almost all, the company returned the same answer, positive but non-committal: if the promoters could secure a route and adequate finance, the HR would be pleased to work it, on reasonable terms. In some cases it was more forthcoming: the company agreed to construct the proposed Forsinard, Melvich & Portskerra Light Railway, and sanctioned the appointment of Murdoch Paterson and his assistant William Roberts as engineers in connection with the promotion and construction of the Culrain & Lochinver Railway.[8] The Highland's real attitude to all of them was one of deep reservation. With its resources already fully extended, it had no intention of contributing capital, and, despite the encouraging words (as the Lybster and Dornoch directors would discover) had its own interpretation of what constituted reasonable terms. To get Board of Trade approval, and a grant, a light railway had to show that an existing railway company was prepared to build and operate it with a long-term commitment. The HR's standard response was to indicate that this could be arranged, but the money had to be found by the promoters. In the course of 1897 the Highland took up almost all these local plans, in a somewhat loose and non-commital embrace, the main purpose of which was to see that they did not fall into the arms of anyone else, who might then claim running powers over the HR to get access. Nothing had changed since the days of the Garve & Ullapool.

The resignation of David Jones, through ill health, was regretfully accepted in September 1896. From thirty-three applicants, Peter Drummond was appointed locomotive superintendent, at £700 a year, on 7 October. In March 1897 the Duke of Sutherland, who had already sold a large number of shares, informed the board that he expected his holding to fall below the level of £100,000, and enquired if he could still be a director. The board's reply was that he had been elected by the shareholders and could remain a director as long as that continued to be the case.[9] The eastern frontier remained unsettled. The Railway & Canal Commissioners had still not come forward with an arbitration from the disputes of 1895, and the GNSR introduced yet another

Bill for running powers from Elgin to Inverness, offering to pay for doubling the line. While this was under consideration, the commissioners produced their findings, in December 1896. Although they made Keith and Elgin the exchange points for an equal number of trains, the advantage seemed to be with the Great North inasmuch as the Highland was required to accept through coaches at Elgin from the GNSR's coast and inland routes. But when Steel promised that the Highland Railway would abide by the commissioners' terms, the Great North's Bill was rejected. However, the HR did abide by the new terms, and the old feuding abated from this year. In 1898 a new director was elected, the thirty-one-year old William Whitelaw, who had been Conservative MP for Perth from 1892 to 1895. He was then living in the old keep of Huntingtower near Perth, but moved to Monkland, Nairn. Anglo-Scottish, educated at Harrow and Trinity, this scion of an industrial family was to discover that his true *métier* was running railways, and he became deputy chairman in April 1900. In May 1898 Steel resigned, to move to the Great Northern of Ireland, and was replaced by Thomas Addy Wilson, of the North Eastern Railway, at £1,500 a year.

Interviewed by the *Railway Magazine* in its January 1899 issue, Wilson remarked that: 'I have already learned that the Highland line requires an experience of its own, and many things I learned during my service on the North Eastern, I have had practically to unlearn, or at least to suppress…' He was particularly struck by the density of the short summer traffic compared to the rest of the year. By this time the company was routinely carrying more than two million passengers a year, but improvements to the track, the double-track section, the direct line, the arrival of the new 4-6-0 'Castle' express locomotives developed by Drummond from a design of Jones's, and the construction of new bogie carriages, all helped to increase carrying capacity. By April 1904 the *Railway Magazine* was writing:

Mr T. Wilson, the General Manager of the Highland Railway, is doing wonders with that line. Four years ago the Company was not only paying nothing by way of dividend on its Ordinary stock, but it had in its balance-sheet suspense accounts to an amount of £46,000. By 1902 the whole of the latter had been liquidated by transfer from revenue, and it resumed the payment of dividends on the Ordinary stock. For the second half of 1902 a distribution of 1 per cent was made. In the first half of 1903 that was repeated, and the company has announced for the second half of the year a distribution at the rate of 1¾ per cent per annum… Not only is this the best of the Scotch group, but if we except the Barry and Rhymney Railways, it shows the largest improvement of any railway in Great Britain for the past half-year.

Such comparisons were valuable in the process of restoring confidence among investors, many of whom still looked askance at the meagre rewards of the 1900s compared with 5 per cent and more in Dougall's time. In the whole decade from 1900 to 1910 the Ordinary dividend never reached 2 per cent. 'Shareholder' complained in the *Highland News* on 26 September 1908 of the board's meagre information and suggested that a 'scouring-out' was needed, but the half-yearly meeting in October was attended with cheers and applause, and lasted under half an hour. The *Financial News* commented that the HR 'did less badly than the Caledonian Railway or the Glasgow & South Western'. Even so, the results were only possible by the practice of strict economy. The Highland had always gone in for small economies; in 1882 the manager had instructed stationmasters to cut up old timetables for toilet paper in staff lavatories. Much of the economy drive focused on Lochgorm Works,[10] which built no main line locomotives after 1901, and whose last new engine was the 0-4-4 tank No.46, in February 1906.

Late in 1901 the Invergarry & Fort Augustus Railway was completed. It had been anticipated that the West Highland would work its trains, but the two companies failed to reach agreement, and the directors of the I&FAR turned to the Highland Railway. A Parliamentary battle ensued, as the North British was no more keen to see the Highland at Spean Bridge than the HR was to see the NB at the south end of Loch Ness. On 21 July 1903 the Highland obtained an Act authorising it to work the line, at a charge of £4,000 a year; services had begun on the 3rd of the month. A Highland 'Yankee Tank' had to take carriages and wagons round by Crianlarich to reach the line, where it was to operate three trains daily in each direction. Traffic was scanty. There were inconveniences attached to running an isolated service, including the supply of additional wagons and engines for occasional special sheep trains. In an effort to provide a through service, the Highland applied in 1905 for a Bill to operate its own steamer service between Inverness and Fort Augustus. Macbraynes, already running the mail steamer (which did not use the railway pier), opposed, as did the West Highland and the Invergarry Railway itself, and the Bill was rejected. At the half-yearly meeting of 27 March 1907, the HR announced its intention to withdraw from working the I&FAR, under Article 9 of the Working Agreement. Losses on the service were running at £2,000 a year. On 1 May the West Highland took over. By then there was so little chance of a connecting line to Inverness being built that the Highland could feel reasonably secure. Despite a maverick ploy to build a line to the north end of Loch Ness in 1908 (see Appendix D), the Great Glen through route was to remain a might-have-been.

Almost all railways were feeling the pinch in the 1900s, and it was the prospect of reduced costs through shared facilities that pushed the Highland and Great North of Scotland into serious merger discussions in 1905. By now the dominant HR directors were Whitelaw (chairman 1902-12) and R.M. Wilson (chairman 1913-15). With new men running both companies, the old frictions had largely disappeared. Although the two boards were in favour, the idea was received with coolness or hostility by many HR shareholders. The Highland Railway was a larger concern than the GNSR, but Aberdeen was a considerably larger city than Inverness, and the Great North had just completed extensive and costly new locomotive works at Inverurie. There was no doubt where the head office and main works of the joint enterprise would be, and hostile feeling in Inverness and its hinterland was strong. Was it for this that the 'Great Railway War' had been fought, and won? At that time, in 1894, the *Inverness Courier* had observed that the Highland workshops' employees were paid around £70,000 a year: 'Remove them and you plunge the northern capital into crisis'.[11] It is unlikely that many people were convinced by Whitelaw's claim, at the half-yearly meeting on 27 September 1905, that the Highland Company wanted amalgamation in order to develop its interests north of Inverness: '… we cannot proceed, in the interest of shareholders, prudently with the development of the North of Scotland, if we stand on our own feet'. The merger was debated throughout the North, but among town and county councils, only Wick supported the proposal. But it was doubt on the shareholders' part whether a joint company would do any better for them that scuppered the project. A letter to the *Scotsman* on 29 September 1905 from Kenneth Macdonald, a shareholder, set out the case, centred on the respective value of GNSR and Highland shares, and the Great North's heavy commitment to capital expenditure at Inverurie and the Joint Station in Aberdeen. He accuses the Highland board of 'throwing away the property of their Ordinary shareholders'. Darker suspicions were rife, about a 'Glasgow syndicate' that had bought many shares in the HR at par, only to find them drop in value, and which hoped to recoup its losses in amalgamation. Though Whitelaw was vociferous in supporting the merger, R.M. Wilson was seen as 'the power behind the throne.'[13] A joint Parliamentary Bill was promoted in the 1906 session, for a Highland & North of Scotland Railway. At a special meeting the GNSR shareholders approved. On 7 March 1906 it was the turn of HR shareholders. The leaders on both sides came armed with large numbers of proxy votes, and the result was: for Amalgamation £1,527,000; against it £715,217. The extent of capital not voting at all was £1,595,000. Although a majority was in favour, it was not a sufficient one – a 75 per cent majority of those voting was required under the Wharncliffe Act, which governed such transactions. Cheers greeted the result: 'some flung hats in the air, others executed a wild war dance'.[14] The Highland Board put the best face on it, saying they had decided to abandon the idea, 'considering that in a matter of such importance they ought not to proceed except with the approval of such a majority as would amount practically to unanimity'. In fact, they had no option. At the half-yearly meeting on 28 March, there were a few calls for the board to resign, to which Whitelaw's reply was: 'What is the use of all this talk?' He did not care a brass farthing if he was put off the board tomorrow, but he was not going out because of a noisy minority.[15] At this meeting, for the first and only time, the votes of those present rejected the re-election of retiring directors; but board proxies swiftly re-established the normal order of things. The Bill was withdrawn, but a climate of co-operation remained between the companies. From 1906, GNS trains and engines ran all the way on some services from Aberdeen to Inverness, and Highland 'Bens' hauled expresses to Aberdeen. A joint meeting on 4 December 1908 agreed that the Great North would look after Highland engines at Keith and the HR reciprocate for GNS engines at Forres (locomotive superintendents were asked to consider consequent staff reductions), and the companies agreed each could use empty wagons belonging to the other.[16] The often-discussed joint station in Elgin was never built, however, and passengers continued to have a 100-yard walk between the HR's through station and the GNSR's terminus. From the merger attempt onwards, however, there was a rift between the board and the town of Inverness, together with an 'old guard' of ex-directorial families, like the Mackintoshes of Raigmore and the Macpherson-Grants, who felt that the board no longer represented wider Highland interests.

T.A. Wilson had a flair for publicity, and advertising campaigns in the North of England promoted special-price holiday excursions on the Highland line. Easter excursions from Lancashire towns to Inverness cost 21*s* for four days, or 30*s* 6*d* for nine days. Wilson's bargain tours were always aimed at extending the season, but circular tours, often taking in steamer and coach trips, were available all through the summer. Features were obtained in papers like the *Wigan Examiner*, whose readers were told on 26 June 1905 that: 'The Highland Railway has arranged a most extensive tour scheme by which the unparalleled grandeur of the Beauty Spots of Scotland may be visited and intellectually revelled in at a most reasonable capital expenditure'. On 1 June 1906 he arranged for a special train to take a press party from London to Dornoch; drawn by two decorated engines, it was the first to run non-stop from Perth to Inverness. A similar press tour was laid on for the opening of the Highland Hotel in Strathpeffer in 1911. In 1909 the HR published a guide to golf courses in the Highlands, and the summer timetable of that year blandly assured the intending visitor to the 'Highland Riviera' that:

> The temperature of the South of England is a little higher during the winter months than that of Nairn or Forres or Tain, but the Northern Climate is, by reason of its won-derful Dryness, infinitely superior to the Climate of Cornwall. Some persons suffering from bronchial troubles who have spent winters in the Canary Islands and in Nairn, do not hesitate to declare their decided preference for the latter.

From 1908 Wilson also used an Albion motor van, emblazoned with slogans like 'The Highlands for Fishing', to tour northern English cities with pamphlets promoting Highland holidays. In 1913 the board accepted Mr A. Paterson's offer of 9 May for a 'Cinematographic View of the Line'.[17] These were innovative ideas, which also showed the company as a forward-looking and dynamic one. But the internal combustion engine was eating deeply into the first-class traffic receipts, as wealthy residents and visitors began to attempt the Highland Roads in motor cars.[18]

A new set of top officials emerged between 1910 and 1914. Thomas Addy Wilson, whose 'health had not been good for some time'[19] resigned in October 1910, at the board's request, his going eased by a retirement allowance of £500. Robert Park, Company Solicitor since 1901, now became General Manager and Solicitor, at £1,500. Peter Drummond moved to the Glasgow & South Western Railway in 1912, and his assistant, Frederick Smith, took over. In January 1914 William Roberts retired and Alexander Newlands, his assistant since 1902, became engineer, at £700 a year. Building of new lines had come to an end and the engineer's task was to maintain and strengthen the tracks, and to continue improving station facilities. With the reinforcing of the Oykell viaduct in Spring 1913, all locomotives could work through to Wick. The reorganised management had new problems to cope with, including the company's first known strike, when thirty fitters walked out from Lochgorm Works in February 1911. The *Highland Leader* explained that all were former HR apprentices, being paid less as journeymen than trained men recruited from the south.[20] It was a stormy year for industrial relations on the railways. The bitter and violent 'Scotch Strike' of railwaymen on the Caledonian, North British and G&SW Railways in December and January 1890-91, had not involved the Highland Railway's men, who continued to work normally. In the railway strike of August 1911, which affected almost all British railways, the Highland again continued to work normally, though the Seaforth Highlanders at Fort George, in common with other military depots, were put in a state of readiness in case of any trouble. The *Aberdeen Free Press* wrote that on Sunday 20 August:

> ... a largely attended meeting of Highland Railway employees connected with the Society [Amalgamated Society of Railway Servants] took place in Inverness for the purpose of considering the situation. A full and free discussion took place in which it was said that Highland Railway workmen would loyally support their brethren in the South.

But the *Highland News*, closer to events, observed on the 19 August that 'the ASRS has only a small membership in Inverness'. While they were still considering, Government intervention ended the strike, and, like other companies, the Highland was obliged by the settlement to operate conciliation boards, with equal staff (elected by their fellows) and company representation, to deal with complaints and requests from the work force. Later in that year, the *Dundee Advertiser* noted that there was grave disaffection among the Highland Railway men, with many taking part in the ASRS ballot on a further national strike. The men were also reported to be preparing a petition to the HR Board. The miners' strike of early 1912 overshadowed the men's grievances; Robert Park issued a precautionary fortnight's notice to all waged staff on 14 March, though promising reinstatement on the previous terms once the coal strike should be concluded. This action in the end was not required.

In 1913, its last year of operations unaffected by war or post-war disturbance, the HR sold 72,198 first class, 2,150,505 third class and 13,092 workmen's tickets, plus 107 first-class and 816 third-class season tickets. Its total receipts were £602,580 5s 3d, to which passengers, mail and parcels contributed £366,359, or 60 per cent; and operating expenses were £340,920 17s 8d, in which the largest elements were locomotive running, £107,477 7s 4d (the company's 152 engines ran a total of 3,657,995 miles), traffic expenses, £87,279 16s 8d, and permanent way maintenance, £56,934 5s 1d. Cartage by Wordies cost £7,484 14s 9d, and printing, advertising, stationery, stamps and tickets cost £6,665 11s. The hotels and refreshment rooms made a profit of £9,070 9s 2d on a turnover of £45,251 6s A dividend of 2.5 per cent on the Ordinary stock was declared.[21]

The Highland Railway had been in being, under that name, for fifty years on 29 June 1915, and in August of that year the *Railway Magazine* published a fifteen-page article on the company by J.F. Gairns, a correspondent familiar with the HR. A survey of the history, scenic aspects, locomotive and carriage resources of the line, it also offered photographs of ten officials, headed by the schoolmasterly looking Robert Park, the only clean-shaven face among the moustaches (though by 1915 only one is still bearded). There were outlines of the careers of Park, Newlands, Smith, and Thomas McEwen, the traffic manager. Of these senior men, only Newlands had been with the Highland from the very start of his career. It looked forward to 'Mr Smith's forthcoming 4-6-0 locomotives' which, by the time the article appeared, were being refused access to the line by Newlands. Most of the article covers familiar ground, but one aspect of the Highland Railway is singled out:

> ... the number of houses and cottages built for the use of employés, in many cases in locations where no village is adjacent to the line at places where staff accommodation is required. Of these there are 473, usually erected in blocks of four to designs which have become more or less standard.

Like many other writings on the Highland, it several times mentioned its 'unique' qualities without quite establishing what these might be. Gairns judged it a well-managed line, though a jubilee article was scarcely likely to convey much criticism, and he even found a kind word for the coaching stock, 'good and comfortable, but not ornate'.

# SEVEN

*The First World War*

War was declared against Germany and Austria on 4 August 1914. The railway companies had made administrative preparations for this eventuality, and a Railway Executive Committee, intended to operate the system as a national one in the case of emergency, had been in existence since 1912. But the Highland Railway was almost totally unprepared for its role as a strategic wartime route.

Military preparations began almost at once. The use of the Cromarty Firth as a naval anchorage, and the development of Invergordon as a major naval depot required the movement of materials and men on a large scale. The construction of large army camps south and north of Invergordon, at Alness and Nigg, and the creation of a full-scale naval dockyard at Invergordon itself, required the haulage of large amounts of building materials. Half a mile south of Alness Station a gravel pit was opened up to provide stone for reclaimed ground on the Invergordon foreshore. Great quantities of cement, steel, corrugated iron sheeting, and other building materials, as well as armaments and munitions, were also needed for the camps and defensive systems on Orkney. The first distribution centre for naval supplies was Dingwall, which had more siding space than most stations, and from where goods could be despatched both north and west, but once the Grand Fleet was stationed at Scapa Flow, Dingwall was too far south, and Thurso became the key holding point. The very limited siding and storage space there, and the lack of a rail connection on the two and a half miles between the railhead and the harbour at Scrabster, which was in any case a tiny one, made it very difficult to keep up an adequate flow of supplies.[1] While the Highland line was used to the utmost, other methods also had to be employed. From 15 January 1915, Aberdeen became the Grand Fleet's main point of supply, with all kinds of stores and supplies, other than coal, shipped on from its docks to Scapa Flow. Coal for the fleet was shipped from the Caledonian Railway's docks at Grangemouth, equipped for coal handling, which had been completely taken over by the Government. But even with these diversions of the bulk of Orkney-bound naval and military goods traffic, the Highland was still used far more intensively than its builders had ever imagined. The Carrbridge line now proved to be of great value, but three serious problems were always present: congestion on the single line, exacerbated by a lack of siding capacity; the inadequate number of locomotives; and a shortage of trained staff, especially signalmen. In the course of the war, the company saw 756 men[2] – about a quarter of its total number of employees in 1913 – leave to join the armed services. Of these, 87 were killed in action.

Despite the railway's evident strategic value, and despite the choice of Orkney and the Cromarty Firth for two great naval bases, no government had paid any attention to the resources of the Highland Railway as a potential military artery. As a result, no provision had been made for the demands which war service would thrust upon it. Its freight traffic had never been heavy, and passenger traffic in the 'winter' period was much less than during the tourist season. This had customarily been the time when locomotives and rolling stock were overhauled and repaired. Now the line had to be run on an intensive, year-round basis with a dramatic increase in traffic. Although long-distance troop trains were made up from rolling stock of other railways, there was considerable movement of troops and forestry personnel within the Highland's own area, and also a much greater demand for goods wagons. The Great North of Scotland Railway's alternative route to the south was also used. Sir Malcolm Barclay-Harvey noted that 48,440 loaded, and 9,033 empty, wagons were taken over the GNSR lines rather than down the Highland main line;[3] and GNSR locomotives ran a total of half a million miles on Highland metals, during the war period.

The first wartime works were two sidings at Invergordon, the extension of the platforms at Fearn, and the laying of new sidings at Kildary, in both cases to serve the large camp at Nigg; and the extension of the Invergordon harbour branch into the new naval dockyard area, in autumn 1914. In 1915, Inverness was designated as the ammunition storage centre for the Grand Fleet. A new line to serve the depot, with storage sidings, was laid by the permanent way staff to the harbour area. Branching off at Welsh's Bridge, it joined up with the old harbour branch at its northern end. Around Invergordon further new works were under way in the autumn of 1915, including extension of the platforms, and further sidings. The fertiliser works at Invergordon and some of Dalmore Distillery's buildings were commandeered as naval workshops, and a short branch was built to provide access from Invergordon, with a junction at Belleport, a mile north of Alness,[4] and terminating at a lower level than the siding from Alness Station.

Among the first responses to wartime conditions was the free buffet for troops in transit (excluding troop trains which had their own catering stops). The first of these was opened at Perth General Station on 7 August 1914, while the first mobilisation was getting underway. It began with spontaneous gifts of fruit to the troops passing through, and in a few days, tea and cakes were added. Before long it was a twenty-four hour service, and the example of the 'Perthshire Women's Patriotic Committee', later the 'Perthshire Barrow Executive Committee', was followed throughout the country. At Dingwall Station, a brass plaque still records that 134,864 cups of tea were served to troops between 20 September 1915 and 12 April 1919, by the Ross &

Cromarty branch of the Red Cross. Before 1914, women were normally employed only as cleaners or crossing attendants, like Mrs Masson, gatekeeper at Brodie, who got 2s 6d a week plus a free house. Wartime brought a modest influx of female staff. On one day in December 1916 nine women were taken on as porters at Inverness, and numerous others followed; others became clerkesses, engine cleaners, and ticket collectors.

Although steam coal for the Grand Fleet warships was not carried, the Highland's coal traffic soared because of the demands of the military camps, and the need to supply coal to fishing vessels, minesweepers, mine-layers and other small coastal vessels and warships based at Inverness, Invergordon, and Wick. As Edwin Pratt noted, reduction of shipping capacity, and the wartime increase in shipping rates to three times that of the railways, meant that the bulk of this traffic was transferred to the railway: 'There were occasions when nearly all the stations between Inverness and Wick were blocked with coal wagons, loaded or empty, which could not be moved owing to the congested condition of the lines'.[5] The company's own need for locomotive coal was also far greater than ever before.

Timber traffic also increased greatly. The difficulties of importing timber led to a massive exploitation of the forest resources of Northern Scotland. Wood was required for every sort of purpose. Some of these were within the region: the defensive booms at Scapa Flow and between the Sutors of Cromarty required massive timbers, and the military camps needed building wood. But most of the lumber was sent south, where there was especially a vast demand for pit-props. There were few expert forest workers, and the lack was supplied from North America. During 1916 the 224th Canadian Forestry battalion was set up, and worked in the Highlands as well as other forest areas; later in that year a 238th battalion was also raised. In 1917 they were supplemented by a Newfoundland battalion and by ten sawmill units from the New England states of the USA. The Americans were based at Ardgay. In addition, large numbers of German prisoners of war were employed in forestry work. In 1918 the Highland Railway transported a total of 403,560 tons of timber. This, as Pratt calculated, was equivalent to 80,712 five-ton wagon-loads; or 2,690 trains of thirty wagons each.[6] It was ten times the normal pre-war timber traffic, carried at a time when other traffics were also at a wholly abnormal peak level. From late 1915, additional sidings were laid at a number of stations, including Tain, Dingwall, Beauly and Keith, to cope with the timber traffic.

In January 1915 the Highland was confident enough to introduce a new express service, leaving Perth at 11.45 a.m. on Fridays, and running non-stop to Kingussie, stopping thereafter at Grantown, Forres, Nairn and Inverness, arriving at 3.55 p.m. The *Railway Magazine* reported that, 'This caters for traffic of the "winter sports" character as the district served offers facilities very similar to those available in Switzerland and other countries for ski-ing... there is good reason to expect that this development in Highland facilities will justify itself.'[7] The company's difficulties also became apparent in early 1915. At one point, lack of signalmen meant that three of the crossing loops between Perth and Inverness were out of service. The increased traffic of winter

1914 had made it impossible to carry out the usual programme of fairly leisurely maintenance and repair procedures on the locomotives. There was a lack of trained fitters at Lochgorm Works. Perhaps because of this, unlike most other railway works, Inverness does not appear to have undertaken any war work beyond that of normal locomotive repairs. Engines sent south to have repairs made at private locomotive shops were held up by pressure of wartime work. By the end of August, there was a crisis. Of the company's 152 serviceable engines, 50 were in such need of repairs that they had to be withdrawn from service; and another 50, though still at work, were also in need of repair. Some requests for trains had to be refused because no engines could be provided to pull them. The engine shortage also exacerbated the congestion on the line. The Highland had to inform the Railway Executive Committee of its inability to meet the commitments demanded by the government. A meeting was convened at Perth, at which the general manager, the chief engineer, and the locomotive superintendent met officers from the London & North Western, the Great Central, the London Brighton & South Coast, and the Caledonian Railways, to discuss their plight and what might be done. It was agreed that twenty locomotives would be supplied, through the agency of the Railway Executive, from other companies; that efforts would be made to temporarily second fitters from other companies to the HR, and that the War Office would be asked, in view of the strategic importance of the railway, to release former Highland Railway fitters from military service. Nothing came of the two latter points, but a number of engines were supplied. A letter from Thomas Brown, the assistant locomotive superintendent, to the Rev. A. Warburton ('Scrutator') written on 15 December 1915, usefully lists the guest engines, with some details of services:

> We've got on loan 7 N.E. engines 6 of them goods 0-6-0 Fletcher class with steam brakes, and one 0-4-4 tank, also Fletcher. This shunts at Invergordon and took the place of a 0-4-4 G.N. of Scotland tank which was wanted back at Aberdeen. We have 7 C.R. Engines Goods, one of them 4-6-0 from Callander and Oban Rly. No. 56. Perhaps you will know it. 2 N.B.R. engines Holmes goods reboilered by Mr Reid and 3 L.&N.W. Webb, 2 of them 0-6-0 17"x24", 5ft. wheel and 1 2-4-0, 17"x24", 6ft 6in. Precedent Class named "Auditor" which runs the 9.50 a.m. relief to Tain as the regular 9.50 a.m. to Wick never leaves before 11.30 a.m. owing to the south connection being so late. In fact we run a daily express to Thurso now leaving about 11.30 a.m. with seamen and officers; stops are Invergordon, Bonar, Helmsdale, Georgemas.[8]

He lists nineteen engines, from the North Eastern, Caledonian, North British and London & North Western as well as the Great North. In autumn 1916 there were still nineteen engines from other companies at work, but forty-two of the HR's own locomotives remained out of service. The situation was made worse when the company's new 'River' class express engines were refused access to the line (see Chapter 9). In all, about forty-three engines from other companies were in use on the Highland at different times between 1915 and 1919 (the Caledonian 4-6-0 remained until 1922). Even in September 1919 Robert Park was trying to stave off returning two engines to the North British: '... if we were to send your engines home the goods and mineral traffic on the line would very soon get into a state of chaos. [9]

Brown's letter hints at the somewhat chaotic nature of the passenger service, both for troops and civilians, that prevailed in the first years of the war. Not for the first time in the HR's experience, delays often began south of Perth, but the Highland's own difficulties compounded them. It was not until the winter of 1916–17 that troop transport was put on a more efficient basis. From 5 February 1917, a London–Thurso naval special left Euston every weekday at 6 p.m. and reached Thurso next day at 3.30 p.m. In winter the times were advanced by three hours, to avoid shipboarding in the dark. But often a second and occasionally a third train was needed, and the journey time was frequently extended by delays along the way. The train, particularly when northbound, was known to the men as 'The Misery'. The ship *St Ninian*, requisitioned from the North of Scotland, Orkney & Shetland Steam Packet Co., left Scrabster Pier at 5.30 p.m. and berthed alongside the post-office and personnel reception ship HMS *Imperieuse* in Scapa Flow at 7.30 p.m. The return train service left Thurso at 11.45 a.m., reaching Inverness at 5.35 p.m. and Perth, where the North British took over, at 10.15 p.m. [10] In Highland folk-memory this train is known as the 'Jellicoe', after the admiral in command of the Grand Fleet, but during the First World War, the 'Jellicoes' were the coal trains trundling up from England to Grangemouth. In the Second World War, with the coal trains no longer needed, the resuscitated 'Misery' was often referred to as the 'Jellicoe Special' or 'Jellicoe Express'.

The Naval Special was a regular service, but the deployment of ships and men required many non-scheduled trains. Invergordon dealt with 1,020 special trains, each carrying between 300 and 400 men, between 4 August 1914 and 4 August 1919. Not included in this number were ambulance trains despatched to the south; and royal trains bringing King George V on two visits to the naval depot. Ambulance trains ran frequently, though usually lightly loaded, except during the influenza epidemic in the Grand Fleet in spring 1918, when over 27,000 men were classified as 'cot cases'; and in the immediate aftermath of the Battle of Jutland, when two trains with several hundred wounded, many of them severely burned, were sent south from Invergordon on 3 and 4 June 1916. Among other special services were seven trains on 4–5 October 1917, carrying 2,993 men and 161 officers, of the Russian and Serbian armies, disembarked from three vessels which had come from Northern Russia, where the Bolshevik Revolution was in progress. Eleven trucks contained field kitchens, water carts and other military equipment. An additional train took 300 refugees, mostly French, to London. It also carried an amount of gold bullion on its way to the Tsarist embassy in London. On at least two occasions bullion shipments were sent outwards from Invergordon, having arrived on trains with a military guard.

The flow of mail to and from the naval depots made a substantial traffic in itself. From June 1915 to the Armistice of 11 November 1918, the total volume of letters and parcels delivered to Fleet Post Office 'A' on the *Imperieuse* was 80,000,000; the amount sorted and dispatched south was 41,000,000. A special newspaper supply service was also organised, once the naval train was in daily operation. Early copies of the next day's *Daily Mail*, printed in Manchester, were got to Preston in time to be loaded on to the train at 10.15 p.m. At 3.15 a.m., parcels of the *Glasgow Herald* and *Scotsman* were picked up in Edinburgh, making it possible for 'today's papers' to be read on board the ships at Scapa.[11] For mainland depots, a mail centre was established at Inverness Station, in a purpose-built shed, but later spreading into the premises of the Station Hotel laundry. To help entertain the troops and sailors in their camps, far from any town, let alone a city, cinema huts were built and film canisters were carried up by train to provide newsreel shows as well as the latest silent movies of the time. Such items were merely the top-dressing on a vast range of freight transported into, out of, and within the district north of Inverness. From 25 July 1916 the entire region north and west of the Great Glen was declared a restricted military area which could not be entered by a non-resident without a special pass.[12]

In 1917, the company was informed of another massive traffic load to be imposed. Improvement in the design of explosive mines, and the capacity of the now-belligerent United States to mass-produce these weapons, led the Admiralty to plan the massive 'Northern Barrage' – a minefield laid all the way across the northern North Sea, and primarily intended to stop German U-boats reaching the open ocean. It was 235 miles across and would require some 70,000 mines. The components were to be made in the USA, shipped to western Scotland, carried to the east coast, assembled there and despatched on mine-layers. Two assembly bases were set up in January 1918: 'US Naval Base 18' which took over the Muirtown Basin and Glen Albyn Distillery close to the end of the Caledonian Canal at Inverness; and 'US Naval Base 17', which took over the Dalmore Distillery, three quarters of a mile north of the station at Alness. Component parts for Base 18 were unloaded at Corpach and sent by lighter up the Caledonian Canal; for Base 17 they were unloaded at the pier at Kyle of Lochalsh and sent across the country by train.

Both bases required new railway works. Muirtown Basin already had its branch, laid alongside the canal wharf. A trailing connection was installed close to where the branch diverged from the main line, leading to a group of sidings inside the American base. Wagon-loads of assembled mines were then shunted out of the assembly area back to the canal for transference to lighters, which took the high-explosive cargo out to waiting ships in the specially dredged Kessock Roads. The works between Alness and Invergordon were more substantial. The single line between these stations was already under severe pressure. Alness had been equipped with extra siding capacity, and the long spur built in 1878 to Dalmore Distillery was in use from mid-1916 to supply an engineering shop set up to form new armour plating for warship repairs. This line ran and terminated at too high a level to serve the shore-front. Now 6,500 casks of whisky were moved out of the bonded warehouses, and new huts and sheds also built, requiring the transport of 7,000 tons of material by rail. A new access track was laid for two miles along the fore-shore, diverging from the line laid from Belleport, and connecting with the harbour branch at Invergordon. The junction with the main line faced north, so that trains from Kyle had to reverse direction twice on their journey, first at Dingwall, and again at Belleport. Completed mines were carried to Invergordon and, as at Muirtown, trans-shipped to lighters for ferrying to the mine-laying ships. A 220-yard railway jetty at Dalmore, still known as the 'Yankee Pier', was not completed until after the Armistice, and was used only for the landing of recovered mines and as a relief to the congested port at Invergordon. Rails for the new lines were provided from the closed line between Buckie and Aultmore. But the naval lines were not operated by the Highland. The Admiralty bought five 0-6-0 tank locomotives, of Stroudley's design (and therefore tracing their ancestry from Lochgorm), from the London Brighton & South Coast Railway, three for use at Dalmore and two at Muirtown. A novel vehicle for the Highland was a steam railcar, No.45 of the Great Western Railway, which was provided in January 1918 to run between Invergordon, Alness, and Dingwall, transporting dockyard workers and military personnel. This was not a public service and did not appear in the published timetable.[13]

During this year the port of Kyle of Lochalsh was commandeered by the Admiralty, as was the Dingwall & Skye line. The Highland Railway was allowed to run a single public train each way on weekdays, for passengers and mails, but no goods traffic was permitted. To the anger of the inhabitants of Skye and Lewis, all goods traffic for the islands had to be routed via Oban or Glasgow, causing considerable delays. Mines began to be landed at Kyle in early May 1918, and the traffic continued until November. The HR steam and hydraulic cranes were dismantled and replaced by new equipment, and new siding space was blasted out of the rocky site. Four locomotives were despatched from the London & South Western Railway to work the mine-trains: William Adams's 4-4-2 radial tank engines, well suited to a line with many tight curves. The South Eastern & Chatham supplied 150 12-ton coal wagons, and four brake vans came from other companies. Train-loads were limited to eleven wagons. Apart from the mine components, a very wide range of other goods for the US bases arrived in the American supply-ships: everything from hydraulic barber's chairs to hospital equipment, motor vehicles, foodstuffs, and chewing gum. The total tonnage moved between May and November 1918 was 32,800, of which 24,000 tons went directly to the Dalmore base and the balance to Inverness, Alness or Invergordon. Around 400 trains carried the traffic, with no recorded accident of any sort.[14]

A desperate shortage of wagons was increasingly apparent as the war continued. The three largest Scottish railways, the CR, GSWR, and NBR, had entered into a common-user scheme of pooled wagons on 5 June 1916, based in its essentials on the German railways' *Wagen-Union* which they had investigated in the pre-war years. This scheme, for general-purpose wagons, proved highly successful and was joined by the Highland and GNSR from 2 January 1917. From the pool, the Highland was allocated a total of 700 extra wagons. But in the early summer of 1918, 200 of these, from the Glasgow & South Western, were recalled; and notice was given that the others would also be needed by their owners before the end of the year. Once again the Highland applied to the Railway Executive Committee, and from September, an extra 1,150 wagons were made available to it for general goods purposes. The extra stock provided by the REC at no point did more than stave off complete collapse. Between mid-1915 and mid-1919, the HR carried on all its operations on a hand-to-mouth basis, with the operating staff, particularly on the Main and Further North lines, always struggling to keep priority traffic moving and avoid excessive delay to the rest.[15]

From 1913 until 1915 R.M.Wilson was chairman of the board, though serious illness kept him away for some of that time. Whitelaw resumed temporarily in the winter of 1915-16, until in March 1916 W.H. Cox, a Dundee jute tycoon, took over, and held the chair until the dissolution of the company. Wartime circumstances reduced the scope of the board's control and a heavy responsibility was borne by the managerial triumvirate of Park, Thomas McEwen the traffic manager, and Alexander Newlands, the engineer.

The company's hotels, now inaccessible to tourists, were also taken over for war use. The Station Hotel in Dornoch was used from 1915 to billet troops in training, and later for Canadian forestry workers. The Admiralty used the hotel as well as every other facility at Kyle of Lochalsh. The Highland Hotel in Strathpeffer was also used at first to hold troops in training,[16] but was later taken over by the Admiralty, and used by the US naval authorities as a surgical hospital.

The government's financial arrangement with the railway companies regarding wartime traffic, controlled under the aegis of the Railway Executive, was first based on the companies' revenues (net receipts) for 1913 (or the first half of 1914, if a company should have earned less in that period than in the corresponding period of 1913). The government would compensate companies for any deficiency on these figures during the war emergency, while any surplus would be paid to the state. Thus the Highland Railway was guaranteed a net revenue of not less than what it had earned in 1913, while carrying an immense amount of additional 'free' traffic on behalf of the government. Edwin A. Pratt's estimate of the figures involved was as follows, with the actual earnings of 1913 and the notional earnings of subsequent years, based on traffic levels (he excludes mail, parcel and livestock receipts):

| Passenger earnings | Goods earnings | Combined earnings |
|---|---|---|
| 1913: £243,716 | £193,531 | £437,247 |
| 1914: £306,872 | £213,527 | £520,309 |
| 1915: £464,452 | £239,608 | £704,060 |
| 1916: £577,560 | £340,539 | £918,099 |
| 1917: £598,710 | £426,894 | £1,025,604 |
| 1918: £632,073 | £442,593 | £1,074,666 |

The 1917 and 1918 figures allow for the 50 per cent increase in fares imposed by the executive. The number of passengers went from 2,222,703 in 1913 to 3,344,480 in 1918, while the goods tonnage went from 653,589 to 1,232,437 in the same period. As nearly all of the traffic increase was directly related to the war effort, the extent of the HR's involuntary contribution to victory is evident.

If the shareholders lost out on these financial arrangements, the main beneficiaries of the war were the staff. The various national agreements made during the war years provided the HR workers – never among the best-paid of railway servants even by Scottish standards – with substantial pay increases in line with all other railway workers. From 13 February 1915 those over eighteen earning under 30s a week were awarded a wartime 'bonus' of 3s a week; those earning above that level received 2s. In June, boys received a bonus of 1s 6d. As a result of trade union representations, the bonus payments were increased to cope with the rising cost of living and by April 1917 they had risen to 15s a week for men and 7s 6d for boys. By November 1918 the respective figures were 33s and 16s 6d. For most grades on the Highland Railway, that represented an increase of 150 per cent or more on their pre-war wages. Somewhat belatedly, bonus payments were also granted to women railway workers, reaching 20s 6d for those over eighteen by November 1918, and half that for girls. Bonus payments were eventually consolidated into normal wages. Perhaps such increases prompted the company to stop the provision of food for engine crews of the naval trains, from 6 May 1917. On 16 December, the meals were reinstated, for men who had been on duty for at least twelve hours.[17] Demands on staff were heavy. Goods guard William MacGregor left Inverness on 19 May 1916, with the 9.10 a.m. to Perth. He booked off there at 12.40 p.m. on the following day, after more than twenty-seven hours of continuous duty. Ordered to work the 9 p.m. back to Inverness that night, he refused, and returned home 'on the cushions'. The fare of 9s 10d was deducted from his pay.[18]

In his evidence to the Parliamentary Select Committee on Transport, in October 1918, Sir Herbert Walker, acting chairman of the Railway Executive Committee, remarked that, 'Certain companies, such as the Highland, have had very heavy burdens thrown upon them in the way of traffic… I think the Highland has been hit more than any other company'. This committee, appointed to consider what steps should be taken for the improvement of the post-war transport situation, made as its first conclusion that the organisation of railways, in particular, should not be allowed to revert to the pre-war position.

As a postscript to the war years, it may be noted that a number of HR men received official honours for wartime effort, including the stationmasters at Invergordon and Kyle, Fraser and Riach, and William Macintyre, the assistant traffic manager, who became MBEs.

### The Last Years

Government control of the railways was not relinquished immediately on the end of the war. In September 1916 it had been decided that state control of the railway system would last until two years after cessation of hostilities, with maintenance of the revenue guarantee during this period. It actually lasted almost another three years, and during this time the Railway Executive Committee remained in being, though only meant to concern itself with operating matters. On 15 August 1919, a Ministry of Transport was established by Lloyd George's post-war government, under Sir Eric Geddes, with authority to retain state control over the railways for a further two years. All the former powers of the Board of Trade with respect to railways were transferred to the new ministry.

From 1 February 1919, despite intense opposition from the railway companies, an eight-hour working day was conceded to all grades of railway staff. Dissatisfaction among railway workers remained high and a national rail strike was called for 26 September. This time the Highland was not unaffected, and on 26 September about 500 men met on Castle Hill in Inverness, with 'quiet underlying determination to carry on the strike'.[1] One train ran from Perth and one from Helmsdale taking railwaymen home to Inverness, and carrying passengers but no mails. Newlands and Cumming were on the Perth train but did not interfere with the union men in charge. On 29 September management staff drove one train, under military guard, to Perth; another went to Lairg on 1 October, driven by the manager of the Inverness Electrical Works. On 2 October the Aberdeen *Free Press* said that Inverness Station was full of confused and stranded passengers. The Strike Committee had offered to discuss their plight. McEwen's answer was: 'What has the Strike Committee to do with stranded passengers? Let them look after their business and we will look after our own.[2] On 5 October the strike was called off, but already it had been noted that, 'Big motor traffic is going on throughout the Highlands'.[3]

Quite apart from the pan-British debate being conducted at Westminster, the part played by the railways in the war, the running-down of their resources, and their future role in the nation's life, were all important issues in the Scottish context. The Secretary of State had already set up the Rural Transport (Scotland) Committee in February 1918 to consider this last point. It was to, 'consider and report on the rural areas of Scotland which are most in need of transport facilities for the promotion of agriculture, forestry, and other rural industries, and the means of improving communication in those areas.' Both light and narrow-gauge railways were listed among the options to be considered, as well as improved roads and motor transport. The committee reported in April 1919, shortly before the Ministry of Transport came on the scene, with a different agenda. Its findings, recommending numerous schemes, with capital costs to be paid from public funds, make an ironic counterpoint to the wider theme. The glimmer of government cash, elusive as fairy gold, prompted a new flush of interest in light railway schemes: even now, the 'Friends of the Garve-Ullapool Railway' published a 'statement and appeal... There could be no scheme with greater promise'.[4] It was not to be realised. Bold new ideas were also aired, like the electrification of the Perth–Inverness line, using power from hydro-electricity,[5] but all remained speculative.

Far greater sums of money were in question in a separate but not wholly detachable issue. Furious argument, with heavy pressure from companies and much political 'spin' from the government, was directed to the question of compensation payment to the railways for their special wartime activity and the resultant dilapidations. A Ministry of Transport Departmental Committee under Lord Colwyn shocked the nation by suggesting that the railways would demand £150,000,000. In the event, £60,000,000 was provided for this purpose in the Railways Bill, and the railway amalgamation tribunal was given the extra task of apportioning it. It proceeded by splitting the fund into two parts, one repayment to be based on net receipts in 1913, plus an assessment of special needs; the second to be based on the extent of arrears in the maintenance of permanent way and works, and of rolling stock, again with an element of provision for any special cases. The sum ultimately assessed as due to the Highland Railway on all counts was £361,681 plus £436 interest; almost exactly the same as that awarded to the Great North of Scotland. Payment was made in two equal instalments at the end of 1921 and 1922. [6]

The Rates Advisory Committee of the Ministry of Transport, making a report on general revision of railway rates and charges in 1920, made the point that the increased costs of operating railways was likely to make some lines uneconomic, as they would either have to charge more than customers would pay, or operate at a loss. The Scottish railways were especially affected, and the Highland was specifically referred to:

> They pointed out that the rise in cost resulting from standardising the hours of labour and the wages paid had fallen much more heavily upon them than upon the principal English companies, estimating that the relative increase in expenses was 25 per cent greater in their case than in that of the average of the English companies. This was due to the fact that wages had been lower and hours longer in Scotland than in England. As an instance we were told that a signal box on a branch line of the Highland Railway with very few trains passing each way had, before the war, been worked by one signalman at 21s a week wages, but that now, as the last train passed more than eight hours after the first train of the day, the company was required to employ two men at weekly wages exceeding £7. [7]

The railways were returned to private control on 15 August 1921, and four days later the Railways Act received the Royal Assent. This provided for amalgamation of the hundred-plus independent railway companies into several large groups. Initially, companies were left to sort themselves into suitable groups, to be approved by the Ministry of Transport; an Amalgamation Tribunal was established to deal with unsatisfactory proposals, or with failures to agree. Discussion had already been intense and now became torrid, with 1 July 1923 set as the date by which all should be accomplished. Shareholders, trade unions, economists, industrialists, passengers, politicians all had views and, to varying degrees, vested interests.

As one of the smaller companies, though still regarded as a 'Constituent Company' of its proposed new group, rather than just a 'Subsidiary Company' as were the Dornoch and Wick & Lybster companies, the Highland scarcely had a voice in this debate. The only Scottish railwayman on the Railway Advisory Committee, representing companies' points of view to the new Transport Ministry, was Donald A. Matheson, general manager of the Caledonian. In the White Paper of June 1920, and for some months after, the notion of a Scottish Railways Company, combining all five in a single group, had been canvassed. But the companies themselves, backed by both staff (who feared pay cuts) and customers (who feared heavy increases in carriage rates) were unhappy about this. The North British and Caledonian preferred to group themselves with bigger and more prosperous and powerful companies to the south rather than to dominate a smaller, economically poorer Scottish system. But in any event, it was clear that Inverness's years of railway independence were coming to an end. To general surprise, however, the Bill introduced to Parliament on 11 May 1921 proposed two separate independent groups of Scottish railways: a western group, comprising the Caledonian, Glasgow & South Western, and the Highland; and an eastern group merging the North British and Great North. This proposal was at once heavily attacked and on 17 June, at the Standing Committee stage, it was accepted that combined Scottish–English groups were permissible. In the Highland Co.'s history, its links had always been closer with Euston than with King's Cross, and there was a general acceptance that it would form part of the 'West Coast' combination, whose biggest elements were the London & North Western and Midland Railways. In November 1922 a special Shareholders' Meeting was convened at Inverness to consider the terms of amalgamation. For every £100 worth of HR Ordinary shares (totalling 2,564,383), the LMS was offering £32 6s 8d. All the various outstanding Preference and Debenture stocks, totalling £4,306,739, were converted into LMS 4 per cent Debenture stock. Employees' superannuation rights and Savings Bank deposits were protected under the Act. Voices from the floor urged rejection of the terms, and appeal to the tribunal established to adjudicate on contentious cases; but Whitelaw, also speaking from the floor, was firmly insistent that this was the best deal the company could get. The voice that had eased many a controversial issue through such gatherings was listened to, and the meeting approved the deal. Like some proud but impoverished mountain heiress, the Highland brought only its 506 miles of track to swell the London Midland & Scottish Railway's 7,790-mile total, but also a vast extent of territory, making the LMS geographically, as well as in other respects, the largest of the 'Big Four' companies. In fact it was the largest non-state railway business in the world.

From 12 January 1923 the regular service advertisements in local papers, with Park's name at the bottom, were given a new rubric: 'LMS (Highland Section). Arthur Watson, General Manager'. The Highland Railway Co.'s final meeting was held in Inverness on 28 February 1923, when a last dividend of 2 per cent on the Ordinary shares was declared. The vice-chairman, A.E. Pullar, of the Perth dye-works family, presided. Pullar, who had been elected as a director of the LMS, expressed formal regrets at the termination of the, 'long, interesting and honourable history' of the company, and expressed suitable hopes for great developments in the future.[8] The shareholders present agreed to the payment of £4,512 to the retiring directors, to be divided as might be agreed among them.[9] So the Highland Railway, as a company, came to an end. Some of its officials prospered in the new regime. Alexander Newlands eventually became the LMS's chief civil engineer. William Whitelaw would become chairman of the LNER. But the effect of absorption into the LMS was to transform the Highland Railway Co. into an operating district of a vastly larger concern.

# PART II

# EIGHT

*Mitchell's Road*

In September 1867 Joseph Mitchell read a paper to the British Association, at Dundee, on 'The Construction and Works of the Highland Railway'.[1] Interestingly, he concentrates on the northern countryside's economic assets as the reason for building railways, rather than the needs of the travelling public: the pastoral agriculture, producing large numbers of sheep and cattle; and the fisheries: 'The object of the promoters, therefore, was to sweep the fertile shores of the Moray Firth, and to send the produce to the country by the most direct route'. Discussing the gradients needed, he observes that although long and steep climbs were unavoidable, there was no gradient exceeding 1 in 70, which as his audience would know, was well within the compass of the contemporary locomotive. He went into some detail on the trickier aspects of construction:

> The principal difficulties that arose in laying out the line were in passing through the narrow defile at Dunkeld, the beautiful demesne of the Duke of Athole, and again in penetrating through the picturesque Pass of Killiecrankie, where the mountains, as it were, close in upon each other for a great height; likewise in passing along the narrow, precipitous, and rocky valley of the Garry, close to a large and rapid mountain-stream; also the Park at Castle-Grant, and the defile at Huntley's Cave near Grantown. These points in particular required much study, with repeated trial and contour levels, so as to obtain a knowledge of the precise formation of the ground, and to choose the best direction at the lowest possible cost. At the Pass of Killiecrankie the banks were so precipitous and steep that the line has to be supported by breast or retaining walls to the extent of 690 lineal yards, and to the average height of 26 feet, the extreme height of one being 55 feet; and in order to carry the railway at the narrowest point in the Pass where the precipices close in, as it were, on either side, and afford scarcely any space beyond that occupied by the channel of the river, instead of supporting the line by breastwalls, it was deemed prudent to construct a viaduct of ten arches, 60 feet above the river, which with a tunnel at the north end carries it successfully through the pass.

At two other points on the line, in running up the sides of the Garry, breastwalls had to be formed, respectively 94 and 35 yards in length, and 15 feet in average height. All these breastwalls, extending to 1650 lineal yards, are built with lime, and set on a solid foundation of dry gravel or rock, at right angles to the face of the wall, which batters at the rate of 1½ inch to the foot.

The spaces behind the walls are filled with rubble stones, set by hand for 10 feet wide, and further back with dry gravel, it being important that all earth or clayey substances should be excluded. The writer prefers the curved to the straight batter, as it gives more effectual resistance if well built; but breastwalls are to be avoided wherever earth embankments can be substituted, as, in his experience, there are subtle influences in the Scottish climate of alternate frost and wet in winter, which operate imperceptibly to their destruction, and they require careful and constant inspection. Except where those breastwalls became necessary, the whole of the lines were formed in cuttings and embankments, and for considerable distances along the slopes of valleys, where the ground was precipitous or irregular in the cross section, level benchings were formed, 10 feet in width, immediately under the permanent way, in order that the sleepers should have an immediate and solid bearing throughout.

In running through so large an extent of mountainous country, the line, as might be expected, had to pass over some lengths of soft ground and morass. The principal of these were for two miles near the town of Nairn, also for about two miles near Keith, one mile on Dava Moor, and about a mile crossing through a hollow at Drumochter on the summit of the Grampians. In all places where the ground was particularly soft, a uniform mode of treatment was adopted. Two parallel drains were first cut outside the fences, about 50 feet apart, from 4 to 6 feet deep, and with slopes of 1 to 1. This drained off the surface-water; and, after making up the holes and other irregularities of the surface with turf, the space for the railway to a breadth of about 15 feet was covered with two or three layers of swarded or heather turf, having the sward side of the lower layer undermost, and that of the top layer up, the joints breaking band. In this way a good sustaining surface has uniformly been obtained... On this bed of turf the ballast was laid for 2 or 3 feet in depth. This was quite sufficient to support the traffic, but as in some cases the bed of moss was from 20 to 30 feet in depth, the railway merely floated on the surface, and was in the first instance undulating, and yielded in some parts from 3 to 4 inches under the weight of the engines passing over. To obviate this undulation longitudinal beams of timber were tried at one place, 30 to 40 feet long, below the sleepers, but this was found objectionable, as rendering it more difficult to raise or repair the surface of the road: and an additional sleeper (making the sleepers 2 feet 6 inches from centre to centre, instead of 3 feet) was found preferable. There was nothing for it, at the worst, but to lift the road every other week as it sank, until it had acquired a solid bearing. In many places we had to lay on 4, 5 or 6 feet in depth of additional gravel, and in one place no less than 27 feet, before the road became solid. In the course of two or three years, however, with due attention, the rails being fished, the lines through these mosses were all that could be desired for solidity and permanence.

The later widening of the line to double track between Blair Atholl and Dalwhinnie brought considerable change to that section of Mitchell's original road, but his account is important as showing the techniques used not only by him but also applied by Murdoch Paterson on the lines to Kyle, Sutherland and Caithness. Mitchell also gave details of the major viaducts that had been built to date, and dwelt on the problems of securing the foundations.

> … the beds of the rivers in the north of Scotland differ in many respects from what is common in England, consisting frequently of depths of 10 or 12 feet of gravel and boulders, the solid and compacted debris of successive floods, below which, if the country is of rocky formation, there is usually hard clay and then rock, or, as in one case at the mouth of the River Ness, after penetrating twelve feet of shingle and boulders, a sort of admixture of whitish clay and sand was obtained.[2] In some cases we had to deal with soft clay and mud of great depth, but these were exceptions. Nor was it possible in general to ascertain, by boring, the precise nature of the foundations, because many of the boulders in the gravel were large size, and were often mistaken for rock. The only way in which an approximate knowledge of the foundations could be obtained was by driving iron rods at various places, and when the bed of the river admitted it, wooden piles. Still we worked very much in the dark; but the writer's long experience of these rivers, and of the nature of their floods, was of great advantage in enabling him to fix the depth of the foundations and the precise description of works, to secure necessary stability of construction. In only two or three cases was there any fear of sinking. What had chiefly to be guarded against was sudden and impetuous floods, sometimes accompanied with floating ice and trees, undermining the foundations and damaging the piers; it was therefore important to provide ample waterway. The construction of these bridges ranged over twelve years, and during that time there had been considerable changes in bridge building, by the adoption of iron cylinders for piers, and lattice girders in spanning the waterways, so that, as the works progressed, these improvements were adopted where found suitable.
>
> In planning these works, the writer, while having every regard to economy, felt the importance of their being of the most substantial character, seeing they were exposed in these districts to every vicissitude of climate and flood; but indeed he feels that all permanent public works involving the safety of the lives of the community should be of undoubted stability. On the whole system there are only three timber bridges, which he was forced to adopt, chiefly with the view to save time, but these are very substantial of their kind. All the other bridges are constructed of stone, and where iron is adopted the piers are in general constructed of masonry.

John Fowler's accusations of extravagance would still be rankling with Mitchell twenty years later. At that time at least two large bridges, over the Spey south of Newtonmore, and over the Beauly, were of timber. For long the only remaining timber bridge was Paterson's massive trestle structure[3] at Aultnaslasnach, near Moy, where extreme bogginess precludes conventional masonry foundations. Later history on the Highland line itself would prove Mitchell's concern with floods to be amply justified.

Eight larger bridges on the Forres–Dunkeld line are described by Mitchell; their total cost, at £76,182, was just about 10 per cent of overall construction coast. The metal bridges were considerably more expensive than the masonry ones: the girder bridge over the Tay at Dalguise cost £39 12s per lineal foot, compared with £11 5s for the stone Killiecrankie viaduct, and £21 9s for the loftier Divie Viaduct, but Mitchell considered the long spans well worth the extra cost. The most expensive of all his bridges was the I&AJR Spey Viaduct at £52 5s per lineal foot. Among his many masonry bridges, Mitchell's favourite was perhaps that over the Conon, on the Ross-shire Railway: its proximity to his mentor Telford's fine road bridge[4] gave a challenge to his engineering skills:

> From peculiar circumstances it was necessary that this bridge should cross the river on a skew of 45 degrees to the stream, and as there were rock foundations, there was no difficulty to contend with beyond that of 4 or 5 feet of water in the channel of the river to reach the rock, which was successfully accomplished. The peculiarity of the skew with the river at this place would have been more easily provided for by the adoption of iron girders from pier to pier, but as the writer found at the time that iron girders would be fully as expensive and not so permanent as a stone bridge, and as there were admirable quarries in the neighbourhood, he resolved to construct this bridge, as already said, on a skew of 45 degrees with the river, by a series of right-angled ribs or arches spanning from pier to pier. This is no new arrangement; but the writer is not aware of the plan being adopted for a series of arches of so large a span in any previous instance. The bridge consists of 5 arches of 73 feet span each, the arches being constructed of four ribs, each 3 feet 9 inches wide; the arch stones are 4 feet deep at the springing, and 3 feet deep at the crown. The keystones of the centre part of each arch were made to connect with each other, as were the stones in the haunchings of the arches, and some cramps of iron were inserted at the joints to connect the ribs. The work was successfully accomplished, and constitutes a very perfect piece of bridge masonry.

The bridge cost £11,391, or £22 2s per lineal foot. A tin box with some mementos was placed behind one of the facing stones. Mitchell was obviously proud of his skew, which he felt, with some justice, to be a daring and remarkable piece of bridge design, worthy of notice by the engineering world. His final comment, that when the centring was removed, no joint showed any indication of settling, courts a deliberate comparison with Brunel's famous and controversial bridge on the Great Western at Maidenhead.

Joseph Mitchell was dead before the direct line via Carrbridge was begun, but its bridges, designed by Murdoch Paterson and Sir John Fowler, are in his tradition. Of the five principal ones, three are masonry and two are lattice-girder structures on masonry piers. The longest masonry viaduct in Scotland crosses Strathnairn just south of Culloden Moor Station, built of local red sandstone, 600 yards in length, 130ft in height, with twenty-eight arches of 50ft span and one of 100ft span over the river. A nine-arched stone viaduct runs above Tomatin village, followed by the fine curving viaduct over the Findhorn valley, 105ft high and 445 yards long. Just south of the summit at Slochd is Slochd Mhuic Viaduct, of eight arches, 105ft high and 400ft long. The girder bridge over the Dulnain at Carrbridge has a 180ft-span and is 56ft high; a more modest version of the Findhorn Viaduct.

Ballast stone for the Highland lines was usually readily available; there were numerous ballast and sand pits, and ballast sidings were laid at Ralia, south of Newtonmore, Bowmanhill, south of Forres, Orbliston on the Fochabers branch, Bunchrew, Rogart, and Marrel near Helmsdale. On the Duke of Sutherland's Railway, William Baxter simply dug shingle from the adjacent beaches. In 1904 the HR spent £4,000 on a two-mile aerial ropeway from Gateshead Quarry, on Lord Breadalbane's land, to Aberfeldy, which carried 80 tons a day for ballasting between Murthly and Struan.[5] Ash collected from the various engine depots was also widely used in re-ballasting, except on wet ground. Fortunately for the appearance of the line, it was cheaper to quarry stone for construction work than to buy and transport bricks from further south. As a result, its structures were built primarily of local stone and this helped to fit the railway harmoniously into the landscape, especially after the cut stone surfaces had weathered and the initial rawness of cut and piled ground was replaced by vegetation cover. By comparison, for all their elegance of design, the concrete viaducts of the West Highland's Mallaig line lack this sense of material integration with the terrain. On the Perth line, rails weighing 75lbs to the yard were first used; north of Inverness, with the expectation of lighter traffic, the original rails were 70lb to the yard. The sleepers used on all the lines were of larch or fir, from the extensive plantations in various parts of the eastern and southern Highlands. In 1863, the cash-strapped I&PJR bargained with the Duke of Atholl for sleepers in return for £3,000 worth of shares. A central creosoting plant for sleepers was set up at Forres in 1875.

On all the lines which formed the Highland Railway, apart from the Perth & Dunkeld, design and construction of buildings were part of the engineer's responsibility. At the majority of stations, especially in the early decades of the company, the employees' houses were the only stone buildings, and travellers were likely to find the station building was an unassuming wooden one-storey structure with a waiting-room, office and parcels room. This was part of the Mitchell formula: the budget for stations was limited, and what was important at first was to have a station at all. Even larger stations, like Nairn and Dingwall, were originally of wooden construction. For the same reason platforms were short and low, and remained so at many HR stations until the 1960s. Carriage floors were well above platform level, and wooden stool-like mounting blocks had to be provided for the less supple passengers. In the stone station buildings, many of which still survive, three influences can be seen. Mitchell had learned his profession from Thomas Telford, and something of Telford's plain, low-cost, but decent and solid style is apparent in his masonry designs. A more up-to-date influence in some cases was the more decorative approach then being applied by Victorian architects to the gate lodges of castles and shooting boxes: a sort of junior

Scots baronial. Lastly there was the new vernacular architecture of the Highlands, where the traditional freestone and turf 'black house' was being replaced, first by one-storey cottages with thatched roofs and then, later in the nineteenth century, by remodelled versions of these, with slate roofs and dormer windows lighting bedrooms in the roof-space.

Most stations had a short awning, to provide some shelter, and these were at first supported by pillars, later by cantilever brackets. By the 1880s, the basic design comprised two end-blocks separated by a central range which was recessed so that a verandah roof could be built over the gap. One of the end-blocks normally had a bow-window built out on to the platform, so that platform, signals and oncoming trains could be seen from inside. This general layout was common on other railways, but the northern lines had their own typical features. At some of the local stations on the Keith line, like Orton, the stationmaster's house was the major feature, built at right angles to the platform, and with a small office extension, complete with a short verandah. At Blair Atholl, the central section was built up into a chalet-style two-storey construction, and this effect reappeared in simpler form on the Ross-shire Railway as a two-storey block, its gable at right angles to the platform, with single-storey extensions on each side. Alness, Fearn and Bonar Bridge were of this type, their overhanging roofs and ornamental barge-boards reminiscent of Swiss chalets, giving tourists an exotic and alpine impression. Sometimes the stationmaster's house was incorporated in the station buildings; sometimes it was a separate structure close by. This depended on how much space was needed for the station office: the access hall with its ticket window, the parcels office, and the waiting room, or rooms. Certain stations required first-class, or even private, waiting rooms. At Blair Atholl the duke had his own waiting room, as part of the agreed package. Grantown, with numerous local lairds, had a large first-class waiting-room. As time went on, additional buildings, toilet blocks or lamp sheds, reflected the trend to provide more amenities for passengers and a more extensive signalling system.

To the small towns and villages which they served, the stone-built stations, of brown rubble-stone or red or grey sandstone, were worthy additions. Good masonry was just as apparent in them as in the bridges and retaining walls. Mullions, window frames and door frames were cut and shaped, though the walls were made of roughly cut and squared stone blocks of varying sizes, typical of the time and region. Gables were often crow-stepped in traditional Scottish style and finished with devices like thistles, as at Aberfeldy. The most elaborate station is perhaps Pitlochry, where the influence of freemasonry has been detected in the various devices, crescent, star, and so on, used as finials (similar effects are seen at Nairn and Dingwall, where stone buildings replaced the original ones in the 1880s). Pitlochry's station was built to convey the late-Victorian feeling for the Highlands. Otherwise, special architectural effects tended to be kept for stations used by local aristocrats, like the part-baronial, part-Tudor building at Beauly, nearest station to Lord Lovat's Beaufort Castle. A special effort was made at Castle Grant, a mile and a half north of the station at Grantown, where a bridge carrying the line across a roadway was integrated with a new gatehouse and gateway for the castle. Mitchell treated it all as a single architectural unit in baronial style, complete with turrets and false battlements. Two bridges on the Invergordon line were done in special style, the handsome Alness viaduct, incorporating crenellations and a Munro crest; and the third of three contiguous bridges at Rosskeen, over the roadway to McLeod of Cadboll's Invergordon Castle, its ashlar masonry looking rather effete alongside its rough-hewn neighbours. Between Invergordon and Tain, where the railway passed through the policies of Balnagown Castle, the bridge over the river was given crenellated parapets and the owners' Cromartie and Sutherland crests. On the railways north of Bonar Bridge, no frills were allowed for, but, perhaps because of its temporary status as a terminus, Golspie, with its great tent-like pitched roof and tall chimney stack, seems almost flamboyant by comparison with the cottage-style Rogart and Helmsdale. It too had an exclusive ducal waiting-room. The biggest bridge on this section was that crossing the Oykell, at the west end of the Kyle of Sutherland, an imposing lattice girder construction of 225ft-span, 55ft above the highest spring tide level. On the opposite end of the scale, many small openings under the line, known as 'creeps', were built on all the lines to allow sheep and cows to pass or be driven under the railway; Murdoch Paterson's report to the S&C directors of 9 October 1873[6] mentions eight of these as not yet built.

With the installation of crossing loops and second platforms at more stations, the buildings on the new platforms were invariably of wood, though at some larger stations, like Pitlochry and Nairn, they were handsome pavilions rather than the utilitarian sheds and shelters found at most other places. Other buildings on the station sites were almost always of wood. Goods sheds were built over a siding, with an inner loading platform, and side doors through which items might be transferred to and from carts. Locomotives were forbidden to enter them. They normally had slated pitched roofs, sometimes hipped. Their wooden sides were painted black, or creosoted. Signal boxes were built in the same manner as the wooden station buildings, with flat plank sides, the joints protected by narrow rounded battens. They were not part of the early station scene, not being required until the HR began to install interlocking signals and points from the early 1880s.

Locomotive sheds were generally built of stone, though Howard Geddes's research into Blair Atholl's railway history shows that the first engine shed there, in 1863, was wooden,[7] but it was intended as a temporary structure. It was only after much badgering from the duke that it was replaced by a new stone-walled shed, using roofing materials from the shed at Keith, in summer 1868. The station buildings were completed at the same time, almost five years after opening of the line. The small engine sheds at Kingussie and Aberfeldy were of wood; as were, later in the nineteenth or early twentieth centuries, the sheds at Dingwall (burned down and rebuilt), Helmsdale (blown down by a gale in 1921 and replaced), Fortrose, Dornoch and Lybster. There was only one brick engine shed, at Portessie. At the company's second biggest shed, with eight tracks at the north end of Perth Station, the stone façade was replaced by a wooden one early in the twentieth century, but the stone side-walls remained. Water supplies to replenish the tender tanks had to be provided at suitable intervals along the line, usually about every ten to twelve miles, though some gaps were longer, like the fifteen and three quarter miles between Blair Atholl and Dalnaspidal, or the twenty-three and a quarter miles between Kyle of Lochalsh and Achnashellach. Water tanks were normally of iron, set high on a masonry supporting structure. In most cases, the tank supplied metal water columns, set up at the platform ends, but at a few locations, like Forsinard, the supply bag came straight from the tank. Often the Highland's water columns were fitted with built-in coal stoves, to keep the pipes from freezing in winter. Drivers had to watch the tender water-levels carefully, as sometimes supply tanks were dry. With double-headed trains, they were instructed whenever possible to use different watering points for each engine, though in the 1890s, water columns in tandem were set up for both directions at Aviemore and northbound trains at Blair Atholl.[8]

## Operations

As first built, the Highland lines were single track, eventually forming much the most extensive single-track system in Britain. Apart from the seven miles between Inverness and Dalcross, doubled in 1864, the provision for double tracking on the I&N and I&AJR was never used. Double tracking was also laid north of Inverness from Clachnaharry to Clunes (1913-14), leaving a single line over the Caledonian Canal and Ness Bridges; and progressively between Blair Atholl and Dalwhinnie on the Perth line from 1897 to 1909. The direct line, originally intended to have double track between Inverness and Culloden Moor, was built with doubling to Daviot. The maximum extent of double-track line was forty-seven miles. Outside these sections, crossing loops were required for one train to get past another. These were relatively rare at first. In 1855 there was none between Inverness and Nairn. With the opening to Forres and beyond, when two trains might be on the line at once, some form of train control was required, and by 1858, the I&AJR was using a combination of the written or printed 'Crossing Order' and telegraphic methods. The Inverness & Nairn Railway, on 19 January 1858, considered a letter from the Electric Telegraph Co. of 9 September 1857, 'for the erection of the Telegraph from Inverness to Keith'; their tender (unspecified) had been accepted after much haggling by the I&AJR,[1] and the I&N also approved it. The system was used between Keith and Elgin from the opening of the line, and extended to Inverness some weeks later.[2] The railway company opened a public telegraph office in Inverness on 22 June 1859. Most railways were still using a 'time interval' system for train despatch, and for its time, the I&AJR's was an advanced method;[3] but others usually had double-track lines. The I&AJR had above all to guard against what the Americans referred to as a 'cornfield meet': a head-on collision on the single track. Crossing orders, set out in the Working Timetable, stipulated where each train should wait until another specified train came past, or overtook, it. In the case of long delays, the normal instruction could be supplanted by changed orders telegraphed from the control centre at Inverness. The system was maintained by 'block instruments', supplied by the Electric Telegraph Co., and two of these ('Up' and 'Down'[4]) were installed at most stations, whether or not they had a crossing loop. A dial with a needle indicator represented the state of the line, with two indications: 'Line Blocked' (i.e. occupied by a train) and 'Line Clear'. A third 'Neutral' position was reverted to when no train was due. The instruments at adjacent stations were interlinked, and an electric bell operated by a plunger handle was incorporated in each instrument. The instruments at adjacent stations were interlinked. Each station could advise the next one of the arrival of a train, and the next one could accept it by 'taking block', and setting his instrument to 'Line Blocked' which would automatically be repeated on the other station's dial. Once the train had arrived at the next station, the signalman there would unpeg the needle from 'Line Blocked' and point it a few times to 'Line Clear' to indicate the change. Both instruments would then revert to the 'Neutral' indication, until a further train was signalled. There were twenty-six block sections between Wick and Inverness in 1881; five between Dingwall and Strome Ferry; twenty-three between Inverness and Perth; and six between Forres and Keith. The block instrument system was paralleled by telegraph circuits, most of them connected to Inverness. Sending messages in words, they dealt with regular company business but had some value as an emergency default system if the block telegraph failed. Each station had its own calling code. Use of telegraph messages was carefully controlled, and non-urgent communications went by letter. It is recorded, though, that Inverness could send up to 800 telegrams in one day.[5] From 1863 at least, a telegraph clerk was on duty day and night at Inverness, and the Working Timetable of 1881 records the same for Perth, except on Sundays between 6.30 p.m. and 11 p.m.

The office of the superintendent of the line, at Inverness, controlled all train movements between stations. Each train was numbered; thus in 1881: 'No. 1 UP TRAIN from Blair-Athole at 6.35 a.m. will stop at Murthly for No. 7 Down Train from Perth to pass, and must arrive at Stanley before No. 8 Down Train from Perth is allowed to pass that Junction.' The 6.35 from Blair Atholl, a mixed train, was timetabled to leave Murthly at 7.47 a.m. (as was the Down Mixed from Perth), and had thus just under seventy-two minutes to cover twenty-four and three quarter miles. But it was required to pick up wagons as necessary at Pitlochry, Ballinluig and Dunkeld. The compilers of the Working Timetables did their best to provide for every kind of routine eventuality.

The greatest problems to normal working were caused by floods and snow. Of these, flood damage was less frequent but more potentially disastrous, and the Highland was lucky to have had only one serious accident caused by a bridge washout.[6] Regular line patrol was necessary in vulnerable areas, but floods could rise with terrible speed. Apart from the Baddengorm Burn, most washouts were spotted before an accident could happen; typically, on 22 August 1866, Buttle notified a breach in the line two miles north of Dava Station, after heavy rains. It had been reported to the Dava stationmaster two hours before the 12.50 p.m. Down train was due to pass. Considering the number of rock cuttings, falling rocks appear to have been quite rare, though soon after the opening of the Sutherland & Caithness Railway, on 6 August 1874, rocks were washed onto the line in a cutting near Altnabreac, derailing the engine and first two vehicles of the 12.10 a.m. mixed train from Wick. Drifting snow was the most regular source of obstruction. The diary of William Smith,[7] a young assistant engineer employed at Inverness in the 1880s, gives a graphic account of the potential hazards of snow-clearing, from 20 January 1881, and incidentally shows that snow blockages did not only happen up in the hills (his punctuation has been modified a little):

> Hurricane Snow and drift from N.E. Fearful morning about 5 a.m. – lulled at 8 a.m., Bar rising. Left at 10.20 a.m. special for 5.40 train which was stuck in snow at Castle Stuart. Train at Newton, Engines at Castle Stuart, pushed on to Nairn where we had some heavy cutting between Lochdhu and Nairn, and stuck in cutting East of Nairn, when we had Collision with 9.30, three engines and snow plough from Forres. Terrible scene – cutting full of men busy cutting when train was heard tearing along at a fearful speed throwing the snow in all directions; just time to get the men up when clap went the Engines into our Engine that was stuck, sending it back on to our second Engine, which sent our Van and a 3 class carriage three or four hundred yards away. Four cylinders of Engines broken by Buffers but nothing off the road. Got all clear at last and started for home arriving at 7 a.m.

How two trains were admitted into the section is not explained, but presumably the telegraph line was down. The problems caused by weather could of course be human as well as operational. At the very end of 1908, the 1 a.m. goods left Wick for the south on Tuesday 30 December. It ran into heavy snowdrifts between Scotscalder and Altnabreac, and was not extracted until Saturday 3 January. A relief train from Wick was stuck between Tuesday morning and Thursday evening only two miles from the start. Passengers coming north via Helmsdale on Tuesday were unable to proceed past that station. They were offered the use of the general waiting room, 'about 10 feet square' wrote a correspondent in the *Northern Ensign*, 'and the floor swimming in water'. The first-class waiting room was kept locked; a guard was quoted as saying it was for first-class passengers only, and the rest could rough it, as he had to. There were sixteen passengers, including a mother with a month-old baby. On Thursday, the first-class waiting room was unlocked, and its fire lit. By this time several more trains had arrived from the south. Tickets through to Wick and Thurso had been on open sale for twenty-four hours after the snow block had first been advised to the superintendent. The station was becoming crowded with cold, tired and hungry people. An appeal must have gone to headquarters, as the general manager, Thomas Addy Wilson, sent a telegram to the stationmaster at Helmsdale: 'Company cannot admit any liability for home expenses'. Helmsdale villagers, and some of the passengers, helped by providing or paying for food and drink. The affair became a scandal, and the local newspapers played the story hard. Wilson was forced to respond to the torrent of complaints, and claimed, in a letter to the town clerk of Wick quoted in the *Northern Herald* of 25 February, that the first-class waiting room had been opened on Wednesday, not Thursday, though otherwise his answer was rather surprising: '... the only excuse I can make is that the Helmsdale stationmaster seems to have been utterly incompetent to deal with a situation that was without precedent'. It was reported that the stationmaster had been dismissed, and when the local MP, R.L. Harmsworth, wrote to protest about this scapegoating, Wilson simply replied, on 27 February: 'Dear Sir, I beg to acknowledge receipt of your letter of the 25th inst. Yours faithfully, T.A. Wilson.'[8]

But was he actually sacked? Exactly a year later, the *Northern Ensign* reported the retirement of 'a popular and much-respected employee of the Highland Railway Company, Mr J. Macdonald', after fifteen years at Helmsdale; '... always recognised as a most kindly and obliging official, doing his duty, sometimes under difficult circumstances, as in the case of the snow-block a year ago'.

By 1909, the Highland had long been using the electric tablet system on the main lines. It had not done so willingly or promptly; methods of train control, and running mixed trains, formed two protracted rearguard actions fought with the Board of Trade. In the former case, since the early 1860s, the Board had been pressing railways to adopt the 'train staff and ticket' system, whereby the driver of a train was provided with a staff or token to show that the line was clear for him. At the end of the section he gave up the staff and received another for the next section, and so on. The Highland Railway however, rejected the system, both for existing and new lines. Capt. Tyler had recommended it on the Dingwall extension in 1863, to no avail; and the same thing happened with the opening of the Sutherland & Caithness Railway in 1874. The company was not being wilfully obstructive: the operating officers considered the system to be unsuitable for the traffic flow and long sections between stations. Also in 1874, the Board of Trade acquired powers to compel the use of tokens on new single lines, except those worked by one engine in steam. When it insisted on the use of tokens on the Portessie line in 1884, the HR, despite having installed crossing loops, huffily applied the 'one engine in steam' principle rather than instal a token system From 1878, the electric token or tablet system became available. The tablet, a metal disc about 6in across, was stamped with the name of the section which it controlled, and was held in an electrically operated instrument which was interlocked with that of the next station. Once a tablet had been withdrawn from the instrument, neither that instrument nor the next one could be opened for the release of another tablet until the one in use had been placed in the instrument at the next station. The released tablet was carried on the engine, and it was usually the fireman's job to give it up at each station and pick up the tablet for the next section. It was a good system and was steadily improved through the 1880s. However, the HR's attitude remained founded on the fact that it had worked successfully with the block telegraph since the beginning, without a single fatality. Having been sent a draft BoT order to get the current HR view on the changes considered necessary by the Board, Andrew Dougall replied on 7 July 1890:

> ... the block system of working has been in use on this line since its commencement, 35 years ago, and has been found in every respect satisfactory. My Directors are not therefore prepared to make any change seeing that the expense would be considerable and no benefit would be given to the public.[9]

Dougall too had been working on the line for thirty-five years, and there is some reason to feel that he considered the experience-based knowledge of Inverness as superior to the theoretical and generalised wisdom of the Board of Trade experts; also some reason to feel he was becoming somewhat arbitrary in his judgements. At this time he was also defending the company's method of running mixed trains (see Chapter 12). The Black Isle branch, opened in 1894, used a combination of staff and block telegraph. It was over a year after Dougall's resignation, in 1897, that the HR used the electric interlocking tablet system for the first time, on the Aberfeldy branch and the new extension from Strome Ferry to Kyle of Lochalsh. By this time, one of the potential objections to the tablet system had been removed. Many HR trains ran non-stop through crossing loops and small stations, at quite a smart pace, and to slow down or even stop for a manual exchange of tokens would add substantially to train timings. But in 1893, James Manson, then the locomotive superintendent of the Great North of Scotland Railway, with John Duncan, a blacksmith at the Inverurie Works, had developed a column-mounted, lever-operated automatic tablet-catcher which could exchange tablets at speeds of up to 50mph. What is more, the philanthropic Manson had refused to take out a patent on the device: it was free to use in the interest of safety.[10] In 1898 tablets were installed betweeen Aviemore and Daviot, between Keith and Mulben, and between Forres and Aviemore. The change was speedy: by the summer of 1899, virtually the whole main-line system was being worked by electric tablet, of Tyer's No.6 design, using a combination of manual exchange, with the tablet in a hooped pouch, and automatic exchange by Manson's tablet-catcher, with the tablet in a stout leather case. From that time all main-line locomotives were fitted with tablet-catcher gear on the left-hand cab side.[11] The 'tablet wire' between stations was also used to enable adjacent stations to communicate by telephone on traffic matters.

Between 1890 and 1910, the majority of HR stations had taken on the appearance that they would retain until the implementation of closures in the 1960s and after. All had once had only a single platform, even where there was a crossing loop (a situation later perpetuated only at The Mound). They now presented a neat pattern of twin platforms with paved edges, lamp-posts, normally oil-lit but occasionally by acetylene or town gas; a latticed iron pedestrian bridge (most of them made by Rose Street Foundry in Inverness), tablet-catcher posts, two signal boxes and a set of semaphore signal posts, starting a mile or so out from the station itself. Much of this 'traditional' scene was actually very new in the 1890s, following an extensive modernising process that, as we have seen, embraced the train control system but extended far beyond that. The first overbridges linking platforms were put up at Pitlochry and Nairn in 1884, coincidental with the rebuilding of the stations, and it was at least 1910 before all two-platform stations had bridges.[19] Dunkeld Station, which had kept its original overall roof until 1878, lost it when the Down platform was extended. In 1879 the wooden building at Aberfeldy was destroyed by fire and a new stone building was put up. New stone buildings were also put up at Dingwall in 1886, Kingussie in 1891, with an elaborate wide awning and end screens, and Brora in 1895 (following a fire: hence the difference between its pavilion-and-colonnade style and the other

Sutherland stations). In all these cases, the buildings on the facing platform remained, or were rebuilt, of wood. Fires at wooden stations were always a hazard, and not always accidents; among others burned down were Burghead (1871), Struan, Strome Ferry in 1891, when its overall roof was destroyed; Newtonmore in 1893, and Muir of Ord in 1921 when an arsonist destroyed the buildings on both platforms.

HR signal posts were generally of squared wood, very ocasionally of latticed iron, in both cases painted white, and topped by an elegant bulb-and-spire finial. In the early decades, provision of signals was very sparse and they, like points, were normally operated by adjacent levers, sometimes in the open, sometimes in a tiny 'pointsman's box'. Since many of the company's improvements were made after heavy nudging by the Board of Trade's railway inspectorate, it is pleasing to record that its adoption of interlocking points and signals appears to have been a spontaneous move. Minor collisions at stations were quite frequent, sometimes resulting in passenger injuries and consequent claims. One of the first of these, at Pitlochry on 14 October 1865, when Up and Down trains collided, resulted in a stream of compensation claims which took almost two years to settle. From the late 1870s the board increased the extent of interlocking.[13] The purpose of the interlocking lever frame was to ensure that no unsafe combination of point-setting and signals could be made. Thus a signal cannot be made to show the line is clear if the points are not set accordingly. Some crossing loops required only one signal box, but most needed two, as Board of Trade regulations limited the distance between mechanically worked points and the levers to 180 yards. In 1881 a tender was accepted from Mackenzie & Holland of Worcester for interlocking at eight stations on the Perth line, and the process was extended through the 1880s. First to be interlocked were not the bigger stations, but the smaller ones with more non-stop trains.

At certain stations like Altnabreac, Dalnaspidal, and Killiecrankie, the signal wires were carried on high posts rather than the conventional ground-level arrangement. This has been seen as a precaution against snow, but wires to the distant signals were not raised. As a more obvious snow protection, the rods which worked the points were often enclosed in wooden casing. Digging out the points and keeping them free of snow and ice was always a prime task of station staff when snow fell. Out on the open moors, snow fences were put up from the mid-1860s. In his half-yearly report of 28 February 1866, Buttle noted that 1,700 yards of snow fence had been erected at Dava, and 1,400 yards between Dalwhinnie and Dalnaspidal. Long stretches of these fences were also set up on the Sutherland & Caithness line. Constructed of old sleepers, they were set well back from the railway, to block the movement of drifting snow towards the track. A more scientific device was the patent 'snow-blower' devised in 1889 by W.L. Howie, a pair of long wooden facings set at an angle within the walls of a cutting, which effectively maintained the wind force and pressure across the line so that snow deposits did not build up. One of these was installed near Altnabreac. Another was also found to be extremely useful on the Burghead branch, where the problem was not snow, but drifting sand from the coastal dunes.[14]

# NINE

*Motive Power – the Early Years*

The Highland Railway at its biggest owned 173 locomotives and in its almost seventy-year history, it acquired or built a total of 247. This relatively modest number, combined with the intrinsic interest of many of the locomotive classes involved, has meant that the company's engines have been more intensively studied, recorded and discussed than any other aspect of the business. Over the years a number of specialist books have been devoted to Highland engines, apart from many articles in railway and engineering journals. With such detailed works available, the present book gives only an overview of the subject, and owes a substantial debt to the Cormack and Stevenson volumes and the Stephenson Locomotive Society's chronological listing, in particular. In the sixty-seven years between the inauguration of the Inverness & Nairn Railway and the grouping of 1 January 1923, three distinct phases of locomotive development can be traced; the early era, from Alexander Allan to William Stroudley; the classic era of David Jones and Peter Drummond; and the 'modern' era from F.G. Smith to the Highland's last locomotive superintendent, D.C. Urie.

Allan, born in Montrose, had learned his trade as a wheelwright there before moving to Liverpool and later Crewe. He joined the Scottish Central in 1853, and his involvement with Inverness began from December 1854. The early locomotives of the I&N and the I&AJR were all of his design, or selection, and followed his established practice. They were small and lightweight (around 27 tons without the tender) 2-2-2 engines of the 'Crewe' type – with double frames; the cylinders mounted between the frames, and the wheels attached to the inside frame – which would typify most Highland engines for decades to come. The downward curve of the smokebox front was extended outwards to encompass the cylinders, giving a rather pear-shaped look when viewed from the front. The single driving wheels were of 6ft diameter, boiler diameter was 3ft 7in at the maximum and steam pressure was a relatively modest 100psi. Allan's own form of 'straight-link' motion or valve gear was used on these and on all subsequent HR locomotives with outside cylinders until 1915. A tall thin chimney with a neat rim-cap was fitted. There was no cab for the enginemen, only a so-called 'weather board' offering a little frontal protection. A tradition of the line was inaugurated by naming both I&N engines after directors, *Raigmore* (Eneas Mackintosh) and *Aldourie* (Fraser-Tytler) respectively: Highland proprietors were eponymous with their estates. On 8 August 1856 Joseph Mitchell reported to the I&AJR Board that he had been in touch with Allan on the matter of locomotives for the extended line: 'His opinion is that for the Mail and Passenger trains one could not have a better engine than the present one now in use between Inverness and Nairn'. Nos 3 and 4, from the same builders, Hawthorns of Leith, and supplied in 1856 and 1857 respectively, followed the same design. The cost of No.4 was £967 10s. Both the I&N and the I&AJR had their engines painted dark green, with black retaining bands on the boiler.

Allan had also submitted a tracing of a goods design in a style he felt suitable for the severer gradients of the Keith line. Between February and September 1858 the company's first six goods engines were delivered, again from Hawthorns. These were of 2-4-0 configuration, with coupled wheels of 5ft diameter. Though from 1882 the HR would give up naming its goods engines, these carried names and were known as the 'Seafield' class after the first to be delivered: the others were also named after directors. In line with what seems to have been typical Scottish practice at the time, the goods engines had steam domes while the passenger engines were domeless. The 'Seafields' had a boiler pressure of 120psi and their estimated tractive effort was greater, though their adhesion weight (that resting on the driving axles) was about a ton less than that of *Raigmore*. As most of the I&AJR trains were mixed, it is likely that the 'Seafields' ran as much on passenger as on freight service. The early engines had been fitted with Clark's Patent Consuming Apparatus to minimise their output of smoke, but in April 1861 the board agreed on a comparative trial with a locomotive whose firebox had been fitted with a brick arch, as developed on the Midland railway by 1860; and following this a Locomotive Committee Meeting of 8 November 1861 agreed that the consuming apparatus could be dispensed with.[1]

Eleven locomotives were sufficient to maintain services until 1862, when the opening of the Ross-shire line as far as Dingwall brought further demand for motive power. Two more 2-2-2s, *Belladrum* and *Lovat*, and two 2-4-0s, Nos 14 and 15, came from Hawthorns. Both pairs were essentially slightly modified versions of the 'Raigmore' and 'Seafield' classes; the passenger engines had their boiler pressure raised to a still fairly modest 120psi. *Belladrum* and its sister were the first to come fitted with cabs for the engine crew, with short, domed roofs. The goods engines lacked this amenity. In 1862 the I&AJR also acquired its first tank engine, the little 0-4-0T that had belonged to the Findhorn Railway, which became No.16. A second tank was bought from Hawthorns in 1863, an off-the-peg purchase at £1,475, with the Burghead branch in mind. The company's first inside-cylinder engine, it was an 0-4-0 with side tanks, and operated on the Burghead line until 1873.

At this point it may be useful to note that, as befitted a line which had to operate economically and conserve its cash, old engines rarely died on the Highland Railway. Nor did they entirely fade away. Lochgorm Works never threw anything away, and, over the years, the early members of the locomotive fleet underwent considerable change, in some cases more akin to resurrection. Spare part surgery was a speciality, and by the time a Highland engine was sold for scrap, one can be sure that every possibility of use had been exhausted. To narrate the history of every locomotive is impossible, but the two pioneers, Nos 1 and 2, were converted into 2-4-0 engines in 1869, and *Aldourie* was thoroughly rebuilt in 1871, emerging in Cormack and Stevenson's view as 'to all intents and purposes a new engine' though retaining the wheels and the outside framing of the original. In October 1894 it was again rebuilt, with a reconditioned boiler and firebox, while its own already venerable boiler was transferred to another engine, and it was finally withdrawn in 1903. The longevity of boilers on the Highland engines was unusual, and can be traced to the soft and pure water available at almost all the company's depots and watering points, which minimised scaling and furring of the tubes. Many of the Highland's locomotives of the 1860s and '70s, especially those built or rebuilt at the company's own works, were, or became, equipped with various body parts from older engines. Quite apart from the genuine economies achieved by this practice, 'rebuilding' gave the company a new engine without having to debit the capital account, which was always closely scrutinised by shareholders; instead the cost disappeared among the innumerable charges against operating costs. Such creative accounting was by no means exclusive to the Highland.

Preparations for the direct line to Perth brought about the locomotive conference between Dougall and Allan in June 1862, surprisingly with no director recorded as being present, considering the capital expenditure at issue. Dougall was certainly no engineer, and the resultant engines were Alexander Allan's response to the challenge of Dava Moor and Struan Bank. The passenger engines were 2-2-2s, forming the 'Glenbarry' class. They weighed 31 tons, of which 14 rested on the single driving axle, with 6ft 1.5in wheels. Boiler pressure remained at 120psi. They were fitted with Giffard injectors to force feedwater into the boiler; these were still a novelty in 1862, but in other respects the engines were not at the cutting edge of design. With the new goods engines of the same year, they were the first I&AJR locomotives to have six-wheel tenders, giving in their case a capacity of 3.75 tons of coal and 1,800 gallons of water against the 2.5 tons and 1,200 gallons of the four-wheel tenders fitted to the 'Seafields'. The 'Glenbarrys' had small, squared cabs with flattened-dome roofs. They were quite inadequate for any but the lightest trains on the new main line; their lack of adhesive weight and tractive power making it very difficult to start, or maintain speed, on gradients, especially if the rails were wet or icy. On the Great North, Robert Cowan was already building 4-4-0s for a less demanding route. Nevertheless, by the end of 1864 there were eighteen of the 'Glenbarrys', by far the company's largest class, to struggle up what was already known as 'The Hill' from Struan.

The companion class was the 'Small Goods' 2-4-0, built by Sharp, Stewart, in Manchester, ten-strong by November 1863, and numbered from 18-27. These were enlarged and more powerful versions of the 'Seafields', with coupled wheels of 5ft 1.5in diameter. Boiler pressure was upped to 150psi, and although the amount of heating surface was slightly less than in their predecessors (1,164sq. ft compared to 1,188.75), their firebox grate area was 16sq. ft against 12.5sq. ft, and their nominal tractive effort, at 13,181lbs, was over 37 per cent more. Though many later alterations were made, they were Allan's best contribution to the Inverness stable. All the 'Small Goods' class had names, from stations on the direct line and the Ross-shire Railway. One of them, No.21, was the only HR engine to suffer a boiler explosion, on 4 January 1872, a mile beyond Fochabers Station, while hauling the 6 a.m. Inverness–Keith goods. The driver and fireman were seriously injured, and a brakeman on the footplate, John Gerrie, was killed. Wreckage was flung up to 300 yards away. Defective condition of the stays on the left side of the firebox was identified as the prime reason, but some stays had been renewed two months previously, and maintenance in general seems to have been good. The *Elgin Courant* of 5 January reported that clearing up was rapid: 'About fifty surfacemen arrived from Inverness, with all the necessary implements for the occasion'.[2]

So far, locomotives had been numbered in sequence of acquisition, but certain names were from an early stage regarded as transferable. Among the 'Glenbarry' class a new *Seafield* appeared, and the original bearer of the name became *Tain*. Renaming locomotives was a propensity of the Highland, which seems to have done it mainly in order not to have its directors identified with the more elderly engines; and also sometimes to reinforce the local identity of a branch engine. Thus there were four *Sutherlands*, five *Bruces* and three *Lovats*, each taking the name from an earlier engine. The first *Strathpeffer*, named to run the new branch in 1885, had already been *Belladrum* until 1864 and then rebuilt as a 2-2-2 tank engine, *Breadalbane*, for the Aberfeldy branch in 1871, and it lost its name to another *Strathpeffer* in 1890; this in turn was renamed *Lybster* on its transference in rebuilt form to the Wick & Lybster Light Railway in 1903. One had also to be aware of the nuances of nomenclature in the Highlands: *Caithness*, first used on an engine in 1864, was in honour of the eponymous earl, but was renamed *Blair Atholl* in 1874, at a time when Lord Caithness and the Highland Railway were temporarily not friends; *Caithness-shire*, used in 1874 on a Class F 4-4-0, was for the county, though at an unknown point (perhaps when the earl became a director of the S&CR); this engine's name was altered to *Caithness*. In a similar way, the company could simultaneously have a *Sutherland* and a *Sutherlandshire*.[3]

On 24 September 1863, the I&AJR Board authorised the purchase of a further ten 2-4-0 goods engines, the Class 36 or 'Medium Goods'. The differences from the 'Small Goods' were scarcely great enough to merit the title and scarcely worth the cost of having to maintain separate sets of spare parts, like coupling rods 3in longer, though the coupled wheels were the same diameter in both classes. These were also built by Sharp, Stewart, and delivered with promptitude between April and June 1964. All carried names (of stations) for a time; the last of the line's goods engines to do so. Their haulage capacity was rated the same as that of the 'Small Goods' – twenty loaded wagons or 200 tons unaided up 'The Hill'. Both goods types were often used as pilot engines to assist passenger and mixed trains, and as snowplough engines.

Allan, from his Perth base, and Barclay remained in charge of locomotive affairs for ten years. But Barclay's fall from grace in May 1865 also spelled the end of Allan's design involvement, though he continued for a time to be a locomotive broker for the company, reporting in November 1865 that he had got Dübs of Glasgow to agree to cancel an order for the Aberfeldy branch engine on condition they got the next order. The new locomotive superintendent, William Stroudley, had no need of a consultant – not only because of his professional abilities but because the company had neither space nor money for more locomotives. He inherited a stock of fifty-five engines, of which thirty-eight were less than two years old. Between October 1864 and February 1869 no new locomotives were added to the roster; and only one was added in 1869. This was the sole engine designed and built in Stroudley's four-and-a-half-year term of office, a small 0-6-0T, numbered 56 and named *Balnain*, the first locomotive built at Lochgorm Works. Its boiler, which had to be shortened, came from the 'Raigmore' class No.3, *St Martins*, now retired. Frames and cylinders were bought in. *Balnain* and two broadly similar engines, *Lochgorm* and *St Martins* (1872 and 1874 respectively) are of interest to locomotive historians as precursors of Stroudley's famous 'Terriers' on the London Brighton & South Coast Railway: to the Highland they were its first shunting engines, and they had lengthy lives. Later renamed *Dornoch* and *Fort George*, the first and third were the inaugural engines on those respective branches. *Lochgorm* was at work, mostly around the yards at Inverness, for sixty years. In 1869 Stroudley also 'rebuilt' the company's No.1, *Raigmore*, as a 2-4-0, of increased power, and fitted it with the prototype of the Highland's big, sheltering cab. The locomotive superintendent was responsible for locomotive running and managing all aspects of the department, so Stroudley was probably busy enough without making new designs. One important change he made was to have steel rather than wrought-iron tyres fitted to the locomotives' driving wheels; this was done in 1867 at a cost of £15,434, which would have been repaid by much longer running. But his duties at Lochgorm cannot have been over-taxing, and he found time to devise one of the first methods of locking facing points, for greater safety. The Highland Board corresponded with the Board of Trade about this (one of the few discussions between the two bodies to be initiated by the railway) and it was patented, but it does not seem to have been widely used. Stroudley's locks were recorded as fitted at Broomhill, Boat of Garten, Boat of Insh (Kincraig), Guay, and Dalguise, all on the Forres–Perth line.

More useful in the end was Stroudley's prompt reaction to the board's plea for better snowploughs after the almost week-long blockages of February 1866. On 8 March the board asked him and Buttle, the civil engineer, for, '… any suggestions which occur to them with reference to improving the appliances which the Company have for clearing the Line'. Barclay had already built snowploughs for attachment to locomotives, one of them described in the *Nairnshire Telegraph* of 22 February 1865 as, 'consisting simply of two sheets of iron, five feet in height, rivetted together in the form of a wedge'. Stroudley applied his scientific intelligence to the question and provided three models – Small, Medium, and Large. On 20 March 1865 he was authorised to build new ploughs and adapt the old ones. 'Small' fitted under the engine's front buffer-beam. 'Medium' was attached to the buffer beam and smokebox sides, and rose to about half the height of the smokebox. Both of these were used on locomotives as they hauled trains. 'Large' was a massive plough reaching a height of 11ft 3in, secured to the frame and smokebox sides. Engines fitted to carry it had an additional upper lamp bracket fixed to the chimney, as the lamp at the smokebox top would have been completely hidden. The ploughs were made of solid 3in-wood planking mounted on a strong timber frame, and the largest model was reinforced with iron plates on its sloping and 'cut-water' faces. The small plough, travelling at about 25mph, could clear drifts up to 2ft deep; the middle size could clear 5ft. These two both fitted within the loading gauge, but the large plough's maximum width was 11ft 9in, and its outer side pieces had to be hinged in order to avoid fouling platform faces and other lineside fixtures.[4] Though they were locomotive attachments without independent wheels, three snowploughs (presumably the Large version) were included separately in the Carriage List given in the next half-yearly report.[5] Stroudley's ploughs gave the company excellent service for many years. A report in the *John o' Groat Journal*, of snow-clearing in Caithness later in the century, refers to the big plough as 'Leviathan'[6]; there is no other evidence for this name, which may be a journalist's invention. But surviving photographs leave no doubt of the awesome visual impact of the big plough being forced at speed through drifts (known then as 'wreaths') by up to four engines. Other photographs show that even so, it sometimes got stuck.

### Motive Power – the Classic Era

In January 1870, David Jones was aged thirty-six and had been employed at Lochgorm since 1855, when he had been taken on as a driver. He had been apprenticed at Longsight, in his native Manchester, with a brilliant chief in John Ramsbottom; then with the London & North Western at Crewe. Although the opening of the Dingwall & Skye line was imminent, it was not deemed to require additional locomotives and the Locomotive Committee's brief to Jones was unchanged, to keep the existing engines in repair and running order. The works extensions and new tools supplied in 1865 eased this task considerably, but Jones, with a limited staff, was always keen on making maintenance as easy as possible. One of the first general tasks was to follow up on Stroudley's last recommendation, which the board had approved on 4 January 1870: this was to fit the Le Chatelier steam brake to the company's engines, at an estimated cost of £2 apiece. This form of braking, devised by an eminent French engineer, seems to have been successful on the HR. It enabled the driver to slow his train on long downhill stretches by admitting steam into the cylinders to retard the pistons. The board also authorised him to introduce lateral movement to engine axles, to reduce wear and tear on curves.[1] In 1872 Jones converted the 2-2-2 *Glenbarry* to a 2-4-0; two more followed in 1873, and ten more were given the same treatment between 1874 and 1881. In 1873 a 'Seafield' 2-4-0, No.10 *Westhall*, was fitted with a four-wheel bogie, to a design established by William Adams, then of the North London Railway, making it the first Highland engine with a non-rigid wheelbase. Renamed *Duncraig*, the new 4-4-0 was tried out on the Strome Ferry line and found much more suitable to its sharp curves than the rigid-framed 2-4-0s. A second conversion, of No.7, was made in 1875. The following year saw the opening to Wick and further engines were now certainly required; these were Jones's first locomotive class, the 4-4-0 type variously known as 'F', '60' and 'Duke'. The board had approved the construction of six new engines on 1 October 1872, and this was increased to ten, all built by Dübs & Co. of Glasgow, at £3,470 each, and delivered between June and August 1874. Scotland had been the proving-ground of the 4-4-0 in Britain, but Jones's engines, now and later, did not follow the conventional form. In yet another of those interesting resemblances between the HR and colonial and North American lines, he opted to retain outside cylinders. Almost all British designers of the time used inside cylinders, whose hidden drive, though less accessible for maintenance, and prone to crank-axle breakages, was admired for its 'effortless' effect with the engine in motion. David Jones's sturdy 4-4-0s and their successors flailed along with no inhibitions about showing where the driving force came from. Only the valve gear, retaining the Allan link motion, was inside the frames. The front four wheels were mounted on an Adams bogie. Driving wheel diameter was 6ft 3in, and the original boiler pressure was 140psi. A soon-to-be-familiar feature was a more substantial chimney than hitherto, with a set of horizontal louvres cut in its frontal arc. Inside the outer chimney was the exhaust pipe, and Jones's theory was that air rushing in through the louvres would rise up in the interstitial space and help lift the exhaust smoke and steam, which on long downhill grades might otherwise impede the driver's vision. He stuck manfully to the design for the rest of his career, but no other railway ever took it up. Above the blast-pipe was also a cone-shaped wire spark arrestor, a response to the board's anxiety over lineside fires. This problem is first recorded as being referred to the locomotive superintendent on 7 October 1865, following a complaint from McLeod of Cadboll that some of his dry grass had been set on fire. The new engines were a definite success and set the basic pattern for Highland main line engines for twenty years. A further seven, with minor modifications, were built in Inverness at intervals between 1876 and 1888. These were known as the 'Lochgorm Bogies'; though the first of the set was a nominal rebuild of original No.4, the 2-2-2 *Ardross* of 1857, the others were new.

Bogie engines were more expensive than 2-4-0s, and it was at the board's behest that Jones built two engines of the latter configuration in 1877 for use on the Ross-shire line. For accounting purposes they were considered rebuilds of locomotives Nos 1 and 3 of 1855-56, and the wheels of old *Raigmore*, though padded out with steel tyres to 6ft 3in, continued to revolve on the new engine of the same name. The same wheel arrangement was adopted for three shunting tank engines built at Lochgorm, one at the end of 1878 and two in 1879, though they were later converted to 4-4-0T for branch line working, the first in 1885, the second two in 1887. One of these, No.59, which carried the name *Highlander*, was the last engine with the old Crewe-style front to survive, being withdrawn in 1933.

On 5 October 1880 the directors saw fit to draw the locomotive superintendent's attention to the number of accidents being caused by locomotive breakdowns.

Jones's response is not recorded, but he might well have reflected on his ageing stud of converted and unconverted 2-2-2s, some of them over twenty years old. Although two converted bogie engines had been running on the Strome road since 1875, it was 1882 before this line, with its limited traffic, had its locomotive requirements looked at again. From September 1880 the D&SR had been merged with the Highland and a more ambitious timetable of two trains each way was in operation. A single new 4-4-0, No.70, was introduced in 1882 and became the prototype of Class L, the 'Skye Bogies'. Though small-wheeled, with 5ft 3.5in-drivers, and not designed for speed, these were actually more powerful and heavier than the 'Dukes': weighing 43 tons compared to the 'Dukes'' 42 tons. They proved excellent performers on the Skye line. Eventually the class numbered seven, with Lochgorm turning out one a year between 1892 and 1895, two in 1897 (year of the extension to Kyle of Lochalsh), and the last in 1898. This one, No.7, later renumbered 34, was also the last to survive; with a handful of 'Straths' it continued to display the old Jones-style rounded front end, and outside frames, until the middle of 1930. Though they were mixed-traffic engines, the 'Skye Bogies' were not named. They ran most services, but did not monopolise the line, and 'Dukes' and 'Lochgorm Bogies' made occasional appearances.

By 1886 the Highland Railway had eighteen 4-4-0s on its books, and a further eight passenger engines were added with the Class E or 'Clyde Bogies' of that year. The first engines to be built by the Clyde Locomotive Works in Glasgow (later taken over by Sharp, Stewart when they moved from Manchester), they were a development of the 'F' class, with which they shared cylinders, motion and frames. The boilers were shorter, with slightly less heating surface (1,140sq. ft in total, compared to 1,228sq. ft, but, pressed to 160psi, they delivered rather more power). The price of the 'Clyde Bogies', £2,395 apiece, seems a bargain. They were the first Highland engines to be fitted with vacuum brakes from the start, and incorporated a standard feature of the Jones main line engines, a joint in the upright brake pipe where it was fixed to the front buffer-beam, enabling it to be laid back in a horizontal position. The reason for this was operational, to make it easier for the fireman to reach the coupling when detaching a pilot engine without stopping. The feature was retained on main line engines to the 'Clans' of 1919-21.

Something of a curiosity in Jones's otherwise very consistent design development was a small inside-cylindered 0-4-4 saddle tank engine built at Lochgorm in 1890 for use on the Strathpeffer branch. Nothing quite like it was seen on the HR before or afterwards. In 1901 it was substantially rebuilt and in this form went to work the new Wick & Lybster Light Railway in 1903. It survived until 1930. A chance to increase the company's stock of tank engines for branch working was seized in 1892, when Dübs suffered cancellation of an order for five 4-4-0 tanks by the Uruguay Eastern Railway. Two were already built, and the HR tried them out, found them satisfactory, and bought them for a bargain £1,500 each. The other three followed in 1893. Known as the 'American' and later 'Yankee' Tanks, their outside cylinders made them look quite at home on the Highland system, though they did not have the bulbous front end and had inside frames. The unmistakable Jones line was back with a new class of twelve passenger engines, also in 1892, the 'Straths'. Their cylinders, 18in x 24in and their 6ft 3in–driving wheels were standard with the 'Dukes', 'Clydes' and 'Skye Bogies' and the double frames were as used on the 'Clyde Bogies'. But the boiler was larger. Most were named after straths and glens, though the first two, *Sir George* and *Tweeddale*, were named after directors: Sir George Macpherson-Grant and the Marquis of Tweeddale. Their arrival coincided with the increased traffic requirement following the opening of the Carrbridge route from Aviemore.

By 1895 the HR had forty-four 4-4-0 locomotives. Only ten of the engines built since 1855 had been sold, scrapped or withdrawn, though one sole veteran, the 2-2-2 No.32 of 1863, was still running without reboilering or other significant alteration (it was scrapped in 1898). Only three single-driver engines remained in 1895, one of them a tank engine. Forty-two 2-4-0s were still in service, hauling goods trains. But over the next few years the ranks of the oldest locomotives would be reduced more rapidly. The policy in introducing new passenger locomotives was to employ them on the Inverness–Perth line, where trains were heaviest and traffic most intensive; and to pass older types on to the Keith and Wick lines and the branches.

Stationing and route availability of locomotives were also conditioned by the length of turntables. The line was quite well equipped with these, but they were of varying length. Twenty-seven locations had turntables in 1901, but these ranged from the 60ft one at Inverness to the 18ft one at Golspie, installed to turn *Dunrobin*. The total wheelbase of a 'Big Goods' was 48ft 5.5in, and in 1901 it could not have worked beyond Helmsdale on the North Line, as Wick had a turntable of 46ft 3in diameter and Thurso's was slightly shorter. Wick got a 55ft turntable in 1902. The turntable at Kyle of Lochalsh was 50ft, which meant that the passenger 4-6-0s were too long for it. The 'Clans' were of 50ft wheelbase, but positioning one on a turntable of identical length would have been tricky. The Kyle turntable was also cut from solid rock, allowing little room for overhang.

In 1894 Jones had been locomotive superintendent for almost twenty-five years and his work had been of immense benefit to the company. Apart from passenger and goods vehicles, he had provided it with a series of standard engines of quality and reliability comparable with best practice on other British railways, and less costly in maintenance; he had rebuilt nearly all the old locomotives; and had presided over an effective running department which even in an era of well-kept engines was celebrated for the spick-and-span appearance of its locomotive fleet. He was sixty in that year, and marked it by a radical new departure in his own work. To replace the fast wearing-out 2-4-0s on goods service, he produced a design for the largest and most powerful locomotive yet to work in Great Britain. This was the 'Big Goods' 4-6-0. Engines of this wheel arrangement had been built in Britain before, but only for export; it was considered a rather 'American' type. Undoubtedly a large part in the design was played by Jones's chief draughtsman, David Hendrie, who had been apprenticed at Lochgorm, and acquired valuable experience with Glasgow builders before returning to his home town in 1893 (he eventually became locomotive superintendent of the Natal Government Railway). On American and colonial railways, 4-6-0s were invariably fitted with outside cylinders, and Jones's preference for these probably encouraged him to embark on the six-coupled design. The board approved the purchase of fifteen in January 1894 and within a month, Sharp, Stewart's tender of £2,795 each was accepted. By July, five engines were ready and all were finished before the end of the year. The distinctive but by now old-fashioned Crewe front end and double frames were abandoned, for a long steel boiler set on inside frames, though Jones's louvred chimney was retained. The cylinders, 20in x 26in, were tucked under the running plate and the smokebox front paid a small but elegant gesture to former practice with curved wing-plates on each side. Though said to stabilise the structure, they were frequently removed in later years. The initial boiler pressure of the 'Big Goods' was 170psi, and the coupled-wheel diameter was 5ft 3.5in, the same as with the 'Skye Bogies'. Total engine weight was 56 tons and they put 42 tons of adhesion weight on the track. Alarm was caused in the summer of 1894 when trials of the first two engines suggested that they were incapable of steaming effectively. After intense activity between the locomotive department and the builders, the problem was traced to the exhaust blast-pipe. The dimensions of this vital orifice were altered and retested until Jones was satisfied and the engines were accepted. The class was a triumphant success, and though largely employed on goods trains, all fifteen were fitted with vacuum brakes for passenger working, and remained in main line action for forty years. Ernest Lemon, a vice-president of the LMS Railway, who worked for a time at Lochgorm early in his career, remarked of the 'Big Goods' that, 'I have never known a locomotive which was so simple to dismantle or to re-erect or so light on repairs as the "Jones Goods"'.[2] In Lemon's estimation, Jones was far ahead of his time as a practitioner of standardisation and accessibility. Despite being the Highland's most celebrated class, as goods engines they never received names. The first to be delivered, No.103, is the only Highland locomotive to be preserved.

Another one-off buy-in was that in 1895 of the little Kitson 2-4-0T *Dunrobin*, which had been stabled at Golspie to work the Duke of Sutherland's saloon (and occasional local HR services between Golspie and Wick) since 1874. It was sent to Sharp, Stewart for rebuilding as a side-tank engine, and on return was numbered 118, named *Gordon Castle* and put to work for a time on the Fochabers branch. Jones introduced a new 4-4-0 passenger class in 1896, which was intended to do for express services what the 'Big Goods' was doing for freight. There were fifteen, all built by Dübs & Co., at £2,940 each, and all delivered by September 1896. In appearance they followed the goods engines, though their shorter length and marginally smaller boiler diameter (4ft 7in compared to 4ft 9in) gave them a less rangy appearance. Boiler pressure was 175psi and the driving wheels the standard 6ft 3.5in. As built, they had piston valves, the most up-to-date form of valve-gear control, but these were not wholly satisfactory in operation, and were replaced by balanced slide valves by the end of 1899. Named after lochs, the class leader being No.119 *Loch Insh*, they were among the most powerful passenger engines of the day, and went into service on the southern main line. Twenty years after the class had first appeared, three new 'Lochs' were built to the order of the wartime Railway Executive, in 1916, to help relieve pressure on the Highland's locomotive stock. The 'Lochs' were not the end of David Jones's plans for Highland locomotives, but he was not destined to bring any more to fruition. While out on a test run on 7 September 1894 with one of the 'Big Goods' he suffered severe scalding to one of his legs, and his health was so weakened that he resigned from the HR on 31 October 1896. Hamilton Ellis records that in 1890, he had refused an offer to succeed Stroudley as chief mechanical engineer at Brighton.[3] His departure from Inverness, after almost forty years, was much regretted;[4] both as a manager and an engineer, his record had been outstanding.

His successor was Peter Drummond, a forty-eight-year old Glaswegian, assistant works manager at the Caledonian Railway's St Rollox works in Glasgow. He was not the first Drummond at Lochgorm; his elder brother Dugald had been works manager under Stroudley. Dugald was now the imperious locomotive chief on the London & South Western Railway, but, rather like certain Renaissance artists, he maintained a sort of family *scuola* in which common techniques and devices might be employed. His reputation in his day was greater than it has been since, and the Highland Board may have felt reassurance in the closeness of the brothers' working relationship. In the event, Peter Drummond gave the Highland some very good engines. He has been criticised for changing company design to inside-cylinder locomotives, of the standard Drummondish appearance which his masterful elder brother had left imprinted on the North British and Caledonian, but these were what he knew most about. Peter Drummond's first Highland class was a passenger 4-4-0 type introduced in 1898 and known from 1908 as the 'Small Bens'. In *Scottish Locomotive History*, Campbell Highet remarked that, 'These were so similar to the new engines his brother had just put into service on the L&SWR that they might be considered to have been made from the same drawings'.[5] As the latter were the famous T9 'Greyhounds', the Highland was unlikely to complain; nor does it appear that the South Western was troubled by the resemblance. The 'Small Bens' dispensed with the Jones louvred chimney, and replaced Allan's valve gear with Stephenson link motion; their coupled wheels were 6ft in diameter, and their working pressure 175psi. Three were built by Dübs in 1898, eight (five by Dübs, three at Lochgorm) at various stages in 1899, three at Lochgorm in 1900, and three more in 1901, and the final three by the North British Locomotive Co. in 1906 (NBL was formed by Dübs, Neilson, Reid & Co., and Sharp, Stewart in 1904). They worked principally on the Aberdeen and Wick lines. The first of the class was briefly named *Ben Nevis,* until second thoughts prevailed: Scotland's highest mountain was well outside Highland Railway territory. *Ben y-Gloe* was substituted before the locomotive entered service: the Highland was not short of mountains of its own.

Drummond, who had reported to the board that seventeen of the 2-4-0 goods engines were worn out and needed replacing, made a useful addition to the goods service with a class of six 0-6-0 engines delivered by Dübs in February 1900 and supplemented by four more in 1902. With 5ft-driving wheels, they shared the motion, boilers and tenders (the 1900 batch) of the 'Small Bens'. Boiler pressure was 175psi. The 1902 engines had Dugald Drummond's patent type of water-tube firebox installed. A further two more came from NBL in 1907. The Highland 0-6-0s from an early stage acquired the nickname of 'Barneys'. Another Drummond innovation on the Highland was an eight-wheel tender with inside bearings; these were interchangeably attached to the 'Barneys' and 'Bens'. The eight-wheel tender weighed 40 tons, and held 5 tons of coal and 3,200 gallons of water; the six-wheel version weighed 37 tons, also held 5 tons of coal, but 3,000 gallons of water. The 'Barneys', costing £2,750 each for the first six, were of course new engines, but the later six, with the cosmetic attachment of the numbers previously carried by scrapped 2-4-0s, were charged to revenue. Their use was chiefly on the Keith and Wick lines, and they frequently did snow-clearing service with the medium plough. Cormack and Stevenson quote a pleasant story from the *People's Journal* of 25 January 1958 about a trout which lived in the tender tank of a 'Barney' for five years between 1909 and 1914, fed by the enginemen.[6] The longest-surviving 0-6-0 was No.136, of the 1900 batch, withdrawn in January 1952.

'Peter Drummond's best locomotives were the 4-6-0 Castles, first built in 1900, of which he designed the tenders', wrote Hamilton Ellis, rather unfairly.[7] In all crucial respects this was Jones's design, retaining his outside cylinders, Allan straight-link vale gear, and boiler. Poor Drummond – had he given it a louvred chimney and a Jones cab as well, he would doubtless have been accused of slavish imitation. Had he tried an express 4-6-0 of his own design (Dugald had not yet attempted such) it is unlikely to have been as successful as the 'Castles'. Once again, David Jones, now retired in far-off Hampstead, had done a first-rate job. Apart from the chimney, cab and eight-wheel tender, there were a number of Drummond features, including Dugald's steam reverser, and marine-type big ends. The driving wheels were 5ft 9in, quite small for an express locomotive (only in the last three, of 1916, was this increased to 6ft) and the boiler pressure was 175psi. No.140, *Taymouth Castle*, was delivered by Dübs in June 1900, with five others; four more came from the same builder in July 1901. All went straight into service hauling trains on the new direct line over Slochd Summit. Further additions were made to the 'Castles', one each in 1910 and 1911, four in 1913, and three in 1916. If to those nineteen can be added the fifty built to exactly the same design by NBL for the *Etat* Railway in France in 1911, one can say it was certainly the most numerous class of Highland locomotives to be built. Most of the castles were the homes of directors or Highland grandees (of one sort or another: Skibo Castle was the self-made millionaire Andrew Carnegie's Highland home); only one, *Urquhart Castle* of 1911, commemorated a ruin. Like the 'Big Goods', the 'Castles' stayed on the main line to the end of their careers, though latterly as pilot engines. The last survivor was *Dalcross Castle*, withdrawn in 1947.

The early years of the twentieth century, though they saw the company system at its maximum extent, were not the healthiest financially. Lochgorm Works had to maintain a familiar tradition of making new boots out of old leather. Drummond built three 0-6-0 side-tank engines, two in 1903 and one in 1904, which rejoiced in the name of the 'Scrap Tanks' and in which wheels, cylinders, motion and other parts were taken from dismantled 2-4-0 goods engines; and the boilers from passenger 2-4-0s which themselves had acquired new ones. Consequently, they had un-Drummondish outside cylinders. The scrap tanks did useful work, mostly in the Inverness yards, until 1930. Lochgorm also built four inside-cylindered 0-4-4 tank engines, three in 1905 and one in 1906, for branch line work. Weighing 35.75 tons, with 4ft 6in wheels and 150psi boiler pressure, they were intended for light railway work. These were the last of the forty-two engines to be built at Inverness and also the last Highland engines to remain in service. No.45, completed in December 1905, was at work on the Dornoch branch until 1957. In 1908 Drummond brought out an enlarged form of the 'Bens', duly known as the 'Large Bens'. Built by the North British Locomotive Co., six in number, weighing 52.3 tons, 6.3 tons more than their predecessors, they had considerably larger boilers, with a heating surface in original condition of 1,648.2sq. ft as against 1,175; and a pressure of 180 psi. They had relatively brief careers compared with the 'Small Bens', all being scrapped by 1937, while most of the 'Small Bens' worked into the late 1940s and two, *Ben Wyvis* and *Ben Alder*, survived until 1952 and 1953 respectively. In 1909, NBL also built four powerful 0-6-4 tank engines to Peter Drummond's design, intended for use as banking engines; and four more were delivered in 1911. These were the HR's largest tank engines and worked mostly between Blair Atholl and Dalnaspidal on banking duties, and on local services between Blair Atholl and Perth. They were withdrawn between 1932 and the end of 1936.

On 27 May 1910 a comparative trial was made between the Highland 4-6-0 No.146 *Skibo Castle* and the North British 4-4-0 express locomotive No.867. The test was run between Blair Atholl and Dalwhinnie, each engine pulling a load of eight bogie carriages, saloon, and brake van. As neither railway possessed a dynamometer car, the tractive efforts and speeds of the engines could not be scientifically recorded. However, maybe to the surprise of the Highland, the North British engine was recorded as taking forty and a half minutes to cover the twenty-three miles, while the 'Castle' took forty-four minutes. The normal allowance for the Down Mail, non-stop between these stations, and usually pulled by two engines, was fifty minutes. A test on the NB's Glen Farg bank also showed a better result for the 4-4-0.[8]

Having contributed fifty locomotives of his own design to the Highland Railway's stable, plus the 'Castles', Drummond resigned in February 1912 to assume command of locomotives, carriages and wagons on the Glasgow & South Western Railway. Between 1905 and 1912, a great deal had changed in locomotive design, primarily because of the introduction of the superheater, but also through developments, pioneered by the Great Western Railway at Swindon, in boiler design, valve gear, and sheer size. The Highland had been the pioneer of the 4-6-0 in Britain, but now they were becoming common.

J.A.B. Hamilton referred to 'the hated Peter Drummond',[9] but there seems no evidence for this. When he left Inverness, Drummond was presented with a solid silver tray and his wife with a silver epergne, at a special musical evening. But he attracted negative stories. The Stephenson Locomotive Society's *Highland Railway* records that Drummond had wanted to employ two 'Bens' on T.A. Wilson's non-stop press publicity train of 1 June 1906. But, '... the two top-link crews who were delegated for the duty refused to have this class of engine... their designer had to yield to pressure both from management and train staffs'.[10] The train was hauled by a 'Loch' and a 'Strath', with larger tenders attached for the purpose.

*Motive Power – The 'Modern' Era*

Drummond's successor was Frederick George Smith, aged forty, who had been Works Manager at Lochgorm since December 1903. Born in Newcastle-on-Tyne, Smith had been apprenticed at the North Eastern Railway works in Gateshead, and had also gained experience of electrical engineering before his arrival in Inverness. This knowledge was useful, not because the HR ever seriously contemplated electric traction, but because of its increasing application in machinery and in carriage lighting. His first task, as far as new locomotives were concerned, was to order four new 'Castles' from NBL. The design was modified to increase the boiler pressure to 180psi, and extended smokeboxes were fitted. They were delivered in April, July and November 1913, but in that year Smith was already projecting a design which would be a generation on from that of the 'Castle'. Philip Atkins has thoroughly researched the 'Rivers' class, and his work is drawn on here.[1] The board, on 29 July 1913, had agreed to seek quotations for 'Four new engines after the Castle type. Remitted to the Chairman [R.M. Wilson] and Mr Smith.' Smith immediately began discussions with the North British Locomotive Co. on a modern 4-6-0 type, to weigh 66 tons and with a 16-ton axle-load. An NBL copy drawing dated 'Aug. 26 1913' is noted in that company's Sketch Register, and a copy of the drawing is preserved.[2] No new engines were ordered during 1913, however. In January 1914 the board sanctioned the payment of £200 to the North British Railway for the production of 'Castle engines drawings'. By this time the HR's pursuit of economies had greatly scaled down the drawing office at Lochgorm Works,[3] which cannot have made design supervision any easier. On 29 September 1914 the board accepted a tender from Hawthorn, Leslie of Newcastle for six new engines at £4,920 each, for delivery in May, June and July 1915. The choice of builder presumably reflects a competitive estimate. Since a 'Castle' would have cost around £4,200, it must have been apparent by then that the new engines were something different. On 30 March 1915 the board resolved to name them after rivers. While the 'Rivers' were building, planning for further engines went on: the Locomotive Committee on 27 July 1915 instructed that rough specifications of the 'Loch' type, with superheater, be sent to Hawthorn Leslie, North British Locomotive Co., and Andrew Barcley of Kilmarnock, to submit drawings. On 14 September *River Ness* was despatched to the Highland shed at Perth, arriving probably around 17 September. For eyes attuned to the lines of the older HR 4-6-0s, it was a startling sight. Its massive boiler allowed only for a chimney and dome that were wide and squat by traditional standards, and it incorporated all the most up-to-date features of the steam locomotive: superheater, feedwater heater, Belpaire firebox, external Walschaerts valve gear, a high running plate that exposed most of the wheels, and a massive, high-sided six-wheel tender. It looked like nothing the Highland had ever seen before, except that its front vacuum brake column could be hinged back. In fact, with the 'Rivers', the future had arrived. Unfortunately, it was more than the HR could cope with. In full working order, engine plus laden tender weighed around 130 tons, fully 10 tons more than a 'Castle'. From the makers' information, the engineer's department at Inverness established the engine's weight as 71.6 tons, and the maximum axle-load as 17.3 tons. The weight discrepancy between the projected design of 1913 and the finished product of 1915 seems to be explained by a failure, at some stage of preparing the design, to appreciate that if 66 tons were the weight in working order, the empty weight would necessarily have to be 5 or 6 tons less. A triumphant arrival in Inverness was delayed while Newlands's men began urgently to work out the stress factor on bridges caused not only by the weight but by the anticipated 'hammer-blow' effect of the reciprocating parts on the rails. It also appeared that the engines did not quite fit within the loading gauge.[4] Once these facts were known, Newlands placed an embargo on use of the new engines. The second, *River Spey* (or perhaps *Tay*), was despatched by the makers on 30 September 1915. Despite one claim that it was seen at Aviemore, it is most unlikely that it ran on Highland metals at this time.

For the Highland Railway the affair was deeply embarrassing. For Smith it was professional doom. On 24 September an emergency board meeting at Perth, chaired by Whitelaw, with seven other directors present, considered the fact that the new engines were, 'now found to be considerably heavier than the Directors anticipated'. Smith was invited to put his own case, but his explanation was not considered satisfactory and he was given until the following Monday to decide between the alternatives of resignation and dismissal, in either case with immediate effect, though three months' salary would be paid. He opted for resignation, and returned to Newcastle, where he ultimately set up his own business in the iron-and-steel trade, and lived until 1956. The Highland's financial predicament in having £30,000-worth of unusable engines was alleviated by rapidly selling them to the Caledonian at a profit of £480 on each, and the matter, though no doubt gossipworthy throughout the national railway community, was almost wholly ignored in the railway and local press. Some sarcastic questions were asked at the Shareholders' Meeting of February 1916, but Whitelaw brushed them aside in the breezy style of which he was a master.[5]

The 'Rivers' affair remained a mystery for many years, its drama heightened by allegations of personal strains between Smith and Newlands.[6] It has been suggested that Smith had ordered, on his own authority, a new turntable for the Inverness roundhouse which was larger than the pit and trackwork allowed for.[7] Smith's post was filled with remarkable speed by Christopher Cumming, district locomotive superintendent of the North British Railway's Fife and Northern Section, whose appointment (at £550 a year) was announced in the minutes of the same board meeting, 7 October 1915, that recorded Smith's resignation. Whitelaw was almost certainly instrumental in this almost instant translation to Lochgorm. The 'Rivers' were generally reputed to be an excellent design, and could be regarded as the best engines the Highland never had, except that they did appear on the Perth–Inverness line in 1928, by which time some culverts and the Dalguise viaduct had been strengthened. Locomotive-caused stress on bridges was also better understood by then. Meanwhile, unable to avail itself of an ultra-modern design, the HR Board ordered six engines from the North British Locomotive Co. on 7 October 1915, three of the 'Loch' class, originally of 1896, delivered (without superheating) in 1916; and three 'Castles' with 6ft driving wheels, delivered in 1917. The meeting also resolved to contract with Hawthorn, Leslie for two 4-4-0 engines. Smith had been working on a design for these in 1915, but the new design was produced by Hawthorn, Leslie. [8] As his would also have been, they were the first 4-4-0s in Britain to have externally mounted Walschaerts valve gear. Delivered in 1917, named *Snaigow* and *Durn* after directors' houses in southern Perthshire, they cost £5,321 each and were intended to work the mail trains between Inverness and Wick. The first operational Highland engines to have superheaters and Belpaire fireboxes, they were later employed on goods and shunting work at Aviemore, and withdrawn in 1936 and 1935 respectively. In 1916, Cumming had commissioned a design for a goods 4-6-0 with 5ft 3in driving wheels, and the first four were delivered in 1917, with a further four in 1919, all from Hawthorn, Leslie. The relative costs of the two batches give an indication of the way prices were increasing at the time: the first four cost £6,957 each; the second set cost £9,676. The extra cost was partly due to copper fireboxes: wartime shortage had meant steel fireboxes for the first set. They were intended to take over express workings from the 'Big Goods' on the Inverness–Perth line, though they also operated some passenger services. On the toughest section of route, climbing between Blair Atholl and Dalnaspidal, they were allowed to pull thirty-three loaded wagons, as compared to twenty-eight for the older 'Big Goods'. It proved a durable class, of which three lasted until 1952. From 1928, with the withdrawal of the 'Skye Bogies', they ran most services on the Kyle line, sharing the task with 'Small Bens'. The final class of Highland engine was also from Hawthorn, Leslie: the express 4-6-0 'Clan' class, sufficiently similar in general appearance to the preceding goods type for that to be back-named the 'Clan Goods'; in fact all three classes, from the same builder, showed a consistent style combining both modern and traditional aspects. The eight 'Clans' had 6ft driving wheels and 175psi boiler pressure. They were 9.5 tons lighter than the 'Rivers', and were the most powerful engines to be used by the Highland Railway. Although the builders had quoted £8,059 as the price, that was back in 1917; on delivery of the first four in 1919 the cost had risen to around £9,100 for each engine, and the second quartet, delivered between July and August 1921, cost £11,251 apiece. During 1921 No.53, *Clan Stewart*, was temporarily fitted with 'Scarab' oil-burning apparatus, perhaps with the thought of using only oil fuel north of Inverness. [9] But the Railways Act had already been passed, and such a major step was not to be undertaken. The 'Clans' were a very successful and hard-worked class, allowed to take a maximum load of 240 tons, unaided, from Blair Atholl to Dalnaspidal, compared with 205 tons for a 'Castle' and 160 tons for a 'Loch'. No.49, *Clan Campbell*, ran 822,393 miles in the course of its twenty-eight-year life. No.55, *Clan MacKinnon*, survived in action until February 1950. Cumming retired early through poor health, in 1922, and was succeeded by

David Urie, the Highland's last locomotive superintendent, who had been assistant to the chief on the Midland Great Western Railway of Ireland. During his nine months of office, before the company was amalgamated into the LMS at the end of the year, he prepared plans for fitting superheaters to the 'Big Bens', but did not produce any new locomotives.

At the end of 1922, the HR had 173 engines on its books, of which 89 had been built since 1900. Of the pre-1900 classes, the oldest were No.27 (by then on the duplicate list as 27A), and No.35 (35A since 1910), both first built in 1863. Their presence on the duplicate list indicated that they were not in revenue service, and both, like other veterans, were kept for their parts, for a notional place in the accounting books which could allow for their 'rebuilding' and consequent charge to revenue; and ultimately for their scrap value. Altogether twenty-three engines were on the duplicate list, many of them stored in scrap sidings at Culloden Moor Station. Most had not pulled a train for years, though one or two achieved a new lease of life. The 'Skye Bogie' No.70, renumbered 70A in 1916, was renumbered 67 in 1923 and fitted with the boiler from the old No.67, *The Duke* (built in 1874 and scrapped in 1923). This boiler had been fitted to The *Duke* in 1916, having been taken from another 4-4-0, No.74, *Beaufort*, which was built in 1885 and scrapped in 1913.

During all its existence, the Highland Railway painted its engines green, but there was considerable variation, both in the shade of green and in the additional colours of 'lining' applied to it.[10] In summary – and consequently with many individual exceptions and variations, especially as different engines were repainted at different times – the following six phases can be discerned. From 1855 to 1865 engines were painted dark green, with edging in black. Between 1865 and 1870 Stroudley introduced his 'improved engine green' for passenger engines, which has been described as 'mustard yellow' and 'dark yellow', with crimson frames, and with a double lining of white (inside) and red. He painted the goods engines in olive green, with either the double lining or single white lining. When Jones took over in 1870, he painted the passenger engines in a shade of mid-green, with a triple white-black-red lining; then from 1884 he used a paler apple-green with the same lining as before, a darker green border, and a bright vermilion panel on the front buffer beam. Until 1883 his goods engines were dark green, lined out as the passenger engines; after that they were painted in the same way as the passenger engines. From 1896, Peter Drummond generally reverted to olive-green for all engines, with a triple white-black-white lining-out. But the economy drive of 1903 and after did away with lining-out, and the engines were painted in unlined olive-green, in a rather darker shade than before. In 1912, F.G. Smith opted for a paler green, still unlined, but somewhat alleviating the drab effect. In his time, the use of brass number plates was replaced by painted numerals; though some locomotives retained their plates, many were removed and melted down for re-use. Christopher Cumming used either a 'moss green' or light green paint (the latter in the 'Clan' engines of 1921). Incidentally, though it was after the Highland period, many observers felt that the Highland Railway locomotives looked extremely well when repainted in the LMS's original crimson-lake livery.

The names of the engines were always painted on, in lettering styles that varied over the years. As has been noted, names came and went with some abandon, and not all locomotives carried their names all the time. The inception of uniform 'class' names with the 'Lochs' in 1896 stabilised naming for the later classes. However, repainting of Gaelic names caused occasional problems. No.133 *Loch Laoghal* was wrongly redone as *Loch Laochal*; and No.61 *Ben na Caillich* as *Ben na Caillach*. A curious case is No.17, *Ben Alligan*, which seems to have borne that name from the beginning, but there is no Ben Alligan, only the lofty Ben Alligin (Beinn Ailiginn) in Torridon. Although sometimes said to be derived from Gaelic *àilleagan*, 'jewel', the name has always been spelt with the *–in* ending. Slioch, the fine mountain that rises above Loch Maree, appears to have been gratuitously prefixed 'Ben' for the sake of consistency. The naming of the first 'Clan' after Clan Campbell also raised a few eyebrows in the north, as the Campbells were chiefly associated with Argyll, which was well outside Highland Railway territory. *Clan Chattan* has also puzzled some non-Highlanders: this was the name of an ancient clan confederacy dominated by the MacIntoshes.

## Lochgorm Works

Being isolated from any other railway, the Inverness & Nairn had to make provision for locomotive repairs from the beginning. The Inverness & Aberdeen Junction Railway, in its first years, also had no connection to lines beyond Aberdeen. Consequently, a locomotive repair shop was necessary, and this, in 1857, was the genesis of Lochgorm Works. It was always part of the locomotive superintendent's domain, along with the running sheds and the carriage and wagon works. In William Barclay's time, it can have been little more than a big forge, but William Stroudley, from 1865, began the process of equipping it with machine tools.

The most detailed description of the works comes from the February 1902 issue of the *Railway Magazine*, in the course of an interview with Peter Drummond. These 'interviews' were not personality pieces and there are no insights from the locomotive superintendent. But there is a very full description of Lochgorm Works just at the end of its heyday. The following résumé gives an indication of the numerous activities and trades required in a modest-sized railway engineering shop at that time. The forge contained a 2-ton double-action steam hammer. The smiths' shop had eighteen fires, and beside it was a spring shop. In the yard in front of the smithy there were a punching and shearing machine, a hot saw, and a tyre-heating furnace, to expand the steel tyres before they were fitted to the wheels. At the other side of the yard was the boiler shop, with a 10-ton travelling crane, and the machine shop, where four rows of assorted machinery were driven by a double vertical engine with 11in x 20in cylinders. A tramway ran from the boiler shop into the erecting shop, which was equipped with two 30-ton travelling cranes, three wheel-turning lathes, and a hydraulic machine for pressing wheels on to axles. The paint shop, which dealt with rolling stock as well as locomotives, had four rail tracks. Attached to it was a trimming shop for leather-working, which also had a 'hair-tearing machine'. There were also coppersmiths' and tinsmiths' shops, the iron store, pattern shop, and brass foundry. Power for all the machines was supplied by three coke-fired locomotive-type boilers. Much of the machinery was then new, installed under Drummond's control. On the other side of the Rose Street curve was Needlefield Carriage Works, with its timber yard, drying shed, saw-mill, and the carriage and wagon building shops.

The same article deals with the 'Accident Train', the HR's breakdown unit, which was kept in a state of readiness for any emergency occurring on the lines radiating from Inverness. It is described as, 'one of the most complete in the country', and the Highland built a set of cottages, Railway Terrace, right by the station, to house its crew. The principal item was the 15-ton steam crane, built by Cowans Sheldon of Carlisle, which was capable of travelling under its own power at 3mph. It was attached to a six-wheel bolster wagon, carrying chains, slings, planking, and other items. Then came a six-wheel tool van, 30ft long, with a staff compartment, complete with writing desk, and containing provisions and cooking gear as well as all the tools and implements likely to be needed. The final vehicle was a six-wheel drop-side wagon loaded with rails, rail-chairs, and sleepers. Other vehicles could be attached as required. The crane, delivered in 1887, and believed to have been intended originally for a colonial railway,[1] itself toppled off the rails on to the side of an embankment when helping with a derailment on 2 August 1888 at Dunachton, near Etteridge, and had to be partially dismantled before being re-railed. It was used for heavy permanent way repairs as well as accident work. Another HR special vehicle was the 'portable stone breaker', a combination of stone crusher, engine and bothy, mounted on a bogie wagon, and normally kept on one of the quarry sidings.[2] It could be used to help in re-metalling track at derailment or washout sites.

# PART III

# TEN

*The Community of the Railway: The Staff*

Every movement of a train was directed, carried out and controlled by individuals themselves working to a rule-book and braced by a system of discipline. The Highland Railway was not just green engines, flat-sided carriages, and low-platformed wooden stations separated by long stretches of track through fields and heather – it was its people. As Brian Fawcett wrote about another much more mountainous, but not more individual, railway:

> '... the work is intensely personal. The systems have organizations of a size not too vast to be seen as a whole. The weight of each officer counts as surely as does each instrument in a chamber music ensemble. The result is a closely-defined 'family feeling' and a pride in the importance of individual effort. The capability of every colleague is known to everyone.

These lines, from *Railways of the Andes*, are as true of the Highland as they were of the Central of Peru.

In the first years, the new men from the south, stationmasters, drivers, clerks, had not only to teach their neophyte colleagues the basics of each job, but to ingrain into them the interdependence of all tasks on the railway, and, above all, the importance of the rule-book and the system. In the Highlands, even more than in most pre-railway societies, daylight and dark, wind and weather, seasonal and local custom and individual judgement ruled everyday human activity. '*Cha b'e là na gaoithe là nan sgolb*', says a Gaelic proverb, 'The windy day is not the day for thatch-wattles', but new employees of the railway had to learn that the trains must run to time, that nothing, whether wind, weather, or the chance of a good conversation with a passing friend, must be allowed to cause delay. When the first I&N rule-book was issued, in November 1855, employees who failed to have it with them while on duty were liable to a fine of 5s.[1] Highlanders understood working together in a disciplined force, however. The leaders of the British Army knew this very well: while the

Inverness & Nairn Railway was building, the 93rd Highlanders formed the 'thin red line' at Balaclava.

As men gained experience and were promoted within the company, the recruitment of southerners virtually ceased. From the late 1850s on, the names of the railway's staff bespeak their Highland origins in the vast majority of cases. Later, they were often the sons of men already employed by the railway. Very often, particularly as clerks and stationmasters, they were moved around the system, ending up a long way from their native place. John Macdonald, the poetically inclined stationmaster at Dalguise,[2] came from Easter Ross, though he remained at his little station for many years. Young men earmarked for promotion were moved most often. In the *Highland Railway Journal*[3] John Roake traces the career of one Donald Maclaren, whose father Alexander was the night pointsman at Struan. Donald was appointed as a clerk at Blair Atholl on 26 June 1901. On 6 April 1902 he went to Dunkeld as parcels clerk, and in the same capacity to Forres on 10 October 1903. In November 1904 he was at Struan as clerk. In April 1907 he was appointed booking clerk at Ballinluig, and in the same post at Aberfeldy, in October 1911, and at Nairn in April 1913. In June 1919 he was appointed stationmaster at Plockton. The railway looked to its own staff to progress towards posts of responsibility. The second superintendent of the line (1875-90), Thomas Robertson, had started as a porter at Ballinluig; his successor, William Garrow (1890-1900), had been a pointsman. Only after 1895 did this policy change for appointments to the highest ranks. In this respect the Highland Railway was just the same as other railway companies: among its senior officials it wanted at least some who had experience of other lines; and who had acquired techniques of railway work and systems that might be put to good use on the Highland; also, it might be added, who had not acquired bad habits on the Highland.

Many railwaymen played a vigorous part in local life, especially in sporting and church organisations. From the beginning, however, stationmasters, or agents as they were for long known, had a reason to be regarded somewhat askance in the communities where they were placed. In many smaller places, it was an accepted perquisite of the stationmaster – accepted by the company – that he should deal locally in coal. In small places like Brodie where there was no coal merchant, and the inhabitants had previously burned wood and peat, the availability of coal at the station was a benefit, to those who could afford it. For the stationmaster, it provided a modest additional income and the activity involved was nothing that could not easily be fitted into his working day. Looking back at Kincraig in earlier times in the *Badenoch Record* of 4 January 1964, George T. Hay, a former resident, wrote, 'Later in the same month [October] there always arrived the winter's coal. This the stationmaster, as local coal merchant, retailed at his leisure, using the wagons as depot'. Some stationmasters appear to have gone beyond this to act as chandlers in other goods which had to be brought up by rail in bulk – like oil, or animal feed. In his *Highland Main Line*, Neil T. Sinclair notes that Perthshire merchants complained to the company in 1873 that stationmasters between Stanley and Struan were dealing in 'coal, lime, grain, potatoes and manure to the detriment of local traders'. Such protests were first made in 1867, when the board resolved on 18 October to 'peremptorily' circulate a prohibition, unless stationmasters had been granted a special dispensation. The traders were complaining again in December 1879. The author Beatrix Potter, a regular and observant summer visitor to Dunkeld between 1871-81 and in 1892-93, wrote in her diary about how the stationmaster, John Kinnaird, overcame the problem:

> His brother Mr James Kinnaird… sits in a zinc shed labelled "Manures and Feeding Stuffs", coals being discreetly in the background. It need hardly be said that Mr James is but a cover or blind for Mr John. It is contrary to regulations for a stationmaster to carry on business.[4]

But some stationmasters became popular local figures. When, after the Rogart accident of 3 October 1876, the stationmaster, Mr Fraser, was transferred elsewhere, a local petition pleaded for his retention, but the HR board was unmoved.[5]

The railway itself could provide a sense of community to those workers who lived close to one another, and most railway cottages, other than stationmasters', were grouped in terraces of three or four. Often the railway houses were partly isolated from other dwellings, as the Highland stations could be some way from the villages they served, as at Grantown or Fearn, and even when they passed right by, as with Newtonmore and Golspie, they might be situated at one end of a long street rather than centrally as in Kingussie. Mutual proximity and shared interests held the little pockets of railway folk together just as the same conditions did for fishers down by the harbours and piers. Lillian M. King described childhood life in the railway cottages at the County March in Druimuachdar Pass during the early 1940s, in a style unchanged since the HR's time, with its two mile-walk to school, and the weekly shopping trip to Kingussie:

> Ours, being the ganger's house, had four rooms, one more than the others. The main room which we called the kitchen, was our living room, dining room, and sometimes in winter, our parents' bedroom… the room was lit by a paraffin lamp with a glass bowl which took on the colour of the paraffin. In summer we ate in the stone-floored scullery, where the sinks were, and also the huge bins for flour and oatmeal, and for the chicken food.

In many ways it was just like other workers' and small farmers' homes in the Highlands, but its closeness to the railway made it distinctive:

> … the railway meant home and childhood and security, telling the clockless time by the trains – the 'Mails', the 'one o' clock', and the 'London'; lying in bed listening to the heavy goods trains labouring up the hill from the station and having to stop to build up a head of steam before the final pull up to the summit. It was cans on fence posts for engine drivers to throw lumps of coal at, sitting on the snow fence waving to passengers; shopping and sheep in the guard's van on Saturdays; waking up to the whistle of the 'Midnight' and going back to sleep again.[6]

Highland Railway staff were the largest single employee group in Inverness. Their first recorded non-railway group activity seems to have been the forming of a 'railway battery' in the Inverness Artillery Volunteers, in the late 1860s. Dougall was Captain for a time, followed by his assistant, William Gowenlock. Naturally, in the manner of a pre-cinema generation, they found means of entertaining themselves when off duty. The HR Literary Society was founded in 1874, by John Simpson, a clerk in the accountant's office. It held regular meetings at first in what was known as the 'Janitor's Room', presumably not as much of a broom cupboard as the name suggests. In his time, Dougall was honorary president and, at the annual social, according to 'J.E.C.', '... nor did he ever fail to give a rendering in his own inimitable way of the fine old Scotch song, "When the Kye Come Hame"'.[7] The Society celebrated twenty-five years in 1909, when it indulged in a 'Nicht wi' Burns' on 25 January, with William Whitelaw in the chair. This was its main annual event, along with the dinner and dance, but regular meetings were held, to discuss such topics as 'Should every Man be trained as a Soldier?' (10 December 1909), or 'Is Roller Skating Beneficial to the Community?' (January 1910). In 1911 it had 137 ordinary and thirteen honorary members. There were also Railway Clerks' Football and Cricket teams, which played in local leagues in the first decades of the twentieth century.[8] In 1913 they received £2 2s and £3 3s respectively from the company, on the understanding that 'Directors and Officials not to be asked for subscriptions'.[9]

In December 1867 the board approved a donation of £20 towards the 'Employees' Annual Festival' and this became a regular tradition, the grant normally being £25 except for the exceptional £40 in 1870. 'J.E.C.' describes this event as taking place in the Music Hall and ending with a ball in the Northern Meeting Rooms:

> This gathering, which brought to Inverness railwaymen and their friends from all over the system, was a great event, both halls being crowded to their utmost capacity." But alas, "Latterly rowdyism crept into these gatherings, and Mr Dougall very rightly ordered that they should be discontinued.[10]

Almost certainly the great majority of those attending would be from Inverness. Forres staff had their own event, described as: 'An excellent tea followed by a chairman's address and a vocal and sentimental programme'.[11] In Keith, where there had long been a mixed HR/GNSR railway community, they had the pleasant custom of a joint annual festival and ball, despite the warfare at official level. The *Banffshire Journal* of 8 January 1900 recorded the thirty-fifth such event, at the Longmore Hall in Keith:

> At the back of the platform, the draperies had been worked into a pretty device. At points in it were suspended railway lamps showing red, white and green lights and signalling flags of red, white and green colours.

Singers, a comedian, elocutionists and 'society entertainers' amused the revellers before the dancing, which went on 'far into Saturday morning'. Even during the industrial unrest of 1911-12, the locomotive department at Inverness launched an annual concert in the Music Hall, on 13 December 1911, with Park in the chair and various other luminaries present (though neither Peter Drummond nor F.G. Smith is mentioned).[12] The flag-draped platform featured several enlarged photographs of HR locomotives. A second concert was held in December 1912. In March 1913, the superintendents, chief assistants, and foremen held a first annual dinner, in the coffee room of the Station Hotel, with J.H. Davidson, assistant traffic manager, in the chair. 'Song and sentiment' followed the meal, which was provided by the staff of Mr Ward, the hotel manager and a fellow diner. Apart from supporting its own staff's functions, the board very rarely disbursed funds to local events and causes, no doubt on the useful principle that as all could not be helped, none would be. An annual £5 5s was given to Dr Gray's Hospital in Elgin; otherwise the exceptions revealed the directors' own interests: the HR annually put up £20 as prize money for the competition of the Highland Rifle Shooting Association, and also gave £10 a year (£20 from 1894) to the Highland Volunteer Artillery (commanded for many years by Raigmore).

From its formation in 1865, the HR was the largest single commercial employer in the Highlands, and by 1922 it had a staff of around 3,500. As a railway business, it was relatively small-scale: by 1922 railways in Britain employed over 500,000 people. The company was big enough for its employees to combine in making demands, but small enough for each department to be administered directly by its head. Thus the traffic manager, the goods managers, locomotive superintendent and the engineer all knew the people in their departments as individuals. Hiring, management and firing of waged staff was their direct responsibility, as was training and promotion, to ensure efficiency. In the crafts, the normal system of apprenticeship and journeyman was used. In the locomotive department, boys began as cleaners and worked their way up; similarly most station staff began as junior porters. Learning was largely done on the job, but the locomotive department in particular, as on other railways, had a Mutual Improvement Society, intended for enginemen to discuss the techniques of their jobs and pass knowledge on to their juniors. Departmental heads were empowered to fine employees for minor breaches of company regulations or procedures. The Locomotive Department Notice Book records numerous such instances as these: 'Dec. 26, 1882. Duncan McMillan, Engineman, is fined 2/6 for damaging the paint of an engine by withdrawing one of the plugs while steam was on and letting the hot water escape'; or from 3 February 1892:

> The 9.50 a.m. up Special train of 27th ult. was booked to cross the 11.50 a.m. Down train at Blair Atholl but owing to the enginemen not keeping the former under proper control it overshot the starting signal which was standing at danger and was only pulled up when outside the south main line crossing, and for this carelessness Donald Mackintosh and Alex. Sim are each fined 5/-.[13]

Such notices, signed by David Jones, were intended to keep his men on the alert. Dismissal was threatened for dilatory or inefficient engine cleaners (many observers commented on the high standard of paintwork and polish on Highland engines).

At its first meeting, on 2 August 1865, the HR Board resolved that servants of the company exposed to risk in discharging their duties should be insured against accident, at an annual expense to the company of £112 14s, half the total premium; the men were required to pay the other half. Railway employees, on all lines, were routinely expected to do work which would be regarded as unacceptably dangerous today. Goods wagons were often moved by the process of tow-roping, in which an engine moved a wagon on an adjacent track, by means of a tow rope. Propping, by which the engine pushed wagons forwards on the adjacent track by means of a rigid bar or frame, was also used, though very rarely after 1900. These props and ropes often broke, and could cause serious injury. The Board of Trade tried to discourage tow-roping, and here again found itself in disagreement with the Highland Railway, which reported to it in 1903 that the system was in regular use at eighty-six stations. Although gradually the installation of extra crossovers between tracks reduced the extent of the practice, it was still widespread on the HR in 1922. Crushed hands and legs were regular occurrences, and while Inverness, Perth and a few larger stations maintained volunteer ambulance teams to give first aid, smaller stations had no such facilities. Even more hazardous was the task of uncoupling a pilot engine when the train was moving. The uncoupled pilot engine accelerated away, in order to reach the crossing loop, be switched on to another line, and allow the points to be reset, before the train arrived. This procedure, involving two separate moving trains within a single block, was completely contrary to Board of Trade regulations, and to the HR's own rule-book. The BoT (and again, the company's rule-book) specified that pilot engines should be attached between the train engine and the train. This cumbersome process was designed to ensure that the pilot could only be attached and detached when the train was standing at a station or crossing loop, and the Highland routinely ignored it. When an engine assisted from behind – two in front and one at the rear was normal for the heaviest trains on Struan Bank – it was supposed to be attached to the rear vehicle. This formality, which again required stops for attachment and detachment, was often omitted. Once again, the single-track line and potential delays were considered as sufficient reason for the company to bend the rules and go its own way. Carried out by experienced men, these procedures were almost invariably managed safely, but the potential for an accident was much higher. There is no doubt that the practices were required by senior staff, who could blame drivers and signalmen for carelessness if things went wrong. The Highland was maintaining its traffic flow at the serious risk of its workers, though the directors, assembled under their gilded ceiling, probably did not see the matter in such terms.

Since the Highland Railway has left a reputation for a certain laxity in its procedures, poor timekeeping and a degree of insouciance about delays, and since these things, to many people, have contributed to the line's special character, it is worth exploring their causes. It has been shown that some dangerous and irregular operations were carried out in the interest of maintaining speed and keeping to time. But these were not what Thomas Addy Wilson had in mind, when as the new general manager in June 1898 he issued an often-quoted staff circular on punctuality, which read in part:

... punctuality is a rare thing on the Highland Line. I do not know whether the Staff have realised this. Usually our trains start late, lose time on the road, and arrive late at the end of the journey... the moment a passenger from another Railway passes on to the Highland Line, he seems to take for granted that there will be a 'leisureliness' which would have excited surprise on other Railways...

By this time the historic reasons for delay were minimised, with almost no mixed trains on the main lines, and far fewer delays at crossing points. Lack of urgency at station stops was seen as the problem, and Wilson, clearly feeling there was a sense of indifference to proper timekeeping that needed to be attacked, made an oblique reference to sanctions, 'I do not like penalties, and prefer to appeal to the Staff in their own interest'. Several years later he was still struggling with the problem,[14] and music-hall comedians like Will Fyffe were still making jokes about passengers getting off and back on the train, not just to pick flowers, but to plant the seeds and then pick the flowers. Of course it is true that the pace of life in the Highlands was generally less pressured than in densely populated districts, that Inverness was a long way off for most station staff, and that there were people in the Highlands capable of exalting unhurriedness to an art form. But this hardly explains the normality of delays to a not over-demanding timetable. Wilson had come from the far busier and more compact North Eastern Railway to the attenuated Highland, with its 400-plus miles of 'main lines' and widely-spaced stations, where trains were infrequent enough for their arrival to be an event rather than a routine. With such an extended system, a very small central management team, and, particularly in the 1900s, tight control on staff numbers, the HR station personnel had to be capable of self-reliance. Put another way, they felt a sense of independence. They did not scorn the control office, but their first priority was to ensure that things were done in the right manner at Kinbrace, or Kinloss, or Kincraig, even if it took a little longer than Control said it should. They did not seek to make delays, but their sense of duty and loyalty was centred on their station, rather than on any abstract notion of timekeeping. Also, the train was the carrier of information from station to station, unofficial as well as official. Exchange of news between guard and stationmaster might take up a few moments after other business had been attended to. Such things created the 'leisureliness' deplored by Wilson, but it was not lackadaisical or negligent, and it is most unlikely that there ever was a general 'don't-care' attitude to delay.

The strictness and severity of the company's discipline are quite hard to assess, especially as what was considered normal or tolerable in the nineteenth century was quite different to present-day standards. When the station at Dava burned down, on 6 September 1867, as the result of the pointsman dropping a lucifer match after lighting the lamps, he was merely reprimanded for carelessness.[15] When Bilbster Station burned down on 16 September 1877, the stationmaster was sacked.[16] The details behind such cases are lost, but it should be remembered that each department kept a staff record, and no doubt first offences were viewed more leniently. There are occasional records of stationmasters being discharged for neglect or incompetence, but there is no record of any being discharged or even disciplined for trading on the side, and it seems that Dougall chose to turn a blind eye to this practice, so long as it did not interfere with their duties. In line with law and tradition, the company was most severe on offences against property and money. Tampering with a station's takings was almost always followed by dismissal. William Collins, ticket collector at Inverness, was sacked on 31 October 1870 for failing to account for excess fares collected by him. Officials who regularly dealt with large sums of money were normally expected to provide a form of surety on being employed. The company also took out insurance against loss through theft by the staff. When David Thomson, parcels clerk at Inverness, absconded to the USA in May 1870, the board noted that the Guarantee Society would make good the deficiency of £23 7s 8d left in his accounts.[17] In May 1868 the stationmaster at Brodie was sacked after being arrested for illegally dealing in grouse with English game retailers, and Donald Mackenzie, stationmaster at Dava, was discharged in September 1869 because his wife had stolen a box of grouse. A pointsman at Blair Atholl was dismissed in March 1868, following the illicit opening of a whisky cask in the goods shed. A greaser, Andrew Bell, was killed by a locomotive on that occasion, presumably while drunk. An engine crew on the Inverness & Nairn Railway were discharged for stopping the train while partly intoxicated and quarrelling on the footplate on Christmas Day 1856 (Scotland, until recent times, took scant notice of Christmas). They were also reported to the procurator fiscal. But the Highland Railway's attitude to drunkenness, at least among the office staff, was not intolerant. When Mr McConochie, stationmaster at Novar, left his station on New Year's Day 1867 without authority and without leaving a competent person in charge, thus causing several hours' delay to Up and Down trains, the board decided to move him to a smaller station at a reduced salary.[18] Another stationmaster with a weakness for drink was transferred to work as a clerk in the secretary's office, under Dougall's eye. In this respect, the company reflected a wider social indulgence of drinking. Distillery workers received a regular dram each day, and the railway carter rarely failed to adjust his arrival time to the serving of this libation. Drunkenness vied with pilfering as prime cause of dismissal among lower ranks of staff.[20] However, no accident on the Highland was ever attributed to drunkenness among operating staff; though a number of the individuals struck down while walking on the line were believed to have been under the influence of drink.

While only two passengers were killed on the Highland Railway until 1914,[21] the rate of attrition among staff was steady. Surfacemen and shunters were most at risk. The platelayers worked in groups of three or four, often with no lookout man, and especially with an adverse wind, could easily be surprised by a light engine or a special train. The 'Engine Following' boards on locomotive buffer beams were intended for their benefit as much as for informing signalmen. Deaths and injuries were regularly reported. The company rarely considered itself responsible: carelessness or incompetence were held to blame. A fund was opened by the Duke of Sutherland, with the £100 awarded to him on the opening of the Perth line, to help the families of those killed or injured in the company's service, and discretionary awards of £20 or

£10 were made, depending on the man's seniority or the circumstances of his death or permanent disablement. On 1 June 1869 it was agreed to give £20 to William Fraser, a fitter and turner, one of the first employees at Lochgorm, 'now laid aside through accident and exposure to weather during extension of the workshops'. Posts might be found for injured men still capable of work: Anthony Lambert's *Highland Railway Album* has a picture of Robert Matthew, who was made stationmaster at the tiny halt of Balnacoul after losing his leg in a shunting accident. Some crossing keepers also were lame. There was no company pension scheme: on retirement stationmasters and porters alike would have to leave their free or cheap houses and fend for themselves. Widows and orphans had to make their own arrangements. Only two groups received some favour, at opposite extremes: those who had given the company good service in senior positions (or the widows of such); and the families of men who had given good service in lower positions, but who now were destitute. For the first group, the board might award a discretionary payment: when Thomas Lowson, the able goods manager at Elgin, died in 1873, his widow was awarded a payment of £50 a year for ten years,[22] and when after that period she re-applied, she was granted a one-off sum of £100. In 1877 Mrs Cameron, widow of the stationmaster at Conon, was awarded £20 after inquiry into her circumstances by Mr Kennedy, the inspector.[23] The employees of the locomotive, traffic and works departments also organised their own benefit societies against disablement or death. In November 1884, the members of the Locomotive Society are recorded as electing a new medical officer, Dr James Murray, to replace Dr James Macrae, who had held the post for some years.[24] At the board meeting of 1 December 1897, the manager drew attention to the contribution given by the company to the three Friendly Societies of the Departments, and, in view of the impending Workmen's Compensation Act, he was instructed to tell them 'not to absolutely count on more support' from the company. A year later, the company was still paying £25 to the three societies.[25] By 1909 the duke's fund had become a Good Service Pension Fund, from which payments could be made to deserving cases: typically Donald Ross, a former surfaceman at Keith, received 2*s* 6*d* a week, an eighth of his pay in service; Mr Wilkie, stationmaster at Alness, received a lump sum of £25 when he had to retire through ill health. From April 1878, top-level staff also had a Superannuation Scheme operated through the Railways Clearing House. David Jones, retiring on medical grounds in 1896, was awarded an annual pension of £293, to bring his income, with superannuation, up to £500. The Highland Railway, while it cannot be considered over-generous in these respects, was perhaps more so than many other railways or large joint-stock companies of the time, if only because, in the small community of its workers, the plight of the destitute was more apparent.

Like some other railways, the company ran a Savings Bank, established in 1887, and managed by Dougall and his successors as a registered Friendly Society. For employees in remote places, and able to make savings, it was a useful facility. An annual report was made to depositors and the HR board; at the end of 1896 the amount at credit was £100,919 and there were 646 depositors.[26]

The normal method for the waged staff of making an approach to the management was to speak to the departmental head through unofficial representatives. If this failed to produce a result, a 'memorial' might be compiled, setting out the nature of the request or grievance, and laid before the directors. Though the ASRS was well established in Inverness by the late 1890s,[27] the Highland Railway never acknowledged the status of a trade union among its employees. In all respects it was typical of its time, and this included a clear distinction between the salaried officials and the waged workers. Because of its relatively small size, and the fact that very often several members of a family would be employed by it, there was a genuine sense of involvement between the workers and the company, which was not fully reciprocated. 'Paternalist' is often the adjective invoked in describing the attitude of the HR management to its men, but this word, with its overtones of the by-then-extinct clan system, is misleading. The Highland directors appear to have regarded their workforce very much as any other railway board did: with a mixture of anxiety and mistrust. Any request was to be initially resisted; any concession was granted reluctantly and hedged with qualifications. Every improvement to its workmen's conditions and pay was made at the request of the men themselves, or as the result of government legislation. Company initiatives were restricted to cutting pay and lengthening hours, when the board felt on safe enough ground to do so. Loyalty and hard work were taken for granted. Commendations from the board for individual merit are notably absent, though it was often noted by outsiders: the *John o' Groat Journal* of 13 January 1875 records the experience of Mr William Adam, of Bank House, Wick, one of only four passengers (and 300 sheep) on the 9 a.m. mixed train to Inverness, on 8 January. With two engines and a 'nose plough', it stuck fast in snow at the County March. The passengers struggled through to Forsinard and its hospitable hotel, but, 'With a pitiless storm soughing down the Halladale valley, with the wind intensely cold coming off these high uplands, these railway engineers and guards stuck nobly by their train through the dreary night'. In the twentieth century, occasional awards were made by the board for special merit: the Traffic Committee awarded £1 each to two drivers, a guard and the stationmaster following a goods train breakaway at Culloden Moor in October 1914, and Driver John Irvine received £1 for action taken to avoid a lineside fire at Little Slochd in July 1915.[28]

Pay rises for some senior staff approved by the Traffic Committee on 1 March 1910 show how much or little things had changed since 1857. Donald Cameron, stationmaster at Wick, went from £85 to £90; Peter Henderson, parcels agent at Inverness, went from £110 to £120; John Cameron, the night telegraph clerk, went from £95 to £110, and Edgar Lowe, the signals superintendent, from £210 to £220. The Scottish railways paid their men less than the English railways did, and the Highland Railway paid less than the bigger Scottish companies. But any comparison needs to take into account the particular case of the Highland Railway. Its nine-hour day in the workshops compared favourably with the ten hours or more of most other companies. Station staff at most places had lengthy periods when no trains passed, and, even though there was still work to be done, it could be proceeded with at a fairly easy pace. For those who wanted to stay on home ground, there was another consideration. The HR had no competing industry of comparable size, and a steady job on the railway, at £50 a year, with clothing provided, and a decent low-rent house (surfacemen paid £4 a year for their cottages: for those at Dalnaspidal it was reduced to £3 in March 1869, because of 'the peculiar character of the district')[29], was preferable in most men's view to a job on a farm, or as a labourer, with lower pay, harder work, no uniform, and a hovel to live in. The railway was also one of the very few organisations in the Highlands large enough to offer prospects of promotion and therefore of 'getting on' within their own region to able and ambitious boys and men. By 1919 (by which time the company was subject to much more government regulation on staff matters than pre-1911) written examinations for junior clerks seeking a higher grade were held periodically at Inverness: candidates were given free travel passes but had to pay for their overnight accommodation.[30]

It was 1889 before the Board of Trade acquired any kind of control over the number of hours worked by railway staff. Section 4 of the Regulation of Railways Act provided for 'Railway companies to make returns of overtime worked by their servants whose duties involve the safety of trains or passengers'. As the definition of 'overtime' rested with the board, the companies did nothing. The Railway Regulation Act of 1893 gave the board greater powers: 'If representation is made to the Board of Trade as to excessive hours, insufficient rest, or insufficient relief of Sundays of any railway servants engaged in working the traffic, the Board of Trade shall inquire into the matter'. It had powers to demand and enforce an amended schedule of working hours. Occasional representations came from the Highland Railway, and the BoT enforced a reduction of working hours for shunters at Elgin and Forres, and surfacemen on the Skye line, in 1896.[31] Excessive working hours on the Highland were regularly criticised at accident inquiries, though the Board of Trade inspectors never found fatigue directly responsible. At the inquiry into the Newtonmore accident of 1894 (see Appendix A) it emerged that the stationmaster was on duty every day from 7.30 a.m. until midnight. In the same year it was found that the signalman at Tain was on duty for fifteen hours a day in each alternate week, less two periods of one hour allowed for meals.

In June 1912 the Inverness Saturday paper *Football Times* reported that three Highland Railway branches of the ASRS (Inverness, Elgin–Keith, and Perth) had entered requests for shorter hours and higher pay. There were separate conciliation boards for the traffic, locomotive, and permanent way departments, and each had a list of demands. The traffic men wanted their day cut from twelve hours to ten; overtime at time plus a quarter; and a pay rise of from 2s to 3s. The locomotive men wanted a ten-hour day and a lodging allowance of from 2s to 3s a night. The demands of the surfacemen, rather pathetically, included the provision of shovels from the company as well as a small pay rise. All claims were contested by the company and therefore deadlocked. Arbitration was provided by Sheriff A.O.M. Mackenzie of Inverness. His judgment was that the Inverness yard shunters should have a ten-hour day and an hour off for meals; that men earning 19s or less should receive an extra 1s;

that the minimum weekly wage of signalmen and brakesmen should be 21s; and that locomotive crews should receive a lodging allowance of 2s a night, to a maximum of 3s per week.

Shortly after the senior staff's first annual dinner, the Highland Railway had its second recorded strike. Thirty-two blacksmiths at Lochgorm Works stopped work in March 1913, in pursuit of a rejected pay claim. A letter to the *Aberdeen Free Press* of 24 April claimed that the total amount of money at issue was £40. The smiths wanted an increase from 27s 3d to 30s a week; the hammermen wanted 21s instead of 19s. The Scottish average rate for these trades was quoted as 39s. The company resorted to outside sources for its forgings, and there was widespread sympathy for the strikers. A relief fund was opened, but after nine weeks the strike was called off, with the men accepting the company's offer of 5 per cent extra. This was followed almost immediately by a strike of men in the coal depot, who were awarded a pay increase from 18s to 21s. This prompted a demand from the men who shovelled coal into the skips supplying locomotive tenders, to have their 20s a week raised to 25s. They went on strike, and were replaced by 'blackleg workers'. The *Highland Times* of 3 July 1913 commented that, 'It is said that trouble is brewing'. This did not materialise, however, and the men went back to work.

## The Community of the Railway: Directors and Shareholders

According to the comfortable fiction of British commercial theory, anyone with £2,000 worth of shares in the company could become a director of the Highland Railway, if elected by the shareholders. In reality, it was impossible unless the candidate were sponsored by the current board, whose own shareholdings, plus the proxy votes they wielded on behalf of others, and the general obeisance paid to them by most shareholders, ensured their control. Thus it was possible, as with J.D. Fletcher, to assure an acceptable would-be director for the next vacancy. The company rules stipulated a maximum of eighteen directors, though around sixteen was more usual. C.J.A. Robertson in *The Origins of the Scottish Railway System, 1722-1844*, wrote in mildly disparaging terms that:

> Rural railways might continue to fill their provisional committees with gentry, culmi-
> nating in the phalanx of peers, clan chiefs and high military officers which graced the
> Highland in the 1860s, but elsewhere the money and the directorial talent which created
> the railways came from the merchant interest. [1]

The real point about the first Highland directors, however, was not their titles or positions as landed proprietors, but their wealth. In the Highlands, there were no merchants of the resources of those in Glasgow and central Scotland. Nor, in the early years, were any rich investors from outside the Highlands likely to put money into railway ventures there. Coal mines, factories, docks, cities – these were what made railways profitable, and the Highlands were notably deficient in all four. If anyone was going to invest in railways there, it was the landed gentry: the only people with the money. Very often, of course, they were first- or second-generation proprietors, [2] whose estates had been bought with the proceeds of commerce or industry: Mammon was never far away. The Inverness & Nairn Railway, a relatively low-cost line, was close to having a board of merchants, but with the I&AJR, the magnates appeared, and dominated from then on. The biggest investors, like Seafield and Sutherland, were not only on the board themselves but so were their commissioners or men of business. In this role Thomas Bruce and George Loch first became directors, their prime task being to make sure their masters' money was being properly spent. They were well off in their own right and (in Bruce's case) well-connected socially, but not men of huge means. Fraser-Tytler and Murray of Geanies were similar types. As committee chairmen they were the backbone of the early board. All shared an interest in the 'improvement' of the Highlands. Marinell Ash records that Matheson bought Ardross in 1846 for £90,000 and spent some £230,000 on reclaiming land and setting up thirty-two farms and fourteen crofts. [3] Their view was that the Highlands could and should be brought to a state of commercial development comparable with that of the rest of the country, and that to make this happen, a railway was essential. It was the utility of a railway, not the idealism of social regeneration, that was in their minds, but there was an aspirational element too: they were prepared both to work and to risk their own credit for it. To typify them as backwoods lairds is obviously absurd. They were provincial but not parochial, and their metropolitan links were strong. The Parliamentary and aristocratic connections of its men of business and grandees was of great value to the HR, and something akin to the 'old boy network' undoubtedly helped in the consistent rebuffing of the efforts of the Great North of Scotland Railway – with a much more mercantile board – to get access to Inverness; perhaps also in the struggles with the Post Office, and in the long emollience of the Board of Trade in the face of the Highland's intransigence.

To be invited to join the Highland Railway Board was certainly considered an honour, but it carried responsibilities, particularly during the hard-pressed 1860s. In the middle of his personal drama, in November 1895, Andrew Dougall gave an interview [4] about his long career, and made this point:

> On the completion of the various lines it was found, that although the proprietors and others in the district had subscribed largely towards them, £1,200,000 was required to equip and open them for traffic. This money had to be raised, and the directors gave their personal security to the banks and insurance offices, the whole of them becoming thus, jointly and severally, responsible for the amount. This obligation continued for ten years.

The account compresses a number of occasions into one, but such a level of commitment from a board of directors is unique in British railway history. A degree of involvement with the business, through personal activity or financial commitment, or both, was expected. The early directors took very large stakes: the Earl of Seafield's holding was £73,370; Alexander Matheson's £73,623; James Merry's £85,000; Mackintosh of Raigmore's £26,500. The Duke of Sutherland eclipsed them all with £355,545. The least involved were the Dukes of Atholl (shareholding £3,150) but with the line traversing so much of their land, it was important to keep them in the fold.

As the first generation of directors died or retired, the composition of the board changed in significant respects. From the 1870s, occasional industrialists like J.W. Kynoch, of the Keith woollen mills, appear, a trend intensified in the 1890s and after. A higher proportion by that time also came from the southern fringe of the Highlands, or beyond the Highlands altogether. This reflected a wider spread of shareholders, and a larger share base, but it also suggests that the influence of northern proprietors had waned. In 1905, with Whitelaw as chairman, his deputy was R.M. Wilson, a Glasgow industrialist, and the other directors were J.D. Fletcher of Rosehaugh, the Marquis of Breadalbane, the Dukes of Atholl and Sutherland, W. Steuart Fothringham of Grandtully, Sir William Ogilvy Dalgleish of Errol Park, Edward G. Fraser-Tytler of Aldourie, Donald Grant, Grantown, Thomas Yool of Auchtertyre, Elgin, James Baillie of Dochfour, Albert E. Pullar of Durn, J.G. Stewart of Aultwharrie, Dunblane, and Lord Lovat. Seven out of the fifteen lived south of Druimuachdar, none had any connection with the municipality of Inverness, and only Sutherland had any links with the region north of Dingwall. At least eight might be classed primarily as businessmen of one sort or another. Fifty years on from the founders, their attitude was very different. These directors had substantially smaller holdings: Baillie's £3,000-worth was typical, and Whitelaw held only the minimum £2,000. For them the railway was not an ambition, a personal commitment, or an act of faith in the future; there was no question of what it might do and what its effect might be: they *had* the railway, it was doing its job, and their task was to keep it at work and in profit. Pragmatism was the order of the day, and aspirations were superfluous. Apart from having a locomotive named after oneself (in territorial or personal terms), the chief perk of a director was a Gold Pass, valid also on other British railways with which the HR had reciprocal arrangements. Their emolument was modest, remaining at £1,250 divided among them as they saw fit, until 1914 when a prominent shareholder, Mr Bosher of Sheffield, a source of regular fulsome tributes to the board at general meetings, moved it be increased to £2,100. This brought a few sarcastic letters in the Scottish press from Ordinary shareholders, who did not feel their scant dividends justified any pay rise for the directors.

The HR directors were always non-executive, with the partial exception of Thomas Bruce, and none of the senior officials was ever invited to join the board. In line with the *mores* of the time, the social gulf between even the salaried staff and the directors was a wide one, though the departmental heads might be invited for the occasional day's shooting; while to the waged staff the board occupied another world. 'J.E.C.', describing Thomas Bruce as 'a sheltered aristocrat of the old-fashioned sort', claimed that on one rainy day, Bruce took a cab from the door of the HR office to the Royal Hotel at the other side of Academy Street, a distance little more than a penalty kick.[5] On the political level, however, all were equal, if they had a vote. The political complexion of the board had been Liberal in the early decades, but with the split in the Liberal party and the rise of unionism and imperialism, it became increasingly Conservative in its sympathies. As the right to vote began to be extended among the adult male population, and especially after the secret ballot was introduced in 1872, the electorate of the Highland counties began to display a stout political independence. By 1889 four crofter MPs sat in the House of Commons, from the northern counties once represented, as if by right, by members of aristocratic families or their nominees, like George Loch. It was the era of the 'Land War' in which, on several occasions, troops and police were sent against demonstrating crofters. Even the most politically Liberal of the Highland Railway's landowning directors viewed such unrest as a threat to their own legal rights and thus as something to be vigorously suppressed. At election times they left no doubt about whom they supported, though there was no coercion as practised for a time by F.W. Webb on the LNWR at Crewe. The moderate extent of political bias is shown by the fuss made in 1910 when the stationmaster at Fort George denied access to the station to the place's only cabman, a Labour supporter.[6] Indeed, the company's most notable foray into Parliamentary politics was a complete disaster. Again in 1910, when Cameron of Lochiel was standing as Conservative–Unionist candidate for Sutherland, the *Northern Times* recorded a 'memorable night in Brora' when the Temperance Hall was packed and 200 people failed to gain entry. The speaker was William Whitelaw, who had come to campaign for Lochiel, on a special train from Inverness, 'accompanied by Messrs. T. McEwen, Traffic Manager, P. Drummond, Locomotive Engineer, and W. Roberts, Engineer-in-Chief'. Whether they knew it or not, Brora was a hotbed of radical Liberalism. The audience was noisy from the start, and a prominent local Liberal, John Ross, had to appeal for a fair hearing. It was in vain: Whitelaw was constantly heckled and in the end, 'the audience rose en masse and riot was threatened'. The police were called, but the Unionists fled the hall, the Radicals mounted the platform, 'and what was intended for a Unionist meeting ended in a magnificent Liberal demonstration'. The special train left for the south in a hurry, with rotten eggs thrown at it. No record exists of whether it was chartered; perhaps with such a formidable supporting party it could have been classed as an inspection trip.

The shareholders were mostly deferential to the board. They enjoyed the pleasant perquisite of two free first-class return passes to Inverness, if they wished to attend the half-yearly meetings (these became annual in 1913), but it was exceptional for more than one in ten to come.[7] Until 1895 these gatherings were rarely controversial, but with the Dougall affair, and the changing composition of the board, a small but vocal dissident group emerged. They had various causes of their own: Mr Laing of Keith, supported loyally by his sister, felt he should be on the board, and ex-Provost Ross of Inverness felt his town was not represented; others, like the Rev. Mr Masson of Edinburgh, Mr Macallan, an Inverness fish merchant, and Neil Mackintosh, son of old Raigmore, waged a more general war against the new order.[8] Unhappiness with the lot of the Ordinary shareholder was an important motive. Only once did the shareholders overcome the board, in the proposed amalgamation with the Great North, and that was as much by passive as by active opposition. The directors' reaction to these regular opponents is typified by the annual meeting of 25 February 1914, when the election to the board of W.H. Cox, the Dundee jute millionaire, was challenged. Laing wanted to know what Dundee had to do with the Highland Railway. Ex-Provost Ross wanted an Inverness man. Mr Keith of Thurso complained that there was no one to speak for Caithness on the board, and there were only fourteen directors. What was to prevent them adding another?

The chairman (R.M. Wilson): 'It is not the intention of the Board to add to the Directorate at present.'
Mr Keith: 'For what reason?'
The chairman: 'For our own reasons.'

And that was that.

# ELEVEN

*Passenger Trains*

On the Highland, as on other railways, the standard of service offered to passengers progressed gradually through the later nineteenth century and made more rapid strides through the first fifteen years of the twentieth. The company operated three types of train, passenger, goods, and mixed. A mixed train conveyed both goods and passenger vehicles, and this was the most common arrangement until the 1890s on all the company's lines. The very first train from Inverness to Nairn had offered passengers a choice of covered or open carriages, but only because of a temporary lack of the former. On normal services, passenger carriages had roofs. All the early vehicles were flat-sided four-wheelers, either first or third class. In 1848, Robert Somers, in *Letters from the Highlands*, had observed that, 'there are only two ranks of people – a higher rank and a lower rank – the former consisting of a few large tenants… and the latter consisting of a dense body of small cottars and fishermen'.[1] There was no need for second-class accommodation until the opening of the Perth line, when the railway was required to honour second class through bookings from the south. Like all British railway companies, the HR was obliged to run at least one 'Parliamentary' train daily, stopping at all stations, at a fare of a penny a mile for adults.

By the end of 1864, the passenger rolling stock consisted of 161 vehicles, of which 60 were third class, 38 first class, and only 4 second class. There were three saloons, one family carriage, nine composite first-second class and twelve composite second-third carriages; also four mail vans and thirty brake vans, some of which incorporated a third-class compartment. Most were also provided with dog boxes. A third-class carriage held fifty people, in five compartments; first class held thirty-two, in four compartments. If, improbably, all carriages were in use at once, the line's carrying capacity would be around 5,500 people. Passengers were not expected to stand, and the bye-laws provided for a fine of 50s on anyone who persisted in trying to enter a full carriage or compartment, against the objection of a seated passenger. Smoking was allowed only from October 1868, in compartments specifically designated.[2] While seats in first class were padded, in third class they were of wood. From early 1865 trains were fitted with an alarm system, consisting of a wire strung between the carriages and terminating in a gong fixed to the right-hand side of the locomotive's tender.[3] For once, the HR was acting in anticipation of legislation, as such communication was first stipulated in the Railway Regulation Act of 1871. The system was phased out with the general introduction of vacuum brakes in the early 1900s, at which point each compartment was equipped with a chain which, when pulled, could partially engage the brakes.

The extension of lines to Wick and Thurso prompted the next increase of coaching stock, fifty-one vehicles, in 1873, and at that time the HR acquired its first six-wheel carriages, all first class, though it continued to build four-wheelers. A further twenty third-class four-wheelers were ordered in 1878, and also six 'tri-composite' carriages to hold all three classes of passenger, in separate compartments, were ordered. These were presumably intended for use on short trains or branch lines. In the same year, the Pullman Co. offered to place drawing room cars on the summer mail trains, at a supplement of 2s 6d to the first-class fare, but the board rejected the idea.[4] Also in 1878, three sleeping cars were built. These seem to have been the HR's first corridor coaches,[5] though without interconnecting vestibules; and they accommodated nine persons each. Two ran between Inverness and Perth, and one from Wick to Inverness, though lack of patronage caused this service to be withdrawn within the year. The Perth service was more successful and in 1885 the HR sleepers were supplanted on it by two six-wheel Pullman cars. Formerly in use on the east coast main line between London and York, they were given the names *Balmoral* and *Dunrobin*, and the charge was 5s a berth, in addition to the first-class fare. By 1888 the HR sleepers were converted to first-class compartment carriages. In the early 1890s, the Pullmans were fitted with four-wheel bogies, becoming the first HR bogie vehicles, though the trains between Perth and Inverness had for some years incorporated bogie carriages of other railways on through services. Passengers with HR tickets were not supposed to use these superior vehicles.[6] David Jones, with a taste for the distinctive in carriage design as in engines, introduced his six-wheeled 'coupé' carriages around this time. Sometimes referred to as 'chariot-shaped' or 'boot-shaped', there were ultimately sixteen of them, with bow ends, and the side-panels curved outwards at the lower corners to provide a straight buffer-beam. The bow ends incorporated large windows, which made them good observation cars if attached to the rear of a train. If a coupé were next the engine, the compartment adjoining the tender was kept locked, in case of flying lumps of coal. The first set had five compartments; the second set had four, with access to two central lavatories: the first HR carriages to have this facility. At the same time Jones built eight composite coaches, running on bogies, with two first-, one second- and two third-class compartments. These were said to be the first HR carriages to work through to Edinburgh and Glasgow,[7] and for this purpose they had Westinghouse air-brakes, as used by the Caledonian and North British, as well as vacuum brakes. Only the first-class compartments had access to toilets: it was 1900 before the Highland began to provide lavatories in third-class carriages. Those carriages of 1889 are probably the ones referred to by Foxwell and Farrer in their famous book,

*Express Trains, English and Foreign*: 'The *third class* carriages of these Highland express trains are equal to the very newest of the wealthiest English companies – are perhaps unequalled in the amount of space between opposing knees'.[8]

At first the sole amenity afforded to passengers was rather dim lighting, from oil-burning 'pot-lamps' inserted ready-lit at the starting stations, through round lids in the carriage roofs. Carriage heating was not on offer: passengers were expected to do as they would once have done on the stagecoach, and wrap themselves up in several layers of clothing. From around 1862 foot warmers began to be provided, at least on longer-distance trains. 'J.E.C.' suggests that this practice was borrowed by the Highland from the GNSR.[9] They were metal cases, filled with fused acetate of soda; solid when cold, but when the can containing it is heated by immersion in hot water it liquefies, and in the process absorbs heat which is given out again as it gradually reverts back to the solid state. They were placed in the compartments at Perth and Inverness, and boilers were installed on the platforms at Blair Atholl and Aviemore to warm up replacements. At Inverness, this was an additional task for the lamp-room men. D.T. Holmes, in his *Literary Tours in the Highlands and Islands*, remarked on possible inconveniences of winter journeys in the 1900s:

> The Glasgow-Inverness train, for example, may, on the coldest night of the year, break down at Dalnaspidal; and in such a case the passengers will have to sit, entertained by howling blasts, till a fresh engine comes up from Blair Atholl. Such an experience was once mine… Outside were the great snow-sheeted mountains, and the moon was gazing in blear-eyed compassion through a screen of haze. From end to end of the train resounded the rhythmic beat of cold-footed passengers striving to bring some warmth of blood to their toes.[10]

With the journey from Perth to Inverness lasting for more than five hours, and that from Inverness to Wick more than seven hours, in carriages lacking corridors and lavatories, some form of provision had to be made to allow for the physical needs of passengers. Kingussie on the Perth line, and Bonar Bridge on the Wick line, were the main stops for this purpose, and both stations had refreshment rooms. Passengers could send a free telegram ahead to Kingussie, reserving a hot or cold luncheon or dinner basket, with a small bottle of claret. Breakfast baskets were also available, and light refreshments (cups of hot soup in winter) were sold at the carriage doors. While baskets could also be reserved at Bonar Bridge, it was chiefly famous for its plates of hot soup, set out for the arrival of a train. A meeting of the Sutherland & Caithness Railway board in late 1874 asked the Highland Railway to make a fifteen-minute stop at Bonar Bridge, and to request the tenant of the refreshment rooms to have ready: '… hot soup, a round of beef, hot potatoes, and fresh bread – also tea and coffee'. The HR timetable allowed a stop of ten minutes, not excessive for a large number of people to obtain food and use the lavatories. An article by G.W.J. Potter in the *Railway Club Journal* of April 1910[11] records the scene as he travelled south:

Following the stoppage of the train the usual rush of travellers across the bridge and into the restaurant took place, and soon there were loud shouts of 'A sixpenny spoon', 'A spoon', 'A sixpenny spoon, miss', from the knowing ones desirous of partaking of soup, this being the price of a plate of soup. The idea seems somewhat original, as it allows the soup to be placed beforehand in plates upon the tables, so saving time, and yet it ensures that partakers thereof shall pay their lawful sixpences to the attendants…

Dining cars were never acquired; at the Shareholders' Meeting on 30 March 1910 Whitelaw called them 'a luxury the Highland Railway could not afford', but in 1922 a Pullman diner from the more sybaritic Caledonian Railway was included on Glasgow–Inverness trains, running to and returning from Aviemore.[12]

In 1893 the HR abolished second class, following the example of many other companies, and the four second-class and fifty-two composite carriages then in stock were regraded to third, or first-third. It may seem odd not to rename third as second, but in the Highland's case that would have involved the upgrading or replacing of 109 wooden-seated carriages, the great majority of them being four-wheelers more than ten years old, and some of them more than thirty years old. But even before the abolition of second class, the company had begun the upgrading of third, and an article in the *Inverness Courier*[13] complimented the company on the introduction of sprung seats, window curtains and luggage-racks in its new six-wheel thirds. These improvements go some way to explain why third-class passenger numbers doubled between 1875 and 1895, and first-class numbers fell heavily from 84,436 in February–August 1876, to 52,740 in the equivalent period in 1894.[14] Between 1896 and 1899, experiments were carried out with electric lighting of carriages, and in the latter year, also with gas lighting. By 1901 it was decided to proceed with gas, and a gradual process of conversion began. The gas-producing plant was installed at Inverness, and tank-wagons of gas were taken from there to Perth and Wick. Construction of four-wheeled carriages had stopped in the mid-1890s, and during the 1900s many of the oldest were withdrawn, though six-wheelers were still being built. In 1905 the company finally embarked on steam-heating, beginning with the carriages running through from Inverness to Glasgow; the Edinburgh carriages were fitted in 1906, and some 'Castle' class locomotives were adapted to supply steam for the purpose. But the great majority of carriages remained unheated. The two Pullman sleepers were still running in 1906, between Inverness and Perth, but on some nights they were little used, or even empty. For this reason, and also because as the *Railway Magazine* observed, [15] the Pullmans 'were of no pecuniary value to the Highland Railway', Peter Drummond was asked to provide two composite carriages containing four single-berth first-class sleeping compartments and three standard third-class seating compartments: 'a very economical type of vehicle,' commented the *R.M.*, "as it saves the running of an empty sleeper'. They ran between Inverness and Glasgow Central, via Forres, with Edinburgh passengers able to join or leave at Larbert. In 1908, carriages with interconnecting vestibules began to be built for the main south line. On some branch lines and local trains, elderly carriages were still in use, to the annoyance of passengers. In September 1909 Thurso Town Council complained both about the lack of through carriages to the south, and the state of the stock used on the branch. Councillor Shearer was quoted in the *Groat*: 'Why should Thurso not have the same as Wick? They have lavatories in the through carriages from Wick and we have two carriages only fit for making firewood'[16] Between 1911-13, steam heating was finally introduced on the Kyle of Lochalsh and Wick trains. Between then and 1922, many more carriages were adapted for steam heating; and gas lighting began to be phased out in favour of electricity. By the time of incorporation into the LMS, the HR had 295 passenger carriages, of which 92 were composite first-third. There were the two sleeping cars, 103 passenger luggage and brake vans, and nine Post Office vans.

The livery of Highland passenger rolling stock was plain dark green, except for a period from 1897, when the upper panels, between the windows, were painted white. This was abandoned in 1907, during the economy years, though the *Railway Magazine* in March 1907 reported that a 'varnished teak' finish was in use on the company's new third-class excursion saloons. All carriages were built of wood on iron frames, though the earlier ribbed sides were replaced with vertical matchboarding by David Jones, from 1892.

From the opening of the Perth line, Highland passenger services followed a fairly consistent pattern on the three main lines east, north and south from Inverness, but a degree of evolution and expansion can be traced. The following summary, looking at three different years, deals with northbound, or 'Down' services; southbound, or 'Up' services were normally equivalent, except where noted. However, particularly in July and August, there were many special trains, empty stock workings and scheduled trains divided into two or more portions. Perth to Inverness was the busiest route, and in summer 1871 three trains ran each way on weekdays, of which the night train, leaving Perth at 1 a.m. and reaching Inverness at 9 a.m., was mixed. The others were passenger trains: the Mail, leaving Perth at 9.30 a.m., carrying only first and second class, and making the journey in five hours and fifteen minutes, with fifteen stops; and the Parliamentary, leaving at 11.50 a.m. and reaching Inverness at 6.25 p.m., carrying all classes and stopping at all stations. In addition two local services ran between Perth and Blair Atholl, a mixed one leaving Perth at 6.50 a.m. and arriving at 9.30 p.m., and a passenger-only at 4.20, taking a mere two hours for just over thirty-five miles. These connected with the Aberfeldy branch train. At the northern end, a mixed train left Kingussie at 8 a.m. (passenger carriages attached to the 3 a.m. goods from Perth), reaching Inverness at 12.35 p.m. The mixed southbound night service from Inverness left at 7.45 p.m. and reached Perth at 5.50 a.m., having crossed the northbound train at Blair Atholl.

On the Keith line, the first service was a mixed train from Inverness to Forres, leaving at 6 a.m. and arriving at 7.30 a.m. A Parliamentary train left Forres at 7.45 a.m. and reached Keith at 9.05 a.m.. A mixed train left Forres at 11.21 a.m., offering a belated connection with the night train as well as with the Kingussie local, and reaching Keith at 12.51 p.m. The northbound Mail, arriving at Forres at 1.45 p.m., had a quick connection with an eastbound train leaving at 1.55 p.m. From Elgin, this became a mixed train, reaching Keith at 3.15 p.m. An Inverness–Forres local left at 3.40 p.m., arriving at 5.10 p.m. The Parliamentary from Perth also had a Keith connection, a mixed train leaving Forres at 5.15 p.m. and reaching Keith at 7.20 p.m.

Four trains daily went north from Inverness in 1871, but only two went all the way; the first being the 5.30 a.m. mixed train for Golspie, arriving at 11.40 a.m. As far as Tain, it carried first and third class; from there on it was Parliamentary. Following the night train's arrival, another mixed train, conveying first class and Parliamentary, left Inverness at 9.15 a.m. and terminated at Tain at 11.20 a.m. This train connected at Dingwall with the 10.12 a.m. mixed and Parliamentary to Strome Ferry, arriving there at 1.15 p.m. (and thence by steamer to Portree, arriving 6.30 p.m.). The northern Mail, with first, second and third accommodation as well as goods wagons, left Inverness at 3.10 p.m. and reached Golspie at 7.25 p.m. A Strome Ferry connection left Dingwall at 4.15 p.m., arriving at 7.15 p.m.; like the morning service it carried only first class and Parliamentary passengers. The Parliamentary status of both daily trains on the Skye line suggests that the majority of passengers were of very low income. The last train to the north was the 6.50 p.m. mixed to Tain, carrying first and third class, and arriving at 9.20 p.m.

The Sunday service consisted of a single Mail train each way on each line, except that to Strome Ferry, which had no Sunday trains. A 9.30 a.m. departure from Perth, with all classes including Parliamentary, reached Forres at 1.45 p.m., running to exactly the same schedule as the weekday Mail, leaving for Inverness at 1.50 p.m. and arriving at 2.45 p.m. A connection for Keith left Forres at 1.55 p.m., arriving 3.15 p.m. The Golspie train left Inverness at 3.10 p.m. and reached the (then) terminus at 7.35 p.m.

In summer 1880, with the Wick and Thurso line open since 1874, the pattern had altered somewhat. All trains except the Mail between Inverness and Perth now accepted Parliamentary fare-passengers. The night mixed train from Perth now left at 12.40 a.m. and offered sleeping-car accommodation, reaching Inverness at 8.50 a.m., albeit with a disclaimer in the Working Timetable that as: 'being a Goods Train, with only Passenger accommodation attached for the conveyance of those who prefer travelling during night by a train of this description', the company could not guarantee its timing or connections. The Mail still left Perth at 9.30 a.m. and reached Inverness at 2.45 p.m., and the old Parliamentary left at 11.50 a.m. and arrived at 6.25 p.m. The morning Blair Atholl local still left at 6.50 but took fifteen minutes longer. There were two evening services to Blair Atholl, leaving Perth at 4.30 p.m. and 7.25 p.m., arriving at 6.6. and 9.15 p.m. All were mixed trains. A Saturdays-only summer excursion service, operated jointly with the Caledonian, left Dundee at 2.30 p.m. for Dunkeld, arriving at 4.15 p.m., and allowing just over three hours' strolling time before beginning its return trip at 7.35 p.m. The 8 a.m. Kingussie–Inverness mixed now arrived at 12.40 p.m. Between Forres and Inverness, mixed trains were largely replaced by separate passenger and goods services, with passenger-only trains leaving Forres at 9 a.m. and 11.20 a.m., and Inverness at 9.45 a.m. and 4 p.m., running to a faster schedule of either one hour or sixty-five minutes. The early train from Inverness to Forres, now leaving at 5.40 a.m., was goods only, then ran mixed from Forres to Keith, arriving there at 8.55 a.m.

Some speeding-up was also visible on the Keith line, with ten minutes pared from the 1871 schedule in both directions, matching the Mail, which still left Forres at 1.55 p.m. and was in Keith by 3.15 p.m. From Elgin it was passenger only, and the timetable now shows an Aberdeen arrival, at 6.30 p.m. The fastest train was the 12.25 p.m. from Keith, which reached Forres in only one hour fifteen minutes. Eastbound, the services were two passenger trains, two mixed and two goods; westbound, there were three passenger trains, two mixed and two goods. The evening train, though still mixed, was quicker than before, leaving Forres at 5.20 p.m. and arriving in Keith at 6.50 p.m. A mixed train ran from Inverness to Forres at 7.35 p.m., arriving at 8.55 p.m., and running on to Perth as a goods train.

Northbound from Inverness, there were still four trains, with the first being the 5.20 a.m. mixed for Helmsdale, arriving at 1.15 p.m. A Wick train – passenger only – left at 9.40 a.m., arriving at 5.40 p.m. (5.25 p.m. in Thurso). At Dingwall, it connected with the 10.50 mixed for Strome Ferry, arriving 1.35 p.m. The second Wick train, a mixed one, left Inverness at 3.10 p.m., arriving at 10.20 p.m. The Strome Ferry connection left Dingwall at 4.51 p.m., arriving at 7.25 p.m. The final train was a mixed local to Tain, leaving at 7.25 p.m. and arriving at 9.45 p.m. A Saturday service ran from Golspie to Wick, leaving at 7 a.m. and arriving at 10.05 a.m.; it left Wick at 4.15 p.m. and reached Golspie at 7.30 p.m. 'Empty train' workings between Golspie and Brora show that these services were usually worked by the Duke of Sutherland's engine *Dunrobin*, which was stabled at Brora. In Caithness, two trains ran between Wick and Thurso each day, from Thurso at 8 a.m. and 11.40 a.m.; from Wick at 9.30 p.m. and 3.30 p.m. They took sixty-five minutes, except for the 3.30, the only one not to be mixed, which took ten minutes less.

The Sunday service was the same as in 1871, except that the 3.10 p.m. mail train from Inverness now ran to Wick, arriving at 10.20 p.m. (Thurso 10.05 p.m.). In addition, two Sunday trains ran each way between Wick and Thurso, in the afternoon and evening.

Southbound services in 1880 generally balanced the northbound ones, with two important exceptions. A night train ran from Wick to Inverness, a mixed service leaving at 12.10 a.m. and reaching Inverness at 9.35 a.m. It is unlikely to have picked up many passengers at its advertised halts at places like Scotscalder and Kinbrace in the small hours, but its business was also with goods wagons. There was no corresponding Down train. The night mixed train from Inverness to Perth now left at 10 p.m. and arrived at 7 a.m. The evening trains between Perth and Blair Atholl were balanced by two morning trains, at 6.35 a.m. (mixed) and 9.55 a.m. (passenger), arriving at 8.20 a.m. and 11.20 a.m. This was as close as the Highland ever got to a commuter service. Local trains and banking duties made the Blair Atholl locomotive shed a very busy one.

From the opening of the direct line from Aviemore, late in 1898, the traffic planners had to cater for two main lines into Inverness from the south. In the summer of 1909, seven scheduled trains ran each day between Perth and Inverness. The night train from Perth left at 12.50 a.m., with sleeping car from Glasgow, and travelled via Carrbridge, arriving at 5.10 a.m. A connecting train left Aviemore for Forres at

4.00 a.m., arriving also at 5.10 a.m. Nairn passengers went on to Inverness and changed trains there. At 5 a.m. another train left Perth, conveying sleeping cars from London and through carriages from southern railways, running via Carrbridge and arriving at Inverness at 8.35 a.m. This ran only from 13 July to 11 August. Fifteen minutes later the 'normal' night train from London left Perth, and arrived in Inverness at 9.08 a.m. This train was also noted as conveying 'Sleeping Carriages Euston to Strathpeffer'. (These presumably went forward on the 9.50 a.m. Wick service, which had through carriages for Strathpeffer, detached at Dingwall). A Forres connection left Aviemore at 8.25 a.m., arriving at 9.35 a.m. The Mail left Perth at 6.15 a.m. and reached Aviemore at 8.33 a.m. Here it divided, the direct Inverness portion arriving at 10.10 a.m., and the Grantown portion arriving in Inverness at 11.15 a.m. A Saturdays-only train left Perth at 9.25 a.m., reaching Inverness at 1.50 p.m.; its Forres connection left Aviemore at 12.45, arriving 1.56 p.m. A train for Inverness via Forres still left Perth at 11.50 a.m., running non-stop to Newtonmore, which it reached at 1.44 p.m.; Forres was reached at 3.25, and Inverness at 4.15. Only ten minutes later, the old 'Parliamentary' left Perth, stopping at all stations (five on request only) and reaching Inverness via Carrbridge at 4.36 p.m. There were two late afternoon services from Perth, the first leaving at 3.50 and stopping only at Pitlochry, Blair Atholl, Newtonmore, Kingussie and Aviemore, and in Inverness at 7.42 p.m. A connecting train via Forres, perhaps also with through carriages, left Aviemore at 6.50 and arrived in Inverness at 9.15 p.m. An all-stations train left Perth at 4.10 p.m., and reached Inverness, via Carrbridge, at 8.40. Despite the larger number of trains, Nairn felt hard done-by, with no direct overnight service and sometimes long waits at Aviemore, and an additional change at Forres or Inverness. To a resort town, this was important. The winter schedule would of course be much reduced from this.

The northbound locals from Perth now numbered five; the first at 5.30 a.m. to Struan, arriving at 7.33 a.m.; the others stopped at Blair Atholl, running at 9.30 a.m. (arriving 10.54 a.m.), 12.10 p.m. (arriving 1.44 p.m.), and in the evening at 7.15 p.m. and 8.15 p.m., arriving at 8.20 p.m. and 9.40 p.m. respectively. The morning Kingussie to Inverness train was absorbed by the Mail at this time, though in later years, with changed timings, it reappeared. The Saturday excursion service from Dundee (West) now ran to Blair Atholl, leaving at 1.50 p.m. and arriving at 3.53 p.m.

Better relations with the Great North are reflected in the Keith line timetable for summer 1909. The existences, of Elgin as a junction, and Aberdeen as a destination, were acknowledged, and a through train left Inverness at 6 a.m., arriving in Aberdeen at 9.55 a.m. The 9.08 a.m. departure from Inverness divided at Forres into a non-stop train to Elgin, arriving at 10.14 a.m., and a stopping train to Keith, arriving at 11.20 a.m. The Mail left Inverness at 10.10 a.m., reaching Forres at 11.08 a.m. Onward travellers had to wait for the arrival of the 11.05 a.m. fast train, which reached Forres at 11.50 a.m. and went on to Keith and Aberdeen, arriving there at 3 p.m. A similar pattern was followed by the next two trains, the 12.35 p.m. all stations service to Elgin, arriving at 2.07 p.m., and the 1.40 p.m. fast train to the same destination, arriving at 2.40 p.m. At 3 p.m. a train left for Keith, arriving forty-five minutes later, but there were also GNSR connections at Elgin for Portsoy and Aberdeen. Further trains to Keith left Inverness at 2.30 p.m. (arriving 4.55 p.m.), 3.35 p.m. (arriving 5.25 p.m.), 6 p.m. (arriving 8.06 p.m.) and the star performer at 7.25 p.m., doing the fifty-five miles to Keith in two hours flat. The 3.35 p.m. and the 6.00 p.m. both provided Aberdeen connections, via Mulben and the GNSR respectively, so that in total six trains ran between Inverness and Aberdeen daily. In the reverse direction there were seven, the extra service being a 3.30 a.m. departure from Aberdeen, running via Mulben and arriving in Inverness at 7.35 a.m.

In the summer of 1909, services on the Further North line were a little more frequent. There were still only two trains daily from Inverness to Wick and Thurso, both shown as Mail Trains, the first leaving at 5.40 a.m. and reaching Wick at 12.40 p.m. (Thurso 12.33 p.m.), and the second leaving at 9.40 a.m., arriving at the northern termini at 4 p.m. and 3.45 p.m. respectively. On Fridays only, the 'Further North Express' left Inverness at 4.35 p.m. and, stopping only at Tain, Bonar Bridge (one minute: no time for soup), The Mound, Golspie, Helmsdale, Forsinard and Georgemas, arrived at Wick at 9.5 p.m. and in Thurso at 8.40 p.m. (The equivalent Up service ran on Thursday, leaving Wick at 10.25 a.m., with the same limited stops but omitting Forsinard and giving ten minutes for lunch at Bonar Bridge, and reaching Inverness at 3.36 p.m.: five hours and eleven minutes for 161.25 miles). Four local trains ran daily to Tain, at 7.45 a.m., 10 a.m., 4.55 p.m. and 8 p.m., stopping at all stations and taking between two hours and five minutes and two hours and twelve minutes for the forty-four-mile journey. A Saturday excursion service ran from Inverness to Dingwall, leaving at 2 p.m. and returning at 8.12 p.m., and a Wednesday one (July and August only) from Dornoch to Brora, leaving at 11 a.m. and arriving at 12.15 p.m.; and returning at 12.36 p.m., arriving in Dornoch at 1.45 p.m. Kyle of Lochalsh was served by four trains, of which two ran all the way from Inverness, at 9.55 a.m. and 2.35 p.m., arriving at 1.40 p.m. and 6.30 p.m., and the morning service connected with Portree and Stornoway steamers. The others ran from Dingwall, in connection with Tain locals, leaving at 8.50 a.m. and 6.10 p.m., reaching Kyle at 11.42 a.m. and 9.30 p.m.

In 1909 all the main lines, except Dingwall–Kyle of Lochalsh, and the direct line, operated the single Sunday mail train in each direction. The Perth Mails came and went by Forres and Grantown. The Sunday Wick–Thurso trains, apart from the Up and Down Mail connections at Georgemas Junction, were reduced to a single one-way service, also billed as a Mail, leaving Thurso at 7 p.m. and reaching Wick at 8 p.m. In 1920, however, when the Post Office withdrew its requirement for Sunday mail trains, all Sunday services on the HR ceased.

An unusual feature of the Highland Railway, probably as a consideration of its relatively sparse services, was that it allowed passengers to travel in the guards' vans of goods trains. Stationmasters were allowed to issue tickets for the purpose, at first-class rate, and incorporating a waiver of all claims for accident or injury. The practice is first recorded on 18 April 1865 when the board allowed Dr Irvine of Pitlochry to use the facility in carrying out his professional duties. The service was not advertised, and it is unlikely that it was much used, though, as David Stirling notes,[17] the practice was continued into the LMS years.

*Passengers*

In the twenty years to 1875, the number of train passengers on the Highland lines rose to 1 million. Between 1876 and 1906, while the population fell slightly, the passenger numbers more than doubled, to over 2 million. Although a substantial proportion were tourists and visitors, the change reflects a huge shift in mobility within the region.

As early as the second week of November 1855, the *Nairnshire Telegraph* was reporting that: 'The Fisherwomen of Nairn have promptly availed themselves of the facilities offered by the Railway – one train on Tuesday having conveyed 22, with at least 1cwt of fish each.' At an early stage cheap fares – below the Parliamentary rate – were available for male and female fish-sellers, and allowing the free carriage of 1cwt of fish, from Tain, Fearn, Invergordon, Strome Ferry, Fort George, Nairn, Kinloss and Burghead. Later, Wick, Helmsdale, Brora, Golspie, and The Mound were added. In 1881, their return fare Nairn to Inverness was 2s; Fearn to Dingwall 2s 6d. The longest journey provided for was from Wick to Perth (25s 5d); '… on Return Journey nothing is allowed free, except the Empty Creel.' In 1909, the fares had not changed.

In *Down to the Sea*, the authors note that the introduction of ice and the coming of the Ross-shire Railway changed the method of salmon distribution from the seaboard villages served by Fearn Station. New ice-houses were built to provide a year-round supply: 'With it, the fish could be safely packed and carried to Fearn Station en route for the London market'.[1] But most of the white fish catch from Balintore and the adjoining villages was sold locally by village women as itinerant fishwives. For them the railway meant an important increase in selling time and area. At first they walked with their hundredweight loads the four miles to Fearn Station, but,

A horse-brake was put on the road… fitted with two parallel seats running lengthwise where the women sat six aside with the creels in the middle… The fishwives got a hand from the porters at the station to heave their creels into the van as they were not allowed to take them in the carriages. Each fishwife had her own area and got off at the appropriate station to walk round her district. They went as far as Invergordon, Alness, Dingwall, Strathpeffer, and even Beauly, and northwards to Tain and Bonar Bridge.[2]

On a wider focus across Easter Ross as a whole, Marinell Ash notes in *This Noble Harbour* that:

The effect of the railway in Easter Ross was immediate and touched all sections of the local population. For example Cromarty fishermen no longer had to walk or sail to Dingwall to sell their wares; instead they came to Invergordon and completed the journey by rail… When the Channel Fleet paid a visit to the Firth in August, 1863, the railroad company ran many special excursion trains to Invergordon… From this time Easter Ross

became a prime area for fattening cattle and growing seed potatoes for the southern markets opened up by the railway. These changes in agricultural practices were to lessen the
local consequences of the national slump in grain prices of the 1870s and 80s. [3]

Even so, she notes that bad harvests and competition from American grain made it
a difficult and even desperate time for many who made their living from the land:
'… the landlords compensated for the loss of income by the further creation of
deer forests and grouse moors and the sale of land'. For many tenants, emigration
was the answer: 'The railroad allowed local emigrants to travel south to Liverpool
and other ports'. Every local newspaper in the north of Scotland carried prominent
advertisements from emigration agencies from the 1870s right into the 1900s. Ash also
records how, after a slump while the railway was a novelty that attracted everyone's
attention, the ship-owners of Invergordon began to fight back. They cut their prices
drastically, so that a steamer fare to Leith might cost 5s, half the third-class rail fare to
Edinburgh. [4] The railway company began to be perceived as monopolistic and greedy.
The *Invergordon Times*, which had proudly boasted on 25 March 1863 that the town
now marked the northern extremity of the line on Bradshaw's map, was by 1876
referring caustically to 'the all-engrossing railway' which charged so much more than
sea transport.

Like all railways, the Highland preferred first-class passengers who paid the full
fare; but had to accept the reality of popular requirements. In the first half of 1876, its
84,436 first-class passengers paid an average of 5s each, while the 500,255 third-class
passengers paid an average of 1s 9d each. Apart from the fishwives, certain other kinds
of passenger received favoured treatment. Among these were emigrants, normally
bound for the Clyde or Liverpool. Special rates were available on production of passage
warrant or emigration agent's certificate. Low fares were also available for fishermen
travelling between Strome (later Kyle) and Buckie. David Turnock estimates that as
many as 2,500 fishermen from Lewis and Harris were going to work on the east coast,
mostly as hired hands. [5] Large numbers of Moray men also made the rail trip when
their boats were tied up at Stornoway. Sometimes they were sufficiently numerous
to need a special train. Cattle drovers, so long as they accompanied a full van-load of
beasts, were allowed to travel free in the guard's van, but if they were escorting only a
half-load or less, they had to pay the full third-class fare. Clearly there was some abuse
of this caboose-riding, and the Working Timetable of 1881 exhorts stationmasters
and ticket collectors to exercise the utmost vigilance when checking such passengers'
travel permits. Schoolchildren travelling to school on season tickets were charged
one third of the standard rate. A memory of this was left by the writer Alasdair Alpin
MacGregor, in *Vanished Waters*. For a time he and his sister travelled by train to attend
Tain Royal Academy, from Bonar Bridge, in the early years of the twentieth century.
Winters were most memorable:

Central heating was then as foreign to the Highland Railway as was electricity. Passengers
in snowy weather sat muffled up in the compartments with their feet on those huge, flat,

foot-warmers provided by the Company in irregular numbers, and upon quite irregular occasions.

When the northbound train was delayed, 'We regarded it as a great mercy when the goods train came in first and got clear, since the compassionate guard used to take us home in his van…'⁶ Volunteers in uniform, travelling to exercise camps or parades, were allowed privilege prices as (by 1909) were boats' crews attending regattas. By 1909 the HR was also offering special return fares for golfers, travelling up to fifty miles, and able to show a voucher signed by the club secretary; also for curlers attending local matches (available on the day only). Theatrical companies and music-hall artistes, 'duly authenticated', were also eligible for reduced fares. The final class of special passenger was corpses, though reduced rates were not in order here. An adult corpse, with hearse, was charged 1*s* per mile, with a minimum of £1; a child's (under twelve) without hearse, was 6*d* a mile (minimum charge 5*s*). By 1909 a degree of social change is noticeable: the fares were the same as they had been in 1880, but now, additionally, 'The Ashes of cremated Bodies, when carried in a Coffin, are charged as a Corpse'.⁷

The standard fares applied were first class, second class (to 1893), third-class mail, third class, and Parliamentary. The government levied a passenger tax of 5 per cent on all fares apart from the Parliamentary one. Third-class mail was more expensive than ordinary third, because the train was faster. On most companies, including the Highland, third class and Parliamentary fares were the same from 1873, when the Cheap Trains Act exempted all 1*d* a mile fares from duty (the tax had previously been chargeable if the train did not stop at all stations). In September 1883, a company circular announced that: 'On and after Monday, 1st October, all ordinary Third Class Single and return Fares will be abolished, and Third Class Passengers will be booked by the Mail trains at Parliamentary Fares.' From then until the abolition of Second, train accommodation was shown as first, second, and Parliamentary. All trains carried all three classes, except for a few locals which omitted second class. By 1909, with first and third only, on all trains, the 'Parliamentary' designation was dropped. Children under three were free, half-price was allowed only for those up to the age of twelve: 'one child per adult passenger'. From the abolition of second class in 1893, and the arrival of a more demanding type of third-class passenger, the HR made occasional attempts to segregate local and long-distance passengers, labelling certain compartments as for 'Passengers for Inverness and Stations South Thereof Only'. While the convenience of those on longer journeys may have been intended, there is a hint of snobbery about it. Some of the Highland's local passengers might have offered the more genteel travellers more local colour than they had expected. A company circular of 21 April 1898 instructed that certain trains should have compartments marked 'Fish-sellers Only'. With no corridor coaches, the railway maintained ticket platforms at the arrival tracks outside Perth and Inverness stations, where ticket inspectors could walk up and down to check tickets. Departure tickets were checked at platform barriers. Highland ticket inspectors were no respecters of persons. Sir Robert Menzies, a shareholder, was found at Perth station on Sunday, 5 May 1877, attempting to travel to Ballinluig on a Saturday return ticket. At first he tried to get a refund of the excess fare from the company; when this failed he brought an action against the HR for £50 damages, claiming assault by the ticket inspectors. Menzies was a problem passenger. On a later occasion, having missed his connection at Ballinluig through delay to his train, he hired a special run of the branch train to take him to Aberfeldy, and tried, in vain, to make the Highland Railway pay for it.

*Through Carriages, the Sleeper War and the 'Caravans'*

Perth was the southern terminus of the Highland trains,[1] and for long, passengers from or to stations south, east or west of there had to change trains, for North British or Caledonian services. The same applied to Great North of Scotland connections at Keith, Boat of Garten, and Elgin, until some through trains between Inverness and Aberdeen started running in 1906. Apart from the sleeping cars to Glasgow and London, there is no indication in its public timetables, until well into the twentieth century, of Highland passenger carriages travelling south of Perth, though from 1889, new bogie coaches were being built with dual braking systems for use on through service between Inverness and Glasgow or Edinburgh; and Caledonian and North British carriages similarly ran to Inverness and beyond. The through carriages would be shunted at Perth for attachment to the onwards train. In summer at least, carriages from other lines travelled north of Inverness. On 27 July 1893, the second portion of the Wick Mail, having left Inverness at 12.37 p.m. and arrived at Dingwall at 1.15 p.m., was derailed at that station when a North Western saloon jumped the points. The eighteen vehicles in the train included a North British saloon, two North Western carriages, and a North Staffordshire horse-box, as well as a Highland travelling post office and a parcels-post van.[2] Though no HR goods trains ran beyond the 'frontier' stations, goods wagons were transferred, as necessary, from the inception of the I&AJR.

An overnight sleeping car service between London and Inverness was run by the London & North Western and Caledonian companies in 1890, using the accelerated 8 p.m. express from Euston; taken on from Perth by the HR's new 5 a.m. train, and arriving at Inverness at 9.15 a.m., 'in time for breakfast". This was part of their response to the east coast's new Forth Bridge route. A regular sleeper between Inverness and London was not introduced until the summer timetable of 1896, when a speeding-up of services both on the HR and lines to the south made it possible for an overnight schedule to be maintained. Two sleeping cars, one of west coast joint stock, the other of east coast joint stock, bound for Euston and Kings Cross respectively, were sometimes supplemented by a Midland railway car bound for St Pancras, via the Waverley Route and Leeds. They were attached to a train that left Inverness at 4.30 p.m. (later 5 p.m.), and reached their London termini at around 7.30 in the morning. The northbound train reached Perth shortly after 5 a.m. and left again for Inverness at 5.30 a.m. This was clearly a prestige service, but the Highland Railway was also concerned about hauling heavy sleeping cars over Dava and Druimuachdar.

The Midland route was the least used, and officials at Inverness would put Midland passengers into the East Coast car, if there was enough room, forcing them to make a midnight change at Waverley Station in Edinburgh. On the northbound service, if all the sleeper passengers could be accommodated in one (or two) cars from Perth, the Highland had no compunction about making some get out at 5.00 a.m. and change cars. This caused a great deal of protest, from passengers and the English companies, but the HR was obdurate.[3] Despite such treatment, use of the service developed to the point where all three of the Anglo–Scottish routes wanted to provide a regular sleeper throughout the year. While the HR did not object to well-filled sleeping cars, it still jibbed at taking empty, or almost-empty ones. Often there was space in its own northbound car from Glasgow, which was attached to the train at Perth. In 1903[4] it proposed to the southern companies that for the next winter timetable, each route should provide a single car, for two nights each week, in turn. The Caledonian Railway felt this unduly generous to the NB, which ran two of the routes to Perth. Its refusal to co-operate meant that for a time, the Highland conveyed no sleeping cars between Perth and Inverness other than its own, until agreement was finally reached on the basis of the HR's suggestion.[5] The *Dundee Advertiser* of 1 November 1908 noted the winter arrangements. The Great Northern Railway provided a sleeping car to Inverness on the 6.25 p.m. from Kings Cross, Mondays and Fridays. The London & North Western ran one on the 8.00 p.m. from Euston on Tuesday and Thursdays. The Midland ran one via the Waverley Route and Edinburgh by the 7.25 p.m. from St Pancras on Wednesdays and the 9.30 p.m. on Saturdays. Reciprocal services were operated in the southbound direction.

The sleeper 'war' reflected the great seasonal fluctuations in passenger traffic between England and the Highlands. For three months, July to September, intensity was high – the summer timetable of 1909 shows two northbound sleeper trains nightly between 13 July and 11 August – but, after that, it dwindled rapidly. During the prime season, the Highland carried large numbers of carriages from other companies. Quite apart from its own publicity efforts, it made great benefits from the promotion drives undertaken by the west coast and east coast companies to the south. During the 'season' the HR carried an extraordinary variety of rolling stock. Foxwell & Farrer's description of the 7.50 a.m. train from Perth, in 1889, is well-known:

> In July and August this 7.50 train is the unique railway phenomenon. Passenger car-riages, saloons, horse-boxes, and vans, concentrated at Perth from all parts of England, are intermixed to make an irregular caravan. Engines are attached fore and aft, and the procession toils pluckily over the Grampians.[6]

On 7 August 1888, they counted thirty-six vehicles from nine companies, including the London Brighton & South Coast Railway. There were one sleeping car, two saloons, ten assorted passenger carriages, thirteen horse-boxes, a carriage van, a carriage truck, five luggage vans, a Post office van, a meat van, and the guard's van. Twenty minutes late out of Perth, it had lost another fifty-two minutes by Kingussie.

Such a combination of vehicles had its own risks: on 28 July of the previous year, the train was derailed at Aviemore. Though every vehicle was fitted with a continuous brake system, and some with two, they could not be connected up because they were of different kinds.[7]

## Goods Traffic

In 1872, C.Y. Michie noted that: 'Almost the only circumstance that has enhanced the value of wood within the past ten or fifteen years is the reduction of the rate of transport derived by railway communication'.[1] W.M. Acworth, in 1889, was in no doubt about the benefits brought by the Highland Railway's goods service: 'Forty years back it cost 6s a quarter to get the barley grown in Badenoch down to Inverness, while to bring a ton of coal up again was worth from £1 to 25s.' The Highland, however, differed from most main line railways in Britain in that its revenues from goods traffic were consistently less than those from passengers and mail; usually around half as much: in 1903-04, all goods traffic totalled £184,458, while passengers, parcels and mails contributed £334,781. This reflected the low level of industry and trade in the region. In addition, the majority of larger communities were on the coast and could also use sea transport.[2] In the circumstances, the goods service provided by the Highland was very good and frequent: something made possible by its use of mixed trains. Though this practice gave rise to a long dispute, and a great deal of mutual exasperation, between the company and the Board of Trade, for many years the line could not otherwise have provided an adequate goods service over most of the system without incurring heavy losses. As it was, the mixed train gave places like Helmsdale three goods services daily to Inverness, in the summer timetable of 1880. Purely goods trains were relatively few. In the June 1864 timetable, there were two daily each way between Inverness and Perth, two from Perth to Blair Atholl but only one the other way; and one daily each way between Inverness and Keith, and Inverness and Meikle Ferry. By 1871 the morning Perth goods was designated 'English Express': it left Inverness at 10.35 a.m. and reached Perth at 5.40 p.m. The Meikle Ferry goods service now operated only to and from Tain, and the Keith goods ran only to and from Forres. The Blair Atholl goods-only trains had gone. In 1880 three dedicated goods services operated each way between Perth and Inverness, the 10.35 a.m. southbound one being designated 'Express'; one daily each way between Forres and Keith, and between Inverness and Dingwall; and one, southbound only, between Blair Atholl and Perth.[3] The Working Timetables set out rules for the number of goods wagons to be carried on mixed trains, and the stations at which they could be picked up or dropped, though these may not always have been strictly followed.

As the main commercial activity of the Highlands was agriculture – arable in the coastal fringe and some valleys; pastoral in the uplands – this was reflected in the goods traffic. Livestock transport was important enough to be recorded separately and was always a substantial proportion of goods traffic, though not the largest; in the half-year to 31 August 1880, general merchandise accounted for £46,217 0s 6d, livestock for £9,148 18s 7d, and minerals for £14,506 4s 4d. Contact with the farmers was important, and Kenneth Murray of Geanies played an important part in this even before he became a director. In December 1866 he was paid £500 for his services in arbitration with landowners and tenants on the Ross-shire line, and that month he passed on the 'anxious desire' of the Easter Ross Farmers' Club that the company would board up the ends of cattle trucks, and, if possible, roof them. The board agreed to the boarding up, at 28s a truck.[4] However, like the passenger traffic, there was a highly seasonal aspect to livestock transport. August lamb sales and transfer of flocks and herds from islands to mainland and upland to lowland in April and October, all created peaks of demand. On 2 August 1921, two livestock specials went from Georgemas to St Boswells (taking sixteen hours forty minutes to Perth), and on the 10th, Lairg's sheep traffic needed two special trains and the help of eight extra men. This was during the peak passenger season.

A detailed comparison of the railway's sheep traffic between 1889 and 1890, published in the *Inverness Courier* on 28 October 1890,[5] shows a very small decrease, from 502,902 to 498,440. The value of the breakdown is in showing where the animals were shipped from. By far the largest centre is Inverness, with its market, which shipped 81,745 in 1890. Next largest was Portree, with 30,952, then Lairg, with 26,166, followed by Dalwhinnie, with 21,033, Perth, with 19,534, Strome Ferry, with 19,469, Muir of Ord, with 18,423, Dalnaspidal with 17,845, Nairn with 17,593 and Grantown with 14,427. The number of sheep put on trains from the two stations on either side of Druimuachdar Pass is striking. Thirty-five stations shipped more than 3,000 sheep in the course of the year. The Highland's stock of sheep vans was sixty-five in 1889, most of which had two decks; but even allowing for this and for the use of many of the 217 cattle trucks at busy times, intensity of use must have been very high. About half these trucks dated back to the 1860s, and an article by Peter Tatlow[6] on the double-deck sheep van makes it clear that only a few years later, the HR was definitely not complying with amendments issued in 1904 to the Board of Agriculture regulations for animal transport of 1895. Although the company adapted 100 goods wagons for temporary use as sheep trucks, at 10s each, in 1907, it was informed by the assistant secretary to the Board of Agriculture on 15 December 1908 that: 'the improvised goods wagons used for the conveyance of sheep during the busy season do not comply with the provision of Article 4 of the Animals (Transit and General) Amendment Order of 1904'. Nagged at by yet another board, the HR Committee for Traffic, Way and Works had to go back to the drawing board.

A side benefit of the railway to Highland agriculture, though it may not have greatly helped the railway itself, was in the improvement of cattle stocks. Pedigree bulls could be bred in the Highlands and readily transported south. In 1865, however, the railway was blamed for spreading cattle plague, and quarantine points for disinfectant treatment were established at the entry points of Perth and Keith. The old-established seasonal market centres in the north, Georgemas and Muir of Ord, and one or two smaller ones, like Parkhill (Kildary) survived for two or three decades[7] after the advent of the railway, and in the case of Muir of Ord a special platform was installed by the market ground, about a mile south of the station, in

1867, at the request of Lord Lovat.[8] But the rural markets' importance dwindled as that of the town marts increased.

Fish traffic had been one of the high hopes of the railway promoters, and by its nature the Highland had to give it special attention. In 1889 the company disposed of 300 fish trucks, compared with 282 sheep and cattle trucks. They were relatively light-weight four-wheeled vehicles, with a 5 ton-load capacity. A despatching station with eight such wagon-loads was authorised to form a special fish train,[9] which would be treated as a passenger train. The traffic was carefully codified. Fish, like game and other perishables could be consigned either at Sender's Risk or Company's Risk, and the passenger train rate was higher than the goods train rate. There were five categories, depending on the type of fish or shellfish, and whether it was cured, salted, dried or fresh. In 1889, the rate per hundredweight to London varied from 2s 6d for thoroughly cured fish by goods train, at Sender's Risk, to 7s 10d for fresh fish by passenger train, at Company's Risk; or from £2 10s to £7 16s 8d per ton.

The carriage rates for fish were a subject of permanent contention. In January 1855 the *Groat* was reporting fish-sellers' protests at a rate of £4 per ton to London, though it was recognised that the English railway companies were at least partly to blame. In 1889 the issue was still a hot one, accentuated by the high retail prices in England compared to the low wholesale prices at the pierheads. James Caldwell MP, reporting to Joseph Chamberlain on a visit to Wester Ross, noted: 'The fact I believe to be that, even supposing the railway company carried the fish for nothing, the fishermen would receive no more than ½d per lb for the fish, while the consumer would pay no more than he does at present'.[10] W.M. Acworth was also on the side of the railways:

> To put the figures in a form perhaps more interesting to the ordinary consumer: the cost of carriage increases the value of the 10 lb. cod, which was worth half a crown retail in Peterhead, to as much as 2s 10 ¼d. in London. No doubt the benevolent fishmonger laments his inability to supply this fish to his hungry customers at anything less than half a sovereign.[11]

Highland ports, with Lybster at the extreme, were at a disadvantage when a fixed rate per mile was charged, but in *Railways and Their Rates*, E.A. Pratt recorded that in 1904 the railway companies involved equalised their charges to London, so that fish from any Scottish port went thither at £2 15s per ton; the only exception being fresh herring from Aberdeen, at £2 11s 8d. Meat too required special consideration, and in response to customers' demands, the company built twenty improved meat vans in 1881, at £155 each, with fitted hooks to replace the old hampers and cloth packing, and fitted to run with passenger trains.[12]

Manufacturing industry in the Highlands was small-scale and rare. Among the largest was the brick and tile works at Culloden, east of Inverness, which had been in existence before the I&N Railway, and had its own horse-drawn rail track to the beach. In 1857 the I&N concluded a contract to carry 1,200 tons of coal at a reduced rate, from 1*s* 4*d* to 1*s* a ton; and 12,000 tons of tiles at a price lowered from 1*s* 9*d* to 1*s* 3*d* a ton.[13] Among the damaged cargo in the Fochabers boiler explosion of 1872 were containers of vitriol, presumably for use in the cloth-making industry. There were woollen works at Pittentrail (Rogart), and lime kilns at Lairg (the limestone was brought from the head of Loch Shin by a small steamer, assembled on the shore in 1869) and Blair Atholl. The brick and tile works at Brora were brought back into action in 1876. Aberfeldy had Haggart's woollen mills, established before the railway, in 1846. But the only manufacturing industry which really expanded in the Highlands during the later part of the nineteenth century was whisky distilling, and here the railway played an important part. Scottish emigration and the rise of consumer markets had combined to create international demand for this product, in which the unlimited supplies of soft water and peat, and regular harvests of good malting barley, were the chief elements. Although the Great North was the prime whisky railway, the Highland had substantial traffic too, and the importance of the railway in supplying the distilleries, and distributing the product, can be seen by their proximity to it, all the way up the line from Aberfeldy to Wick. Most had been traditional small-scale distilling centres, but there were many more such which did not survive, because with the great increase of demand and output, they were inconveniently sited. Pitlochry's two distilleries, Blair Atholl and Edradour, as well as remote Dalwhinnie, were on the main Perth line, as were Dallas Dhu, Dallasmore and Benromach near Forres. Royal Brackla and Glen Cawdor were close to Nairn, as Glentauchers was to Keith, and Aultmore was set up by the Portessie line. Tomatin Distillery, remodelled and enlarged in 1909, had a siding on the new direct line. Ferintosh, Dalmore, Glenmorangie, Balblair, all old-established distilling locations, acquired railway sidings on the Ross-shire line. Dalmore's long siding, almost a mile, was put in from Alness station early in 1878. An HR Board minute of 5 February for that year records that Mr Mackenzie, the proprietor, would provide the labour, and the HR the materials, for laying the siding, on condition that he took all his coal and other traffic by railway and worked the siding with his own horses. Further north there were distilleries at Clynelish by Brora and Pulteneytown in Wick. Coal and barley were carried in; barrelled whisky and draff, the mashed grainy residues used in animal feed, were carried out. Elgin, commercial centre of the whisky trade, also had traffic of crates and bottles, and at Burghead there were large maltings.

In 1887, Dr Cameron Lees noted that the industries of Inverness were two breweries, a woollen factory, some meal and flour mills, and various distilleries (three large ones by 1892, Millburn, Glen Mhor and Glen Albyn). It is typical of the apparent invisibility of the railway that he did not mention the locomotive and carriage works which then employed several hundred people; nor did he list the two iron foundries. While the old Falcon foundry eventually disappeared, the Rose Street Foundry, of which the HR was the largest customer, flourished, and developed into a well-known welding business whose advanced and specialised techniques made up for its distance from other centres of industry. Almost all works and factories, however small, required coal, and this was one of the prime long-haul items. Coal-burning gasworks were built at Dunkeld, Aberfeldy, Pitlochry, Forres, Nairn, Elgin, Keith, Dingwall, Wick and Thurso, and of course Inverness. The large Perthshire County Asylum, built at Murthly in 1864, had its own gas-plant, served from mid-1867 by a siding from the station[14]. The railway itself was a heavy user of coal in locomotives and its own workshops and buildings. In 1886 it hauled nearly 33,000 tons of locomotive coal[15]. To fill all the tenders and bunkers in the 1890s would require around 600 tons, at a time when the maximum permitted load for a 'Big Goods' locomotive on the 'Hill' between Blair Atholl and Dalnaspidal was 250 tons. Interestingly, the company appears to have supplied its locomotive coal to Wick by steamer rather than by train until the winter of 1897[16]; presumably it was cheaper to make a monthly shipment from Methil or Grangemouth. Apart from coal, and paraffin oil for lighting and cooking, inward freight consisted chiefly of manufactured goods: farm and domestic equipment, cloth, linoleum, clothing, basic foodstuffs like flour, tea and sugar; all kinds of everyday retail items from knives to zinc buckets; and, as time went on, packaged goods, tinned foods, and all the requirements of a society gradually acquiring the habits of consumerism.

However modest the scale of traffic, communities in the Highlands came to be dependent on the railway for goods supply and despatch. When the direct line from Aviemore was being planned, a letter from the company to Mackintosh of Mackintosh, on 4 March 1884, informed him that if he agreed to a proposed deviation to the original survey at Tomatin, the company would erect stations at Moybeg (Moy) and Easter Craggie (Daviot) with goods sidings and loading banks. Loading banks, hand cranes, and goods sheds were features of all but the smallest stations. Most also had a separate short dock with animal pens. At country stations, people made their own collections and deliveries, or hired a local carter. In the towns, however, where there was a more consistent, substantial and varied pattern of demand, the enterprising William Wordie provided a service. His first contract as a dedicated railway carter had been with the Edinburgh & Glasgow Railway in 1842. In 1858 he was made official carrier to the I&AJR, his tender beating Pickfords' by '£200 or thereby'.[17] 'J.E.C.' records that John Mackay, Wordie's first agent in Inverness, came from Stirling with two horses in the autumn of 1855, and: "For a considerable time he was responsible for the shunting operations in the yard, such a thing as a shunting engine being then unknown in Inverness'.[18] By March 1865 Wordie was also at Burghead, Grantown, Kingussie, Pitlochry, and Dunkeld, and a seven-year contract with the Highland Railway was agreed early in 1869.[19] However, there is no doubt that a contract with the I&N existed prior to 1857, for in that year Wordie, as railway carrier, asked permission of the I&N board to act as carrier to the Aberdeen, Leith & London Steam Packet Co. at Inverness harbour: the board refused to sanction it.[20] Wordie's charges were deducted from the general merchandise takings in the accounts. In a typical half-year, between March–August 1880, collection and delivery of goods cost the HR £1,784 9s 7d, or almost 4 per cent of merchandise receipts for the period. Even before the railway reached these places, Wordie opened depots at Beauly, Muir of Ord, Avoch, Dingwall, Fearn, Bonar Bridge, Clashmore,

Dornoch, and eventually also at Wick and Thurso. By 1909 Wordie's were working from thirty-three stations on the Highland system, the only place where a rival had the concession being Golspie.[21] The carter's men worked closely with goods agents and clerks, to the extent that the Highland Board on 29 November 1865 resolved that Wordie's foreman at Inverness be sacked, 'for inducing his Manager to get a Pass from the Goods Manager, Mr MacKay'. The right to hand out, and to hold, free passes for travel on the line was always jealously guarded and closely monitored.

Management of the goods traffic was in the hands of two goods managers, based at Inverness and Elgin. They in turn employed a number of canvassers, men paid on retainer or commission to promote the HR goods service at markets, fairs and fishing ports. When the Duke of Sutherland's Railway was opened, the duke paid a Mr Butcher of Wick £15 a year to attend cattle markets and get business for his line. At ports, coastal steamship lines provided strong competition, but the GNSR was also active in promoting its alternative route to the south. It sent its own agents as far as Stornoway[22] to persuade shippers to consign goods via Aberdeen. Their case was helped by most people's belief that the HR charged excessively high goods rates. In 1896, when a railway link from Newtonmore to Tulloch on the West Highland was sought by the local people, they wanted the West Highland to operate it, as its coal rate to Tulloch was cheaper than the HR's to Kingussie. Despite the Highland's semi-monopoly, its customers were not passive. In November of 1881, John Gordon, a farmer at Balmuchy in Easter Ross, was in correspondence with the Great North about a consignment of fat cattle for the London Christmas market. He wanted to know how many wagon-loads would be needed to make up a special train, and promised to get his friends to contribute their animals as well. But the special had to run on the Highland line from Fearn to Keith, and Alexander Ross of the GNSR wrote to him on 18 November that: 'The Highland are doing all they can to stave us off, so as, if possible, to prevent us from getting the traffic… raising various flimsy excuses calculated to annoy'. It took a flurry of correspondence, and the intervention of the Great North's general manager, before the special was organised. There was jubilation in the GNSR camp at this rare victory: 'The Highland has succumbed'. John Gordon and his friends were the farmers whose cattle had perished in the Dava snow-block of the previous year, when the Highland would only pay them half the value of the stock. Now they had their revenge.[23]

Ironically, perhaps, the most 'modern' nineteenth-century industrial developments in the Highland area were on remote sites without railway access. They were the establishment in the 1890s of the British Aluminium Co.'s works at Foyers, on Loch Ness, and at Kinlochleven. In both cases the location was determined by the availability of hydro-electric power, and they were served by water-borne transport, though both used narrow-gauge railways within the works area.

# TWELVE

*The Postal Subsidy and the Mail Wars*

Carriage of the mails was an important source of income. W.M. Acworth observed in 1889 that: 'the Highland Company hurries the mails faster than the Italian lines can convey the international special train to Brindisi, faster than the German and Belgian Governments, with the assistance of the Chemin de Fer du Nord, can forward their passengers from Aix to Calais'.[1] He did note, however, that the postal subsidy of the Highland was no less than £55,000 a year.

As railways came on the scene, they naturally acquired the postal contracts, putting the old mail coaches out of business on one route after another. The new speed and convenience increased the postal traffic, as did the simultaneous development of commercial and industrial activity, and this in turn laid more demand on the railways for mail trains. The railway companies and the General Post Office needed each other, and the resulting relationship was always a brittle one. In its dealings with the GPO, the Highland Railway was in the happy position of possessing a monopoly of its territory: there was no rival who could offer a service. If this prompted the HR to set a high price on the mail contract, the Post Office had officials with long experience of dealing with greedy carriers. Mail contracts were rarely agreed at first or even second go; very often they were not agreed at all and a well-tried system of arbitration was brought into play. Money was not the only issue: the postal authorities stipulated the number, speed, frequency, stops and running times of the mail trains on each line, in their effort to ensure an effective national letter delivery system. When Mackintosh of Mackintosh demanded that mail trains should stop at his proposed station at Moy, the HR was able to say that this would be a matter for the Post Office.[2] The GPO also required travelling post offices and sorting carriages to be provided on certain routes. Mail was also to be carried, as required, on other trains. The mail contracts were negotiated for several years at a time, and this made it all the more vital on each side to secure a good price.

In 1808, when a direct mail service between Perth and Inverness had first been proposed, the surveyor had suggested a fee of £200 a year (in the event, no service on this route began until 1836).[3] The first recorded agreement between the GPO and the Inverness & Nairn Railway was sealed on 10 January 1857. The charge was £645, but on the 23rd, a letter from the Inspector of Mails intimated that the company was being given an additional 11s 6d daily for the night mail train between Inverness and Nairn, backdated to November 1856, when the service began.[4] Mail to and from the south was transferred between train and coach at Nairn, and routed via Aberdeen, using the GNSR and Scottish North-Eastern lines. With the completion of the line to Aberdeen, mail to and from the south went via the I&AJR and GNSR. The service was slow; in 1860 the south mail did not reach Inverness until 7.12 p.m., having left Aberdeen at 1.17 p.m. Once the Perth line became imminent, a wordy war was waged between Aberdeen and Inverness as to which route the profitable north–south mails should now take. At a public meeting in Inverness on 12 November 1863, the banker Charles Waterston declared of the Perth line:

> … the railway in question is a national undertaking, it having been promoted and con-
> structed almost entirely at the risk of North country noblemen and gentlemen, not as a
> mere stock-jobbing speculation, but on the broadest view of public interest, and for the
> general benefit of this important province of the empire.[5]

The meeting had been called to urge the GPO to use the new route. Meanwhile the GNSR was offering to cut its rate and speed up its service, in order to retain the contract. The *Aberdeen Herald*, two days after the Inverness meeting, observed, after suggesting there would be long delays through snow blocks, that: '… the enthusiasm on this subject in Inverness has but a very subsidiary reference to postal facilities. The real object is a subsidy of £14,000 a year for the Highland lords and lairds who own the Alpine line'. On 10 October 1863 the Perth–Inverness mail coach ran for the last time, and the I&PJR began to carry the local mail. Next day George Fraser, a Post Office Inspector, rode the 9.30 a.m. Down Mail from Perth, to check the service, and made a cautiously favourable report: 'The working of the trains on this line appears to be getting more regular'.[6] Timings were monitored, and all delays had to be explained. Andrew Dougall had to report to the Post Office that the 1 p.m. Down from Perth had been delayed by rocks on the line north of Killiecrankie tunnel on 3 February 1864: 'The Platelayers were removing some projectory pieces when a larger block fell down than was anticipated, and the train was detained fully an hour before it could be removed'.[7] It was 3 August 1864 before a contract for the long-distance post was executed between the GPO and the Inverness & Perth Junction company, backdated to 1 May. It was worth £10,500 a year to the railway, paid quarterly, with extra for an extension to Tain and Bonar Bridge: 'Forty-two Pounds 12s per annum for every double mile over which the Mails and Officers in charge thereof may be so conveyed'. A detailed schedule of trains and times was attached, with provision for additional mail trains, if requested by the Post Office, at 1s a mile. A room was to be provided at Inverness Station for the use of PO sorters.[8]

Almost from the first, the sorting of some post was done in transit; the first sorter was a single clerk travelling between Inverness and Aviemore from June 1864. By

1865 the Highland Railway had four travelling post offices – short four-wheelers like every other vehicle it owned. Mailbags were stored and letters were sorted in the post office carriages, which were staffed by PO men. Amendments to the contract were occasionally proposed: in August 1866 the Highland offered to cut the mail train's time between Inverness and Perth by one hour and forty-five minutes to four hours, with six stops, if the PO would pay an additional £5,000 a year.[9] The PO declined, as it did more often than not; but the scope of the service steadily increased. By July 1870, two sorters were working between Inverness and Perth. Anticipating a new contract, in February 1871, the general manager was instructed to propose to Mr Benthall, assistant to the postmaster general, that the present service, based on 2s 6d per mile between Perth and Inverness, and 2s per mile between Forres and Keith, and Inverness and Bonar Bridge, for mail trains, be continued, plus £5,000 'for the general use of all the other trains run by the Company'.[10] Dougall went to London and came back with an offer worth around £14,000, which the Board deemed inadequate. Arbitration was requested. The thrusting Thomas Bruce took over as the HR's negotiator, and at the meeting of 6 June 1871, a new rate of £20,000 a year for ten years was agreed by the board.

This rate applied only to the Highland Railway itself. When it opened in August 1870, the Dingwall & Skye company had no mail contract. Soon it noticed that Post Office men were using the trains, with mailbags carried as luggage. The D&S charged them parcel rates for the mailbags, which the PO men were instructed to pay 'under protest'.[11] An interim arrangement was reached, that the mail guards would pay full fare, plus excess baggage charge for mailbags between Dingwall and Strome, and second-class fare for bags dropped off or collected at intermediate stations. But in April 1871 the GPO proposed to send the bags as parcels, without mail guards. Wrangling went on until a contract worth £1,000 a year was agreed, from 25 September 1871, including steamer conveyance to Portree. The frequent variations in steamer service caused prolonged disputes, resolved in April 1873 when the GPO reluctantly agreed to pay for up to fifty-six additional trips a year of the Portree boat, in addition to a thrice-weekly regular service. The GPO applied the same methods when the Sutherland & Caithness Railway opened at the end of July 1874. A mail train, with a single sorting clerk, had been running on the Sutherland and Duke of Sutherland's lines from Bonar Bridge to Golspie, and then Helmsdale. On 11 July 1874, the gentlemen, tenant-farmers and merchants of the north met in Inverness, to ask the postmaster general to accelerate postal services north of Helmsdale in order to provide two deliveries a day, as standard in the rest of the country. The PO was unwilling to provide this level of service in such a thinly populated area, and the meeting's view was that the PMG 'was not behaving in the liberal manner which might have been expected", now that the railway made it possible. In un-liberal style, the Post Office dropped its subsidy for the Bonar Bridge-Helmsdale mail train and refused to make a contract with the S&CR. Instead, it sent mailbags forward from Bonar Bridge 'under the custody of the servants of the company' without designating the trains as mail trains. The last mail coach 'of the regulation build and carrying

HM's mails'[12] left Wick for the south on Friday 1 August. Next day, a former coach guard got on the southbound train at Wick with the mailbags. As he had neglected to buy a ticket, he and his bags were turned off the train at Kildonan. The northbound mailbags were unloaded at Bonar Bridge and slowly and solemnly weighed by the Sutherland Railway, while the Wick train steamed off. On the night train from Wick, the postal official again failed to buy a ticket and was put off at Bilbster, in the small hours. As it was then Sunday, no one would help him as he humped his bags back to Wick. The Post Office, in its own view, was simply following the Regulation of Railways Act of 1873, which required railways 'to carry mail by any of their trains, and to afford all reasonable facilities for the receipt and delivery of mails at any of their stations, without requiring them to be booked or interposing any other delay'. Aware that mailbags were being taken out and weighed at Bonar Bridge, Golspie and Helmsdale, the Post Office threatened legal action, and controversy grew between it, the railway companies, and the public. The dispute reached the columns of *The Times*, on 12 August 1874, in a story hostile to the GPO. It said that the Post Office was willing to go to arbitration, but only on the question of what the rate for mailbags, as parcels, should be. Allegedly, PO men had taken the mailbags off at Tain, to go forward by road via the Meikle Ferry, but 'the ferryman was found to be in an inveterate state of deafness, especially to the call of the postman's horn'. A reply from John Tilley of the GPO was published, to put its point of view, claiming it was all the fault of the railway companies' refusal to conform to the law.[13] On 17 August, T.C. Bruce contested Tilley's interpretation of the law (strangely, his letter makes no mention of his railway connection). As the Highland Railway was working the northern lines, it could not avoid involvement, and a letter from Andrew Dougall, on 19 August, made clear the dispute was not over a trifle – the number of mailbags was from 150 to 200 daily. A deputation of northern gentry, led by Sir Tollemache Sinclair and George Loch, waited on the postmaster-general in London, to be told on his behalf by the Rt Hon. William Mossel that the Post Office had made a profit of only £23 on its £10,500 contract with the Highland Railway. He said that the Post Office would not accept arbitration in case the arbiter might agree to what the railways were asking for, and threatened that unless the Highland Railway came to terms, it would lose all its mail business.[14] The Rt Hon. Edward Ellice, proprietor of Glenquoich, protested against the one-sidedness of the Post Office view, and added: 'If we are going to have the letters stopped by the Highland Railway it is war to the knife with the Post Office for everybody North of Perth, and you do not know what a nest of hornets you are bringing about your ears'. Mossel's final word (for the moment) was: 'I do not think we should be justified in submitting to what would certainly involve an expenditure very much beyond that what is proper to the income it made and is entitled to.'[15]

By the end of August, the Post Office was proposing a limited compromise; Tilley wrote to Loch, who had offered himself as an honest broker (despite being an HR director), offering to pay for a Sunday train if the companies would run a weekday service as before. The HR accepted the Sunday train but would agree to take mailbags, with PO guards, on its ordinary trains only if a charge was negotiated through arbitration. The PO refused, and the matter was eventually referred to the Railways and Canals Commission. C.T. Simpson, the attorney-general, represented the PO and Sir William Harcourt, lately solicitor-general, represented the Highland Railway. The three commissioners found the railway had been obstructive, in terms of the 1873 Act, but recommended arbitration to determine the proper level of charging for the northern mails. Lord Selborne, in arbitration, awarded a charge of £5,490 to the railway companies from 21 September. This was worked out on the basis of 5*d* a mile for two trains each way daily between Bonar Bridge and Wick; three between Georgemas and Thurso; 4*s* 5*d* a mile for a Sunday train each way between Bonar Bridge and Wick/Thurso, and a sum of £1,289 divided among the companies.[16] By 24 September the *Groat* reported that two mail trains were running daily from and to Wick and Thurso, and one on Sunday. The HR's own timetable, advertised on 15 October 1874, refers only to a Down mail train, the afternoon service from Inverness. To the railway company, however, there was a difference between a train carrying mail, and a Mail Train: the latter was run under GPO contract and supervision.

The HR seems to have formed the view that if it was not intransigent, it would be walked over. In October 1874 it embarked on a new dispute with the GPO, refusing to pay for the conversion of two compartments of a carriage into an additional sorting vehicle, to run between Inverness and Dingwall. In retaliation, the Post Office began to withhold £250 from its quarterly payments.[17] In July 1875, this was resolved with the agreement to operate a sorting carriage on the day mail from Inverness to Bonar Bridge. A somewhat weary GPO internal memo of this time refers to this as: 'Among the other difficulties which the Department has experienced in its dealings with the Highland Railway Company'; but if the Post Office found the people at Inverness difficult, it had mostly itself to blame. Somewhat more temperate relations resumed, and in October the Post Office also agreed to pay an extra £1,500 on top of the Selborne award, to prevent the HR from cutting back services on the Further North line. Formal mail contracts with the three northern lines, to run to 1881, were executed on 25 April 1876. A letter from Benthall, read to the HR board on 3 October 1876, agreeing a rate of £2,000 a year for daily conveyance of mail between Scrabster and Stromness, except Sundays, confirmed a vital element of the Orkney steamer project, though he rejected a similar service between Strome and the Outer Hebrides. In the early months of 1881, the HR and the PO again locked horns over a new postal contract. In February the Post Office proposed £22,000, which the Highland board declined. In June, the offer of £26,200 for seven years, exclusive of £1,550 for the Skye Line, was accepted;[18] in the following month the company gave a year's notice of its intention to terminate the Orkney mail contract.

By 1881, the four travelling post offices had been rattling through the mountains for nearly twenty years. At the Post Office's behest, the company was due to install automatic bag-catching apparatus at certain stations, and David Jones informed the board on 6 September that the old vehicles were too weak to support the catchers. He proposed buying two supplementary second-hand vehicles from the Caledonian Railway at £100 each, and this was done. At this time, the Parcel Post was about to be introduced, and in late 1881, negotiations were also going on with the Post Office for carriage of its parcels. By 1883, the company was earning around £150 a month from the parcel post: a useful sum but not to be compared with the letter contract. In August 1882 the HR persuaded the GPO to increase the mail subsidy to the Skye line by £250 a year. Benthall and his colleagues dealt with virtually all of the country's 100–plus railway companies, and for minor provincial lines they often encountered town clerks or country solicitors. For the Duke of Sutherland's Railway, seventeen miles long, which did not operate trains, they found themselves confronted in 1883 by the redoubtable figure of William Cawkwell, General Manager of the mighty London & North Western Railway.[19] Somehow, the DoSR received a postal subsidy of £1,000 in its last independent year.

Controversy arose again when it was time to negotiate a new mail contract in 1888. By then, the contract of 1881 had been amended several times and the Highland Railway, now incorporating the three northern lines, was receiving a total of £43,080 annually. The board set their sights on £48,080, while the GPO felt it was already paying too much. Negotiations led only to deadlock. The Post Office suspended letter sorting north of Inverness except on the northbound night mail and the southbound Day mail, and on these it was done only to and from Dingwall. On 1 July, arbitration was agreed, and the Earl of Derby, a prominent Liberal politician, was appointed to hear the case. To the outrage of the Post Office managers, who had confidently expected a reduction,[20] his judgement, given on 20 December 1888, awarded the railway the sum of £55,526, as from 1 July 1888, annually for three years. This was a triumph for Bruce, who had led the Highland's case. The GPO resolved to reopen the matter 'at an early opportunity', but it was to learn the meaning of an old Highland motto, 'What I have, I hold'. The huge award remained in force after the renegotiation of 1891, though it bound the company to send north mail by the Carrbridge route, when finished, and 'the time gained by the shorter route shall be utilised in such manner as the Postmaster-General may direct'. During 1890, the Perth–Helmsdale sorting carriage on the Night Mail was restored, with a Day sorting carriage between Inverness and Bonar Bridge. Now the company was pledged to run sorting carriages in both the Night and Day Up and Down Mail trains as far north as Helmsdale; also to provide a daily van for the Post Office between Perth and Wick and Thurso for sorting parcels: 'such train to be selected by the Postmaster-General'. Rooms for mail bags and guards were to be provided at Inverness, Forres, and other important junction stations.[21]

By the 1890s, the Post Office's parcel business had grown enormously. Payment to the railways was administered by the Railways Clearing House, which received 55 per cent of the gross revenue and passed the money on to the companies according to its assessment of their proportion of the traffic. In 1894, the Highland company formed the view that it was receiving substantially less than its proper share, to the tune of some £12,000 a year. The other railway companies refused to alter the apportionment or to permit arbitration. The Highland had enough belief in its own case to promote a private Bill in Parliament, for amendment of the Post Office (Parcels) Act of 1892, in January 1896; and three months later attempted to have it turned into a public Bill in the Lords, with the help of Lord Morley. By June, however, faced with large costs and little likelihood of success, it dropped the Bill.

Eventually, automatic apparatus for the non-stop collection and dropping of mailbags was installed at seventeen stations: Murthly, Dunkeld, Ballinluig, Pitlochry, Struan, Dalwhinnie, Newtonmore, Kincraig, Aviemore, Dunphail, Fort George (Gollanfield), Clunes, Muir of Ord, Conon, Novar (Evanton), Delny and Nigg – not all at the same time: Novar was last, in May 1910. Post Office staff were responsible for working them, and they were situated well beyond the railway's tablet-catching apparatus. Although it was originally intended for both directions, the apparatus in later years was used only for dropping off northbound mailbags. In the twentieth century, relations between the HR and the Post Office were on the whole peaceful, despite frequent delays; but there was discontent among the remotest customers. In the summer of 1909 demands came from Orkney, seconded by Wick, for a speeding-up. The postmaster-general replied that greater punctuality was hoped for, but not a faster service. In fact the summer timetable of that year gave slightly later arrival times for the Night and Day mails to the Far North. Debate rumbled on.[22] Thomas Addy Wilson, still striving to make timetables correspond with reality, wrote to Alexander Bruce, Town Clerk of Wick, on 21 June 1909: '… the 5.40 a.m. mixed train from Inverness, although timed to arrive at Wick fifteen minutes later, will arrive, it is believed, earlier than formerly…' A letter from the postmaster-general's office on 16 August informed R.L. Harmsworth MP that the mail train was late in Wick 156 times between January and July, though on 33 of these, the delay did not exceed five minutes. But, it added, an improvement on last year was discernible. In 1910, Stornoway was also complaining about late mails. Although part of the blame for a 'belated and benighted service' was put on the Macbrayne steamer *Sheila*, late trains at Kyle were also held responsible.[23]

The GPO continued to keep a close eye on the service. In November 1912, the HR withdrew the 10.50 p.m. Inverness–Perth, which, though not a designated mail train, carried a lot of mail from Orkney and the North, estimated at 61,800 letters and 2,787 parcels weekly. The postal officials found that the company was running a train 'for its own purposes' from Aviemore to Perth at a suitable time for the mail, and served a notice on the HR to run a connecting train from Inverness, daily except Saturday and Sunday. The HR complied, and a special was run from November 1912 to April 1913, when the 10.50 p.m. was restored. It tried to charge the GPO 7s 6d a mile for this train, but unfortunately for the railway company, the Post Office was able to show that the rate of 1s a mile for such trains, negotiated back in 1864, had never been altered.[24] For once, English guile won the day. In general, apart from rare contretemps like the mail van falling into the sea near The Mound,[25] the Highland ran its postal services safely if not punctually. Among the few other dramas was a fire in one of the sorting carriages on the 6.15 a.m. Perth–Inverness Mail on 2 October 1914, between Ballinluig and Pitlochry. Fire from the gas light broke out in the middle one of three post vans, and quickly took hold. The communication cord was pulled, but it broke.

The train was well past Pitlochry before the enginemen realised something was wrong. They stopped, and backed to that station for water. But the van, with 60 mailbags and 100 packages for the Grand Fleet, was burnt out.[26]

By the end of 1922 the company was operating nine mail vans, including three built at the Needlefield works in 1916. One of these was not withdrawn from the Perth–Helmsdale route until 1961: the last Highland Railway vehicle in regular service.

## Mixed Trains and Continuous Brakes

For a variety of operational and commercial reasons, the Highland Railway had a preference for running mixed passenger and goods trains whenever possible. Its goods traffic, as we have seen, was of less importance than the passenger traffic. It had a limited stock of goods wagons and could not afford to keep them standing about for very long; it had a small stock of locomotives; and a single line track with very limited siding capacity at all stations. A substantial proportion of the goods traffic was livestock or fish, needing prompt transit. To keep things on the move, mixed trains were the essential and only answer. The resultant variegated appearance of the trains made a strong impression on many observers, and added to some visitors' sense of the line's 'quaintness'. The somewhat haphazard quality of operations that this suggested was quite misleading: the working of mixed trains, like everything else, was governed by rules set down in the Working Timetable, and intended to ensure that the trains ran to time and did not carry excessive loads. Two typical examples relate to night trains in the Working Timetable of autumn 1880:

12.10 a.m. Train from Wick – In addition to Passenger Traffic, this Train will work Goods Traffic as follows:- 1st, Will take to Inverness direct all Perishable Traffic for England, also Fish for Edinburgh and Glasgow, and Live Stock off Caithness Line for Great North of Scotland Railway; and will, in addition, so far as it can keep time with, all Live Stock from North of Tain to destinations direct for Stations north of Inverness, and to Inverness for Stations beyond. Those that cannot be taken forward by 12.10 Train beyond Helmsdale or Bonar-Bridge, to be picked up there by 6 a.m. Train. Such must be so placed in the Sidings, however, that they will be the first Wagons to pick out. 2d. Will, in addition to the foregoing, work General Goods Traffic up to Helmsdale, and drop there all Wagons for Stations up to Bonar-Bridge inclusive, but will take the length of Bonar-Bridge all Wagons from Stations north thereof for Stations beyond that point.'

The 12.40 a.m. will have no Pilot from Blair-Athole; load must not exceed Twenty-two through vehicles. When necessary may take Twenty-seven from Perth to Blair-Athole, and from Grantown to Forres. Should this Train, for want of Through Vehicles, have Wagons from Perth to Stations between Dalwhinnie and Forres, and Engineman able to take them up the Struan Bank, they must not be left at Blair-Athole, but taken up to Dalwhinnie, and left there. No intermediate work will be done between Perth and Forres by this Train, except putting off at Blair-Athole and Dalwhinnie, and making up a full load at Grantown. Will have Passenger Carriages attached from Perth to Inverness.

Will not work Goods Traffic at Intermediate Stations between Forres and Inverness, except leaving off Through Wagons at Nairn.

Such instructions needed clear understanding and close collaboration between station staff, train guards, and engine crews. The trains were marshalled with the goods wagons next the engine, then the passenger carriages, and finally the brake van. [1] This made it easier to carry out shunting operations while leaving the passenger part of the train at the station platform, with the brakes on in the van. Brakes on trains, by the 1880s, had become a contentious issue. In the first years of railways, the only brakes were hand-operated ones on the locomotive's tender and the brake van: carriages, wagons, and the engine itself had no brakes at all. The role of the guard, or brakesman, in bringing the train to a halt was vital. On 17 November 1865, following the accident at Pitlochry caused by a train overshooting the platform through lack of brake-power, the board resolved to have continuous brakes fitted to the carriages used on the 10.18 and 12.40 Up and the 9.30 and 12.50 Down trains. This was the Newall brake, invented by the carriage superintendent of the East Lancashire Railway in 1852, applied by a wheel manually turned in the guard's van, [2] and linked by rods and springs to brake-shoes fitted on the two preceding carriages. By the later 1870s, steam brakes were being fitted to new HR locomotives, in addition to the Le Chatelier counter-pressure system, which was intended to slow, rather than stop, the train. But carriages remained unbraked, and on several railways, though not the Highland, fatal accidents occurred when couplings broke and carriages ran away. Individual goods wagons became fitted with hand-brakes, which required pinning down by brakesmen to operate. In 1869 George Westinghouse had successfully demonstrated his automatic braking system in the USA, and in a much-publicised set of tests in 1875 at Newark, on the Midland Railway, it proved superior to its rivals, but for the next twenty years this improvement was ignored by most British railway companies. Cost was the reason, and accidents and passengers' sense of insecurity contributed to the growing unpopularity of railway companies with the general public. By 1880 the Highland was experimenting with different braking systems. On 6 July that year, David Jones was asked to report on fitting the Westinghouse automatic brake on Inverness–Perth trains, and in September, the London & North Western Railway was asked to lend a train fitted with the Clark & Webb patent chain-brake, for testing, which it cordially agreed to do. The *Elgin Courant* of 5 November reported tests of Newall's continuous brake, between Inverness and Dalcross, when the coupling of the engine was slipped, and the train brought successfully to a halt. This appears to have been the Newall system already in use, which was not an automatic one, and so did not meet the Board of Trade's requirements. Jones reported in April 1881 that the Clark & Webb brake, as used on the borrowed LNWR test train, also had not fulfilled Board of Trade requirements. On 30 November, the board resolved that: 'having regard to the frequent and urgent representations of the Board of Trade and the state of public opinion on the subject, the Board cannot with propriety further delay the adoption of an efficient Continuous Brake for Through Passenger Trains'. Whereupon it promptly postponed consideration to the January meeting, when a committee was set up, chaired by the Duke of Sutherland, to supervise two test trains, one fitted with the Westinghouse compressed-air system, the other with Smith's vacuum system. The committee visited Edinburgh, Newcastle, Crewe, Derby and Doncaster to look at other companies' practice.

In February 1887 the HR decided to fit the automatic vacuum-brake system to the vehicles forming the 7.50 a.m. train from Perth and the 3.00 p.m. from Inverness. In the previous year the latter train had conveyed fish wagons on 275 occasions, and in March the board agreed that all fish wagons, carriage trucks and horse-boxes should be fitted with the vacuum brake. At last, on 3 December 1889 David Jones was instructed to progressively equip all passenger stock with vacuum brakes, or at least with brake pipes to transmit the vacuum.[3] In this system, brake shoes were fitted to the carriage wheels, and a pump on the engine created a vacuum in a pipe that ran along the train, with flexible hose joints between vehicles. Any admission of air into the vacuum, caused for example by couplings parting, resulted in immediate automatic application of the brakes on all carriages and on the engine. The Highland was the only Scottish railway to adopt this system, as the other companies thought it might 'freeze up' in cold weather, a view not accepted by the HR.[4] This created problems when other companies' carriages, if not dual-fitted, were included in its trains. Perhaps cost considerations were behind the decision.[5] Over the next fifteen years, most Highland carriages and locomotives were fitted with vacuum-brake equipment. However, no general goods vehicles were so fitted, and this meant that passenger carriages marshalled in the rear of mixed trains had no automatic braking provision.

Such a practice was considered unacceptable by the Board of Trade, which at first could only remonstrate and recommend against it. It resulted in an accident at The Mound, on 26 November 1885, when a southbound train, climbing up the curve towards the station, suffered a derailment to one of the leading wagons, and several wagons, passenger carriages and a mail van broke off and ran backwards downhill, tipped over, and fell into Loch Fleet at high tide. Fortunately the passengers escaped, wet and shaken, but uninjured. The Highland Railway took the accidental parting of trains seriously enough to include instructions in the Working Timetables to cope with goods trains 'breaking away and retrograding' on Struan Bank and between Forres and Dava: but no mention is made of the possibility of passenger vehicles being involved. From the passing of the Regulation of Railways Act in 1889, the Board of Trade had power to compel railways to use automatic brakes on passenger trains. It also wanted to eliminate mixed trains altogether, or at least drastically reduce their number: the Highland, operating seventy-six mixed trains daily, was squarely in its sights. From 24 October 1889, when the board sent out a circular to all railway companies, there ensued an extraordinary eight-year sequence of delays, prevarications, and refusals to co-operate by the Highland Railway in the matter of continuous brakes on mixed trains. '… There appear to the Directors to be many difficulties', began a letter from Andrew Dougall to the BoT on 12 December 1889. The board itself was not unduly hasty. In November 1890 it sent to the HR the draft of an Order it proposed to make, compelling the company to run mixed trains with the passenger carriages placed directly behind the engine and fitted with continuous brakes; and placing various other restrictions on the composition of such trains. The company's reply was that the proposed restrictions were, 'so unnecessary and oppressive that our passenger traffic would be seriously injured and rendered almost unworkable. The Directors therefore protest in the strongest possible manner against the application of the Order in its present form'.

Both sides had reasonable arguments to make. The Highland Railway's working would be drastically impaired if it first had to detach passenger carriages before proceeding to shunt wagons at intermediate stations, quite apart from the fact that there was nowhere to place them, unless on the wrong side of a crossing loop. Its safety record was good – up to this time, no passenger had been killed as the result of a train failure or collision. The Board of Trade was quite correctly treating passenger safety as the top priority. It was also concerned to see that all main line railways adopted best practice, and here, unfortunately, the railways' general bad record in investing in safety played against the Highland. Locally, however, public opinion was largely in favour of the railway company, if only because the choice seemed to be between an already modest service of mixed trains, and a drastic reduction in the service, particularly on the Skye and Wick lines. On 16 February 1891 the BoT issued an Order to the HR to comply with its requirement, giving the company until 16 August 1893 to complete its arrangements. During this time the company did nothing other than protest, and orchestrate further protests from at least some of its customers and the local authorities. Its case was not helped by an accident at Achnashellach on 14 October 1892, when a train of seven goods vehicles, three passenger carriages and a van, with a defective Newall brake, ran away when the engine was uncoupled for shunting purposes. The engine set off, in reverse, to retrieve it, but the train, having run to the foot of the 1 in 60 gradient and partly mounted the next slope, was now returning in the original direction and collided with the engine. Only nine passengers were on board, but eight complained of bruising and shock. The engine driver, Alex. McDonald, was fined £1 by David Jones, and the incident lent weight to the Board of Trade's attitude. Dougall, however, argued the position, writing to the BoT on 8 December 1892 to say that had the carriages been next the engine, the effects of the collision would have been worse. He repeated this in further letters, to the astonishment of the London officials, who considered that to send the engine after the runaway train had been a piece of dangerous foolishness; and that even if this had been done with the carriages attached to the engine, the passengers would surely have been taken off first and left in the care of the stationmaster. On 24 January 1893 Dougall blandly wrote to the President of the BoT that:

> I need scarcely point out that in any view it is impossible to carry out the necessary changes upon our railway system and methods of working by 16th of August next... The directors therefore venture to request that you will cancel the order so far as it relates to the marshalling of mixed trains or at all events to suspend it indefinitely.

Partly as a result of representations by the area's Liberal MPs, further extensions were granted while the HR management did its best to prolong the discussion; even attempting, in August 1894, to deny the validity of the original BoT order made against it in February 1891, on the ground that the Board of Trade had not, as the Act required, properly consulted them and taken regard of the company's circumstances. This claim was rejected, though it brought a further few months' respite. Andrew Dougall, of course, always wrote on behalf of the directors, and it is not clear how far the company's policy was formulated by him.[6] He certainly defended it with vigour, up to his resignation in December 1895. By the end of 1894, following further mixed-train accidents at Dalnaspidal and Tain (see Appendix A), the Board of Trade was demanding action, and the HR responded by cutting a few mixed trains, including the midnight train from Wick to Inverness, which ceased to carry passengers from 1 January 1895. Time finally ran out for the railway company with the BoT's last extension, at the end of 1896. Charles Steel, the new general manager, had made dispositions for the Board of Trade's requirements to be met, without putting them into effect. Numerous cases were reported in 1897 of breach of the regulations. By far the most serious was the incident between Achterneed and Raven Rock on 25 September when the 6.15 p.m. Dingwall–Strome Ferry train broke in two following the failure of a coupling, and four goods wagons, four passenger carriages, a luggage van and brake van began to roll backwards down the 1 in 50 gradient, through Achterneed station and on towards Dingwall. The passenger carriages had been placed at the rear, with no automatic brake. Luckily the alert Fodderty pointsman, who had set the junction for the returning Saturday evening Strathpeffer–Inverness excursion train, heard the runaway coming and reset the points. Somehow negotiating the tight double curves at the foot of the hill, the train hurtled on. The gate-keeper at the western level crossing in Dingwall quickly opened the gates, but the train smashed through the eastern crossing gates before finally coming to a stop about 200 yards short of the junction with the Wick line, having almost certainly achieved the fastest six miles ever run on Highland Railway metals. No one was hurt but everyone had been terrified.[7] That marked the end of the company's resistance. On 30 September, William Garrow, superintendent of the line, was told by Steel to implement the new arrangements immediately. The mixed train service was greatly reduced from 1 November 1897. By this time, the installation of more crossing loops, and the lengthening of others, was making it possible to increase the number and size of trains without causing delays. In 1922, the company was still running forty-three mixed trains a day, all of them on branch lines with the exception of three between Inverness and Kyle of Lochalsh.

# THIRTEEN

*The Railway in the Community*

'Did Highland landlords lack enterprise and capital?' In part-answer to his own question, Eric Richards[1] notes that capital was not the problem.

> … Some of the most successful entrepreneurs of the age were drawn to the Highlands. They included men full of zeal, urgent to crack the problem of the Highlands, prepared to plough their commercial and industrial wealth into the region. But the return on their investments was always derisory.

Most of the early backers of railways in the Highlands were keen improvers, with Alexander Matheson and the third Duke of Sutherland as prime examples. They were liberal capitalists, with a strong Utilitarian strain in their thinking. As landowners on a large scale, they saw the potential benefits of the railway for themselves, but it had to be a sufficiently convincing investment in its own right. The return was by no means derisory. The same view was held by others who invested small amounts of capital. Debentures issued by the company were bought by a wide range of individuals and organisations in the Highlands. In the record of 4 March 1867, St Duthus Lodge of Freemasons, Tain, purchased £400-worth, and the Kirk Sessions of several parishes also invested in the company. By this, on a modest but far from insignificant scale, wealth which might have drained out of the Highlands was retained and re-circulated within the region.

The writer of the 'Open Letter to Sir Robert Peel' in 1849 saw the railway as an instrument of social policy that would have to be funded by government. But he was wrong. The first lines were built without government aid, not as instruments of social or economic policy or philosophy, but because it was anticipated that they could profitably provide a service, as, indeed, they did. In Lord Seafield's case, in the 1850s, he was interested in cheap transport for his huge reserves of standing timber, and, like all others, he expected railway access to increase the value of his land. [2] Economic benefit was still evident in the Wick & Lybster Light Railway's prospectus in 1898:

The route followed by the railway will not only be very convenient for the large croft-ing area between Wick and Lybster… but also will draw all traffic from the district as far south as Dunbeath… The want of reasonable transit facilities has severely prejudiced the value of sheep and cattle reared in the district.

The value of fresh fish landed at Lybster in 1898 was £8,074; that of cured fish £12,889. The hope was that speeded-up transport would increase the fresh fish element both proportionately and absolutely, by making the port more attractive to fishing vessels; and, in the process, generate revenue for the railway. It was perfectly sound thinking, but the coming of the steam drifter, independent of winds, and needing bigger harbours, changed the whole situation.

None of the railways forming the Highland system were built with the expectation of making a loss, or to be justified by social value alone. This applies to the Sutherland railways as much as to the other lines, and explains why the duke was so keen to complete the line into Caithness. Even Joseph Mitchell, who believed that railways should be built and owned by the state,[3] held this view not because of their social benefits but through dislike for wasteful competition and in the hope that the state's resultant profits would reduce taxation. Naturally, thoughtful investors considered that the railway would be an economic stimulus in a general sort of way, and perhaps benefit industries in which they had a personal stake. Such secondary benefits are hard to quantify, and often slow in appearing. Comparing changes in land values in parishes in the two northernmost counties, with and without railway access, Wray Vamplew concluded that:

If Sutherland and Caithness are adequate guides, the construction of the Highland rail-ways had generally a long-term benefit on the land values of the parishes through which they passed… its benefits were perhaps more to aid gradual development than suddenly to increase values relative to the parishes without railways.[4]

Such a gradual process was of more interest to landowners and tenants than to other prospective shareholders: to raise capital, railway promoters had to demonstrate the possibility of more direct rewards through dividends. The lack of corporate and private willingness to support a railway which, though undoubtedly of social benefit, was of highly questionable profitability, is shown by the fate of the Garve & Ullapool proposal.[5]

In action, the HR showed the extent and limitations of what a railway could do. Throughout the lifetime of the company, the region continued to be a 'problem', its pattern of social life at variance with the rest of Scotland; its population in gradual decline while that of the rest of the country had never been growing faster; its economic basis insufficiently able to provide a general standard of living comparable with other regions. These difficulties had begun before the nineteenth century, persisted after it, and are by no means resolved yet. The issues of landownership and land use were always at the heart of the matter. Virtually all the land in the region was held in large estates, whether owned by 'old' families, newcomers, or corporations.

Even in the mid-1850s, as the Inverness railways began to be built, the last of the population clearances were still taking place in Ross-shire, and earlier episodes remained a vivid and ugly memory.

In broad economic terms, however, a trend of improvement was beginning. Richards notes in *The Highland Clearances* that during the period from 1850 to 1882, wool prices rose by a third, cattle prices doubled, land values and rents rose, and the standard of living improved for almost the entire community. For many of course, the standard in the 1830s and '40s had been destitution: improvement was strictly relative. Evidence of this producer-based prosperity is seen in the rise of the sheep population. In Sutherland it increased from 168,170 in 1853 to 240,096 in 1875, and comparable rises took place in Ross & Cromarty and Inverness-shire, where by 1869 there were over 760,000 sheep. The railways were the beneficiaries but also part-creators of this growth, as they were for other market-aimed produce. From the mid-1870s, however, the sheep population began to decline, hit by falling wool prices and the development of refrigerated transport from Australia. At this time began the sharp increase in the amount of land given over to deer forest, as the landowners sought to maintain the value of their ground. By 1884, Charles Withers records that there were 1,975,209 acres of deer forest in the Highland counties.[6] In 1914 this had grown to almost 3,000,000 acres in around two hundred separate 'forests', each with at least one, and often several, large houses available for renting. Economic pressures on the proprietors were relieved by the social trend: 'Sporting estates gave higher rents than sheep farms or returns from crofting. The general rise in sporting rents led to an inflation of land prices as well as change in land use'.[7] Sporting estates were let for the season, or the month, and new shooting lodges were built to accommodate the large groups who came for the stalking, fishing, and other country pursuits. Although both indoor and outdoor staff were needed, the numbers were not high, and the last thing the estate-owners wanted was a fringe of independent crofters or smallholders, clinging to the Highlanders' legendary right to catch their own venison and salmon. In *Scotland Since 1707*, R.H. Campbell notes that: '... population continued to fall, by about 10 per cent in the crofting counties between 1881 and 1911, and the fall was concentrated in the younger age groups'.[8] Most commentators at the time were unworried by this trend. In *Scotland of Today*, Anderson and Watt, overstating one case: 'The Highlands are now becoming more and more the playground of Britain', were quite complacent about another:

> ... there are few districts in the Highlands in which there is room for any considerable development of the crofter system... he has really nothing to lose, but everything to gain, by exchanging his crofter life, as many Highlanders do, for that of a Lowland policeman, or an emigrant to the colonies.

Campbell also comments that: '... though railways did not penetrate the Highlands extensively, their influence, where they did go, was great'. Alas, he does not enlarge on this statement. But it is plain that the existence of the Highland Railway played a vital part in the development of tourism and of the 'shooting box' economy of the region between 1880 and 1915. In reverse, however, the statement is also accurate: the seasonal influx and departure, its consumer demands, and, to a lesser extent, the outward flow of venison, salmon and other dead game for marketing, all played a vital part in the continuing life of the Highland Railway Co. Writing as an impartial observer in 1890, W.M. Acworth was in no doubt about the benefits of the railway in this respect: 'Nowadays the railway is sued for damages if the salmon that was caught or the grouse that was shot in the farthest corner of Ross-shire on the Monday afternoon is not punctually delivered in Leadenhall or Billingsgate markets on the Wednesday morning'.[9]

The Highlands were not a rich area, and so the Highland was never a rich railway. The company's income was derived from a wide range of sources. Summer and autumn tourists and house parties were very important, as were sheep, and coal, and the Royal Mail. But it also needed, and had to provide for, the fishwives of Burghead, the migrant workers who went to help in the harvest on lowland farms, the townsfolk of Inverness who fancied a Saturday trip to Strathpeffer, the Tayside smallholders taking calves or poultry to the Perth market. Each small source of income was necessary. The company survived by providing a service which responded to every viable level of demand. Emigration from the region came into this category. The HR was not concerned to stop it, but to sell emigrants' tickets at a rate which undercut coastal shipping. Part of a stationmaster's job was to look out for any local event which might generate extra business, from the Forres town holiday to the Dunkeld rose and pansy show and the Caithness annual art exhibition. Special trains were laid on. It had to be the whole community's railway, to survive.

In its own time, the Highland Railway was certainly not seen as having a social mission. Most of its customers believed it was exploiting a captive market. Iain Sutherland records that it:

> ... had not got a good reputation in the North, either among the public, with whom it dealt in a very autocratic manner, or among the companies with whom it had business dealings where it had a reputation for ruthlessness. It had of course the monopoly of rail travel in the North and exploited this position at every opportunity. [10]

The Lybster and Dornoch companies could bear witness to the fact that the HR's first and prime loyalty was to itself. To the directors this was entirely proper. They knew very well that the company, compelled by law to contribute to the poor rates in every parish in which it owned land, was already paying into the social budget. But occasionally the needs of the railway and the community went hand in hand. The company wanted to ensure water availability at certain stations, and worked with local boards to improve the supply. At Invergordon, it made a subscription of £60 to the waterworks in August 1867, and carried the pipes at a reduced rate. At Blair Atholl, it provided the village's water supply as well as keeping its own tanks full: a situation that continued into the post-British Railways era. [11]

Discussing late twentieth-century industrial projects in the Highlands, James Hunter writes that: '... oil-related industrial development can be seen as a continuation of the pattern of Highland exploitation established more than two hundred years ago'. [12] He has in mind the transience of these industries and the almost casual opportunism with which they engulf a community and then move on, leaving a site bulldozed in human as well as physical terms. Though Hunter gives it no credit, the railway was the first large Highland industrial enterprise to establish a permanent presence. By providing its services, staying independent and solvent, and paying its wages and dividends, the Highland Railway made a long-term contribution to the regional economy. As the biggest business, it kept a large amount of money in circulation. Many other local businesses were at least partly sustained by its patronage, from iron founders and timber suppliers to glaziers and printers. The cashier's payment details provide lengthy lists of regular expenditures with local companies. The existence or growth of other businesses, hotels, woollen mills, suppliers of tweeds, tartans and fishing gear, as well as those detailed in Chapter 11, were made possible by the railway.

Not everyone was grateful. Prof. John Stuart Blackie, celebrated advocate of crofters' land rights, had this to say:

> The increased facilities of intercourse between the Highlands and the Lowlands which steam communication and the railroads now so amply afford has no doubt proved of no small pecuniary advantage to certain classes in certain districts, and must be a matter of congratulation. But there are serious drawbacks to this sort of Celtic prosperity which must not be concealed... the class of Highlanders who hang upon the skirts of professional tourists in the Highlands, as in other countries, is both morally and physically an inferior type to the sturdy rural population whom the big farm mania has displaced.

He went on to comment on the adverse balance of trade created by the railways, both economic and social: 'A lusty Highland lass never can be improved by being taught to dress herself like a dainty lady's maid'. [13] The lasses are unlikely to have agreed, but Blackie was only one among many observers who regretted that mechanical progress and greater ease of access were robbing the Highlanders of some of their virtues, and most of their distinctiveness. One of those distinctive aspects was the continuing use of the Gaelic language. The census of 1891 revealed that, in the counties of Sutherland, Ross & Cromarty, Inverness and Argyll, 31 per cent of the town population could speak Gaelic; in the villages this rose to 65 per cent and in the countryside to 76 per cent. Apart from some in the oldest generation of country-dwellers, these people were bilingual. In the Western Isles, the proportion of Gaelic speakers rose to 93 per cent. Particularly on the Skye line, the HR had a large number of Gaelic-speaking customers, but it behaved as if the language simply did not exist, apart from the names of the nine 'Ben' (but not *Beinn*) 4-4-0 engines built between 1906-09, from *Ben Udlaman* to *Ben a' Chaoruinn*. Its tourist handbook makes no reference to Gaelic, even as a 'quaint' something to be overheard during a visit to the Highlands. The board refused to put up station names in Gaelic, [14] though most of its stations had scotticised Gaelic names, as with Kingussie for *Cinn a' Ghiuthsaich*, or *Inbhir Nìs* itself. Nor did it make use of the Gaelic heritage in its promotional literature and advertising. As the language of an impoverished under-class of peasants and fisherfolk, groups that the railway company had to cater for, but felt no need to court, Gaelic was not only ignored, but its decline was hastened by the social mobility which the railway made possible.

The concept of the iron road, *rathad iarainn*, was well-known, but the reality might still something of a shock. On first seeing a train at Garve, and being asked by a busybody what he made of it, an old man from Coigach said: 'I'm not quite sure, but maybe it is the Devil's funeral'. He was probably being sardonic rather than naïve.[15] Even when no longer a novelty, the railway station was still a place of interest, especially Inverness, which with its relatively frequent arrivals and departures of trains, its times of bustle, the consequential air of its porters and officials, the comings and goings of important personages, all to an accompaniment of hissing steam, the shrilling of guards' whistles and the slamming of carriage doors, was a natural focus of attraction for those with nothing much to do, as well as for beggars and hucksters. A 'southern visitor' is quoted in the *John o' Groat Journal* of 1 October 1874: 'The station at Inverness seems to have become, owing to the remissness of the authorities, a lounge in the evening for all rowdies in the place''. But anti-social behaviour might even extend to passengers; he went on to complain that the evening Forres train was 'full of drunken people – yelling, kicking and stamping all the way'. He may have chosen an unfortunate day; one might well suppose that the occupants of a train at the end of a market day, or even more one of the specials run in connection with the feeing fairs at which agricultural labourers were hired for the season, would mostly be well topped-up with whisky and ale.

The role of the railway as a conduit of cultural change was largely a passive one. Trains made it possible for the commercial traveller and the clothes shop to replace the weaving of homespun and the trades of the itinerant tailors and cobblers. Newspapers and magazines could be much more widely distributed. Many manufactured items became cheaper as well as more readily available. Inevitably, ideas and attitudes from beyond the Highlands were an invisible import. When Highland custom or attitudes conflicted with commerce, however, the railway company was quick to show its teeth. Sabbatarianism was not confined to Scotland in the nineteenth century, and there were many protests against Sunday trains in England; but the Calvinist Sabbath had taken a particularly strict hold over the north of Scotland. Very few people would have used trains on a Sunday, and it was in deference to their practice rather than their opinions that the HR also observed a day of rest. Nevertheless, to fulfil its Post Office contract it ran one Sunday mail train each way between Inverness, Wick and Perth, and between Forres and Keith. No Sunday trains ran on the branches, except between Wick and Thurso. None ran west of Dingwall, except when fish traffic required a special train from Strome Ferry. This practice had gone on since the opening of the line, despite occasional protests, which the HR Board allowed to 'lie on the table'. The local mood was aggravated by the fact that west-coast fisherman normally lay up on Sundays, while those from the Moray Firth fished on. Matters came to a head on the night of Saturday–Sunday, 2 and 3 June 1883, when three shiploads of herring from Stornoway arrived at Strome in the early hours. Unloading of the vessels was prevented by a band of local men, who, forewarned of the consignments, disabled the crane, held the porters back, and pushed the fish wagons away towards the station. After a telegraphed appeal from the stationmaster, the chief constables of Ross-shire and Sutherland, with six policemen, came by a special train from Dingwall. Together with the fish porters, they tried to force a way past the demonstrators, but failed. Faced with around 150 determined men, Chief Constable Munro of Ross-shire recommended prudent inaction, and they stood by until the demonstrators, having held open-air prayers, dispersed at midnight. Eighty tons of fish, valued at £1,750, were delayed. With a similar action expected on the next Sunday, the company appealed for help. This was the time of the 'Land Wars' of Skye, where troops and gunboats had been sent against a civilian population, and the public authorities were jumpy. Some two hundred police, from as far away as Moray and Lanarkshire, were sent up, and a detachment of seventy troops from Edinburgh was moved to Fort George, with a train ready to bring them to Strome if their presence was found necessary. The early dawn of Sunday 10 June was tense, with the police holding an estimated crowd of 400 at bay while the fish boats were unloaded. Once the train had been got away, at 8.30 a.m., the angry crowd dispersed, and the police departed. In the course of the next days, ten men were arrested, and taken to Edinburgh for trial. The jury found them guilty but recommended leniency; the judge imposed four-month sentences for mobbing and rioting. Their sentences were partially remitted and they returned as martyrs on 25 September. The forces of law and order returned to Strome on the next four Sundays, but there were no further disturbances.

The Strome 'riots' aroused great antipathy to the Highland Railway locally. The incident was widely reported and discussed across the Highlands and far beyond, and even the majority who thought the Sabbatarians had gone too far also felt generally that the authorities had been excessively heavy-handed. But the same authorities were behaving in an even more over-zealous and confrontational way on Skye. To them the Strome events, though arising from very different motives, were all of a piece, and the sanctity of property had to be protected. The Highland directors would have said Amen to that. They were unrepentant. Business was business. Fish was fish, and would not keep.

Quite apart from such idealistic if illegal actions, the railway was subject to various other undesirable attentions, though those reported at the directors' meetings were quite rare, and vandalism seems only to have been an occasional problem. On 4 June 1867, stationmasters were instructed to clean all writing off water-closet and waiting room walls, and to try to prevent recurrences. In 1910 four boys were admonished at Inverness Sheriff Court for 'touting and plying passengers for employment' on the station platforms – something said to be a great nuisance to the Highland Railway.[16] (In some ways, for the English visitor, arrival at Inverness may have been a not dissimilar experience to arriving at Naples, or Aleppo, and little less foreign). A more grandiose example of the same thing was noted by David Thomson in *Nairn in Darkness and Light*; at Kingussie '… a piper in grand Highland dress got on and walked up and down the corridor playing his bagpipes'. More serious things did happen sometimes, mostly as a result of juvenile delinquency. The magistrates at Dingwall fined a fifteen-year old boy £3 on 4 September 1897 for trying to derail the Strathpeffer train by laying a coupling chain on the rails. In 1911, a small boy, said to be 'of the tinker fraternity', whose family had been camping close to the new direct line, was accused of placing a large stone and a rail chair on the line, with the intention of causing an accident (the engine split the stone and was not derailed) but as the only witness was his even younger brother, he was discharged for lack of evidence. As noted elsewhere, wooden buildings were sometimes set on fire. Organised or gang crime was virtually unknown in the Highlands, and petty pilfering was the worst form of theft, though common enough for 'constables' or night watchmen to be employed at vulnerable points.

Within the continuing slow decline of the Highlands' population, certain places showed an opposite trend, because of the railway. Pitlochry, recorded as Pitlochrie in *Black's Guide* of 1863, had a population then of 334, and a single hotel, Fisher's. By 1894 the population is 1334 and six major hotels are listed, including the Atholl Palace ('omnibus meets trains'). [17] The presence of the railway, combined with an entrepreneurial spirit, made all the difference. Pitlochry was perhaps helped by being less than thirty miles from Perth, making it quite accessible in time and cost to places like Dundee, but its growth overtook the older town of Dunkeld, which was even closer to Perth. Here it was Birnam, across the river and by the station, which grew, and a large hotel was built, owned in 1892 by the ubiquitous Edward Cesari (see Appendix B). Day or weekend outings from Glasgow, combining trains and healthy walks, popularised by such characters as 'Tammy Trampalot' in the weekly papers, helped these southern Grampian resorts. Places north of Druimuachdar grew more slowly, but the Spey valley also set out to attract visitors. Newtonmore in 1863 was Newton of Benchar, hardly more than a road junction; by 1894 it is 'a long village'. Kingussie, merely the site of a new inn in 1863, is now 'a large village annually growing in size', with around 800 inhabitants, one excellent hotel, and two smaller ones. Aviemore in 1892 had yet to become famous, but Grantown on Spey is recorded in the HR *Handbook* of that year as having undergone considerable expansion since the opening of the railway. Although only one superior hotel is noted, plus an excellent inn, the guide remarks that in the season: 'every house in the town and every farmhouse in the Strath (many of which are new and most commodious) readily find tenants'. Nairn seized advantage of the railway: Bain's *History of Nairnshire* comments that:

Few of the smaller towns in the north have benefited by the opening up of the country by railway communication as Nairn has done. Its prosperity dates from that develop-ment. A new drive was given to the enterprise of its citizens. It was then seen that the future progress of the town depended on its development as a sea-bathing place. [18]

Nairn was lucky in having a fine sandy beach, but the key was the drive and persistence of Provost Grigor in ensuring his town developed the right facilities (including a glass-roofed salt-water swimming pool) and became known for them: 'The Brighton of the North' was the town's slogan. The growth of Strathpeffer, 'The Harrogate of the North' to the *Weekly Scotsman* in 1911, has already been noted. Not all towns began to flourish just because they had a station. Elgin, with 7,543 inhabitants in 1863, had only advanced to 7,894 in 1894. Dingwall and Tain, with 2,400 and 2,300 respectively, scarcely grew at all. In the same period, Thurso advanced from around 3,400 to 4,000 people, and its main inn, the Royal, had by 1892 been rebuilt and extended into 'the Largest and Most Commodious Hotel in the North… fitted up with due regard to the comfort and convenience of Commercial Travellers, Tourists, and Visitors'. [19] Wick, by 1892, had a permanent population of 8,000, reaching 14,000 at the height of the herring season.

The place to grow most was Inverness, which by 1894 is recorded as having a population of 19,215, and would exceed 20,000 before the turn of the century. In the fifty years from the opening of the Nairn railway its population almost doubled, and this was largely due to the railway, both directly through the offices, running shed and works (the station alone accounted for the employment of seventy people), and indirectly through its position as a nucleus of distribution in all directions. Isabel Anderson wrote in 1885 that:

> Since the opening of the Inverness and Nairn railway in 1855, not only have a number of strangers come to reside in the Highland Capital, causing a spirit of competition to arise, and an impetus to be given to progress and activity, but their ever-extending arrival and settlement have caused a gradual but complete revolution in the ways of what had for many years been a quiet exclusive little town. [20]

Until the 1860s, the town had only one respectable hotel, but the Station Hotel was the first of several new large hotels which occupied dominating sites in the town centre or on the river. Despite the railway's contribution to the town's growth and prosperity, relations between the Highland company and the Town Council were rarely good. [21] The HR's monopoly position was partly responsible, as the council was dominated by merchants who felt they were being overcharged for the carriage of their goods; the company in turn resented the town's 'disloyalty' when it backed the competing Glasgow & North Western scheme in 1882, and the I&FA extension in 1897. It was not until 1923, when the Highland Railway ceased to be, and Inverness became the outermost satellite of Euston, that the town perhaps fully appreciated the prestige and the economic value it had enjoyed in being the railway's headquarters.

Though the community of the Highlands – agrarian, introverted, and until the 1850s largely self-contained – had changed greatly by 1900, it retained many old-fashioned aspects and obsolescent customs. Only a few hours away was the new world of urban conglomerations, smoke-stack industry, and mass organisation and activity in all fields from manufacturing to holiday outings and football-watching, with Glasgow, once a pleasant little city rather smaller than Inverness now was, as the prime and awesome example. The Highland Railway was a two-way conduit between these worlds. From the north it led ultimately to the factory, the mine, the counting-house, the clanging streets, but also to the places of opportunity, power and wealth; while from the south it was the way to a great, airy quietness, to wide landscapes where deer herds drifted across mountain brows; to green fields of grazing sheep and golden fields of barley lying between the hills and the sea, to lonely beaches where seals sprawled or sea-otters scrambled. Here, where isolated hills of Archaean rock rose above the moors, were also remnants of an older human world, untouched by the hustle of elsewhere. Perhaps not every stockbroker or manufacturer, travelling north for the annual massacre of grouse, nor every commercial traveller heading with his cases (conveyed at special rate) for Inverness, thought in such terms, but their thoughts are of no interest. For those with imaginations, the exotically named green engines, the mist-hung stations, the brief vistas of grey lochs reaching back towards far-off peaks, the rivers flowing south, then north as the watershed was passed, the hill torrents tumbling under the track, the glimpses of snow-patches in high summer, were elements of a uniquely evocative journey. By some chemistry of colour, form, and association, the trains ran in harmony with the landscape. David Thomson, as a young summer visitor, felt that the stations from Perth to Nairn 'became like a poem in my head'. [22] It was the way of escape, or at least, it was so in peace-time. The soldiers and sailors who rode the wartime 'Misery' put the magic firmly into reverse. But for some of them too, northwards was also the way home. Few natives of the North, even with more than a hundred miles yet to travel, did not feel a sense of home beginning to slip about them, like a soft cloak, as the hills closed in around the train at Dunkeld.

This was the railway seen by some people as a 'lairds' line' and nothing more. [23] The origins of this label go back to the jibes of Aberdonian newspapers in the 1860s, repeated by the advocates of the Glasgow & North Western scheme in the late 1880s. In 1913 the railway enthusiast Lord Monkswell wrote of the Highland in *Railways of Great Britain*:

> No doubt its construction was primarily due to the great landlords, who wanted a means of access to their estates… A railway of this kind cannot be looked on as a strictly commercial undertaking, and its founders no doubt regarded it as a convenience, for which they were, in the last resort, ready to pay, without hoping for much direct return on their capital.

There was just enough of appearance to make this view stick: the titles and territorial appellations of directors; even the largely middle- and upper-class status of non-local passengers. But it was a travesty of the origins and local significance of the line. To suppose that a man of Joseph Mitchell's social ideas conceived it and put his heart and soul into building it as a convenience for the local proprietors was absurd, as was the notion that the founding directors invested in the company on behalf of their many fellow-members of the landed gentry who used its trains without doing so. The railway's effect in opening their country to the world beyond made it a portent and agent of profound and widespread change for the people of the Highlands, as well as an essential part of daily life. Appreciated sometimes, vilified on occasion, criticised often, taken for granted most of the time – with all its idiosyncrasies, it was very much the Highlands' railway.

# APPENDIX A

## SOME NOTABLE ACCIDENTS

Like all railways, the Highland had to notify the Board of Trade of accidents involving passenger trains, and, later, of virtually all accidents causing injury to staff. From the returns, it can be seen that its record was comparable with or better than most other railways. But some accidents stemmed directly from its methods of working. Certain accidents are also noted in the main text: see 'Accidents' in the Index for references.

### Pitlochry, 21 October 1865

The station is on a southwards-falling grade of 1 in 300, but north and south this steepens to 1 in 85. The 12.40 p.m. Inverness–Perth passenger train, with one engine, a horse-box, brake van, eight carriages and a second brake van, was approaching the station, when the driver saw the distant signal at danger. He whistled for the brakesmen to apply their brakes, but said he felt the train 'pushing', though he applied reverse gear and sand. The train ran past the platform as the 4.24 p.m. Down mixed train from Perth was entering the loop, with two cattle trucks, a horse-box, five passenger carriages and a guard's van. Its driver saw the oncoming train, 'with fire flashing from the wheels', shut off steam and put his engine into reverse. Although the combined speed was estimated at only ten miles an hour, one passenger carriage of the mixed train was smashed and two were derailed. Nine passengers were injured, none seriously. Capt. Tyler, investigating, attached mild blame to the driver of the Up train, but mentioned wet rails and leaves on the line. He put in a plea for a continuous brake system, and said that he had recommended this when inspecting the line before it was opened. This led to the HR's adoption of the Newall brake.

### Rogart, 14 September 1876

A collision between the 10 a.m. Wick–Inverness train and a sheep wagon special, which had been allowed to go beyond the crossing loop. Several passengers were injured and claims had to be met. In the aftermath, the HR Board Meeting of 3 October resolved: '… to convey to Mr Barclay, farmer, Davoch, the thanks of the Board for his kindness to the injured passengers, and to present him with a handsome meerschaum pipe bearing a suitable inscription, and also with a supply of tobacco'.

*Dalnaspidal, 23 September 1893*

Snow, even in September, was a contributory cause of this accident. The 12.50 a.m. Perth–Inverness goods was due to cross the 10.30 p.m. mixed train from Inverness to Perth here, at 3.25 a.m. Slowed by snow and adverse wind, and running more than an hour late, the southbound train, double-headed, collided head-on with the goods (also double-headed), at 4.43 a.m. It had overrun the home signal, set at danger, by 155 yards. Like all other HR collisions, this happened at relatively low speed, about 5-7mph, and the only injury was sustained by the driver of the mixed train's pilot engine, whose foot was squeezed between the engine and tender foot-plates. This train had fourteen goods wagons and a brake van, followed by eight passenger carriages, with no automatic brake. Snow was falling quite heavily, and when the signalman set the distant signal to danger, frozen snow prevented the balance weight from falling, and it continued to show the road as clear. Although the home signal was at danger, the engine crews failed to see it until the pilot engine was passing it, blaming the poor visibility and a dim light. At that time, the HR's system of interlocking points and signals meant that when a train entered a crossing loop, the points at the other end had to be set in that train's favour, until the train had stopped, at which moment they could be reset to let the oncoming train enter on the through line. Meanwhile the oncomer would be warned by the distant signal at danger, that it might have to stop at the home signal. If it overshot the home signal for any reason, it would be diverted on to the loop. The inspector pointed out the deficiency of this procedure. He also noted – with the ongoing dispute over mixed trains in mind – that if the mixed train had been marshalled with the passenger carriages behind the engine, its braked weight would have been 230 tons out of 350 tons, and it would very probably have come to a stop before colliding with the other train. The HR, of course, took the view that the goods vehicles had 'cushioned' the carriages. The same opposing views were expressed six months later, after an accident at Tain, on 28 March 1894. A passenger and two enginemen were slightly injured when the 5.30 a.m. mixed train from Helmsdale ran past the distant signal at danger, and hit the 8.16 a.m. Down Goods which was shunting outside the loop. The passenger coaches were again marshalled at the rear, with no continuous brake.

*Newtonmore, 2 August, 1894*

The HR's first accident in which a passenger was killed, had a close resemblance to the Dalnaspidal collision. An excessively tight wire had prevented the distant signal to the south of the station from going to the 'danger' position, and the 11.50 a.m. Perth–Inverness passenger train, running fifty minutes late, and formed of sixteen vehicles drawn by two engines, ran past it. An Up goods train, also with two engines, normally crossed at Kingussie, had been accepted into the crossing loop, and according to the standard practice, the points at the south end of the loop were set in favour of this train. Although the home signal was at danger, the enginemen, expecting it to be clear, did not look out for it until too late. The passenger train ran past the home signal, was diverted on the crossing loop, and collided with the goods train. The collision might have been worse had not the driver of the goods pilot engine, David Adams, seen what was about to happen and managed to get his train moving backwards. There was a tragic irony in the event. The rule to set the points in this way had just been cancelled, following the fitting of a new interlocking system at the station, but the pointsman had not yet been told. A passenger, Professor Dobbie, had a horse in a box immediately behind the engines. At Blair Atholl he had gone into the groom's compartment of the horse-box, to keep an eye on his animal, and he was killed in the collision. Six other passengers were injured, as well as Adams and one of the passenger train's firemen.

The Circular to stationmasters regarding the new arrangements to be implemented reads:

> Dear Sir, Your station is now fitted up with the new system of interlocked working, and it is necessary that you and your staff should understand that at the off and opposite end of the loop to that at which a train is entering a station, the 'admitting' lever only must be pulled for the purpose of crossing and stopping of trains, and under no circumstances are you to give the 'setting' or other levers, unless for a non-stopping train. After trains have passed out of the station loop, all signals must at once be restored to danger, and the points put to their normal position, which, in all cases, is for the left-hand road. Please note, instruct all concerned, and acknowledge receipt.

### Baddengorm Burn, 18 June 1914

The most serious accident to befall the HR was caused by a massive cloudburst in the hills to the north-west of Carrbridge, an area drained by the Baddengorm burn, which was crossed by a single-arch railway bridge built in 1893, skewed at an angle of 65°, about a mile beyond that station. The water rose with extraordinary speed, and the bridge and its abutments, between two cuttings, became a combination of dam and sluice. At about 3.30 p.m. the 'direct line' portion of the 11.50 p.m. Perth–Inverness passenger train, formed of six vehicles, was crossing the bridge, at around 20mph, when the enginemen felt a lurch to the left. At the same time the automatic brake came on, and the train drew to a standstill. The driver, Murdo Ross, jumped down on the upstream side and walked back to see what had happened. His engine, with a horse-box and two carriages, was past the bridge, which had partially collapsed on the downstream side, pitching the fourth carriage into the furious rush of water. The fifth carriage and the brake van were on the far side. Ross went back to the engine to confer with his fireman, Charles Ross. Just then the bridge collapsed completely, in a turmoil of water, rocks and rubble, and the third carriage toppled down the bank at an acute angle. The roof of the fourth carriage was ripped away and the muddy water swept through it. Four people escaped from the fourth carriage, but five were drowned. Two of the bodies were retrieved from the water more than four miles away.

Rumours of a disaster quickly reached Inverness and a crowd of around 2,000 people gathered at the station, drawn by anxiety or morbid interest. At the inquiry, Donald Campbell, surfaceman for the section, described the storm in apocalyptic terms: 'I am safe to say, I never was out on such a day. They were not altogether hailstones – they were lumps of ice. They were something in the shape of a saw – ragged, jagged lumps of ice. It was very dark, and there was a tremendous roaring in the hill… it was fearsome.' The very solid foundations of the arch had been completely scoured out. An 8 ton-mass of brickwork had been carried over 200 yards downstream, and one of the bogies of the fourth carriage was found completely buried under stones. The sense of a natural calamity made the event a national sensation. Accepting the accident as, 'an event that could not have been foreseen or guarded against', the inspector, Lt-Col. Druitt, exonerated the Highland from any blame. The company nevertheless paid £1,000 to victims of the smash. It also acted quickly to restore the line, using McAlpines as contractors. The bridge was rebuilt in even more massive fashion, and the line was reopened within three weeks.

### Dava Viaduct, 17 August 1914

The 10.10 Inverness–Aviemore passenger train, drawn by two engines, was approaching Dava when the fireman of the train engine, William McIntosh, who had been stoking, noticed that the driver, George Begg Michie, had left the footplate. Assuming that the driver had gone forward to the pilot engine, he worked the train into Dava station, but Michie was not to be seen. A surfaceman found his body, with severe head injuries, at the north end of Dava Viaduct. In his inquiry report, Mr Armytage of the Board of Trade remarked that: 'it appears that the practice of going from a train engine to a pilot engine is not unknown amongst some of the drivers on this line'. But Michie was known as a 'steady man', and the cause of his fall was never ascertained. The company issued an order forbidding crews to climb from one engine to another on a moving train.

# APPENDIX B

## HOTELS AND REFRESHMENT ROOMS

While local inns had mostly improved in accommodation and catering standards, their capacity was adjusted to small parties travelling by gig or wagonette. The railway train, holding 100 people or more, presented new problems. These were foreseen by the company itself, which of course had precedents elsewhere to study. Refreshment rooms were a source of income as well as a necessary service to passengers. In establishing the Station Hotel at the end of 1855, the Inverness & Nairn Co. was following an example already set at Euston and Swindon. The refreshment rooms opened in January 1856, operated by the hotel tenant, at a rental usually around £25. By 1863 there were refreshment rooms at Invergordon, Nairn, and Elgin, and from 28 February 1864 the Dunkeld rooms also came within the ambit of the I&PJR. Once the station ceased to be a terminus, the Invergordon rooms were unprofitable to operate and they were closed from Whitsunday 1870. Dingwall acquired its refreshment rooms from July that year, with the opening of the Skye line. All rooms were run on a tenancy basis, and the company often found a wide gap between its anticipation of rent, and what the tenant was prepared to pay. At Inverness in May 1867 the company sought an annual rental of £250; the hotel manager, Mr Marshall, disputed it, and after arbitration the sum of £80 was agreed at the board meeting of 29 June, or £96 8s, 'if the hotel licence would also cover the refreshment rooms'. There was a similar gap of expectation with the Station Hotel itself, and from October 1877 the HR took direct control. The second hotel manager, Edward Cesari, appointed in May 1878, was a dynamic figure who quickly became the company's catering czar. In 1878 the Nairn refreshment rooms were closed. By 1882 the Station Hotel's revenue was over £12,000 and the profit of £1,080 was substantially more than the old rental. In the following year the board resolved to take all the refreshment rooms into the company's own management as the leases expired, starting with Dunkeld and Dingwall. At that time, there were rooms also at Bonar Bridge, Ballinluig, Elgin, Forres, Inverness, Keith, Kingussie and Perth. Cesari was in overall charge of these establishments, and visited them regularly. Bonar Bridge's he deemed to be too small for satisfactory service, and the board gave instructions on 1 January 1884 for plans for new first and third class refreshment rooms there.

In 1890 the HR joined with the Caledonian and NB in taking a one-third share in building and running the Station Hotel in Perth. With the surge in tourist travel of the 1890s, several large new hotels were built, and in 1889 Cesari obtained permission from the board to operate the large Birnam Hotel on his own account, with a manager. In the reformist investigations of 1896, large shortages in his stocks were identified, including seventy dozen cups and saucers missing at Kingussie. He blamed passengers: in July and August, around 8,000 cups of tea would be consumed at Kingussie, more than half as platform sales. Cesari resigned in April 1897, and removed to his hotel at Birnam. The HR board refused his request for a pension (always a sign of its dissatisfaction or suspicion), but the citizens of Inverness presented him with a silver salver, and 300 guineas, plus a gold bracelet for his wife. Mr Brunton, Assistant Manager of the St Enoch Hotel, Glasgow, was appointed in his place but attracted severe criticism from certain directors and left in the following year, to be succeeded by Mr Woolf and then Mr Ward. In October 1899 the bars at Forres and Dingwall were made one-class only. By 1909 there were refreshment rooms also at Kyle of Lochalsh, though Dunkeld and Elgin are no longer listed (by then the Highland station at Elgin was linked to the larger GNSR station). Light refreshment stalls were advertised at Pitlochry, Newtonmore, Alves, Invergordon, Lairg, and Helmsdale; and Perth, Dingwall and Inverness also had fruit stalls. Boys with trays would walk alongside the train, so that passengers could buy fruit or chocolate without having to get out.

Achnasheen, where the refreshment rooms first opened by Alex Matheson had grown into a hotel, remained a special case, run by tenants rather than by the company. The HR opened its hotel at Kyle in December 1897, the larger Station Hotel in Dornoch in 1904 and the even bigger Highland Hotel, Strathpeffer, in 1911. The two latter were open to visitors only from July to October, and provided further reason for the HR's ardent efforts to extend the Highland tourist season. During 1913 the HR considered buying Dunskaith House and its golf course at Nigg Bay, but decided the water supply was inadequate. In that year the hotels and refreshment rooms earned £45,251 6s, and cost £36,181 16s 10d to run: making a useful profit of over £9,000.

Neil Sinclair notes that Dunkeld had a bookstall as early as 1858 (under P&D auspices), and bookstalls were established at some other HR stations from 1868, the company letting the concession for northern stations, presumably including Inverness and Elgin, at £150 a year for three years; and southern stations for £28 7s 11d a year. A further modest income was made by letting the advertising concession on HR property to Messrs Critchley of Inverness.

# APPENDIX C

## THE STRANGE STORY OF THE SS *FERRET*

Following the agreement with David Macbrayne of April 1880, the Highland Railway was left in possession of its ships *Ferret* and *Carham*. The disposal of *Carham* is noted in the main text. *Ferret* was chartered on 5 October 1880, through Greig & Sons, Shipbrokers, to Mr George Smith, of 14 Brunswick Square, London, for a six-month winter cruise in the Mediterranean, at a rate of £270 a month, complete with her HR captain and crew. Smith provided excellent bank references, and no deposit was requested. However, when the first instalment of the charter fee became due, no payment was made. Enquiries by Andrew Dougall to 14 Brunswick Square were returned marked 'Addressee Unknown'. Smith's bank account had been closed and another reference from a shipbroking firm turned out to be a forgery. The secretary turned to the Board of Trade and Lloyds of London for information, and Lloyds confirmed that the ship had been recorded as passing Gibraltar on 11 November 1880. A lookout was kept, and a message came from Malta via the Board of Trade to report that *Ferret* was there on 24 January 1881. By now four months of the charter fees were owed, and Dougall telegraphed to a shipping agency in Malta asking them to arrange detention of the vessel. They, however, replied that *Ferret* had not appeared there. In February, wreckage was picked up in the Straits of Gibraltar and identified as having come from *Ferret*. Presuming that the ship had foundered, the HR lodged a claim with the insurance underwriters. But on 28 April 1881 the company was startled to receive a telegram from Lloyds, to say that the *Ferret* had been detained in Melbourne, Australia, and that Mr Smith was being held under arrest.

The Highland Railway paid £300 to the Crown Agents to have Smith and his associates returned to Scotland for trial. But, as Australian law also had a claim on them, they were tried in Melbourne. In the course of this, the full story emerged. The ship had sailed to Cardiff, where most, though not all, of the crew were discharged before it set off again. Having passed Gibraltar, Smith did an about-turn and steamed back into the Atlantic, at night and without lights. Two lifeboats and other items with the ship's name were thrown overboard to suggest a wreck. The funnel was repainted, efforts were made to alter the look of the superstructure, and the ship was renamed *Bentan*. At Santos in Brazil, using forged papers, Smith picked up a cargo of 3,092 bags of coffee destined for Marseilles. Instead, he changed the ship's name again, to *India*, and headed for Cape Town, where he sold the coffee for £11,000; and hoped also to sell the ship, but could not find a ready buyer. Hoping to repeat the coffee exploit, but never daring to stay too long in any port, they crossed to Mauritius, Albany in Australia, and finally Melbourne, where their permanent head of steam, in case of instant departure, aroused the port authority's suspicions. The ship was detained on 20 April. Smith and his associates fled but were arrested and brought back to Melbourne, where they were put on trial in July.

Although charged with conspiracy to defraud the Highland Railway Co., they were found not guilty: a seemingly perverse verdict perhaps explained by the absence of any witnesses from the HR. But on the counts of conspiracy to defraud intending purchasers of the *Ferret*, and of deceiving the Australian Commission of Trade and Customs, they were found guilty. Smith was sentenced to seven years in prison, and Wright, the master of the ship, to three and a half years, as was Walker, his purser. The *Ferret* was sold by local agents on behalf of the HR for £8,000, and had a lengthy career in the coastal trade, until wrecked on the Yorke Peninsula in 1920. A sum of £2,100 in respect of five months' charter and damages for detention was also paid, so the company's persistence in following the matter was rewarded. Four seamen, members of the original crew, sued the Highland Railway for unpaid wages, and were awarded £263 19s 8d by an Australian court. Somewhat indignantly, the HR contested this, and the case eventually reached the Judicial Committee of the Privy Council, which ruled that the company was bound to pay.

# APPENDIX D

## PROPOSED, BUT UNBUILT OR UNCOMPLETED
## RAILWAYS IN THE HIGHLANDS

From the 1840s on, numerous railway schemes were suggested or proposed, without coming to fruition. Some of these were scarcely more than talking points, or lines drawn on maps, but others were seriously considered, surveyed, and formally proposed. The Light Railways Act of 1896 resulted in a rush of interest. Numerous lines were proposed in 1896-97, and in some cases Parliamentary or Ministerial approval was given and some work was done. The promoters invariably came to see the Highland company, which, carefully keeping its financial distance, gave them fair words and few promises. In 1897 the HR 'adopted' most of the northern mainland schemes, and Steel, giving evidence to a Parliamentary Committee in March of that year, said that the HR had 247½ miles of branch line proposed in the North and 'though there was no possibility of these lines paying, they looked forward to the run over their line to Inverness, where they gathered the traffic, to recoup themselves' (*Inverness Courier*, 12 March 1897). The fact remained that the Highland had no intention of investing any of its own money in these enterprises, and therefore had nothing to lose; and chiefly wanted to ensure that no other company should have the chance to act as patron. The embrace was a smothering one, and these might-have-been lines are part of the HR's history. The proposals are listed in alphabetical order (for the Garve & Ullapool, see Index).

### The Achnasheen & Aultbea Railway

The Ullapool line's great rival. A large public meeting at Aultbea to support the plan was reported in the *Scotsman* of 19 November 1889. A preliminary survey of this thirty-nine-mile line was done by Murdoch Paterson and a Parliamentary one was undertaken by Thomas Meik & Co. in 1893 for the promoters, Sir Kenneth Mackenzie of Flowerdale, the Earl of Lovelace, Paul Liot Bankes of Letterewe, Duncan Darroch, Torridon House, and John Dixon of Inveran. A Bill was entered to Parliament in the 1893 session, putting the cost at £350,000 including pier works at Aultbea, but its preamble was not proven. Branching from the D&S line at Achnasheen, the line was to pass south of Loch a'Chroisg and cross the watershed into Glen Docherty, then follow the south bank of Loch Maree to Poolewe, then round Loch Ewe to the pier at Aultbea. In 1896 and 1918-20 the idea of the line as a light railway was revived, but not pursued.

## The Cromarty & Dingwall Light Railway

Although Fortrose is only about ten miles from Cromarty, difficult topography and a lack of intervening settlements prevented any plan for extending the HR's Black Isle branch to the tip of the peninsula. But in 1896, local interests proposed an eighteen-mile railway along the north shore, with the aim of linking the old but decayed burgh of Cromarty with the county town of Dingwall. The original proposal included a long bridge over the Conon Estuary, directly into Dingwall, whose only purpose can have been to avoid joining the Highland Railway at Conon and using its line – at whatever price the HR might impose. Understandably, the Light Railway Commissioners saw no reason not to take the much cheaper option of making the junction at Conon, and a Light Railway Order was obtained on that basis, on 1 August 1902, while negotiations with the HR were still going on. Progress was extremely slow, through difficulties over land acquisition, and a large deficiency of capital. Powers for the line lapsed and had to be reacquired twice, in 1907 and 1910. The C&D became something of a local political football, when the Young Scots Society, during the first 1910 election campaign, claimed that the project was only ever heard of when Sir Arthur Bignold required to be re-elected as MP for the Northern Burghs (which included Dingwall). On 17 January 1912 the *Scotsman* reported that work was about to start, with a Treasury grant of £32,000 plus an interest-free loan of £16,000. The county council proposed to invest £10,000 and Cromarty and Dingwall town councils had each pledged £5,000. Other capital amounted to scarcely more than £1,000. The total estimated cost was £96,000 and the consulting engineers were Forman and McCall of Glasgow. The directors of the line were Sir Arthur Bignold, Col. Ross of Cromarty, Jonathan Middleton, and A.R. MacIntyre, with Provost Ross of Cromarty as secretary. Inauspiciously, in March that year the Black Isle Motor Car Service was introduced between Cromarty and North Kessock, and Cromarty and Dingwall. A notice in the *Ross-shire Journal* on 30 January 1914 invited shareholders to attend a meeting in Cromarty to ratify the Working Agreement with the HR, and the contract with Mr Nott, the constructor; and approve the issue of £7,000 in debentures. Lady Bignold cut the first sod in a ceremony at Cromarty in March 1914. By August rails originally destined for New South Wales had been purchased, and about six miles of track had been laid from Cromarty (with a contractor's locomotive at work), and works had been prepared on a further two miles. On the outbreak of war, construction was suspended. It was locally assumed that the Admiralty would take a keen interest in the line, but this turned out not to be so, and in 1917 the rails were commandeered for use in France. After the war Col. Ross, now a general, made valiant efforts to resurrect the line, but though £28,812 19s 6d was paid in compensation for commandeered material, costs had risen and the company could not raise additional money. A final meeting on 2 February agreed on liquidation of the company. With the government waiving repayments of its advance, there was enough to pay off the shareholders and distribute £2,613 15s 5d as the company's one and only dividend.

## The Culrain & Lochinver Railway

This forty-one-mile line seemed to be a likely one for completion. It had been under active discussion since 1890 and received some encouragement from the commissioners in that year. The HR offered (to the Special Commission on 27 July 1891) to construct and work the line at an annual charge equivalent to 3 per cent of a construction bill of £200,000. In fact the estimate was £420,000, none of which was on offer from the Highland. On 29 March 1892 the *Inverness Courier* observed that: 'In the eyes of the Committee, the only scheme immediately practical is the line from Culrain to Lochinver'. But it was not to be. After the Light Railways Act, the Committee for this line made representations to the HR for assistance in April 1896; they were told to come back once they had heard from the Treasury and the Secretary of State. Later that year the HR confirmed to the Easter Ross District Council that the line had been surveyed (*I.C.*, 8 December 1896). But the proposal languished when in the following year Sutherland County Council backed the alternative Invershin–Lochinver line, and the HR switched its limp-wristed support to the rival. Had there been a united effort behind the Culrain & Lochinver, it might have been built.

## The Fearn & Portmahomack Light Railway

A public meeting in Portmahomack in December 1896 launched this eight-mile project and vocal support was initially given by Tain Town Council and the Easter Ross District Committee, but a dispute broke out as to whether the junction should be at Tain or Fearn; or even at Nigg, with a longer line going via Balintore. Asked to survey a route, the HR replied asking them first to select one (6 January 1897). Tain Council lost interest when the proposed junction was moved to Fearn. In September 1898 the HR was asked to survey, and agreed, if the promoters would bear the costs. A Provisional Prospectus for a Fearn & Portmahomack L.R. was issued, with a capital of £24,000, of which the Government was confidently expected to contribute one third as a free grant. It also stated that, 'It is expected that the Highland Railway Company will construct the line at actual cost and after completion sufficiently work it for a period of 3 years also at actual cost' – the HR had only said 'on terms to be agreed' but these were the terms extended to some favoured lines. Murray of Geanies and McLeod of Cadboll were willing to allow free access to their land. On 26 May 1897, Galloway Weir, MP for Ross & Cromarty, informed Steel that he had obtained a Certificate of Approval under Section 5 of the Light Railways Act, from the Secretary of State. Inability to raise capital, and continuing dispute over the route, left the proposal stillborn. New hope of government funds revived the scheme briefly, as with some others, in 1918-19.

## The Forsinard, Melvich and Portskerra Light Railway

Although the third Duke of Sutherland was six years dead when this railway obtained its Order from the Board of Trade on 13 July 1898, and the North of Sutherland Railway Co. was formed, it was a scheme perfectly in accord with his philosophy. Running fourteen miles almost due north from Forsinard, into and down Strath

Halladale to the Pentland Firth townships of Melvich and Portskerra (where a small harbour had been begun in 1894), it promised to open up a wide stretch of almost unpopulated country that had been blighted by the clearances. As with all schemes involving the Duke of Sutherland, the Highland was more forthcoming than usual, though it offered no investment or guarantee. An Agreement was reached in October 1898, that it would construct and work the line for the first three years, at actual cost. Though £20,000 was offered by the Board of Trade, and the fourth duke had offered £10,000 in 1896, the balance had to be found by other promoters. The line was fully surveyed and pegged out, and one or two bridges were constructed. But failure to raise the necessary capital meant that work came to an end, and when construction powers lapsed, they were not renewed. On 12 October 1901 the directors and shareholders held a final meeting at Golspie and agreed to abandon the project.

## The Inverness & Lochend Light Railway

Francis Darwin of Muirtown had proposed a line to Dores on Loch Ness at the HR Shareholders' Meeting on 22 October 1892. This line of seven miles three furlongs, promoted in November 1898, was intended to link Inverness with a pier at the north end of Loch Ness, in effect forming the northern end of the never-built Great Glen line. The proposed share capital was £60,000 in £5 shares and construction cost was estimated at £46,776. No Treasury money was asked for. The promoters were Sir Kenneth Matheson (better known for his Lochalsh interests but who also owned land here), James Baillie of Dochfour, Francis Darwin (both HR directors), Provost McBean and Bailie Macdonald of Inverness, and Donald Grant, solicitor, Inverness. The North British and Invergarry & Fort Augustus Railways both opposed the scheme. The promoters had made no arrangement for a Working Agreement with the HR, and in fact the scheme was in blatant defiance of an HR Board Minute of 26 October 1898, when the company agreed with the NB and the I&FA Railways 'not to promote any Bill in the ensuing session which would revive the controversy with regard to the district between Inverness and Fort Augustus'. The HR kept its distance, though the board did resolve on 4 January 1899 to try to acquire the right to purchase the line at or below cost, should it be put up for sale. At the Public Enquiry into the proposal, on 20 May 1899, the two civic dignitaries had to admit that neither the Chamber of Commerce nor the Town Council supported the scheme. The Enquiry rejected the proposal, on the ground of insufficient public advantage proved.

## The Invershin and Lochinver Light Railway

An alternative to the Culrain & Lochinver, of similar length but following the north bank of the river Oykell as far as Oykell Bridge, and thus in Sutherland territory all the way. Sutherland County Council backed it at a conference called in Golspie in September 1896, and chaired by the duke. The only dissenter was Mr Gilmour, proprietor of Glen Cassley, who saw no need for a railway for 'a few discontented crofters'. The backing for this line seemed sufficiently firm for the HR to sanction the appointment of Paterson and Roberts as engineers to it, on 3 March 1897. But the competition with the Culrain line enabled the Treasury to ignore its claims and the scheme faded away, though the Scottish Rural Transport Committee were 'greatly impressed' by Lochinver's case – still forty miles from a railway – in 1918 (*Highland News*, June 15, 1918).

## The Lairg & Loch Laxford Light Railway

First proposed in June 1891, and one of the six lines examined and despaired of by the Special Committee, it was intended to follow Lochs Shin, Merkland, More and Stack north-west to Laxford Bridge, with an extension to the fishing harbour of Kinlochbervie, about fifty-three miles in total. In March 1896 the HR made its most common answer to renewed application for involvement and assistance: it would work the line, if built, 'on reasonable terms'. Sufficient capital was never likely to be raised, and a Light Railway Order was not applied for.

## The Newtonmore and Tulloch Railway

The twenty-six-mile gap between Newtonmore and Tulloch on the West Highland was the focus of a vigorous local campaign for a railway in the later 1890s, to help 'open up' the Glen Truim and Strath Mashie district. The West Highland was favoured as a sponsor, but neither it nor the HR were interested, and the scheme fell into abeyance.

## Scrabster Branch

Joseph Mitchell's map of 1864 shows Scrabster, not Thurso, as the northernmost branch terminus. But Scrabster was not included in the Sutherland & Caithness Railway's Act of 13 July 1871, and travellers and goods for the Orkney steamer had to be transferred from Thurso Station to the harbour by wagonette and Wordie's cart. In April 1896 the Harbour Board wrote to the HR to say it had a light railway in mind: would the HR build it for them? The HR Traffic Committee felt that the company might like to build it for itself. A report in the *John o' Groat Journal* on 15 May 1896 indicated that a survey was under way. But no further action was ever taken.

## Wick & Gills Bay Railway

At the HR half-yearly meeting of 30 October 1891, a shareholder had recommended Gills Bay as a harbour, and the chairman had replied that the company was in touch with the authorities. For no clear reason, this project seems to have been more warmly embraced by the Highland Railway than most others (the HR knew that Wick Town Council had flirted with the Great North in the early days of the Lybster line proposal). Although a branch from Thurso was also suggested, the projected route was from Wick, passing a string of tiny crofting and fishing settlements to Gills, where there was (and is) a pier. Iain Sutherland makes the plausible suggestion that the line is related to the desire of the North of Scotland, Orkney & Shetland Steamship Co.'s desire to transfer their weekly steamer call at Wick to another Caithness port, since Wick harbour was so congested with fishing boats. But capital was never forthcoming.

# NOTES AND REFERENCES

*Abbreviations*

D&SR: Dingwall & Skye Railway Committee and Board Minutes

*Groat: John o' Groat Journal*

HRA: Highland Regional Archives, Inverness

HRB: Highland Railway Board Minutes (NAS)

*HRJ: Highland Railway Journal*

*I.A.: Inverness Advertiser*

I&AB: Inverness & Aberdeen Junction Railway Board Minutes (NAS)

I&AC: Inverness & Aberdeen Junction Railway Committee Minutes (NAS)

I&NB: Inverness & Nairn Railway Board Minutes (NAS)

I&NC: Inverness & Nairn Railway Committee Minutes (NAS)

I&P: Inverness & Perth Junction Railway Board Minutes (NAS)

*I.C.: Inverness Courier*

J.E.C.: Campbell, *The Iron Track Through the Highlands*

*JRCHS: Journal of the Railway and Canal Historical Society*

JRD: John Ross Diaries

*JTH: Journal of Transport History*

NAS: National Archives of Scotland

NHA: North Highland Archive, Wick

PMP: Printed Memoranda of the Proceedings that led to the Appointment of the Committee of 1891 (File GD40/16/29 in NAS)

RCR: Railway Commissioners' Reports (National Railway Museum)

*R.M. Railway Magazine*

Rem.: Joseph Mitchell's *Reminiscences*, Vol. 2

## PART I

### ONE

### *The Great Scheme and its Failure*

1. Quoted in Vamplew, *Railway Investment in the Scottish Highlands, JTH*, Vol. 3, No.2. July 1970.

2. *Rem.*, 151.

3. Ibid., 152. By his own account; others also were promoting the SCR.

4. *I.C.*, 8 September 1863.

5. *Rem.*, 159-60.

6. Ibid., 161.

7. Ibid., 163.

8. Ibid., 164.

9. The preamble summarised the aim and proposed route of the line.

10. *Rem.*, 181.

## The Inverness & Nairn Railway

1. *Rem.*, 181-82.
2. The GNSR had proposed a separate company to build from Elgin to Inverness, in March 1845, and it is likely that some potential Elgin supporters were won over to the Inverness scheme.
3. I&NC, 10 January 1854.
4. Ibid., 30 January 1854.
5. Ibid., 21 February 1854.
6. Ibid., 9 March 1854.
7. The bridge is illustrated in *HRJ*, Nos 39 and 40.
8. I&NB, 3 December 1854.
9. RCR, 1855.
10. Highland Railway Soc., *Eastgate II*, 5-6.
11. I&NB, 1 November 1855.
12. *I.C.*, 8 November 1855.
13. Culloden was renamed Allanfearn in 1898; Cawdor station opened early 1856, was renamed Kildrummie in 1857, but closed on 1 January 1858.
14. 'J.E.C.' reports an injury (26) but this is almost certainly a confusion with a later accident during an Inverness trades excursion to Elgin, on 10 September 1858, when a young man, drunkenly larking in an open wagon carrying banners, fell back, struck his head on a cross-bar, and died from his injuries. See I&AB, 14 September 1858. This was the first passenger fatality.
15. I&NB, 1 November 1855: 'It is the intention of the Directors to carry out the original design of a branch to the harbour of Inverness so soon as the negotiations with the Harbour Trust… are sufficiently matured'. It opened on 27 August 1857.

## The Inverness & Aberdeen Junction Railway

1. A new company, unrelated to the old GNSR proposal.
2. Barclay-Harvey, 24-25.
3. *I.C.*, 1 November 1855: 'The Inverness & Elgin has now developed into the Inverness & Aberdeen Junction Railway, now in process of formation.'
4. *Rem.*, 182.
5. I&AC, Westminster, 14 June 1855. T.C. Bruce and the engineer J.C. Gunn were authorised to go to Paris to speak to Locke, and confirmed the arrangement at a London meeting on 18 June with Locke present. His involvement seems to have been largely nominal.
6. I&AC, Westminster, 14 June 1855. It appears that a joint line, rather than two separate lines, had already been an option.
7. On 16 June 1855.
8. I&AC, 9 July 1855.
9. Ibid., 12 September 1855.
10. Barclay-Harvey, 26.
11. I&AC, 9 September 1855
12. Ibid., 15 February 1856. By this point Gunn, identified with the Rothes route, had been dropped and Mitchell was sole engineer.
13. Bradshaw's *Shareholders' Guide*, 1857: '… the number of shareholders who may be noted as having a local interest is 312 and their capital £165,900 out of £243,900 subscribed'.
14. *Rem.*, 185. The Board Minutes of this time show regular complaints from Falshaw about Mitchell's certificates of work done.
15. I&AC., 12 July 1856. The playground had been said, by an anonymous contributor to the *I.C.*, 15 March 1855, to be unnecessarily extensive.
16. RCR, 1858. Letter from Bruce to the Board of Trade, 9 August 1858: '… we now propose to open for public traffic two sections, extending from Keith to the Spey on the east side, and from Orton to Elgin on the west'. He does not explain how passengers would be conveyed across the river.
17. The letters are reprinted in RCR 1858, Appendix No.1.
18. *Rem.*, 186.
19. I&AB, 21 December 1858.
20. RCR, *loc. cit.* The report was written on 23 April 1859. The viaduct was laid with double track, though Tyler notes that only one track was actually used in normal service.
21. Ibid.
22. Letter quoted in *HRJ* 44, 11-13.

23. The guard, who had left the train at Fochabers, without permission from Inverness, was also dismissed (I&AB, 16 November 1858).
24. *Rem.*, 187. Ironically, the blind siding at Mulben had been put in at the Board of Trade's request, for safety reasons.

## 'Further North': The Inverness & Ross-shire Railway

1. *I.C.*, 20 September 1860.
2. Clew, 8.
3. *I.A.*, 14 June 1861.
4. I&AB: 9 November 1861.
5. *I.A.*, 26 April 1864.
6. The 'Open Letter to Sir Robert Peel' had envisaged bridges and embankments across the Beauly and Cromarty Firths, with land reclamation schemes 'in aid of the elevation of the downtrodden and fast-disappearing race of Highland crofters'.

## The Great North Withdraws

1. On 15 October 1858, a meeting of I&AJR Directors complained about the GNSR's inability to provide a through Inverness–Edinburgh service from 1 November, implying that this had been an intention, if not a commitment.
2. Vallance (*GNSR*) refers to 'the high-handed attitude adopted by the directors from Aberdeen' (33).
3. I&AB: Extraordinary Meeting on 20 December 1859.
4. *Rem.*, 190. The story is repeated in Nock.
5. *R.M.*, January 1905.
6. The I&AJR solicitor.
7. Barclay-Harvey, 69.

## TWO
## The Inverness & Perth Junction Railway

1. *Rem.*, 190.
2. Ibid., 190.
3. Ibid., 190-95.
4. Ibid., 195.
5. I&P, 3 December 1861.
6. Few railways had spare capital for outside investment at this time.
7. *Rem.*, 196.
8. Ibid., 196.
9. Ibid, 202.
10. I&P, 6 November 1862.
11. *Rem.*, 197.
12. Ibid., 198.
13. *I.C.*, 8 September 1863.
14. *Rem.*, 199.
15. At that time, engines did not work through, but in three stages, changing over at Aviemore and Blair Atholl. Reporting the I&PJR Shareholders' Meeting, the *I.A.* of 30 October 1863 recorded that Bruce thanked the southern companies for their help, which included providing special connecting trains when the I&PJR trains were late at Perth.
16. HRB, 10 April 1866.

## Formation of the Highland Railway Co.

1. Barclay-Harvey, 26
2. Despite the heraldic language (from an LMS pamphlet of the 1920s) permission to use these arms was never sought from the Lyon Court and so their use was illegal under Scots law. There was no motto but the shields were enclosed within a garter lettered 'HIGHLAND RAILWAY COMPANY', or emblazoned on an eagle's breast.
3. He persuaded Allan to knock £500 off his charge of £3,096 1s 5d for services between 1863-65 (HRB, 5 September 1865).
4. Mitchell's plan (NAS) shows the line going via Bankfoot, with double track between Dunkeld and Murthly.

5. His brother J.B. Barclay, who had joined with him, remained as foreman of the running shed until 31 January 1899, when he received a retirement allowance of 20s a week (HR Loco Committee, 31 January 1899).

## THREE
### The Sutherland Railway
1. He did so in 1874.
2. *Rem.*, 218-20.
3. On 14 February 1866.
4. HRB, Westminster meeting, 19 July 1866.
5. HRB, 21 August 1865. It was to pay off a Commercial Bank bill. But the bank loan was also renewed at the 5 September meeting.
6. HRB, 5 September 1865 had considered a letter from the Secretary of the CR noting his Board's proposal to authorise the acquisition of £50,000 worth of HR Ordinary stock 'as previously arranged'.
7. HRB, 17 November 1866.
8. HRB, 3 September 1867.
9. A copy is preserved in the GPO Archives.

### The Caithness Railway Co.
1. *Rem.*, 213.
2. Ibid., 214.
3. *Groat*, 19 January 1865. In fact the Act did not allow grants for railway investment.
4. *Groat*, 30 September 1865.
5. Also in *I.C.*, 28 November 1866.
6. *Groat,* 5 October 1865.
7. *Rem.*, 221.

### The Highland Railway, 1866-70
1. The Caledonian had abortive merger talks also with the GNSR around this time. See Vallance (*GNSR*), 73.
2. HRB, 20 March 1866.
3. HRB, 2 January 1866. By whose horse is unclear. The HR never appears to have owned horses itself.
4. HRB, 10 August 1866.
5. Vallance (*GNSR*), 55.
6. The MR already had Parliamentary approval for an amalgamation with the GNSR but this was not accomplished until 1881.
7. On 2 August 1899 payment of £1 5s 1d towards the stipend of Rev. James Macdowall, Fortrose, was approved – such occasional payments were presumably responsibilities associated with the feuing of Church-owned land.
8. HRB, 3 September 1867.
9. *HRJ* 29. This arrangement did not survive the opening of the Forth Bridge, with consequent traffic gain by the North British Railway.
10. *Scottish Industrial History*.

### Dingwall & Skye – the First Phase
1. The Matheson fortunes were founded largely on the opium trade.
2. *Groat*, 23 March 1865.
3. Bradshaw gives the figure as £100,000, but Dougall reported to a D&S 'Directors' Meeting' on 22 June 1865 that the CR was proposing to invest £50,000 in the Skye line and the same amount in the Perth line.
4. John Mitchell, 'Telford's Tartar', was reputed to have been a man of flintily uncompromising character.
5. *Rem.*, 212.
6. Bradshaw's *Shareholders' Guide*, 1868.
7. *Rem.*, 211-12.
8. Most debenture holders were from outside the Highlands; the furthest subsriber was in Madras (D&SR).
9. See Thomas, *The Skye Railway*, 41-42.

### The Duke of Sutherland's Railway
1. The site is referred to by Vallance as Gartymore (36), and in Tyler's report the station is described as 'temporary', with a siding. It was probably by the sea, at Gartymore Shore. The OS map dated 1879, though evidently drawn some years earlier, shows the station at its present site, as a terminus, with Goods and Engine Sheds.

2. HRB, 6 December 1870.

3. He was appointed managing director, at a salary of £50 a year.

4. This was a unique privilege, but the DoSR was a unique railway.

## The Sutherland & Caithness Railway

1. *Northern Ensign Almanac*, January 1897.

2. Letter of 26 October 1870.

3. *Groat*, 12 November 1870.

4. Treated in more detail in McConnell, *Rails to Wick and Thurso*.

5. *Groat*, 20 May 1871.

6. An additional reason for stopping at the edge of town may have been that Wick, as a royal burgh, was entitled to charge 'petty customs'.

7. NHA file P482. The *Groat*, 5 March 1874, noted that Caithness contributed less than 5 per cent of the cost of the S&CR.

8. The following details are largely from reports and documents in NHA file P482.

9. Plan in NHA file P482.

10. *Groat*, 9 July 1874.

11. Ibid.

12. Ibid., 30 July 1874.

## FOUR
## The Highland Railway in the 1870s

1. HRB, 7 December 1869.

2. HRB, 6 June 1871.

3. HRB, 7 February 1871.

4. HRB, 3 May 1873.

5. Directors' Report to 31 August 1876.

6. Discussed further in Chapter 4.0.

7. Ellis, Vol.2, page 203.

8. Discussed further in Chapter 3.3.

## Dingwall & Skye – the Second Phase

1. Some histories, including Hamilton Ellis, state that this subscription was paid.

2. Bradshaw's *Shareholders' Guide*, 1878.

3. *The Times*, 18 July 1872. Ninety-two shareholders supported the company; none opposed.

4. Mackay, 346.

5. HRB, 4 September 1877.

6. For the Board Meeting of 7 October 1879.

## The Steamship Venture

1. The S&CR might have been expected to participate in this, but it had no funds.

2. Stephenson Loco Society, *Highland Railway*, 53.

3. Reported by Dougall to the board on 3 April 1877.

4. Letter from Benthall, received on 27 September 1876.

## FIVE
## The Highland in the 1880s: Territorial Defences

1. HRB, 2 March 1880.

2. See Chapter 3.9.

3. HRB, 4 September, 1877.

4. Letter of 9 May 1883, in O'Dell Collection.

5. Letter to Ferguson, 26 July 1883, in O'Dell Collection

6. Barclay-Harvey, 99.

7. Letter in O'Dell Collection.

8. Letter in O'Dell Collection.

9. Letter to William Ferguson, of 2 February 1887, in O'Dell Collection. Protests centred on actions like this: A private saloon carriage party from Euston to Craigellachie wanted to transfer to the GNSR at Boat of Garten, but the Highland refused to take the carriage from Perth unless it was booked to run via Forres. In the end, it was taken to Craigellachie via Forres and Elgin. The GNSR got only the price of twelve and a half miles, Elgin–Craigellachie, instead of thirty-three and a half miles from Boat of Garten; and the passengers arrived at 12.23 p.m. instead of 11.55 a.m.

## The Portessie and Strathpeffer Branches

1. See Chapter 7. The HR Traffic Committee, 27 July 1915, specified 'want of engines and men'. Twenty-two men were employed on the branch.
2. *HRJ* 4, 2-5.

## New Western Schemes, and Frontier Skirmishes

1. A handwritten Private Agreement between the companies, dated 3 June 1889, also notes that the HR would receive £500 against costs incurred in opposing the West Highland (NAS, BR/HR/3/6).
2. Acworth , 75.
3. The commission's prime concern was with agriculture and fishing, but noted: 'Extended Railway Communication is the principal requirement of the fishing population of the western coast'.
4. Hunter, 179.
5. Ibid.
6. O'Dell Collection. Fraser was the moving spirit, but not very dynamic: Ferguson advised him to form a Committee and force the HR to say if it would, or would not, support the line.
7. HRB, 14 June 1890.
8. *Northern Chronicle*, 20 August 1890.
9. Correspondence between them, and other papers, in PMP.
10. Maj.-Gen. Hutchinson, RE, HM Inspector of Railways; Rear-Admiral Sir George Nares, and Henry Tennant, ex-general manager of the North Eastern Railway, formed the 'Special Committee appointed to inquire into certain schemes for the improvement of railway communication on the western coast of Scotland'.
11. For other schemes, see Appendix D.
12. PMP: A handwritten memorandum of a meeting on 13 April at Martin & Leslie's office, between Raigmore, Grant Peterkin, and Andrew Dougall, with Major Houstoun, Mr Fowler and their solicitor, sums it up: 'After discussion the Highland Company agreed to work the G&U Line in perpetuity but would undertake no liability of construction or guarantee construction, even if all capital for this purpose was found for them'.
13. Correspondence in O'Dell Collection. Believers in conspiracy theories might well question the Treasury's motives.
14. Letter in PMP.
15. Letter of 15 May, in PMP.
16. Report of the Special Committee appointed to inquire into certain schemes for the provision of railway communication on the western coast of Scotland. *Parliamentary Papers*, 1892, CXX.

## The Kyle Extension

This section of the HR is well documented in McConnell, *Rails to Kyle of Lochalsh,* on which the précis given here is largely based.

## New Branches: Hopeman Extension, Black Isle Fochabers and Fort George

1. As a wartime economy, Hopeman station was closed between January 1917 and June 1919.
2. The original HR plan, ascribed to Murdoch Paterson and John Fowler (NAS), shows a rail link to a jetty at Chanonry Point. But unlike the GNSR, the Highland had no reason to be interested in a ferry that cut off some thirty-five miles of its own route.
3. JRD: Cash Record, 1892, and Diary 1894.

## SIX
## The Resignation of Andrew Dougall

1. To conserve coal stocks, services had to be curtailed.
2. The following account is based on the HR Board Minutes and associated documents (NAS), and the extensive reports in the *I.C.* of 25 October and 6 December 1895.
3. See Appendix D.

4. It was reiterated in the Directors' Report for February-August 1895, in which the Accounts are certified 'subject to the competency of crediting the revenue of the half-year with interest on cost of works in course of construction, and to an overstatement of traffic for the preceding six months being met out of the Reserve Fund instead of being set against Revenue'.

5. Copy with HRB Minutes of 4 December 1895.

6. *I.C.*, 6 December 1895.

7. HRB, 8 January 1896: 'Mr Waterston has transferred the Stock held by him to the Caledonian Bank and was therefore no longer qualified for the office of Director'.

8. Dougall continued to live in Inverness until 1897, when he moved first to Nairn and then to London. He died on 30 November 1905 and was buried, after a well-attended funeral, in Tomnahurich Cemetery. The *Highland News* called him 'a martyr of circumstances'. (2 December 1905)

9. HRB, 28 October 1896.

## Double Track over Druimuachdar, and the 'Direct Line'

1. By 1922 there were loops at Kingswood, Inchmagranachan, Moulinearn, Inchlea, Etteridge, Dalraddy and Slochd; and at Acheilidh beween Lairg and Rogart.

2. If anything, they were reduced. A Board Minute of 1 February 1899 notes that, having regard to locomotive weights and the permanent way, the General Manager undertook that: 'No train on and after this date would be booked to run at a speed exceeding 50 miles per hour'.

3. Acworth, 75.

4. JRD. On 30 October 1890, he went to the 'Forth Bridge Sale'.

5. JRD.

6. JRD. His tender was put in on 27 November 1891.

7. *I.C.*, 2 August 1892. There was a Scottish Navvy Mission Society, which employed eight missionaries, who also had some medical training. Ross frequently found his men drunk.

8. JRD. Sir Francis Marindin inspected the section for the Board of Trade on 15 and 16 July. Vallance's date of 8 July seems incorrect.

9. It was originally intended to end at Culdoich, about two miles beyond the Strathnairn Viaduct. This would have required a separate signal box.

10. JRD. Ross saw him on 20 July and noted he was 'verey poorly (sic)'.

11. In May 1899 they had the pleasure of entertaining the GNSR directors, who had asked for a tour of the direct line (letter from Moffat to Ferguson, 12 May 1899, in O'Dell Collection).

## Light Railways in the North: Dornoch, Wick & Lybster

1. *British Railway History*, Vol.2, 146.

2. From 13 April 1868 (GPO Archives).

3. It was rescinded, whatever it was, and the subscription was paid (HRB, 29 January and 26 February 1913).

4. William Whitelaw's speech to the HR Shareholders' Meeting, 29 March 1905.

5. Simnett, 253, though the DLR Minutes of 17 March 1923 show £10,785. The DLR never paid a dividend on its Ordinary shares.

6. The following draws largely on working notes (NHA) by Iain Sutherland.

7. Such initiatives, paid for by the county rates, were highly unpopular in parts of the county not served by the proposed railway.

8. They were released from this obligation on 25 November 1914 (HRB).

9. Simnett, 253. The LMS operated the line until 1 April 1944, when it was closed 'as a wartime expedient', but never reopened.

## New Men and New Attitudes: The Highland Railway 1896-1914

1. HRB Finance Committee, 26 October 1898.

2. HRB Traffic Committee, 4 August 1896.

3. A GNSR advertisement for its services via Aberdeen in the *I.C.* of 30 June 1899, stressed its 'EXPRESS TRAINS equipped with first and third-class Corridor Carriages with Lavatory Accommodation, and lighted by Electricity … Passengers are requested to ask for Tickets Routed via Aberdeen'.

4. *I.C.*, 24 July 1896. Despite his forecast of 'large works, which would employ a great many people', all three subsequent schemes for a Loch Ness-side railway followed the opposite shore, via Invermoriston and Drumnadrochit.

5. *I.C.*, 27 November 1896.

6. *I.C.*, 19 March 1897.

7. *I.C.*, 9 July 1897. Its main aim now was to force the HR and NB to take it over or buy it out.

8. See Appendix D. The Duke of Sutherland was a backer of both lines.

9. HRB, 28 March 1897.

10. HRB Locomotive Committee, 30 January 1906: Drummond reported that he could reduce workshop staff by 34, saving £1,700 a year.

11. Both Lord Lovat and the Duke of Sutherland expressed reservations about the loss to Inverness. At a meeting of the Joint Committee established by both companies, at Westminster on 10 November 1905, Lovat threatened to resign from the board if the new HQ were not at Inverness.

12. And Town Clerk of Inverness. The HR Ordinary shares had never been split or diluted, whereas of the GNSR's £7 million of capital, £2 million was 'pure water'. HR Ordinary stock (par 100) went down from fifty-two to forty-eight when the consolidation terms were announced, and back to fifty-two when it was dropped. GNSR shares moved in the contrary direction each time. See also *I.C.*, 5 December 1905.

13. Shareholders' Meeting, 28 March 1906.

14. *I.C.*, 13 March 1906. Around 300 people attended.

15. He rejected the suggestion that the board had been defeated on a major issue.

16. Minutes of HR/GNSR Joint Meetings, NAS.

17. HRB, 28 May 1913.

18. The HR carried motor cars in its one-time carriage vans. Petrol tanks were supposed to be emptied, and a car was destroyed at Dalguise on 25 August 1905 when a porter watched this operation while holding a handlamp (Traffic Committee, 5 September 1905).

19. *I.C.*, 1 November 1910.

20. *Highland Leader*, 9 February 1911. See also Chapter 3.3.

21. Directors' Report, 25 February 1914. To illustrate the fallibility of statistics, the line carried 4741 tons of fish by goods train and 8,000 tons by passenger train (credited to passenger revenue).

## SEVEN

### The First World War

1. Details are largely from Pratt, II, 532ff.

2. Number given at the Annual Meeting, 26 February 1919.

3. Barclay-Harvey, 18-19.

4. Pratt, II, 804. The HR had agreed to lay the ammunition siding, but did nothing until the Admiralty intimated that the first trains were on their way: it was then laid in two weeks during May 1915.

5. Pratt, II, 953. Coal for the fleet went by sea from Grangemouth.

6. Ibid., 952.

7. *R.M.*, January 1915. Sir Arnold Lunn had acquired the Atholl Palace at Pitlochry in May 1914 on behalf of the British Public Schools' Alpine Sports Club. On 24 November 1914, the Traffic Committee agreed to provide a special train from Dalwhinnie to Blair Atholl, for skiing parties of twenty or more, connecting with the 5.30 p.m. to Perth.

8. Quoted in full in Nock, 156.

9. Thomas, *The North British Railway*, Vol.2, 169.

10. Pratt, I, 502ff.

11. Ibid.

12. Inverness Station was closely guarded. The town was much entertained when Capt. Mackinnon, Intelligence Officer for the North of Scotland, arrested and prosecuted his clan chief, The Mackinnon, of Dalcross Castle, for being in the station without intent to travel. He was seeing someone off, and was fined £1 (*I.C.*, 17 October 1916). But in the course of the war, seven spies were arrested here, of whom five were later executed.

13. *HRJ*, 46, 28.

14. Pratt, II, 539.

15. Ibid., 681.

16. Two lock-up cells were still *in situ* in the cellars when the author was a hall porter there in 1960.

17. Hamilton, 108.

18. Ibid. *loc. cit.*, from N.U.R. records then at Inverness.

### The Last Years

1. *I.C.*, 29 September 1919.

2. Ibid.

3. *Aberdeen Free Press*, 2 October 1919.

4. *North Star*, 17 April 1920.

5. A denial of this plan was published in *Modern Transport*, 20 November 1920.

6. Simnett, 264.

7. Quoted in Pratt, II, 785.

8. *I.C.*, 2 March 1923.

9. Ibid. True to form, Miss Laing of Keith rose to protest about ex-directors retaining their free passes; but she was persuaded not to move an amendment. See Chapter 3.4.

# PART II
## EIGHT
### Mitchell's Road

1. Reprinted in the Stephenson Locomotive Society *Highland Railway*, 59-67.

2. This bridge was washed away in an exceptional spate on 7 February 1989.

3. Now with an inner steel support structure.

4. Later demolished.

5. *R.M.*, January 1904.

6. S&CR papers in the NHA. JRD also suggest that creeps were *ad hoc* features: 'Mr Paterson and Mr Gordon on hand, arranging about Drains and creeps' (7 January 1890).

7. *HRJ* 27, 8-15; No. 36, 7-12.

8. HRB Way & Works Committee, 25 October 1898: William Roberts reports that double water columns at Blair Atholl are about to be installed.

### Operations

1. I&AB, 11 September 1857 to 2 February 1858. The E.T.C had installed its system on the GNSR at no charge other than a £4 a mile rental. It proposed £36 per mile and £15 per instrument to the I&AJR. A draft agreement was approved on 2 February 1858 and sealed on 3 March. Completion between Elgin and Dalvey was expected by 14 March.

2. David Stirling has confirmed in a letter to the author that the original Inspection Report of the line, at the Public Records Office in Kew, states that the block telegraph was in operation between Keith and Elgin.

3. During a dispute with the Board of Trade, Alex. Matheson wrote to the *Railway Times* (6 February 1873) that: 'The directors adopted the block telegraph system of working at a very early period, and at considerable outlay, not in consequence of the recommendation of Board of Trade officers, but against their opinion' – a claim rejected by the BoT.

4. 'Down' meant northbound; 'Up' southbound or London-wards. Trains to Keith were 'Up' to Forres and 'Down' after that, and vice versa.

5. Stephenson Locomotive Society *Highland Railway,* 70.

6. See Appendix A.

7. In HRA.

8. Correspondence quoted in *Northern Herald*, 25 February and 4 March 1909.

9. Quoted in Hunter, *The HR in Retrospect*, 32.

10. Vallance, *GNSR*, 156.

11. Drummond's 0-6-4 tank engines, intended to run in either direction, had them on both sides.

12. Twenty-one bridges at £150 each were ordered in 1905 (HRB Way & Works Committee, 28 March and 24 October 1905).

13. Interlocked signalling at junctions had been a feature of the HR since the 1860s.

14. Acworth records an 'assistant engineer' as saying, after a sandstorm: 'The agent and leading surfaceman gave me their opinion that 40 men could not have kept the line clear on Friday night, and that, if the fence had not been there, there would have been at least four feet depth of sand over the rails' (157).

## NINE
### Motive Power – The Early Years

1. By 1862, Inverness town council was discussing the 'smoke nuisance' from the running sheds, and a councillor complained that the company was breaching an Act of Parliament by burning coal instead of coke (it was, but the Act was by then a dead letter). *I.A.*, 10 June 1862.

2. If fifty is correct, they must have been assembled from a wide range of locations.

3. A more detailed article by the author on HR engine names is in the possession of the Scottish Place-Names Society.

4. *HRJ*, No. 6, 5, 10-11.

5. Later reports would list all snowploughs, with a maximum of seventy-one. From 1906 this seems to have included a 'double line snowplough', to work between Blair Atholl and Kingussie, authorised by the Locomotive Committee on 27 March 1906, at a cost of £25.

6. *Groat*, 13 January 1885.

## Motive Power – The Classic Era

1. HRB, 6 December 1870.
2. Quoted in *HRJ*, 11, 3.
3. Ellis, *Twenty Locomotive Men*, 128.
4. Murdoch Paterson spoke of the 'warm loving kindness' felt for Jones in Inverness (*I.C.*, 3 November 1896).
5. Highet, 178.
6. Cormack & Stevenson, 40.
7. Ellis, *The Trains we Loved*, 68.
8. *I.C.*, 28 May 1910.
9. Hamilton, 130.
10. Stephenson Locomotive Society, *Highland Railway*, 79.

## Motive Power – The 'Modern' Era

1. *LMS Journal* No. 7, 52-69.
2. In 1912 the post of Chief Draughtsman was abolished.
3. At the National Railway Museum.
4. *LMS Journal, loc. cit.* Atkins's final assessment is that Newlands was excessively cautious and that the 'Rivers' could have been employed.
5. *Highland Times*, 2 March 1916.
6. A wider anti-English bias has also been suggested; but in a company with warm memories of David Jones, this seems unlikely.
7. Atkins has shown that Smith placed the original order, but it was approved at £595 by Newlands's Way & Works Committee on 25 November 1913. Smith was probably the source of the later request for it to be lengthened from 60ft to 63ft 2in, which required a cancellation and re-order, from Newlands, approved on 24 February 1914, at a price of £750. The wheelbase of the 'River' design was 49ft 4.5ins; its overall length 59ft 6in.
8. See Atkins, 'Hawthorn, Leslie and the HR', in 'Backtrack', March 1998.
9. The suggestion is made in Nock, pp.167-8.
10. For a thorough account, see Geddes & Bellass.

## Lochgorm Works

1. J.S. Brownlie (181) thought this was quite likely as it incorporated features, like side-mounted capstan heads for hauling in scattered wreckage, more common on cranes for colonial than for home lines. As the 'Yankee Tanks' showed, the HR had an eye for bargain items.
2. As 'portable engine wagon' or 'stone crusher' it is listed in the carriage and wagon return in half-yearly and yearly Reports from 1898 up to 1922.

# PART III

## TEN

## The Community of the Railway: The Staff

1. JEC, 23.
2. He published two slim volumes of verse to raise money for charity. See *HRJ*, Nos 66 and 67.
3. *HRJ* 58.
4. Sinclair, 88.
5. HRB, 2 January 1877. It was the second accident in close succession: see Appendix A.
6. *HRJ* 35, 12.
7. JEC, 104.
8. *Highland News*, 11 January 1911.
9. HRB, 26 January 1913.

10. JEC, 105.

11. *I.C.*, 11 December 1891.

12. *I.C.*, 15 December 1911.

13. HR Locomotive Dept. Record Book, NAS.

14. See Chapter 3.8.

15. HRB, 18 October 1867.

16. HRB, 2 October 1877.

17. HRB, 25 May 1870.

18. HRB, 11 January 1867.

19. A practice maintained into the 1960s.

20. HR Staff Register (NAS).

21. Most accounts say only one, ignoring the man killed on the I&AJR excursion in 1858, though his death was not the railway's fault.

22. HRB, 10 October 1873.

23. HRB, 3 July 1877.

24. *I.C.*, 28 November 1884.

25. HRB Finance Committee, 8 December 1898.

26. HRB, 6 January 1897.

27. *I.C.*, 20 April 1897 records its annual festival in the Northern Meeting Rooms with George Clark, engine-driver, in the chair. Its purpose seems to have been mainly charitable.

28. Traffic Committee, 27 October 1914; Loco Committee, 27 July 1915.

29. HRB, 5 January 1869.

30. *HRJ*, 63, 23.

31. *Ross-shire Journal*, 9 October 1896.

## The Community of the Railway: Directors and Shareholders

1. Robertson, 105.

2. Joseph Mitchell noted that in his time he had seen nearly two thirds of the estates in the Highlands change proprietors (*Rem.*, 114).

3. Ash, 129.

4. To the *R.M.*

5. J.E.C., 97. The foot-warmers were made at Lochgorm (150 were ordered by the Traffic Committee on 31 January 1899).

6. *Highland Leader*, 21 July 1910. Questions were asked in Parliament.

7. Over 500 came to the half-yearly meeting of October 1905, expecting to hear details of the GNSR merger, to find that the directors proposed to say nothing about it at all.

8. In May–June 1918 a bitter correspondence on Whitelaw's 'somewhat ambiguous role' on the HR was opened in the *Highland News* by 'N.M.'; and one A. Norman Dormer took up cudgels for the Board against what he termed 'the Old Gang'.

## ELEVEN
## Passenger Trains

1. Somers, 110.

2. *I.A.*, 6 October 1868.

3. *I.A.*, 17 March 1865.

4. HRB, 2 July 1878.

5. Heap and van Riemsdijk (69) record them also as the first side-corridor sleeping cars in Britain.

6. The *Perthshire Constitutional* noted on 25 July 1916 that the HR had been fined £5 in a case involving the forcible ejection of two Perth Academy girls, with season tickets to Ballinluig, from the 'wrong part of the train'.

7. *I.C.*, 3 September 1889.

8. Foxwell & Farrer, 63.

9. JEC, 25.

10. Holmes, 12-13.

11. Reprinted in *HRJ*, 31, 24.

12. Advertisement in *I.C.*, 31 October 1922: 'Lunch, Tea and Dining Facilities' were available for both first and third class.

13. *I.C.*, 24 July 1891.
14. HR half-yearly Directors' Reports.
15. *R.M.*, March 1907.
16. The *Northern Ensign,* 22 February 1910, again reported the council's dissatisfaction with 'the inferior nature of the through carriage accommodation'.
17. *HRJ*, 2, 15.

## Passengers

1. Gordon and Macdonald, 60.
2. Ibid., 45.
3. Ash, 131-2.
4. Ibid., 153.
5. Turnock, 46.
6. Quoted in *HRJ*, 60, 23.
7. HR Working Timetable, Summer 1909.

## Through Carriages, the Sleeper War and the 'Caravans'

1. Stanley Junction marked the end of the actual HR system, but the Highland was part-owner of Perth General Station, with the Caledonian and North British companies.
2. Board of Trade Accident Returns, 1893.
3. Stephenson Loco Society, *Highland Railway*, 70.
4. Vallance (*HR*), 88.
5. By 1905 the HR's public timetable for summer advertised Sleeping Cars daily to Euston, Kings Cross and St Pancreas; the winter timetable merely said London. (*I.C.* 7 July and 5 December 1905)
6. Foxwell & Farrer, 62.
7. Board of Trade Accident Returns, 1887.

## Goods Traffic

1. From *Transactions of the Highland Society*, 1872, quoted in Vamplew, *Railway Investment in the Scottish Highlands, JTH*, Vol. 30, No.2, July 1970.
2. Even small coastal communities without harbours could be reached by smacks and puffers, if there was a beach to lie safely on at low tide.
3. HR Working Timetable, Summer 1871.
4. HRB, 21 December 1866. Later, special 'Valuable Cattle' trucks were provided.
5. Republished in HRJ, 49, 20.
6. *HRJ*, 10, 9.
7. JRD: On 15 April 1890 John Ross went to Kildary Market and noted 'Not much doing'.
8. HRB, 10 May 1867.
9. *Groat*, 30 July 1874.
10. *Scotsman*, 24 May 1889.
11. Acworth, 130.
12. HRB, 5 April 1881.
13. I&NB, 22 September 1857.
14. *HRJ*, 24, 12.
15. *HRJ*, 29, 22.
16. *Groat*, 24 December 1897.
17. I&AJB, 16 February 1858. The *HRJ Eastgate II* supplement notes that in 1861 Wordies had twelve horses working at Inverness; by 1905 they had ninety-five.
18. J.E.C., 25.
19. HRB, 5 January 1869.
20. I&NB, 22 September 1857. Wordie offered his services to the I&AJR on 9 November 1857 (I&AJB, 19 December 1857). Wordie's official historian, Paget-Tomlinson, seems unaware of this.
21. HR Working Timetable, Summer 1909.
22. Letter from William Moffat to William Ferguson, in O'Dell Collection.
23. Letters in O'Dell Collection.

TWELVE
## The Postal Subsidy and the Mail Wars

1. Acworth, 136.
2. HRB Letter of 4 March 1884.
3. Haldane, 297.
4. I&NB, 5 February 1857.
5. *I.C.*, 17 November 1863.
6. GPO Archives.
7. Ibid. Letter of 4 February 1864 to Mr Mawson of the GPO, Edinburgh.
8. Ibid. This caused a significant drop in revenue to the SNE and GNS Railways.
9. HRB, 10 August 1866.
10. HRB, 7 February 1871.
11. GPO Archives.
12. *Groat*, 6 August 1874.
13. *Times*, 13 August 1874.
14. *Groat*, 3 September 1874.
15. GPO Archives.
16. A note in the S&CR Board Minutes for November 1874 records the award of 25 guineas to the Hon. T.C. Bruce 'for acting as Arbitrator for the Company in the recent Arbitration with the Post Office'. He was putting the company's case to the arbitrator. The £1,289 was split as £361 12s 4d to the SR, £23 11s to the DoSR, and £903 16s 8d to the S&CR (GPO Archives).
17. GPO Archives.
18. HRB, 9 June 1881.
19. The duke was a director of the LNWR. Cawkwell received £16 6s 8d for his trouble. The DoSR's total mail earnings for 1883-84 were £1,595, almost a quarter of its entire revenue.
20. GPO Archives.
21. Wilson, *The TPOs of Great Britain & Ireland*.
22. *Groat* and others, June-August 1909.
23. *I.C.* and others, February-June 1910.
24. GPO Archives.
25. See Chapter 12. An account of this accident is also given in the suspiciously picturesque recollections of 'Caberfeidh', pseudonym of the Head Postmaster at Inverness, in *Notes*: Organ of the Association of Head Postmasters, in 1925-26; reprinted in *HRJ* 39, 11-15.
26. Report in *Dundee Advertiser*, 3 October 1914.

## Mixed Trains and Continuous Brakes

1. Long trains would also have a brake van, with brakesman, in the middle.
2. It was the guard's, or brakesman's, responsibility to partially apply the brakes when trains were running down-grade.
3. Highet, C., *Continuous Brakes: A Vexed Question*, from *JTH* Vol. 4, No.1, March 1971.
4. *R.M.*, April 1904.
5. Though the LNWR, often used as a model by the HR, also chose this system.
6. But he was responsible for the HR's failure to report track alterations to the BoT between 1871 and 1889; caught out in that year, the HR pled ignorance and asked for twenty-two other omissions to be recorded. See 'The Impenitent Sinner' by David Stirling, *JRCHS*, Vol.31, Pt 3, No.157, March 1994.
7. The *Ross-shire Journal* of 1 October 1897 called it an 'amusing but highly dangerous incident'.

THIRTEEN
## The Railway in the Community

1. Richards, 320.
2. Vamplew, *Railway Investment in the Scottish Highlands*, *JTH*, Vol. 30, No.3, July 1970.
3. He published a pamphlet on the subject, in 1862, with a new edition in 1865.
4. See Vamplew, above.
5. In local council discussions of Light Railway schemes, laughter greeted every mention of the likelihood of local investment. *I.C.*, 3 November 1896 and many other references.
6. Withers, 247.
7. Ibid., 248.

8. Campbell, 294.

9. Acworth, 143.

10. Sutherland, 26.

11. *HRJ*, 27, 9.

12. Hunter, 217.

13. Blackie, 100.

14. HRB, 6 March 1907. The request, from the Hon. Ruairidh Erskine of Mar, was that station names 'be relettered in accordance with the orthographic and grammatical principles of the Gaelic language, or alternatively that the Gaelic name should be shown'. Under Scotrail, this has been done on most surviving ex-HR stations.

15. *Groat*, 9 November 1865.

16. *Highland Leader*, 17 March 1910.

17. *Murray's Guide.*          .

18. Bain, 433.

19. Advertisement in HR *Guide*.

20. Anderson, 2.

21. On more than one occasion, the Chamber of Commerce took the HR to court and even (1898) to the Railway & Canal Commissioners, over its charges.

22. Thomson, 45. Or Hamilton Ellis: '… at Perth General in the first small hour… one could greet the puissant green engines of the Highland, its austere carriages with their yellow gaslight shining on yellow groove-and-tongue, on curiously autumnal plush trimmings, and through that eagle frozen in frosted glass, with just such a shout of delight as that with which Scott greeted the Eildon Hills on his last return from Italy' (*The Beauty of Old Trains*, 93).

23. Even in 1985, Heap and van Riemsdijk could write, quite incorrectly, 'It was from its beginnings more of a local than a trunk route (74).'

# SOURCES AND BIBLIOGRAPHY

## 1. Archive Sources

Highland Regional Archives, Inverness
John Ross Diaries
National Archives of Scotland, Edinburgh
North Highland Archive, Wick
O'Dell Transport Collection, Aberdeen University Library
Post Office Archives, London

## 2. The Highland Railway: Books

Allchin, V.R., *Highland Railway Locomotives*. Southsea, 1947.
Campbell, J. ('J.E.C.'), *The Iron Track Through the Highlands*. Inverness, 1922.
Cormack, J.R.H., and Stevenson, J.L., *Highland Railway Locomotives*. Book 1: *Early Days to the 'Lochs'*. Lincoln, 1988; Book Two: *The Drummond, Smith and Cumming Classes*. Lincoln, 1990.
Geddes, H. and Bellass, E., *Highland Railway Liveries*. Easingwold, 1995.
Hawkins, C., Reeves G., and Stevenson J., *LMS Engine Sheds, Vol. VI, The Highland Railway*. Pinner, 1989.
Hunter, D.L.G., *Carriages and Wagons of the Highland Railway*. Leeds, 1971.
Hunter, D.L.G., *The Highland Railway in Retrospect*. Edinburgh, 1988.
Lambert. A., *Highland Railway Album*. Shepperton, 1974.
Lambert, A., *Highland Railway Album – 2*. Shepperton, 1978.
McConnell, David, *Rails to Wick and Thurso*. Dornoch, 1990.
McConnell, David, *Rails to Kyle of Lochalsh*. Oxford, 1997.
Nock, O.S., *The Highland Railway*, Shepperton, 1965.
Sinclair, Neil T., *The Highland Main Line*, Penryn, 1998.
Stephenson Locomotive Society, *The Highland Railway Company*. London, 1955.
Tatlow, Peter, *Highland Miscellany*, Poole, 1985.
Thomas, John, *The Skye Railway*. New edition, revised by John Farrington, Newton Abbott, 1990.
Vallance H.A., *The Highland Railway*. Revised and extended. Dawlish & London, 1993.

## 3. Journals, Newspapers, Pamphlets, Annuals etc.

*Backtrack Magazine*.
Bradshaw's *Shareholders Guide, Railway Manual and Directory*.
Clew, Kenneth, *The Dingwall Canal*. Dingwall Museum Local Studies No. 1, 1988.
*Div Ye Mind?* Caithness-Glasgow Association.
*Football Times*.
*Highland Leader*.
*Highland News*.
*Highland Railway Society Journal*.

Highland Railway Society: *Highland Railway Stations, Locations and Dates*. Revised September 1995.
Highland Railway Society, *Highland Railway Acts of Parliament*. 2003.
Highland Railway Society, *Eastgate II: A Brief History of the Inverness Site*. 2003.
*Highland Times*.
*Inverness Advertiser*.
*Inverness Courier*.
*John o' Groat Journal*.
*Journal of the Railway & Canal Historical Society*.
*LMS Journal*.
*North Star*.
*Northern Ensign*.
*Railway Magazine*.
*Railway Times*.
*Ross-shire Journal*.
*The Scotsman*.
*The Times*.
*Transport History*.

## 4. Other Works consulted or referred to

Acworth, W.M., *The Railways of Scotland*. London, 1890.
Ahrons, E.L., *Locomotive and Train Working in the Latter Part of the Nineteenth Century*, Vol. 3. Cambridge, 1952.
Anderson, Isabel H., *Inverness Before Railways*. Inverness, 1884.
Ash, Marinell, *This Noble Harbour*. Invergordon, 1991.
Bain, George, *History of Nairnshire*, 2nd ed., Nairn, 1928.
Barclay-Harvey, Sir Malcolm, *A History of The Great North of Scotland Railway*. 2nd edition, 1949.
Biddle, Gordon, *Britain's Historic Railway Buildings*. Oxford, 2003.
Black's *Picturesque Tourist of Scotland*. Edinburgh, 1863.
Blackie, J.S., *The Scottish Highlanders and the Land Laws*. London, 1885.
Brooke, David, *The Railway Navvy*, Newton Abbot, 1983.
Brownlie, J.S., *Railway Steam Cranes*. Glasgow, 1973.
Byles, C.B., *The First Principles of Railway Signalling*. London, 1910.
Campbell, J.R.D., *Some Helmsdale Memories*. Helmsdale, 1998.
Campbell, R.H., *Scotland Since 1707: The Rise of an Industrial Society*. Oxford, 1965.
Cornwell, H.J. Campbell, *William Stroudley, Craftsman of Steam*. Newton Abbot, 1968.
Drummond, Peter, *Scottish Hill and Mountain Names*. Edinburgh, 1991.
Durkacz, V.E., *The Decline of the Celtic Languages*. Edinburgh, 1983.
Ellis, C. Hamilton, *The Trains We Loved*. London, 1947.
Ellis, C. Hamilton, *Some Classic Locomotives*. London, 1949.
Ellis, C. Hamilton, *British Railway History*, Vols. 1 and 2. London, 1954-59.
Ellis, C. Hamilton, *Twenty Locomotive Men*. London, 1958.
Essery, Bob and Jenkinson, David, *An Illustrated History of LMS Locomotives*, Vol. 3. Poole, 1986.
Fawcett, Brian, *Railways of the Andes*. London, 1963.
Foden, Frank, *Wick of the North*. Wick, 1996.
Foxwell, E., and Farrer, T.C., *Express Trains, English and Foreign*. London, 1889.
Fraser, Alexander, and Munro, Finlay, *Tarbat, Easter Ross*. Evanton, 1988.
Haldane, A.R.B., *Three Centuries of Scottish Posts*. Edinburgh, 1977.
Hamilton, J.A.B., *Britain's Railways in World War I*. London, 1967.
Heap, C., and van Riemsdijk, J., *The Pre-Grouping Railways*, Vol. 3. London, 1985.
Henderson, T.F., and Watt, F., *Scotland of Today*. London, 1907.
Highet, Campbell, *Scottish Locomotive History, 1831-1923*. London, 1970.
Highland Railway, *Handbook to the Highland Railway and West Coast*. Inverness, 1892.
Holmes, D.T., *Literary Tours in the Highlands and Islands of Scotland*. Paisley, 1909.
Hunter, James, *The Making of the Crofting Community*. Edinburgh, 1976.
Lees, J. Cameron, *A History of the County of Inverness*. Edinburgh, 1897.
Lenman, Bruce, *An Economic History of Modern Scotland*. London, 1977.
McAskill, E.H.I., and Craig, Noel, *The Highland Transport Revolution*, 2 vols. Inverness, 1988.
Macdonald, Jessie, and Gordon, Anne, *Down to the Sea*, 3rd ed. Dingwall, no date.
McDowall, R.J.S., *The Whiskies of Scotland*. London, 1971.

MacGregor, Alasdair Alpin, *Vanished Waters*. London, 1942.

Mackay, T., *The Life of Sir John Fowler*. London, 1900.

Mackenzie, W.C., *The Highlands and Isles of Scotland*. Edinburgh, 1937.

Macpherson, Duncan, *Gateway to Skye*. Stirling, 1946.

Malcolm, Eric H., *The Cromarty & Dingwall Light Railway*. Cromarty, 1993.

Mills, J., Maclean, M., Hesling, H., and MacLeman, K., *Rosehaugh: A House of Its Time*. Avoch, 1996.

Mitchell, Joseph, *Reminiscences of My Life in the Highlands*, Vol. 2 (1884). Reprinted Newton Abbot, 1971.

Monkswell, Lord, *The Railways of Great Britain*. London, 1913.

Murray's *Handbook for Scotland* (1894). Reprinted Newton Abbot, 1971.

Nock, O.S., *Scottish Railways*. Revised edition, Edinburgh & London, 1961.

Paget-Tomlinson, Edward, *The Railway Carriers*. Lavenham, 1990.

Pratt, Edwin A., *Railways and Their Rates*. London, 1905.

Pratt, Edwin A., *British Railways and the Great War*, 2 vols. London, 1921.

Richards, Eric, *The Highland Clearances*. Edinburgh, 2000.

Robbins, Michael, *The Railway Age*. London, 1983.

Robertson, C.J.A., *The Origins of the Scottish Railway System, 1722-1844*. Edinburgh, 1983.

Ross, John, *Travellers' Joy: The Morayshire Railway*. Elgin, 2003.

Scottish History Society, *Scottish Industrial History: A Miscellany*. Edinburgh, 1978.

Simms, Wilfred F., *The Railways of Caithness*. Rustington, 1998.

Simnett, W.E., *Railway Amalgamation in Great Britain*. London, 1923.

Somers, Robert, *Letters from the Highlands*. London, 1848.

Sutherland, Duke of, *Looking Back*. London, 1934.

Sutherland, Iain, *The Wick and Lybster Light Railway*. Wick, no date.

Thomas, John, *The North British Railway*, Vol. 2, Newton Abbot, 1975.

Thomas, John, and Turnock, David. *A Regional History of the Railways of Great Britain*. Vol XV, *The North of Scotland*. Nairn, 1993.

Thomson, David, *Nairn in Darkness and Light*. London, 1987.

Turner, Barry C., *The Dornoch Light Railway*. Dornoch, 1987.

Turnock, David, *Patterns of Highland Development*. London, 1970.

Vallance, H.A., *The Great North of Scotland Railway*. Dawlish, 1965.

Victoria, Queen, *More Leaves from a Journal of a Life in the Highlands*. London, 1884.

Wilson, Harold S., *The Travelling Post Offices of Great Britain and Ireland*. Derby, 1996.

Withers, C.W.J., *Gaelic Scotland: The Transformation of a Culture Region*. London, 1988.

# INDEX

A

Aberdeen, 13, 16ff, 21, 22, 24, 26,
    32, 36, 37, 41, 54, 55, 64, 83,
    85, 90, 110, 113, 118, 185, 186,
    190, 194, 197, 199
*Aberdeen Free Press*, 116, 127, 173
*Aberdeen Herald*, 199
Aberdeen Railway, 16, 18, 28
Aberdeen Steam Packet Co., 22
Aberfeldy, 18, 39, 44, 88, 95, 134,
    135, 136, 141, 147, 182, 190,
    195
Accidents:
    Achnashellach, 208
    Achterneed, 209
    Baddengorm Burn, 138, 223f
    Dalnaspidal, 222
    Dava Viaduct, 224
    Fochabers, 146
    Kincraig, 74,
    The Mound, 207
    Mulben, 32
    Newtonmore, 172, 222f
    Pitlochry, 221
    Rogart, 221
    Tain, 172, 222
Achanalt, 60, 62, 77,
Achnasheen, 62, 77, 226, 229
Achnasheen & Aultbea Railway,
    91, 92, 229
Achnashellach, 77, 137, 208
Achterneed, 60, 77, 88, 209
Acworth, William, 89, 104, 192,
    194, 198, 213
Alexander, William & Co.,
Allan, Alexander, 22f, 30, 43, 46,
    143ff

Alness, 34, 118f, 123f, 135, 136,
    170
Alsh, Loch, 57, 62
Altnabreac, 51, 66, 138, 142, **28**
Alves, 30, 39
Amalgamated Society of Railway
    Servants, 116, 171, 172
Anderson, James, 100
Anderson, Peter, 16, 18
Applecross, 34
Ardersier, 90, 95
Ardgay, 35, 47, 120
Ash, Marinell, 174, 187
Atholl, Duke of, 17, 28, 38, 42,
    43, 73, 134, 175
Atkins, Philip, 156
Attadale, 60, 62, 77
Aultbea, 76, 78, 79, 80, 229f
Aultmore, 87, 124, 195
Aultnaslasnach viaduct, 132
Austin, William, 17f
Aviemore, 41, 83, 84, 86, 88, 92,
    94, 97, 103f, 141, 157, 180,
    181, 184ff, 192, 196, 199, 204,
    217
Avoch, 95

B

Badenoch, 38, 192
*Badenoch Record*, 163
Baillie, J.E.B., of Dochfour, 98,
    110, 175, 232
Ballinluig, 18, 39, 44, 81, 189f,
    204, 225
Balsporran, 103
*Banffshire Journal*, 165
Barclay, William, 23, 46, 147, 160

Barclay-Harvey, Sir Malcolm, 37,
    84, 119
Baxter, William, 63, 66ff, 134
Beauly, 120, 135
Beauly, River, 132
Belleport, 119, 123
Best, John, 93f, 103
Bignold, Sir Arthur, 108, 230
Bilbster, 168
Birnam, 27f, 217
Black Isle branch, 95, 141
*Black's Guide to Scotland*, 57, 217
Blackie, John Stuart, 214
Blaikie, John, 27
Blair Atholl, 41, 43, 103, 110, 132,
    135, 136, 137, 155, 169, 180,
    182ff, 192, 195, 213
Board of Agriculture, 193
Board of Trade, 23, 27, 31, 42, 62,
    63, 65, 68, 74, 85, 93, 109, 111,
    140f, 142, 167, 172, 174, 192,
    206ff, 224, 232
Boat of Garten, 55, 83, 86, 104,
    147
Bogbain Timber Siding, 46
Bonar Bridge, 35, 44, 47, 50, 55,
    107, 121, 135, 136, 180, 186,
    188, 199ff, 225
Bradshaw's *Shareholder's Guide*, 76
*Brand, Charles, 32, 105*
    *Brassey, Thomas, 19, 21, 34, 52f,*
    *64, 66*
*Brassey & Falshaw, 22, 27*
*Breadalbane, Marquis of, 98, 134,*
    *175*
*British Aluminium Co., 110, 197*
*British Association, 130ff*

British Linen Co., 98
Brodie, 54, 163, 169
Brodie of Brodie, 26f, 59
Brooke, David, 34, 105
Broomhill, 55, 147
Brora, 47, 48, 49, 52, 63, 141, 176, 184, 186, 195
Brown, Marshall & Co., 22, 26,
Brown, Thomas, 121
Bruce, Hon. T.C., 25, 27, 31, 36, 40, 42f, 44, 45, 49, 56, 61, 69, 83, 85, 92, 101, 102, 174, 175, 200ff
Buckie, 86f, 124, 188
Burghead, 26, 39, 90f, 95, 142, 144, 195
Burton, Lord, 110
Buttle, J.W., 46, 56, 138, 142, 147

C
Caithness, 50, 64, 67, 176
Caithness County Council, 108f
Caithness, Earl of, 25, 27, 50, 52f, 64ff, 69
Caithness Railway Co., 52f, 63, 64ff
Caledonian Bank, 14, 19, 20, 41, 50, 73,
Caledonian Canal, 14, 15, 33, 34, 45, 61, 73, 123, 137
Caledonian Railway, 15, 19, 43, 49, 54, 55, 56, 58, 60, 74, 76, 81, 83, 94, 113, 116, 118, 121, 124, 128f, 153, 157, 179, 181, 183, 190
Callander & Oban Railway, 76, 82
Cameron of Lochiel, 21, 58, 176
Carrbridge, 104, 105, 133, 134, 137, 184f, 203, 223
Carsewell, 30
Castletown, 64
Cawkwell, William, 203
Cesari, Edward, 74, 217, 225f
Chisholm & Co., 103, 107
Church of Scotland, 82
Clachnaharry, 137
Clunes, 137
Cockburn, Lord, 16
Coltfield Platform, 39
Colville of Culross, Lord, 85, 98, 102
Commercial Bank, 39, 58, 61
Commissioners for Highland Roads and Bridges, 14f, 18
Conon, 170, 230, 31
Conon Viaduct, 133

Cormack, J.L., & Stevenson, J., 143
County March (Druimuachdar), 103, 104, 164
County March (Further North Line), 64, 66, 67, 68, 171
Cowans, Sheldon, 61, 161
Cox, W.H., 125, 177
Critchley, J., 55
Cromarty, 26, 230f
Cromarty & Dingwall Light Railway, 230f
Culloden, 23, 194
Culloden Moor, 95, 104, 105, 133, 137, 159, 171
Culrain & Lochinver Railway, 111, 231
Cumming, Christopher, 157, 158, 159
Cumming-Bruce, Major, of Dunphail, 42, 45
Cummingston, 95

D
Dalcross, 23, 32, 137, 206
Dalgleish, Sir William O., 175
Dalguise, 41, 132, 147
Dallas, A.G., 58
Dalmore Distillery, 119, 123f, 195
Dalnacardoch, 103
Dalnaspidal, 103, 110, 137, 142, 155, 172, 193, 209, 222
Dalvey, 30
Dalwhinnie, 71, 103, 132, 137, 142, 155, 193, 195
Darwin, Francis, 98ff, 110, 232
Dava, 56, 81, 110, 138, 168, 169, 207
Dava Moor, 39, 131, 190, 197
Davidson, Duncan, of Tulloch, 58
Davidson, Leslie & Oughterson, 28
Daviot, 104, 105, 137, 141, 196
Derby, Earl of, 203
Dining Cars, 181
Dingwall, 26, 33f, 55, 57ff, 76, 88, 94, 103, 111, 118, 119f, 124, 134, 135, 136, 138, 140, 141, 175, 183ff, 190, 192, 202, 209, 216, 217, 218, 225f, 230f
Dingwall & Skye Railway, 56ff, 62, 64, 65, 66, 75, 76ff, 87, 148, 200
Dingwall Canal, 34, 61
Divie Viaduct, 40, 41, 133
Dornoch, 47, 106f, 115, 136, 186

Dornoch Firth, 35, 44, 47
Dornoch Light Railway Co., 106f, 128, 213
Dougall, Andrew, 23, 27, 30, 31, 43, 45f, 47, 55, 57ff, 67, 69, 71, 72, 73, 76, 78, 79, 85, 86, 91, 92, 93, 97ff, 140f, 145, 165, 169, 174, 199, 200ff, 207ff, 227f, 35
Doull, Alexander, 51
Down to the Sea, 187
Druimuachdar Pass, 103, 104, 131, 175, 190, 193, 217
Drummond, Peter, 111, 115, 143, 153ff, 159, 160f, 166, 176, 181
Drybridge, 87
Dübs & Co., 147, 149, 150, 153, 154
Duff, Hon. G. Skene, 27
Duff, James, 25, 45,
Dufftown, 37
Duirinish, 94
Duke of Sutherland's Railway, 62ff, 66, 67, 75, 86, 134, 197, 200, 203
Dulnain viaduct, 134, 24
Dunbeath, 51, 108
Duncraig, 94
Dundee, 81, 83, 84, 130, 183, 185, 217
Dundee Advertiser, 116, 191
Dundeee & Arbroath Railway, 23
Dundee & Perth Railway, 19
Dunkeld, 20, 27f, 38, 40, 54, 73, 132, 141, 164, 183, 195, 217, 225f, 9
Dunphail, 50, 55
Dunrobin Castle, 48, 55, 63, 67

E
Edderton, 18, 56
Eden, Bishop, 82
Edinburgh, 15, 26, 29, 93, 179, 188, 216
Edinburgh & Glasgow Railway, 14, 15, 23, 39, 46, 196
Electric Telegraph Co., 137
Elgin, 15, 16, 18, 24, 25, 26ff, 37, 54, 71, 72, 83, 84, 85, 90, 93, 110, 112, 114, 137, 170, 172, 183ff, 195, 218, 225, 16
Elgin Courant, 145, 206
Elgin, Earl of, 40
Ellice, Edward, 42, 201
Ellis, C. Hamilton, 74, 106, 153, 154

Elphinstone, Sir James, 25, 27,
Enzie, 87
Euston, 42, 122, 129, 185, 190f,
    218

F
Fairbairn, William, 31
Falcon Ironworks, 23, 195
Falconer, Provost, 34
Falshaw, James, 20ff, 27, 82
Faulds & Co., 22
Fawcett, Brian, 162
Fearn, 46, 119, 135, 164, 187,
    197
Fearn & Portmahomack Light
    Railway, 231
Fearn, Easter and Wester, 35
Ferguson, William, of Kinmundy,
    84, 90f
Fife, Earl of, 24
*Financial News*, 113
Findhorn Railway, 32, 144
Findhorn Viaduct (I&AJR),
    30, **22**
Findhorn Viaduct (Tomatin),
    105, 134
Findlay, Col., 33
Fleet, Loch, 26,
Fletcher, J.D., 96, 97ff, 110, 173,
    175
Fochabers, 26, 39, 86, 95, 134,
    146, 152, 195
Fodderty Junction, 87, 209
*Football Times*, 172
Forbes, Alexander, 33
Forbes, Duncan, 104
Forgie, 87
Forman, Charles, 110
Forres, 16, 30, 39, 41, 54, 72, 81,
    83, 86, 93, 110, 114, 120, 132,
    134, 137, 141, 165, 172, 182ff,
    192, 195, 207, 225
Forsinard, 51, 137, 171, 186
Forsinard, Melvich & Portskerra
    Light Railway, 108, 111, 232
Fort Augustus, 14, 73, 110,
Fort George, 23, 35, 95, 116,
    176, 216
Fort William, 57, 82, 88f, 92, 93
Fortrose, 90f, 95, 136
Fothringham, W. Steuart, 175
Fowler, Sir John, 48, 55, 60f, 65,
    77, 90, 104, 132, 133
Fraser, Captain William, 58
Fraser, Robert, of Brackla, 33
Fraser, Roderick, 107
Fraser-Tytler, Edward, 75, 175
Fraser-Tytler, William, 21, 25, 27,

33, 38, 42, 45, 75, 174
Free Church Presbytery of
    Lochcarron, 82,
Friendly Societies, 170
Further North Express, 107f,
    186
Further North Line, 35, 36

G
Gaelic, 214f
Gairloch, 34, 76, 78, 79, 80
Garmouth, 39
Garrow, William, 163, 209
Garry, River, 131
Gartymore, 63
Garve, 61, 62, 77, 89
Garve & Ullapool Railway, 89ff,
    92, 111, 127, 211
Geddes, Sir Eric, 126
General Post Office, 70, 76, 79,
    174, 186, 198ff, 215
Georgemas Junction, 66, 67, 121,
    186, 193
Giles, Nethan, 52f
Gills Bay, 97, 233f
Gladstone, W.E., 101
Glasgow, 15, 26, 73, 79, 82, 83,
    88, 92, 107, 114, 179, 181,
    184, 190f, 217
Glasgow & North Western
    Railway, 82f, 218, 219
Glasgow & South Western
    Railway, 113, 115, 116, 124,
    129, 155
Glencarron Platform, 77
Gollanfield, 95
Golspie, 26, 44, 47, 48, 49, 50,
    63, 67, 106, 136, 151, 152,
    164, 183f, 186, 200, 233
Gordon, John, 197
Gordon Cumming, Sir
    Alexander, 27, 33, 38, 42, 45
Gowans & Mackay, 44, 71
Gowenlock, William, 71, 97,
    102, 165
Grandtully, 44, **11**
Granger & Co., 35, 60, 87
Grant, Donald, 175
Grant, Rev. Donald, 107
Grant, James, 15, 18, 26
Grantown, 26, 38, 55, 120, 135,
    164, 185, 186, 193, 217
    Great Central Railway, 121
Great North of Scotland
    Railway, 16ff, 19ff, 24ff, 28,
    32, 36f, 39f, 44, 54, 55, 78,
    83ff, 87, 89ff, 92, 95, 102, 104,
    110, 111ff, 119, 121, 124, 129,

141, 165, 174, 180, 185f, 190,
    197, 199, 233f
Great Northern Railway, 85, 96,
    191, 195
Great Western Railway, 85, 124,
    133, 155
Grier, James, 79
Grierson, James, 54,
Grigor, Dr, 19, 218
Guthrie, Col. Charles, 69

H
Halkirk, 66,
Hamilton, J.A.B., 155
Handyside, Andrew & Co.,
Harbour Branch, 44, 73,
Harmsworth, R.L., 108, 140,
    204
Harris, 57, 79
Hawkshaw, John, 17
Hawthorn & Co., 22, 26, 30,
    43, 143
Hawthorn, Leslie & Co., 156,
    158,
Heiton, Andrew, 28
Helmsdale, 51, 63, 64, 67, 127,
    136, 139f, 151, 186, 192, 200,
    202, 205
Henderson, James, of Bilbster, 69
Hendrie, John, 41
Highet, Campbell, 153
Highland & North of Scotland
    Railway, 114
Highland Hotel, Strathpeffer, 88,
    115, 125, 226
*Highland Leader*, 116,
*Highland News*, 112, 116
Highland Railway Company
    Arms: **5**
    Dissolution, 128f
    Formation, 44f
    Stock Exchange Quotation, 71
    New offices, 72f
    Proposed amalgamation, 113f
    System Map, **1**
Highland Railway Literary
    Society, 165
Hope, James, 14,
Hopeman, 90f, 95
Hopetoun, Earl of, 14
Houstoun, Maj. James, 90
Houstoun, Mrs, of Kintradwell,
    63
Howie, W.L., 142
Hutcheson, David, 62, 76, 79
Hunter, James, 10, 89, 214
Huntly, 16, 18, 24,
Huntly, Marquis of, 83

I

Inchlea, 103
Inchmagranachan, 103
Inglis, Hugh, 33, 45
Inver, 40, 41, 44, 71
Invergarry & Fort Augustus
  Railway, 110f, 113, 218, 232
Invergordon, 33f, 46, 54, 118ff,
  122, 123f, 126, 136, 213, 225
Invergordon Manure Works, 46
*Invergordon Times*, 188
Inverness, 13, 15, 18, 21ff,
  24ff, 32, 33, 34, 35, 36, 40, 41,
  47, 50, 54, 55, 62, 63, 64, 70,
  71, 72, 84, 86, 88, 90, 92, 93,
  97, 104, 107, 111, 112, 113ff,
  119f, 123, 127, 129, 134, 137,
  138, 145, 153, 161, 165, 167,
  169, 172, 175, 178, 180, 182ff,
  189, 192, 207, 215, 218f, **14,
  15, 58**
Inverness Academy, 23, 28
*Inverness Advertiser*, 18, 21, 23,
  34, 40
Inverness & Aberdeen Junction
  Railway, 24ff, 28ff, 32f, 35,
  36f, 40, 41, 43, 44, 47, 57, 76,
  137, 143f, 160, 174, 199, **3, 4**
Inverness & Elgin Junction
  Railway, 24
Inverness & Lochend Light
  Railway, 232
Inverness & Nairn Railway, 20ff,
  24ff, 27, 28ff, 32, 33, 137, 143,
  160, 162f, 169, 174, 194, 199
Inverness & Perth Junction
  Railway, 39ff, 44, 57, 199
Inverness & Ross-shire Railway,
  33ff, 36, 43, 59
*Inverness Courier*, 23, 42, 66, 98,
  103, 113, 181, 193, 229, 231
Inverness Town Council, 82,
  218, 232
Invershin & Lochinver Light
  Railway, 232

J

Jackson, W.L., 91
'Jellicoe' trains, 122
*John o' Groat Journal*, 47, 51, 52f,
  148, 171, 194, 202, 215, 233
Jones, David, 46, 68, 70, 72, 75,
  82, 111, 143, 148ff, 159, 166,
  179, 182, 202, 206ff
  Joseph Mitchell & Co., 43, 47

K

Keith, 16, 24ff, 27, 28, 32, 33, 42,
  54, 55, 83, 84, 85, 86f, 93, 112,
  114, 120, 131, 136, 137, 141,
  143, 165, 170, 175, 182ff, 192,
  193, 195
Keith, William, 98, 176
Kennedy, William, 109
Kildary, 119, 193
Kildonan, **19**
Killiecrankie, 20, 41, 130, 133,
  142, 199
Kinbrace, 168
Kincraig, 74, 147, 163, 168
King, Lillian, 164
Kingswood, 28
Kingussie, 26, 41, 42, 83, 136,
  141, 164, 180, 182, 191, 197,
  217, 225f
Kinloss, 30, 32, 168
Kitson & Co., 63
Kyle of Lochalsh, 58, 90, 91, 92,
  93f, 97, 123f, 125, 126, 137,
  141, 150, 151, 182, 186, 204,
  209, 226
Kyleakin, 80, 94,
Kynoch, J.W., 96, 175

L

Laing, H., 176f
Lairg, 47, 67, 127, 194, 233
Lairg & Loch Laxford Light
  Railway, 233
Lambert, Anthony, 170
Laxford, Loch, 91, 233
Le Chatelier brake, 148, 206
Lees, J. Cameron, 195
Lenman, Bruce, 110
Letterewe, 57
Leveson-Gower, Lords Alfred
  and Ronald, 50
Lewis, 57, 62, 111, 124
Lewis Chemical Works, 57
Lhanbryde, 30
*Literary Tours in the Highlands and
  Islands*, 180
Littleferry, 26, 39
Liverpool, 26, 67, 80, 188
Loch, George, 26, 27, 29, 42, 45,
  48, 49, 52f, 64f, 69, 75, 174,
  176, 201
Loch, James, 48
Lochcarron, 59, 82
Lochgorm Works, 35, 61, 73, 74,
  82, 113, 116, 121, 124, 144,
  147, 149, 153, 154f, 156, 160f,
  170, 173, **6, 30, 32, 33**
Lochinver, 97, 231, 232

Lochluichart, 77
Locke, Joseph, 15f, 19, 24
Locomotives, by number/name:
  11, **39**
  16, 144
  21, 145, **40**
  45, 155
  46, 113
  103, 152
  *Aldourie*, 144f
  *Balnain*, 147
  *Beaufort*, 159
  *Belladrum*, 34, 88, 144, 146
  *Ben Alder*, 155
  *Ben Alligan*, 160
  *Ben-na-Caillich*, 160
  *Ben Udlaman*, 214
  *Ben y-Gloe*, 153
  *Blair Atholl*, 146
  *Breadalbane*, 88, 146, **53**
  *Bruce*, 146
  *Caithness*, 146
  *Caithness-shire*, 146
  *Clan Stewart*, 158
  *Duke*, 159
  *Duncraig*, 148
  *Dunrobin*, 63, 68, 97, 151,
    152, 184
  *Durn*, 158
  *Glenbarry*, 148
  *Gordon Castle*, 95, 152
  *Gordon Lennox*, 95
  *Highlander*, 149
  *Loch Laoghal*, 160
  *Loch Insh*, 152
  *Lochgorm*, 147, **42**
  *Lovat*, 34, 144, 146
  *Lybster*, 146, 150, **57**
  *Raigmore*, 144, 149
  *River Ness*, 156
  *St Martins*, 147
  *Sir George*, 151
  *Skibo Castle*, 154, 155
  *Snaigow*, 158
  *Strathpeffer*, 88, 146, 150
  *Sutherland*, 146
  *Sutherlandshire*, 146
  *Taymouth Castle*, 154
  *Tain*, 146
  *Tweeddale*, 151
Locomotives, by class:
  'Barneys', 153f
  'Big Goods', 151, 152, 153,
    158, 196
  'Castles', 154, 156, 157, 158,
    181
  'Clan Goods', 158, **52**
  'Clans', 150, 151, 158, 159

'Clyde Bogies', 150, 151
'F', or '60' or 'Duke' class, 72, 146, 149, 150, 151
'Glenbarry' class, 145
'Large Bens', 155, 159
'Lochgorm Bogies', 149
'Lochs', 152f, 156, 158,
'Medium Goods', 146
0-4-4 Tanks, 155, **48**
0-6-4 Tanks, 155
'Rivers', 117, 121, 156f, 158,
'Scrap Tanks', 154,
'Seafields', 144f, 148
'Skye Bogies', 150, 152, 158
'Small Bens', 114, 153, 155f, 158, **61, 62**
'Small Goods', 145f
'Straths', 150, 151, 156, **20**
'Yankee Tanks', 113, 150, **54**
London, 16, 17, 21, 25, 26, 36, 47, 49, 57, 84, 91, 115, 122, 185, 190, 194
London & North Western Railway, 19, 56, 68, 96, 121, 129, 148, 176, 190, 190f, 206
London Brighton & South Coast Railway, 70, 121, 124, 147, 191
London, Midland & Scottish Railway (LMS), 129, 152, 159, 182
London & South Western Railway, 124, 153,
Lossiemouth, 15, 26, 39
Loth, 63
Lothian, Lord, 89, 91
Lovat, Lord, 135, 175, 193
Lovat, Master of, 33, 42, 45, 49, 58
Lybster, 51, 64, 106, 108, 136, 194, **57**

M
Macallan, Mr, 176
Macandrew, Sir Henry, 100
Macbrayne, David, 79, 113, 204
McConnell, David, 10,
McDonald & Grieve, 44
Macdonald, A.& K., 60,
Macdonald, Kenneth, 114
McEwen, Thomas, 117, 125, 176
MacGregor, Alasdair Alpin, 188
Mackay & Mackay, 105
Mackay, Donald, 66
Mackay, Hector, 107
Mackenzie & Holland, 142
Mackenzie, Colin, of Findon, 34

Mackenzie, Provost Colin Lyon, 33
Mackenzie, Sir Kenneth Smith, 33, 42
Mackenzie, Sir William, of Coul, 58f, 87
Mackintosh of Mackintosh, 38, 196, 198
Mackintosh of Raigmore, Eneas, 18, 20ff, 25, 27, 33, 38, 42, 58, 85, 92, 97ff, 166, 174f
Mackintosh of Raigmore, Neil, 176
Maclean, Neil, 33
McLean & Stileman, 53, 66
Macleod of Cadboll, R.B., 33, 45, 136, 149
Macleod of Macleod, 58f
Macpherson of Cluny, 21, 22, 33, 42, 45
Macpherson-Grant, John, 98
Macpherson-Grant, Sir George, 73, 94, 102
Manchester, 26, 123, 148
Mansfield, Earl of, 27
Manson, James, 141
Maree, Loch, 57
Martin, Theodore, 21, 25, 55
Masson, Rev. Mr, 176
Matheson, Alexander, 19, 27, 33, 36f, 40, 42, 45, 49, 56ff, 69, 71, 72, 77, 78, 85, 102, 174, 210, 226
Matheson, Lady, of Achary, 90
Matheson, Sir James, 19, 33, 57
Matheson, Sir Kenneth, 93f, 232
Matthews & Laurie, 72
Meakin, George, 34
Meikle Ferry, 44, 192, 201
Menzies, Sir Robert, 189f
Merry, James, 45, 49, 61, 73, 96, 174
Middleton, Lord, 59f
Midland Railway, 96, 129, 144, 190ff
Millburn (Inverness), 21f, 56
Milne, Robert, 26
Ministry of Transport, 127, 128
'Misery', The, see Naval Special
Mitchell, Dean & Co., 27
Mitchell, John, 14, 59
Mitchell, Joseph, 14ff, 23, 27, 31, 32, 33ff, 36, 38ff, 46, 47ff, 51ff, 54, 57ff, 63, 64, 71, 84f, 94, 105, 130ff, 143, 211, 219, 233, **34**
Moffat, William, 83ff
Monkswell, Lord, 219

Morayshire, 24
Morayshire Railway, 26, 37, 55
Moulinearn, 103
Mound, The, 47, 106, 108, 141, 186, 204, 207
Moy, 104, 196, 198
Muir of Ord, 34, 54, 90, 95, 142, 193
Muirtown branch, 73, 123
Mulben, 30, 32, 83, 141, 186
Munlochy, 95
Munro, John, 104
Murray, Kenneth, of Geanies, 61, 63, 66, 69, 174, 193
Murthly, 28, 62, 134, 196
Mutual Improvement Society (Loco Dept), 166

N
Nairn, 16, 19ff, 25, 26, 27, 30, 39, 54, 55, 120, 131, 134, 135, 136, 137, 139, 141, 178, 185, 187, 193, 195, 199, 217f, 219, 225
Nairnshire, 21, 23
*Nairnshire Telegraph*, 147, 187
Napier Commission, 89
National Bank, 39
'Naval Special', 122, 219
Needlefield Carriage Works, 28, 161, 205
Neilson & Co., 43
Ness, Loch, 110, 113, 197
Ness, River, 24, 33, 132, 137
Newall brake, 206ff, 221
Newlands, Alexander, 115, 117, 125, 129, 157,
Newtonmore, 55, 58, 71, 72, 82, 132, 134, 164, 172, 185, 217
Newtonmore & Tulloch Railway, 197, 233
Nigg, 46, 118f
Nock, O.S., 10
North British Locomotive Co., 153, 155, 156, 158,
North British Railway, 56, 74, 82, 83, 84, 89, 94, 111, 116, 121, 122, 124, 128f, 153, 155, 179, 190
North Eastern Railway, 85, 96, 102, 112, 121, 156, 157, 168
North of Scotland, Orkney & Shetland Steam Navigation Co., 80, 122, 234
*Northern Ensign*, 139f
*Northern Times*, 176
Novar, 169

O

Ogilvy, Thomas, of Corrimony, 33
Orbliston Junction, 95
Ord of Caithness, 35, 51,
Orkney, 50, 64, 78, 80, 118f, 202, 204
Orton, 27, 30, 55, 135
Oykell, River, 136, 232

P

Park, Robert, 115, 116, 117, 122, 125, 129, 166
Paterson, A., 115
Paterson, Murdoch, 33, 42, 43, 46, 60, 62, 65ff, 72, 84, 90, 93f, 104, 105, 111, 132, 133, 136, **36**
Peel, Sir Robert, 18, 210
*People's Journal*, 154
Perth, 15, 16f, 26, 27, 34, 38f, 40, 41, 42, 43, 45, 81, 82, 83, 93, 103, 119, 120f, 126, 127, 136, 138, 147, 156, 167, 180, 181, 182ff, 189, 190, 192, 199, 202, 204, 207, 225
Perth & Dunkeld Railway, 27f, 39, 134
Perth, Inverness & Elgin Railway, 16
Perthshire Women's Patriotic Committee, 119
Peterkin, J. Grant of Grangehall, 75, 102
Pitlochry, 20, 38, 41, 73, 88, 135, 136, 141, 195, 204f, 217,
Plockton, 79, 80, 94
Portessie, 83, 86f, 136
Portland, Duke of, 108ff
Portree, 62, 76, 79, 183, 193, 200
Portsoy, 87
Post Office: see General Post Office
Potter, Beatrix, 164
Pratt, E.A., 120, 125, 194
Pullar, A.E., 129, 175
Pullman Co., 179, 181
Pulteneytown Burgh Council, 108ff

R

Railway & Canal Commissioners, 93, 111, 202
Railway Executive Committee, 121, 124, 125, 126
*Railway Magazine*, 112, 117, 120, 160, 181, 182
*Railway Navvy*, 34, 105

*Railway Times*, 15
Railways Clearing House, 63, 71, 96, 99, 203
Rathven, 87
Raven Rock, 60, 209
Redesdale, Lord, 40
*Regional History of the Railways of Great Britain*, Vol. XV, 10
Rich, Col., 68
Richards, Eric, 210, 212
Richmond and Lennox, Duke of, 26f
Roake, John, 163
Roberts, William, 103, 105, 108, 111, 115, 176
Robertson, A. I., of Aultnaskiach, 27, 45, 75
Robertson, Thomas, 163
Rogart, 50, 134, 136, 164, 195
Rohallion, 28
Rose Street Curve, 35, 88, 161
Rose Street Foundry, 100, 141, 195
Rosemarkie, 90
Ross, David, 82
Ross, Donald, 51
Ross, ex-Provost, 176f
Ross, John, 66, 95, 104
Ross and Cromarty, 57, 62, 212
*Ross-shire Journal*, 88
Rothes, 25, 26f, 37, 55

S

Sacré, Charles, 67
Savings Bank,, 170
Scapa Flow, 122f
*Scotsman*, 114
Scottish Central Railway, 15, 17, 22, 39, 43, 45, 143
Scottish Midland Junction Railway, 16, 20, 27f
Scottish North Eastern Railway, 28, 36, 39, 41, 45, 54, 199
Scottish Provident Institution, 54
Scrabster, 50, 66, 67, 78, 80, 118, 122, 202, 233
Seafield, Countess of, 17, 22, 40
Seafield, Earl of, 17, 24, 27, 45, 174, 210
Seaforth, Earl of, 59
Selborne, Lord, 202
Sharp, Stewart & Co., 43, 145, 146, 152
Shaw, Duncan, 100
Shin, Loch, 67, 194
Sinclair, Neil T., 10, 163
Sinclair, Sir Tollemache, 53, 66, 68, 201

Skye, 57, 62, 78, 93f, 111, 124, 216
Sloan, William & Co., 62
Slochd Mhuic, 105, 134
Smith, Frederick George, 115, 117, 143, 156ff, 159, 166, **38**
Smith, W.H., 91
Smith, William, 139
Somers, Robert, 178
South Eastern & Chatham Railway, 124
Spean Bridge, 88, 110, 113
Spey, River, 24, 25, 26, 39, 86, 95, 132
Spey Viaduct, 24, 30ff, 32, 133
Spinks, Mr & Mrs, 74
Squair & Mackintosh, 41
Stafford, Marquess of, 25, 27,
Stanley Junction, 27f, 39, 45, 56, 72, 81, 103, 163
Station Hotel, Dornoch, 107, 125, 226
Station Hotel, Inverness, 29f, 34, 74, 81, 107, 123, 166, 225
Station Hotel, Kyle of Lochalsh, 94, 125
Station Hotel, Perth, 226
Steamships of the HR:
    *Carham*, 76, 78, 79, 80
    *Ferret*, 76, 78, 79, 80, 227f
    *John o' Groat*, 79, 80
    *Jura*, 62, 76
    *Oscar*, 62, 76
Steel, Charles, 102, 112, 209
Stephenson, George, 17
Stewart, Charles, 21, 33, 36, 38
Stewart, J.G., of Aultwharrie, 175
Stewart, John, 28
Stewart of Auchlunkart, 27
Stirling, David, 186
Stornoway, 57, 62, 76, 188, 197, 204
Strathcarron, 62, 77
Strathnairn Viaduct, 105, 133f
Strathpeffer, 58, 60, 62, 77, 86, 87f, 115, 185, 209, 217, 218
Strathpeffer Spa Express, 88, **59**
Strathspey Railway, 55
Strathtay & Breadalbane Railway, 18
Strome Ferry, 58, 60, 62, 76, 77, 78, 80, 81, 82, 87, 88, 89, 91, 94, 138, 141, 142, 183, 193, 202, 209, 215f
Stromness, 79, 202
Stroudley, William, 46, 54, 56, 61, 70, 124, 143, 147, 153, 159, 160

Struan, 42, 55, 56, 72, 73, 134, 142, 163, 207, **13**
Stuart, Sir John, 59f, 77
Sutherland, 25, 35, 36, 48, 66, 106, 142, 176, 200, 233
Sutherland & Caithness Railway, 61, 64ff, 75, 86, 136, 138, 140, 142, 180, 200, **2**
Sutherland, fourth Duke of, 98, 106f, 111, 175
Sutherland, Iain, 213, 234
Sutherland Railway, 47ff, 52, 55, 57, 60, 61, 63, 75, 86, 106
Sutherland Steam Packet Co., 39
Sutherland, third Duke of, 35, 45, 47ff, 51ff, 62ff, 64ff, 75, 85, 86, 106, 152, 169, 174f, 207, 210, 232, **7**

T
Tain, 26, 33, 35, 44, 107, 120, 136, 172, 183, 186, 188, 192, 199, 201, 209, 218, 222, 231
Talisker Distillery, 57
Tay, River, 20, 28, 38, 44, 132
Tayler, W.J., 25, 27, 45
Telford, Thomas, 14, 133, 134
Tennant, Captain R.J., 77
Tennant, Henry, 85
   Thomas, John, 10,
Thomson, David, 217, 219
Thrumster, 109
Thurlow, Lord, 75

Thurso, 35, 50ff, 64ff, 72, 78, 118, 122, 139, 179, 183ff, 202, 218, 233f
Thurso Town Council, 181f
*Times, The*, 68, 71, 102, 201
Tomatin, 104, 134, 195, 196
Tummel, River, 38, 44
Tummel Viaduct, **23**
Turnpike Trusts, 21, 27
Tweeddale, Marquis of, 93, 101
Tyler, Captain H.W., 31, 42, 62, 63, 140, 221

U
Ullapool, 34, 57, 78, 89
Ullie, Strath, 64
Urie, D.C., 143, 159

V
Vacuum brake 207
Vallance, H.A., 10
Vamplew, Wray, 211
Victoria, Queen, 43

W
Wade, General, 14
Wales, Prince and Princess of, 55
Walker, Sir Herbert, 126
Warburton, Rev. A., 121
Wards, 39
Waterston, Charles, 33., 42, 73, 102, 199
Watson & Co., 22

Welsh, H.A., 21f
West Helmsdale, 63
West Highland Railway, 88, 90, 92, 94, 104, 110, 113
Westinghouse brake, 206
Whitelaw, William, 109, 112, 114, 125, 129, 157, 165, 175, 176
Wick, 26, 35, 50ff, 64ff, 72, 78, 81, 108f, 111, 114, 120, 138, 139, 149, 151, 158, 171, 179, 180, 181, 182, 183ff, 195, 196, 201f, 204, 209, 218, 233, **20, 37**
Wick & Gills Bay Railway, 233f
Wick Town Council, 233
Wick & Lybster Light Railway, 106, 108f, 128, 150, 210f, 213
Wilkinson & Jarvie, 82
Wilson, Peter, 56, 66, 72, 77
Wilson, R.M., 114, 125, 156, 175, 176
Wilson, Thomas Addy, 36, 88, 106, 112, 115, 139f, 155, 167f, 204
Withers, Charles, 212
Wordie & Co., 79, 116, 196f
Wynne, Lt. Col., 23

Y
Yool, Thomas, 98